SCIENCE, FOLKLORE AND IDEOLOGY

SCIENCE, FOLKLORE AND IDEOLOGY

STUDIES IN THE LIFE SCIENCES IN ANCIENT GREECE

G. E. R. LLOYD

Reader in Ancient Philosophy and Science
and Fellow of King's College in the
University of Cambridge

CAMBRIDGE UNIVERSITY PRESS

CAMBRIDGE

LONDON   NEW YORK   NEW ROCHELLE
MELBOURNE   SYDNEY

Published by the Press Syndicate of the University of Cambridge
The Pitt Building, Trumpington Street, Cambridge CB2 1RP
32 East 57th Street, New York, NY 10022, USA
296 Beaconsfield Parade, Middle Park, Melbourne 3206, Australia

First published 1983

Printed in Great Britain
at the Alden Press, Oxford

Library of Congress catalogue card number: 82–19808

British Library Cataloguing in Publication Data
Lloyd, G.E.R.
Science, folklore and ideology.
1. Civilization, Greek
[. Title
938 DF77

ISBN 0 521 25314 4 hard covers
ISBN 0 521 27307 2 paperback

AL

IN MEMORIAM
G.E.L.O.

CONTENTS

Acknowledgements   ix
Texts and abbreviations   xi

Introduction   1

Part I The development of zoological taxonomy   7
  1 Introduction   7
  2 Social behaviour of animals in Aristotle's zoology   18
  3 Man as model   26
  4 Dualisers   44
  5 Conclusion   53

Part II The female sex: medical treatment and biological
       theories in the fifth and fourth centuries B.C.   58
  1 Introduction   58
  2 The treatment of women in the Hippocratic Corpus   62
  3 Alternative theories of the female seed   86
  4 Aristotle on the difference between the sexes   94
  5 The post-Aristotelian debate and conclusions   105

Part III Developments in pharmacology, anatomy and gynae-
       cology   112
  1 Introduction   112
  2 Theophrastus, the Hippocratics and the root-cutters   119
  3 Pliny, learning and research   135
  4 The development of Greek anatomical terminology   149
  5 The critique of traditional ideas in Soranus's gynaecology   168
  6 The epistemological theory and practice of Soranus's Methodism   182

Conclusion: Science, folklore and ideology   201

Bibliography   218
Index of passages referred to   239
General index   256

ACKNOWLEDGEMENTS

This book owes much to the criticisms and advice offered by an unusually wide circle of friends, colleagues, audiences and correspondents. Versions of one or other of the sections have, during the past two years, been given as lectures or seminars at several universities in England (Bristol, King's and University Colleges, London), in the U.S.A. (Harvard, Yale, Princeton, Pittsburgh, Chicago, Northwestern, Notre Dame and the University of Texas at Austin), in Japan (University of Tokyo at Kamaba) and in Italy (Pavia). The whole formed the basis of a seminar course I offered at Stanford University in the spring of 1981, and benefited greatly from the constructive criticisms of a lively group of classicists, philosophers and historians of science. To my hosts on all those occasions, to those who participated in the discussions and who corresponded with me after them, my warmest thanks are due, and especially to two successive Chairmen of Classics at Stanford, Professors Marsh MacCall and Mark Edwards, for inviting me to visit that University as Bonsall Professor, to Professors Shigeru Kawada, Shigenari Kawashima and J. Edward Kidder – and to the Japan Society for the Promotion of Science – for making my visit to Japan possible, and to them and all our other friends at ICU, at Tokyo, at Kyoto and at Hiroshima for their imaginative hospitality and kindness to my wife and myself, and to Professor Mario Vegetti for the opportunity to participate in a conference on Hellenistic science at the Istituto di Storia della Filosofia at Pavia. A Japanese translation of a lecture summarising some of the ideas in Part I was published in *Shiso* in 1981, and a much abbreviated English version in *The Sciences* in January 1982; an Italian translation of a section of Part II has appeared in *La Donna Antica*, Torino 1982, and the English text of the lecture, based on the concluding section, which I gave at Pavia is to be published in the conference proceedings (for the Italian version I delivered on that occasion my thanks are due to my wife and to my colleague, Dr Giovanni Contini).

It is a pleasure to express my thanks also for the generous help I have received from those who have been kind enough to read and comment on drafts of parts or the whole: David Balme, Jacques Brunschwig, Ann Hanson, Pamela Huby, Sally Humphreys, Edward Hussey, Mary Lefkowitz, James Lennox, Paola Manuli, Jeremy Mynott, G. E. L. Owen, Gary Rubinstein, Mario Vegetti. I have also had the advantage of consultations on specific points of anatomy, physiology, botany and pharmacology with three of my colleagues at King's, Professor Gabriel Horn, Dr Matthew Kaufman and Professor Max Walters, and with Dr Betty Jackson of the Department of Pharmaceutical Chemistry at Sunderland Polytechnic: none of these individuals, it must be added, bears any responsibility for the use I have made of their advice. Nor should I fail to acknowledge what I believe I have learned about ancient φαρμακοπῶλαι from less formal consultations with herbalists, curanderos and specialists in 'Chinese' medicine, in southern Spain, in Mexico and in Japan, and my thanks go also to Francisco Guerra, to Shigenari Kawashima and to Masako Nabeshima in this regard. Finally I should like, once again, to express my appreciation for the patient and painstaking help I have received from the Officers of the Press, and especially to Jeremy Mynott and to Pauline Hire.

Cambridge, June 1982   G.E.R.L.

The typescript of this book was delivered to the Press at the end of June 1982, two weeks before the tragic death of Gwil Owen. Neither this note nor any of my many other previous expressions of thanks can convey what I owe, over so many years, to his constructive criticism, his friendship and his inspiration. Many of the topics in the study that follows are, as we both recognised, remote from the centre of his own interests. However inadequate, in other respects as well, as a tribute to his memory, the book is dedicated to the man whose work, for me as for so many others, transformed the understanding of all ancient philosophising, including what we now call science.

Cambridge, December 1982   G.E.R.L.

TEXTS AND ABBREVIATIONS

Except where otherwise stated, the fragments of the Presocratic philosophers are quoted according to the edition of Diels, revised by Kranz, *Die Fragmente der Vorsokratiker* (6th ed., 1951–2) (referred to as DK), the works of Plato according to Burnet's Oxford text and the treatises of Aristotle according to Bekker's Berlin edition. Greek medical texts are cited, for preference, according to the *Corpus Medicorum Graecorum (CMG)* editions. For those Hippocratic treatises not edited in *CMG*, I use E. Littré, *Oeuvres complètes d'Hippocrate*, 10 vols., Paris, 1839–61 (L), except that for *On the Nature of Woman* I use H. Trapp, *Die hippokratische Schrift De Natura Muliebri*, Hamburg, 1967. For those works of Rufus not in *CMG*, I use C. V. Daremberg and C. E. Ruelle, *Oeuvres de Rufus d'Ephèse*, Paris, 1879. Galen is cited according to *CMG* and Teubner editions (where these exist), but the reference is also given to the edition of C. G. Kühn, Leipzig, 1821–33 (K), which is also used for works not in *CMG* nor Teubner; the later books of *On Anatomical Procedures*, extant only in an Arabic version, are cited according to the translation of W. L. H. Duckworth (D) (edd. M. C. Lyons and B. Towers, Cambridge, 1962).

Otherwise Greek authors are cited according to the editions named in the *Greek–English Lexicon* of H. G. Liddell and R. Scott, revised by H. S. Jones, with Supplement (1968) (LSJ), though, where relevant, references are also provided to more recent editions, and Latin authors are cited according to the editions named in the new *Oxford Latin Dictionary (OLD)*, supplemented, where necessary, from Lewis and Short. Abbreviations are those in LSJ and *OLD*, again supplemented, where necessary, from Lewis and Short, and with the following abbreviations of works of Galen: *AA (De Anatomicis Administrationibus)*, *PHP (De Placitis Hippocratis et Platonis)*.

Full details of modern works referred to will be found in the bibliography on pp. 218ff. They are cited in my text by author's name and publication date or dates. A double date is used to distinguish, where this has seemed relevant, the original publication from the revised or reprinted or translated version used. Such works are listed in the bibliography by the first date, but cited according to the second. Thus Owen (1961) 1975 refers to the 1975 reprint (with additions) of an article originally published in 1961, Vernant (1972) 1980 to the 1980 translation of a study originally published in 1972.

INTRODUCTION

The essays in this book are self-contained but interconnected studies of issues concerned with the development of the life sciences in ancient Greece. The establishment of science in Greece depended importantly on marking out the subject-matter, aims and methods of rational inquiry from popular or traditional patterns of thought. But although many Greek scientists self-consciously contrast their own investigations with other, especially traditional, systems of belief, they nevertheless often remain deeply influenced by such beliefs and in some cases may appear to us to do little more than attempt some rationalisation of their basis. Many of those who explicitly discuss methodological and epistemological questions emphasise the need to reject all unexamined assumptions and to found their knowledge of the physical world on the secure basis of reason, experience or some combination of the two. But that did not prevent large segments of popular belief from being incorporated into would-be scientific systems – not that those systems are otherwise devoid of genuine grounds for claiming to be in some sense scientific. Ancient science is from the beginning strongly marked by the interplay between, on the one hand, the assimilation of popular assumptions, and, on the other, their critical analysis, exposure and rejection, and this continues to be a feature of science to the end of antiquity and beyond. This interaction provides the first major unifying theme of these studies.

The second such theme concerns the relationship between the products of scientific investigation and the prevailing ideology – taking ideology in a broad sense to cover the ideas or beliefs that underpinned fundamental social structures or that corresponded to the views or ideals of the ruling elite. Here the principal questions that must be pressed relate to the extent, and the limits, of the critical scrutiny undertaken by ancient scientific writers. Did their criticisms extend to, or did they stop short of, the central assumptions implicated in the dominant ideology – at least where those assumptions impinged on one or other possible domain of scientific inquiry? How far did ancient scientists implicitly or explicitly lend positive support to such beliefs? In what contexts and under what conditions did they reject or challenge them?

A major methodological problem that must be raised straight away will indicate the limitations of our inquiry. The difficulty concerns the extent to which any reconstruction of 'popular' or 'traditional' beliefs or practices is possible. Obviously there is no way in which we can gain direct access to the ideas and assumptions of the vast majority of ordinary men and women in the periods we are interested in (which stretch from the sixth century B.C. to the second century A.D.). We have, of course, information in Greek and Roman writers, sometimes quite rich information, concerning their cultures' 'folklore' – not that what may be included under the rubric of 'folklore' ever comprises a single clear-cut category in ancient or modern cultures. But all of that information has already been processed by our ancient literate sources: their prejudices and biases are sometimes blatant, but more often they can only be conjectured.

However, some of the shortcomings of our sources can be countered, if not overcome, by exploiting their very heterogeneity, by examining the contrasts between what we may be told by the natural philosophers on the one hand, for example, and what we gather from the medical writers on the other, or again between the information in different types of medical writing. The preoccupations, concerns and motivations of our various sources differ interestingly, and the intersection of several different view-points sometimes enables us to reconstruct some of the background common to them all. It must, however, be understood at the outset that when we speak of traditional or popular beliefs we are talking about what ancient writers or documents implicitly or explicitly acknowledge, represent or reveal as such. Any more extravagant ambition, to be able somehow to stand the far side of the barriers interposed by our sources, must be renounced. To the objection that this limitation hamstrings the enterprise from the start, the only proper reply is to refer to the results that a critical reading of our complex source-material appears to allow us to propose.

The first group of essays concerns zoological taxonomy. Thanks to much recent and some not so recent work in anthropology, the importance of the role of animal and plant classifications in the patterns of belief of non-literate and literate societies alike has come to be more fully appreciated, even if the understanding of that role still poses plenty of problems. In the ancient world we have a good deal of material from which to reconstruct parts at least of the symbolic systems in which plants and animals figure. At the same time we can study the first attempts at systematic classifications aiming to establish the genera and species of living creatures and plants on purely zoological and botanical considerations. Three aspects of the interactions of such classifications and popular beliefs are especially worth investigating: (1) the reaction or response, in zoological taxonomy, to the tendency to understand animal behaviour and interrelations in human, especially social, terms; (2) the implications of anthropocentricity on zoological taxonomy – the influence of the special role allotted to man as the model, or supreme, animal; and (3) the question of how intermediate or marginal species are dealt with: the particular symbolic significance often attached to these species as boundary-crossers is well known from both anthropological and classical studies, but that symbolic load poses obvious and fundamental problems for any system that purports to give a single comprehensive and consistent account of natural kinds. In each of these three studies the focus of attention will be on zoology rather than on botany. Our most interesting material comes, in each case, from Aristotle, although other ancient taxonomists before and after him will also be brought into consideration.

The next group of studies discusses the scientific repercussions of certain ancient Greek assumptions and value-judgements concerning the inferiority of the female sex. The first investigates how such assumptions and judgements influenced medical practice in the fifth and fourth centuries B.C. What factors inhibited the relationships between, on the one hand, male doctors and female patients, and, on the other, male doctors and various types of female healers, notably midwives? How far were the male doctors aware of such factors? How far did they attempt to overcome the barriers they faced and how successful were they in doing so? These questions will be discussed principally in relation to the evidence in the Hippocratic Corpus, especially that from the remarkable – and still remarkably neglected – specialist gynaecological treatises it contains. The second study turns to topics in biology to consider how far similar assumptions concerning the inherent inferiority of women are in play in the intensive debate on problems of reproduction and heredity in the fifth and fourth centuries. We have comparatively rich sources of evidence, including some extensive discussions in different Hippocratic treatises, concerning the divergent views held on the question of the woman's role in reproduction. The questions we shall concentrate on are to what extent and on what grounds theories on this topic were proposed that break away from or run counter to the common, indeed prevailing, prejudices. The third study returns to Aristotle's zoology to attempt both to summarise where his well-known views on the superiority of the male sex influence his biological doctrines, and then, and more particularly, to analyse how he dealt with *prima facie* counter-evidence to his beliefs. Aristotle may here be represented as providing some kind of rational or rationalising grounds for views that owe much to common Greek assumptions, and our chief concern will be to explore the tensions that such an accommodation sets up. Some aspects of the post-Aristotelian debate on the role of women in reproduction will be discussed briefly in the final study in this group.

The connections between the next five studies are less marked, although all deal with features of ancient scientific methodology and its varying success in freeing itself from extraneous influences. The first two studies tackle problems connected with *materia medica*, especially botanical pharmacology. We have extensive and largely independent discussions of different aspects of this subject in Theophrastus and in a number of late fifth- or fourth-century Hippocratic works. Theophrastus records and comments on a number of popular beliefs and what he considers myths or superstitions concerning the collection and use of certain plants as medicines. The Hippocratic authors offer many prescriptions in which these plants figure but are silent on the folk-beliefs referred to by Theophrastus. The problems that this suggests are complex: first how far can we specify the grounds on which Theophrastus criticises and rejects some beliefs but accepts or rationalises others? Then to what extent can we define the attitudes of the Hippocratic authors: how far were they, or how far were their patients, still influenced by similar beliefs? This will involve the admittedly tricky problem of considering what the Hippocratic writers leave out, as well as what they include in their comments, but the comparison and contrast with Theophrastus offer an opportunity to consider how natural philosophy, on the one hand, and medicine, on the other, reacted to one group of popular beliefs.

The second study considers a similar set of topics in the first-century A.D. Roman encyclopedist Pliny. The two general questions that can be raised here concern first the apparent conflict between, on the one hand, Pliny's adherence, in principle, both to the appeal to experience and the methods of critical research, and, on the other, his actual practice, in his frequent wholesale transcriptions or translations of material from earlier written sources (as can be shown by detailed comparisons with, for example, Theophrastus). Then Pliny's use of literary authorities suggests a second wide-ranging topic, the potentially negative effects of the prestige of the written text and of the distancing from the oral tradition that the acquisition of book-learning might represent. These two general issues can be examined by considering Pliny's extensive discussions, in the *Natural History*, of botanical and pharmacological subjects in particular.

The third study tackles problems concerning the development of anatomical terminology. Popular vocabulary was to prove both too vague and ill-defined, and insufficiently rich, for the purposes of medicine and surgery, let alone those of anatomy and physiology themselves. The principal questions we shall be concerned with here are how far the Greeks were successful in developing a comprehensive, technical and standardised anatomical terminology and what factors inhibited that development. To this end we shall follow the history well beyond the limits of the classical period, down to the second century A.D., where the discussion of some of the problems in Rufus of Ephesus is particularly revealing.

The next two studies also concern later Greek science and discuss first the criticism of traditional ideas, and then the interaction of epistemological theory and practice, in the second-century A.D. medical writer Soranus. The chief interest of the first topic lies in the illustration it offers of the continuing problems posed by the exposure of what Soranus himself represents as superstitious beliefs, and it provides a case-study of the tensions between such a critical approach to traditional beliefs and the concern the medical practitioner shows for the psychological well-being of his patient. There are instances where harmless, and some not so harmless, superstitions are to be tolerated because the patients believe in them and to disabuse the patients of their opinions would upset or disturb them. The second study of this pair considers the impact of the epistemological theories developed in the medical sects – largely under the influence of philosophy – and their adaptation to medical practice. Here it is not popular belief, but philosophical theorising, that constitutes the extraneous influence to which medicine is responding, and the tensions that arise are those that derive from an attempt to accommodate official epistemological doctrines and applied medical methodology.

Each of these three groups of studies will be introduced with a brief discussion setting the particular topics to be investigated in a wider context of current controversies, whether within the specialist field of classical scholarship or, more often, in anthropology and the philosophy and sociology of science. These include questions relating to the comparisons and contrasts between primitive thought and early science, to the growth and development of literacy, to the role of the consensus of the scientific community or of groups within it and to their self-legitimations, to the ideological character of – and to the limits of the ideological influences on – scientific inquiry. No claim can or will be made that the case-studies present more than particular opportunities to illustrate and discuss aspects of these more major controversies. Above all the case-studies themselves will in places show the dangers of transferring conclusions from one field or period of ancient scientific activity to another. But a final study will provide the occasion to return to the more general issues, to broaden the scope of the inquiry, and to take stock of what our particular investigations contribute to an understanding of the development of the life sciences in the ancient world.

Finally, in this introduction, a word of explanation is in order concerning the use of this category of the 'life sciences'. I adopt this term merely as a convenient shorthand for a variety of studies of aspects of the living thing, including, for example, what we should call zoology, botany, anatomy, physiology, pathology and pharmacology. It is not intended to imply that the Greeks themselves regularly distinguished between these and other areas of what they also often included in 'the inquiry concerning nature' (for example element theory, or the theory of compounds, that is what we might call 'physics' and 'chemistry'), even though, for one tradition in ancient thought, 'nature' referred especially to what is alive, and even though under the heading of 'mathematics' they sometimes separated off branches of what we should term the exact sciences (such as optics and harmonics) from other fields of study, including some that they would have held to belong primarily to the domain of 'medicine'. It follows that the reasons for my concentration, in these essays, on aspects of the 'life sciences' are contingent ones, the chief factor being simply the richness of the ancient material available from certain such fields for the investigation of the questions we are interested in. This richness itself reflects the fact that popular assumptions about such subjects as the animal and the plant kingdom are more widespread and more deeply engrained – and they therefore figure more prominently in the background to science as it developed – than corresponding beliefs about what things are made of, let alone about the behaviour of light and sound. The differences are, however, a matter of degree, not of kind. Emerging science is the general field of our inquiry: aspects of the life sciences provide, as we said, particular, but clearly not the only, opportunities to study the topics we have proposed.

PART I

THE DEVELOPMENT
OF ZOOLOGICAL TAXONOMY

I. INTRODUCTION

The debate

The ways in which human experience is understood and ordered by means of categories apprehended in nature have been much debated in recent years by specialists in a variety of disciplines. A series of penetrating studies by social anthropologists in particular has brought out how the organisation of social relations, moral attitudes, cosmological and religious beliefs may all be expressed through the animal code or other codes thought of as given in nature – not that such distinctions between social, moral, cosmological and religious necessarily correspond, or are even likely to correspond, to any distinctions drawn within the societies concerned.[1]

One influential statement was that of Mary Douglas in *Purity and Danger* (1966). There she argued that pollution and taboo only make sense in relation to a 'systematic ordering of ideas', to a 'total structure of thought whose key-stone, boundaries, margins and internal lines are held in relation by rituals of separation'.[2] Taking as one of her chief texts the dietary rules in Leviticus, she claimed that the key to the understanding of these often seemingly bizarre proscriptions lay not in any notions of hygiene, aesthetics, morals or instinctive revulsion, but in the need to express the central notion of holiness as separation.[3] Rules of ritual avoidance make a visible public recognition of the boundaries within the structure of ideas.[4] The interest in natural boundary-crossers, intermediates, anomalies of one kind or another, that leads them to be the particular subjects of prohibitions and taboos, derives in part from their role as models, paradigms or symbols. Essential aspects of the social, moral or religious order are expressed through beliefs and behaviour directed at natural species (usually but not exclusively animals) thus singled out for particular attention. It is not that that process of the expression of ideas

---

[1] Cf. Tambiah 1977, p. 73.   [2] Douglas 1966, p. 54.
[3] Douglas 1966, p. 63.   [4] Douglas 1966, p. 188.

7

concerning the social or religious order via such symbols is a *conscious* one. On the contrary the apprehension of the social and religious order and of the natural order is a seamless whole. But the explanation of much that looks at first sight unintelligible can be found by reading the texts in the context of the whole system of beliefs.

Since the statement of the thesis of *Purity and Danger* the debate has moved on. Mary Douglas herself has modified her ideas, partly in response to criticism, first in *Natural Symbols* (1970) and then in some of the papers collected in *Implicit Meanings* (1975), especially her 1972 Myers lecture on 'Self-evidence'. Thus she has come to lay greater stress on the point that dietary rules or myths marking the special role of certain animals can serve to emphasise the external as well as the internal boundaries of a group, and positive as well as negative evaluations, and to acknowledge that what each society sees as an anomaly or hybrid will itself depend on the society's classification system, and this in turn has been the starting-point of her ambitious attempt to classify cultures themselves in terms of 'grid' and 'group', that is the dimensions of 'individuation' and 'social incorporation'.[5]

Other aspects of this debate can be traced in the work of anthropologists such as Luc de Heusch, Leach, Bulmer and Tambiah, much of it influenced by or reacting to Lévi-Strauss.[6] One particularly attractive, because particularly finely detailed, contribution was a paper of Tambiah in 1969, 'Animals are good to think[7] and good to prohibit'. There Tambiah presented a wealth of field data from north-east Thailand relating (1) to marriage and sex rules, (2) to spatial categories, particularly to rules concerning the organisation and lay-out of the house, and (3) to animal taxonomy and dietary rules, and he showed convincingly how each of these three series or levels exhibits precisely the same structure. The lay-out of a Thai house cannot be understood except in terms of Thai ideas about the relations between blood siblings, first cousins, classificatory siblings,

[5] See Douglas 1978.
[6] L. de Heusch (1964) 1981, Leach 1964, Bulmer 1967, Tambiah 1969. Since Lévi-Strauss (1962a) 1966 and (1962b) 1969, the theoretical and methodological issues have continued to be the subject of extensive debate in France: among the numerous contributions, the work of Foucault (1966) 1970, and Bourdieu (1972) 1977, may be mentioned especially.
[7] Tambiah's expression alludes to a point that Lévi-Strauss had made in his critique of totemism when he had written of animals chosen to convey certain ideas not because they are 'bonnes à manger' (good to eat) but because they are 'bonnes à penser' ('good to think', in Needham's translation, Lévi-Strauss (1962b) 1969, p. 162). As the animals are the instruments rather than the mere objects of thought, the ungainly 'good to think with' seems preferable to 'good to think'.

other persons and rank outsiders – getting further and further away from Ego. Moreover Thai ideas about animal categories relate directly *both* to their ideas about house space (there is consternation if a buffalo or an ox sleeps under the entrance platform or under the wash place, rather than under the sleeping quarters) *and* to their ideas about social relations.

This intensive discussion of a cluster of related problems by anthropologists in the mid-60s to early 70s can be followed both forwards and backwards in time. Forwards the ramifications go into semiology, studies of symbolism, literary criticism – topics that cannot be pursued here.[8] But backwards there are strong links with much earlier themes and theories in anthropology. An interest in some aspects of these questions can be traced back to some of the founding fathers of the discipline such as Tylor and Frazer, even if most of the solutions they offered now seem half-baked. The concept of 'totemism' has, since Lévi-Strauss's devastating critique ((1962*b*) 1969), been recognised as essentially misleading. But although the identification of social groups with natural objects, often though not always animal species, is not the coherent cultural phenomenon that the advocates of 'totemism' supposed, the material discussed under that rubric raised, and raises, fundamental questions concerning the relationship between nature and society, including the relationship between natural categories and social, moral and religious ones. Durkheim's work on primitive classification systems, and his studies of primitive religion, including his thesis that a society's religious beliefs may be understood as expressions of the structure of the society itself, were, after all, contributions to the study of just such questions.[9] In Lévi-Strauss's own classic *La Pensée sauvage* ((1962*a*) 1966) the interaction of social and animal taxonomies and the role of both in belief-systems as a whole are two of the central themes.

Many of the topics thus broached have immediate and obvious relevance to the classicist, and in this area classical studies have not been so isolated from the work carried out in other disciplines as is often the case. Totemism was, unfortunately, a red herring. Although some classicists speculated that ancient Greek society might at one stage have been totemic, the absence of any direct evidence for this whatsoever had deterred most scholars some time before the viability of the whole notion of totemism was called in question by Lévi-Strauss. At the same time classicists have long been familiar with a

---

[8] See, e.g., Barthes (1964) 1967*b* and (1970) 1975, Derrida (1967*a*) 1976 and (1967*b*) 1978, Sperber 1975, Todorov 1977, 1978*a* and 1978*b*.

[9] See Durkheim (1912) 1976 and cf. Horton 1973.

variety of very obvious ways in which the interaction of the natural
and the social worlds is expressed in Greek thought. We have no need
to be reminded of the importance of – we may even feel proprietorial
towards – the major articulating dichotomy of Nature and Culture,
φύσις and νόμος – not that there is an exact equivalence between
these two pairs of expressions.

So far as the animal world is concerned, every student of Greek
literature registers, to some degree, that there is a very heavy use of
animals in similes and metaphors from Homer onwards. Indeed this is
such a familiar point, and one that seems so readily understandable in
terms of features of our own cultural experience (ranging from a
similar use of animal imagery in high literature to the common use of
animals in, for example, terms of abuse[10]) that it is easy to
underestimate its importance. The fundamental points have, however, been brought out in studies of ancient animal similes and of the
use of animals as types. The assumption of the constancy of the
behaviour of each animal species – the lion is always courageous, the
deer fearful, the fox cunning – was remarked on by scholars who, in
most cases, were not concerned to make cross-cultural comparisons or
to illustrate theses about the similarity of the use of animal categories
in Greek thought and what is reported in some anthropological
monographs.[11] So too was the convention that two people when
meeting offer comparisons for each other, often (though far from
exclusively) comparisons with animals.[12] So too, to take a slightly less
familiar, but still absolutely obvious, example, was the recurrent use
of animal paradigms in the vast body of ancient physiognomical
literature.[13]

Ancient animals are evidently 'good to think with' in such ways as
these, and others can easily be added. Just as boundary-crossing
animals are the focus of particular attention in many pre-literate
societies, so too a similar phenomenon can be found in ancient
Greece. One of the most detailed and sophisticated studies of a series
of such marginal creatures is Detienne's *Gardens of Adonis* ((1972a)
1977), a veritable mine of examples of the roles played by anomalous
creatures, and anomalies of all sorts, in Greek thought. Thus to take a
particularly well-known instance, the snake is at the centre of a rich
complex of religious beliefs and practices and was evidently conceived
as an intermediary between this world – and the surface of the

---

[10] See especially Leach 1964.
[11] See, e.g., Fränkel 1921, Riezler 1936, Snell (1948) 1953.
[12] See, e.g., Fraenkel 1922, pp. 171ff, and 1950, II pp. 101f, III pp. 575f, 773f, Rivier 1952.
[13] The chief collection is that of Förster 1893. On the treatise *Physiognomonica* in the Aristotelian
Corpus, see further below, p. 24.

earth – and the underworld.[14] Many other more or less common, more or less exotic, species, such as the seal, the bat, the wryneck, also figure repeatedly in mythology, in religion and in riddles, as *special* creatures, not necessarily the objects of avoidance behaviour, but marked out, nevertheless, as anomalies and used to convey, implicitly or explicitly, messages not just concerning the norms and boundaries that they breach and span, but concerning norms and boundaries in general.

Moreover in line with what the findings of the anthropologists would lead us to expect, it is not the case that the taxonomies implied or adumbrated in early Greek thought are confined to what *we* should call *natural* species. It is true that, as Vernant and Vidal-Naquet have shown,[15] *both* what divides men from animals *and* what divides them from the gods are strongly emphasised. Men are marked out as beings that not only hunt in special ways but also offer sacrifices to the gods. Yet the very marking of the contrasts between animals, men, divine creatures and demi-gods of various kinds, and the gods themselves, is itself evidence that animal taxonomy is subsumed in a much wider framework. The objects to be encompassed in the classification span both what we should call the natural and the supernatural domains, and the interest is as much in establishing the external relations of the groups as in the internal divisions between, for example, the various kinds of animals themselves.

Hesiod illustrates these points very vividly. In the *Works* (276ff) a strong moral contrast is drawn between men and animals: man alone has δίκη, 'justice', the fishes, beasts and birds eat one another. More importantly, in the *Theogony* man is linked, and contrasted, with a whole range of deities. Setting out the genealogies of the gods, the *Theogony* identifies, besides the ancestors of Zeus and his progeny, a veritable menagerie of divine beings. There are the Cyclopes, with one eye, Cottus, Briareus and Gyes, with fifty heads and a hundred arms, the Erinyes, produced from Ouranos's genitals, Giants, Melian Nymphs, a frightening array of children of Night (211ff) and a further awesome group at 265ff which includes the Harpies, Typhaon, Cerberus, the fifty-headed hound, the Hydra, the Chimaera, with lion, goat and snake heads, Pegasus and the Sphinx. These creatures are strongly characterised and differentiated, and they include theriomorphic as well as anthropomorphic beings. But they all find a place in the account of the gods and their offspring.

---

[14] See most recently Bodson 1978, pp. 68ff.

[15] Vernant (1972) 1980, Vidal-Naquet (1970a) 1981, pp. 80ff and 1975; cf. Detienne (1972a) 1977 and (1972b) 1981, pp. 215ff.

Clearly, for Hesiod, man and the animals are to be classified not just in relation to each other, but also in relation to divine and mythical beings. His interest in establishing the kinds of the latter is as strong as, if not stronger than, his interest in the former. We may, if we so wish, reconstruct some classification of natural species and attribute it to Hesiod.[16] But we must acknowledge first that it *is* a reconstruction, and secondly and more importantly that this is to focus on what, for Hesiod himself, is only a part of a much wider and more comprehensive whole.

Hesiod is, undeniably, a highly sophisticated poet, reworking and transforming traditional materials with great creative genius. Nevertheless he provides good enough evidence for one fundamental, if uncontroversial, point, namely the interpenetration of animal and other taxonomic systems in early Greek thought. Nor is there any lack of further evidence from other articulate early Greek authors to illustrate how animals are used to express ideas about the human condition and social relations, and to interpret human character. Thus parts of the animal code in Homer have been explored by Fränkel, Snell and Redfield,[17] and Loraux's subtle study analyses how Semonides, especially, uses certain species of animals (along with other natural objects) to convey a number of value-judgements about the 'race' and various 'tribes' of women.[18]

The problem

It will readily be granted that in a variety of absolutely obvious ways and in some no doubt less evident ones animals were used in early Greek thought as the vehicles for the expression of fundamental social, moral, religious and cosmological categories. At the same time anyone who studies the material from ancient Greece has to confront the further fact that, by the fourth century B.C. if not before, there were Greek thinkers who were engaged in the development of what may be represented as would-be scientific zoological classifications. But the relationship between these classifications and earlier beliefs poses a series of questions. What influences or interferences (if any) were there from popular ideas, attitudes or assumptions? To what extent was the emerging study of zoological taxonomy inhibited or diverted by such beliefs? How successful were the 'scientific'

---

[16] As also for Homer, along the lines of the highly positivist analyses offered, for example, by Buchholz 1871–85, 1 Part 2, pp. 90ff, or by Körner 1917 and 1930.

[17] See Fränkel 1921, Snell (1948) 1953, J.M. Redfield 1975, pp. 193ff and cf. Dierauer 1977, pp. 6ff.

[18] Loraux (1978) 1981, cf. further below, pp. 94f.

taxonomists in freeing themselves from popular assumptions? The questions take on all the more importance in that it is in relation to the Greek material, par excellence, that we can study the transitions, interactions and interferences between popular beliefs and emerging 'science' – not that there was agreement among those concerned about what 'science' consisted in, either on its methods or on its defining characteristics.

First, however, the use of the term 'scientific' in relation to Greek zoological taxonomy requires some justification. The sceptic might object that – whatever the ancient Greeks themselves thought on the subject, that is whether or not they would deem such taxonomy part of ἐπιστήμη, knowledge – we are not dealing with anything that can be called scientific in any strict or strong sense. We are certainly not dealing with experimental science, nor even with the formulation of general laws applicable in practice or in principle to empirically testable situations. Taxonomy was, in the ancient world, and to some extent remains today, descriptive, not explanatory or predictive – descriptive, though not autonomous, as if it could be pure or totally disinterested. Yet it would be a mistake to rule that, for that reason, it falls outside the domain of science. Aristotle, for one, saw the collection of the differentiae of animal species and their parts as a preliminary to the investigation of the causes involved, and he was surely right in the main, even though we may challenge the types of causes he had in mind and – since evolutionary theory – substitute our own rather different model of the kind of explanation eventually to be obtained.

It is true that at a deeper level fundamental questions concerning the notions of the genus and the species, the particular and the general, have to be confronted. The validity of the notion of the species itself is at bottom quite questionable. Yet when all that has been said, there is still a scientific subject here to be studied, the evolution and interrelations of animal kinds and parts. Although some aspects of the philosophical questions that the inquiry poses are *not* raised by ancient writers,[19] the basic distinction between broadly 'scientific' and other classifications is still presentable in ancient terms. Thus Aristotle would no doubt have allowed that such factors as that a particular species of animal is sacred to a particular god, or is the subject of dietary proscriptions, or has a particular symbolic value, positive or negative, might all be relevant to religion, to mythology or to poetry. Yet his view is clearly that no such factor is

---

[19] Thus the validity of the notion of the species itself is not explicitly challenged, despite some interest in and speculation concerning hybrids and sports.

admissible in any attempt to establish the differentiae of the species in question, to define it and to locate it in relation to other species. For the latter purposes it is certain 'physical' characteristics alone that count – using the term 'physical' in the ancient sense to include the vital functions or functions of ψυχή.

The main point is again a simple one, that here, as so often elsewhere in Greek thought, we are confronted with the existence, side by side, of a complex of popular and religious beliefs and assumptions on the one hand, and of what may – if with due caution – be called scientific investigations on the other. Lévi-Strauss, Tambiah and Douglas were not concerned, in the material they were discussing, with any attempt on the part of the people in question to *criticise* and *reform* common assumptions on the basis that they misrepresent what is the case. Yet it is just *that* that can be documented from ancient Greece. It is this that gives the classicists a quite exceptional opportunity to study the interactions of traditional and scientific approaches and to investigate under what conditions, and within what limits, such criticism and reform are possible.

The antecedents of Aristotle's zoological taxonomy

The first writer in whom these interactions can be studied in some detail – the first to have attempted a comprehensive investigation of the differentiae of animals – is Aristotle. It is possible to map out the broad features of much earlier implicit taxonomies in Homer and Hesiod, in other early Greek literature, in the Hippocratic Corpus, and in each case the picture that emerges is an interesting and complex one. Obviously what Homer has to say about animals expresses much more besides symbolic and ritual beliefs and certain assumptions about the characters of different species. Broad group-ings of animals into land and sea, tame and wild, and so on, are adhered to fairly consistently.[20] Nevertheless all of our extant sources that date from before the fourth century B.C., the earlier Hippocratic writers[21] and Democritus[22] included, present, at most, implicit taxonomies.

[20] See, e.g., J.M. Redfield 1975, pp. 189ff.
[21] Burckhardt's study, 1904, exaggerates the extent to which what he calls the 'koische Tiersystem' can be said to be presupposed by certain Hippocratic texts. His main evidence for this, *Vict.* II chh. 46–49, certainly gives a fairly detailed account of the nutritional and digestive properties of the flesh of some 52 different types of animals, in terms of whether the flesh is dry or moist, 'strong' or 'weak', easily digested or not, and so on, and these properties are in turn associated with qualities and characteristics of the animals themselves, for example whether they have an abundance of blood or not. Yet this is some way short of – and some way short of even presupposing – an explicit general classification of animals:

In the fourth century itself, Plato certainly raises, in very sharp terms, the issues of classification and definition, and he illustrates his method of division with zoological examples among others, although how seriously he took these is disputed. But the *Sophist* and *Politicus* do not yield a single consistent dichotomous classification of animals. Rather, different and at points conflicting, dichotomies are suggested at different junctures and for different purposes.[23] In the *Timaeus* (91d ff) broad groupings of animals are suggested – birds, four-footed and footless wild creatures, fish, shell-fish and other water animals – but the context of this is an account of the transmigrations of man's soul as he degenerates, and the first such transformation is from man to woman (90e ff). The hierarchy of animals that follows evidently serves moralising and teleological purposes in the first instance.

Speusippus's interest in animal classification can be inferred from the fragments of his work that have been preserved. Several fragments suggest groupings based on similarities,[24] and one may introduce what may be a new zoological term. μαλακόστρακα, literally 'soft-shelled', appears in one testimony,[25] although priority between

as Burckhardt acknowledges, 1904, p. 390, no animal that is inedible is mentioned – which is natural enough in view of the dietetic interests of the author. While it may be granted that Aristotle often builds on common earlier beliefs and assumptions, Burckhardt rather begs the question of how far an explicit and systematic classification of animals had been elaborated before Aristotle. Harig and Kollesch (1974) have recently suggested a closer connection between *Vict.* II and the work of Mnesitheus and Diocles, and that these last two did do important work in zoological taxonomy is clear from the admittedly fragmentary remains and reports that have come down to us (see Wellmann 1901 for Diocles, Bertier 1972 for Mnesitheus). This is, however, work done around the middle of the fourth century at earliest (Harig and Kollesch accept a mid-fourth century date for Diocles, as does Kudlien 1963, against the conclusions of Jaeger 1938).

[22] Several of our admittedly very fragmentary sources for Democritus indicate that he was interested in zoological questions, and according to Diogenes Laertius (IX 46ff) he wrote a work in three books on the 'causes of animals'. But although Aristotle, for instance, intriguingly reports that Democritus held that the viscera of bloodless animals are invisible because they are so small (*PA* 665a30ff) – which *may* suggest that Democritus himself already used a general distinction between blooded and bloodless animals similar to Aristotle's own – that is far from certain. Indeed it seems more likely that the term 'bloodless' is Aristotle's interpretation, not original to Democritus. Elsewhere, at least, Aristotle notes that the 'blooded' and 'bloodless' groups have no regular common name, see *PA* 642b15f. We are not, in general, in any position to say how far Democritus proceeded towards a classification, nor even whether his interest in the 'causes' of animals included their taxonomy.

[23] In the *Sophist* (220ab), for example, when angling is being defined as a species of hunting, animals are first divided into 'walking' and 'swimming', νευστικόν, and the latter group then subdivided into 'winged' and 'water-animals'. In the *Politicus* (264d ff), however, when different kinds of herding are being classified, animals are first divided into water and land (ξηροβατικόν) and the latter then subdivided into 'winged' and 'walking'. Cf. also *Laws* 823b which implies a *trichotomy* into 'water-animals', 'winged animals' and 'those that go on land'.

[24] The evidence is collected in Lang 1911.   [25] Fr. 8 from Athenaeus 105b.

Speusippus and Aristotle, if Speusippus did use the term, is impossible to establish. Again it is evident from Aristotle's criticisms of the application of dichotomous division to zoological taxonomy in the *De Partibus Animalium* I chh. 2–4 that the possibility of such an application was discussed, along with the problems of classification in general, in the Academy.[26] What is not clear, however, is just how far either Speusippus or anyone else in the Academy went towards implementing such an idea in practice, or how far anyone before Aristotle elaborated a detailed and comprehensive zoological classification. Even Aristotle himself nowhere sets out a complete and definitive taxonomy, but concentrates rather on establishing the main differentiae of the principal groups.[27] Yet it is with Aristotle, certainly, that we have, for the first time in the extant literature, a considerable body of material relevant to our main concerns.

Although it would be a mistake to pin Aristotle down to too rigid a system of classification, the broad distinctions first between blooded and bloodless animals, and then within both the blooded and the bloodless groups are very stable. Thus the latter are regularly divided into four principal genera, cephalopods, crustacea, testacea and insects,[28] and although the groupings of blooded animals are more complex, he normally includes – besides man – viviparous quadrupeds and cetacea, oviparous quadrupeds and footless animals, birds and fish.[29] There are, too, some well-known explicit statements on the subject of how we should arrive at the main genera and species of animals, the method to be adopted. The most famous of these passages come in the programmatic first book of the *De Partibus Animalium* in the chapters of anti-Platonic, or at least anti-Academic, polemic that have just been mentioned. Whether Plato himself intended, and whether he would even have approved, the application of the method of division to the classification of animals are, as we said, controversial questions. But Aristotle's criticisms of dichotomy presuppose active debate, within the Academy, on the correct method in zoological taxonomy.

[26] That the Platonists in the Academy were interested in questions of zoological classification emerges not just from Plato's own dialogues and Aristotle's criticisms of division, but also from the well-known comic fragment in which such interests are mocked, Epicrates Fr. 11, Kock II 287–8.

[27] See, e.g., Balme (1961) 1975 and 1962a. Balme points especially to the lack of intermediate groups between the principal γένη and the individual species. One should not, however, underestimate the point that the principal γένη themselves are, on the whole, remarkably stable, see below, n. 29.

[28] I use the conventional translations of μαλάκια, μαλακόστρακα, ὀστρακόδερμα and ἔντομα.

[29] See, e.g., *HA* 490b7ff, 505b25ff, 523a31ff, 534b12ff, 539a8ff, *PA* 678a26ff, 685b27ff, *GA* 732b28ff.

The chief thrust of Aristotle's criticisms is to object to the artificiality and rigidity of dichotomous division and to restore to such main groups as fish and birds their 'natural' place in animal classification. He evidently thereby favours a procedure that keeps closer to the main genera already picked out in the natural language he used. To that extent he may be represented as recommending a return from a would-be deductive programme to, or at least towards, popular beliefs. At the same time his criticisms are not just directed at Academic deductive taxonomy, but also, on occasion, at Greek popular taxonomy itself. He is clear, for example, that whales and the other cetacea are not fish, that is that the term ἰχθῦς is not, strictly speaking, correctly applied to these viviparous sea-animals.[30] More importantly, he recognises that popular language lacks terms for important groups. His name for the crustacea, μαλακόστρακα, may appear also, as already noted, in Speusippus. But Aristotle's names for two of the other main groups of animals, μαλάκια (literally 'softies', for the cephalopods) and ὀστρακόδερμα (literally 'potsherd-skinned', for the testacea) are not attested in those senses before him. The identifications of, for example, the viviparous quadrupeds, or of the oviparous quadrupeds, and of the group that is, as he puts it, internally oviparous but externally viviparous – the ovovivipara, for example the selachia such as the sharks and rays, and the vipers – correspond to facts that were more or less well known before him, but again involve the introduction of terms of art.[31]

The principal features of Aristotle's zoological classification are familiar enough and up to a certain limited point it is not too inaccurate to represent him proceeding in a manner comparable with that of much later taxonomists such as Linnaeus. His position is, however, in certain respects quite different from that of a Linnaeus. At a number of points, some of minor, but others of crucial, importance, it may be suggested that his theories and procedures must be understood in the light of the popular assumptions that provide the main background to his work – including the type of belief that has been the focus of attention in the anthropological debate I outlined at the outset. It is this aspect of his zoology, the interaction of traditional and critical view-points, that I shall attempt to explore and document here. In the following studies I have selected three topics where Aristotle's treatment appears to reflect a complex reaction to the popular beliefs he inherited, namely (1) his ideas on

---

[30] See, e.g., *HA* 490 b 7ff, 505 b 29f.

[31] As already noted (n. 22) Aristotle himself remarks at *PA* 642 b 15f that the 'blooded' and the 'bloodless' groups have no regular common name.

the social behaviour and interrelations of animals, (2) his use of man
as a model in zoology, and (3) his treatment of intermediate,
marginal or boundary-crossing animals.

2. SOCIAL BEHAVIOUR OF ANIMALS IN ARISTOTLE'S ZOOLOGY

One of Aristotle's principal explicit aims, in his zoology, is to establish
the main differentiating characteristics of the various species of
animals, such a collection being essential as a preliminary to giving
their causes. He clearly recognises in this context – whatever may be
the case elsewhere in his work – that to try to state the definition of an
animal species by means of a genus and a *single* differentia is quite
mistaken and that any such definition will be grossly inadequate. This
is indeed one of the criticisms he makes against the use of dichotomous
division.[32] The form of the species will be captured, rather, by
a – presumably unique[33] – conjunction of differentiae.

Which differentiae he attaches most importance to cannot be
simply stated.[34] He pays more attention to the soul, ψυχή – that is to
the vital functions – than to the body, σῶμα, for ψυχή is the form,
σῶμα the matter, of the living creature. Accordingly he differentiates
groups of animals by their faculties of sensation, their means of
locomotion, their methods of reproduction. These capacities are, in
his view, closely correlated with certain primary qualities, the heat,
coldness, dryness and wetness of the animal. Thus the viviparous
animals, the ovoviviparous ones, the two main divisions of ovipara
(those that produce perfect, and those that have imperfect, eggs) and
the larvae-producing animals are arranged in a descending order of
'perfection', where the hotter, and wetter, the animal the more
perfect it is.[35] Since the possession of a vital faculty or capacity
presupposes certain physical parts or organs, he is also concerned,
naturally, with anatomical structure and morphology[36] – though
not, to be sure, from an evolutionary point of view. On the other
side – turning to what Aristotle leaves out – there is, as we noted, no
question of his paying any attention, in the zoological treatises, to the

---

[32] See, e.g., *PA* 642b7ff, 643b9ff, 28ff.

[33] In another criticism of dichotomy he implies that a species should appear only once in any
division, *PA* 642b31ff, 643a13ff.

[34] Cf. Balme (1961) 1975 for a detailed discussion.

[35] The most perfect animals, the vivipara, are hot and wet and not earthy. Next come animals
that are externally viviparous, but internally oviparous, which are said to be cold and wet.
Oviparous animals that produce perfect eggs are hot and dry, while ovipara that produce
imperfect eggs are cold and dry. The fifth group, the larva-producing animals, are said to be
coldest of all. *GA* 732b28 – 733b16, cf. Lloyd 1961, pp. 76f.

[36] As noted, for example, at *PA* 644b7ff.

religious associations of different species in defining and classifying them.

It is, however, at first sight surprising that, alongside the other principal differentiae which he considers, he includes certain aspects of the animal's behaviour. The first chapter of the first book of *Historia Animalium* sets out a whole range of differences that are to be taken into account, and these include differences in 'manner of life', in 'activities' and in 'character' or 'disposition' (ἦθη) (*HA* 487a11ff). His first example is the differences between land-animals and water-animals, which are partly a matter of where the animal lives and feeds, and partly a matter of whether it takes in and emits water or air. He considers, too, differences between animals that are gregarious and those that are solitary, between tame and wild ones, nocturnal and daylight ones, between carnivores, graminivorous animals and omnivorous ones. There is no reason why any of these factors should not be included in a scientific natural history. But Aristotle goes on to speak of animals' characters:

Some are gentle and sluggish and not inclined to be aggressive, such as the ox; others are ferocious, aggressive and stubborn, such as the wild boar; some are intelligent and timid, such as the deer and the hare; others are mean and scheming, such as the serpents; others are noble and brave and high-bred, such as the lion; others are thorough-bred, wild and scheming, such as the wolf. . . . Again some are mischievous and wicked, such as the fox; others are spirited and affectionate and fawning, such as the dog; some are gentle and easily tamed, such as the elephant; others are bashful and cautious, such as the goose; some are jealous and ostentatious, such as the peacock. (*HA* 488b13–24, trans. after Peck.)

Now in practice, in the body of *HA* and the other zoological works, Aristotle does not pay too much attention to such questions as whether an animal is mean or bashful or jealous or ostentatious (though he has more to say on the topic of animal intelligence). Yet *HA* I ch. 1 clearly suggests that he considers animal character to be part of his subject-matter. Nor is this the only such text in the zoological treatises. In *HA* VIII ch. 1, 588a17ff, he returns to the differences in animals' characters, remarking that there are traces of such differences in most animals, even though they are most clearly marked in man. He specifies differences in tameness and wildness, in gentleness and harshness, in courage and timidity, in fear and confidence, in spirit, in mischievousness and in intelligence.[37]

HA IX in turn provides a further extensive discussion of the question. The longer-lived animals have more recognisable characters, for example intelligence, stupidity, courage, timidity, gentleness,

---

[37] One of the later chapters of this book, ch. 29, *HA* 607a9ff, discusses briefly how location or habitat may affect the dispositions of animals.

harshness, ability to learn and so on (*HA* 608a 11ff). The opening two chapters are concerned especially with charting the *friendships* and *enmities* between animals. Some of the suggestions made are readily understandable in ecological terms: the friendships or enmities are said to depend on such factors as whether two species compete for the same food, or whether one species preys on another (e.g. *HA* 608b 19ff, 609a 4ff, 28ff) – which would be reason enough to consider the species in question to be hostile to one another. But other cases are much more puzzling until we realise that they stem not from literal experience – whether Aristotle's or anyone else's – so much as from literary or cultural experience.[38] Thus he writes of the enmities between the nuthatch and the eagle,[39] and between the crow and the owl,[40] and of the friendship between the crow and the heron.[41]

The remainder of this book deals further at great length with a variety of aspects of animal behaviour, remarking on certain species that are jealous, proud, fearless, quarrelsome, lecherous and so on, but paying most attention to instances of animals' intelligence or craftsmanlike skill. These range from the frankly fabulous to the acutely observed. In ch. 13, *HA* 616a 6ff, for example, he reports what 'those who live in the regions where the cinnamon bird lives' say about it: it brings the cinnamon from somewhere and builds its nest out of it on the tops of trees; the inhabitants attach lead weights to the tips of their arrows and bring down the nests from which they then collect the cinnamon.[42] On the other hand, ch. 37 contains accounts of how the fishing-frog uses the filaments in front of its eyes as bait to catch small fish (*HA* 620b 11ff), of how the torpedo lies in wait, hidden in sand or mud, to narcotise its victims (*HA* 620b 19ff) and, most remarkably, of how the male of the river-fish *Glanis* protects its young, standing guard over the spawn or fry for forty or fifty days and warding off intruders by darting at them and emitting a kind of

---

[38] The associations and dissociations of animals were, as is noted at *HA* 608b 27f, the basis of a well-known technique of divination (see also *EE* 1236b 6ff, and cf., e.g., Aeschylus, *Pr.* 484ff). D'Arcy Thompson (e.g. 1910, note to *HA* 609a 4) went further and suggested that in some cases the enmities and friendships mentioned in *HA* ix have an astrological basis, that is they correspond to the oppositions and conjunctions of the constellations that bear the same names as the animals in question. The theme of the friendships and enmities of animals and of plants continues in many later ancient writers, see, e.g., Aelian, *NA* 1 32, iii 22, iv 5, v 48, vi 22, Plutarch, *De Invidia et Odio* 537bc, and can be paralleled extensively in the Middle Ages, Renaissance and later, see, e.g., Foucault (1966) 1970, p. 24 n. 17, quoting Cardan.

[39] σίττη and ἀετός, *HA* 609b 11ff, cf. D'A.W. Thompson 1936, pp. 260f.

[40] *HA* 609a 8ff. Cf. Thompson's suggestion, 1936, p. 79, that the fable of the war between the crows and owls is oriental.

[41] *HA* 610a 8.

[42] On this and other fables concerning cinnamon, see Detienne's analysis (1972a), 1977, pp. 14–20.

muttering noise (*HA* 621 a 20ff) – an account often later dismissed as fictitious and only vindicated as substantially correct by the work of the naturalist Agassiz in the mid-nineteenth century.[43]

It is true that the authenticity of substantial sections of the *Historia Animalium* is in doubt and the ninth book, in particular, which provides our richest haul of examples of the quasi-human characters of animals, is often thought to be probably *not* by Aristotle. Following Aubert and Wimmer, Dittmeyer and others, Huby has recently made out a case for connecting the material in this book (as also parts of *HA* VIII) with Theophrastus.[44] Diogenes Laertius (v 43 and 49) reports that Theophrastus composed two books, one *On Animals said to be Spiteful* and the other *On the Intelligence and Character of Animals*. Neither is extant, and the direct evidence for their contents is meagre,[45] but in both cases their general subject-matter at least appears to correspond quite closely with topics covered in *HA* IX.

To this several remarks need to be made. First, if *HA* IX is indeed partly or largely by Theophrastus – who was closely associated with Aristotle and no mean naturalist himself – its value as evidence for the interaction of scientific and popular beliefs is scarcely diminished.

Secondly, the kinds of differentiae discussed in *HA* IX conform, in the main, to the general guidelines laid down in *HA* I. This has a greater, though not, it is true, undeniable, claim to be by Aristotle himself. Moreover it contains two forward-looking references that promise further discussion of the differences in the 'manner of life', 'activities' and 'characters' of animals. At *HA* 487 a 11ff he says he will deal with these, and with the differences in animals' parts, in outline

---

[43] See D'A.W. Thompson 1947, pp. 43ff, reporting the work of L. Agassiz 1857.

[44] Following Aubert and Wimmer 1868, Dittmeyer attacked the authenticity of *HA* IX with detailed arguments and suggested that parts of the book correspond to the subject-matter of works ascribed to Theophrastus (Dittmeyer 1887, pp. 16–29, 65–79, 145–62). While many of his points, particularly concerning the terminology used in this book, are suggestive, the force of some of his arguments is weakened first by his assuming too readily that discrepancies between *HA* IX and other parts of *HA* show the inauthenticity of the former: this discounts the possibility of Aristotle modifying his views, and so far as discrepancies between books VIII and IX go (which account for a high proportion of those Dittmeyer discusses), the assumption that VIII as we have it is all authentic is also questionable. Moreover, secondly, many of Dittmeyer's arguments from what he considers the absurdity of the material contained in IX – particularly where it deals with the characters of animals or recounts fables which are 'unworthy of Aristotle' – are dangerously subjective and beg the question of the extent to which Aristotle himself was prepared to incorporate such differentiae into his discussion. While it cannot be denied that parts of *HA* IX may be by other hands, the interests it develops are closer to some we should ascribe to Aristotle himself than Dittmeyer allowed. For further discussion of the inauthenticity of *HA* IX see Joachim 1892, Dirlmeier 1937, pp. 55ff, Regenbogen 1940, cols. 1423ff, and Huby unpublished. Against this the case for considering the contents of *HA* as a whole, including IX, as in the main authentic has been restated forcefully by Balme unpublished.

[45] It is reviewed in Huby unpublished.

first and come back later to attend to each of the groups of animals. Again at *HA* 488b27f, after the examples of animals' characters given in *HA* 488b13–24, quoted above, he says that with regard to the characters and the manners of life of each of the groups of animals he will speak later with greater accuracy. If these passages are genuine, and not editorial additions, they show that some detailed discussion of animals' characters was planned for *HA*, even if the account we actually have in *HA* ix may not be or may not wholly be by Aristotle.

But the third and by far the most important consideration is that Aristotle clearly accommodates differences in character and intelligence within the theoretical framework provided by remarks that he makes in the *De Partibus Animalium*. There, in *PA* ii chh. 2 and 4 especially, he correlates certain such differences with differences in the qualities of the animals' blood or (in the bloodless animals) of its counterpart. Thus at *PA* 648a2ff he notes that the thinner and colder the blood, the more conducive to perception and intelligence it is. Remarking that this applies also to 'what is analogous to blood' in other animals, he says that this explains why bees, for instance, are more intelligent than many blooded animals. Creatures that have hot, thin and pure blood, he goes on to suggest, are superior in courage as well as in intelligence. At *PA* 650b27ff he suggests further that animals with watery blood are timorous, that animals that have blood that is full of thick fibres are high-spirited and 'liable to outbursts of passion' (he instances bulls and boars) and in general that the nature of the blood is 'responsible for many things' in regard both to the character of animals and to perception.

Moreover the correlations between 'psychic' and 'bodily' characteristics are not limited to those that he mentions when discussing the qualities of the blood in *PA* ii. Aristotle is also prepared to take quite seriously the practice of physiognomy – the inferring of character traits from external bodily signs. It is true that in the *Prior Analytics*, 70b7ff, this is discussed in hypothetical terms. 'The practice of physiognomy is possible, *if* one grants that the body and the soul change together, so far as the natural affections go', that is those that relate to passions and desires. Again at 70b11ff he puts it:

if then this were granted and for each thing [change or affection] there is one sign, and if we were able to grasp the affection and the sign proper to each kind [of animal], then we shall be able to practise physiognomy. For *if* there is an affection that belongs properly to some indivisible kind – such as courage to lions – there is necessarily also a sign for it: for it is assumed that they are modified together.

Such a sign might be, he suggests, the possession of large extremities, which may belong to other kinds as well, but not universally, and he goes on to consider the problem that arises if a species has two 'proper' characteristics – such as courage and generosity in the lion – when we have to try to distinguish which sign corresponds to which characteristic.[46]

The treatment of physiognomy in the *Prior Analytics* is hypothetical throughout. Aristotle is interested, there, in the formal structure of inferences, on the assumption of a correlation between certain psychic and bodily characteristics.[47] Yet there are passages in the zoological works, particularly in the first book of *Historia Animalium*, that show that Aristotle was prepared to endorse certain such correlations. In *HA* I ch. 8, 491 b 12ff, for instance, discussing the face, he remarks: 'Persons who have a large forehead [we are to understand 'ox-like'[48]] are sluggish, those who have a small one are fickle; those who have a broad one are excitable, those who have a bulging one, spirited.' The next three chapters deal with the eyebrows, eyelids, eyes and ears. Straight eyebrows are said to be a sign of a soft disposition (491 b 15), those that bend in towards the nose are a sign of harshness, those that bend out towards the temples indicate a mocking, dissimulating character (491 b 15ff). If the parts where the upper and lower eyelids join are long, this is a sign of malice, if they have the part towards the nose fleshy – as kites do[49] – this is a sign of dishonesty (491 b 24ff). As for the eyes, those that are neither very deepset nor protrude excessively are a sign of the finest disposition (492 a 8ff): those that tend to blink indicate unreliability, and those that remain unblinking impudence, while those that avoid both extremes are, again, a sign of the finest disposition (492 a 10ff). As for the ears, those that are intermediate between protruding too much and not standing out at all are the sign of the finest disposition. Large projecting ears are a sign of 'foolish talk and chatter' (492 a 34ff), and he is even at pains to point out that the smoothness or hairiness of the ears does *not* signify character (492 a 32ff).

The correlations proposed in *HA* are quite modest and restrained,[50] especially when we compare them with some of the highly

---

[46] Aristotle's proposed solution is to consider another class to which both affections belong, but not as a whole (that is not to some members of the class). 'For if a man is courageous but not generous, and exhibits one of the two signs, clearly this will be the sign of courage in the lion as well.'

[47] The practice of physiognomy is included in *APr.* II ch. 27 as part of a discussion of inferences from signs, and Aristotle ends by stating the formal relations that must hold between the terms in syllogisms expressing such inferences (*APr.* 70 b 32ff).

[48] Cf. *Phgn.* 811 b 29f.

[49] Reading ἰκτῖνες at *HA* 491 b 25, with Peck, for Bekker's κτένες.

[50] Elsewhere Aristotle himself remarked critically on the lengths to which one physiognomist went in reducing all human faces to those of two or three animals, see *GA* 769 b 20ff. The evidence for the practice of physiognomy in the fifth and fourth centuries B.C. has been

elaborate extant physiognomical treatises.[51] Thus the work *Physiognomonica* – which is included in the Aristotelian Corpus – sets out, for example, detailed suggestions both for how certain characters can be recognised ('signs of courage are: coarse hair, an upright carriage of the body . . . the belly broad and flat', 807 a 31ff) and on how to interpret particular bodily signs: 'when the lower leg is at once well-articulated and sinewy and stalwart, it signifies a strong character, as in the male sex: when it is thin and sinewy, it signifies loquacity, as in birds. When it is full and almost bursting, it signifies by congruity blatant effrontery' (810 a 28ff, trans. Loveday and Forster). There is no reason to suppose that this work is by Aristotle himself. On the other hand its incorporation in the Aristotelian Corpus is understandable. Not only does it repeat some of the specific correlations suggested in *HA*,[52] but the study it engages on is one that has some support, at least in principle, from Aristotle. The chief difference between *Physiognomonica* and the zoological treatises lies in the extent to which the idea of such correlations is elaborated.

A considerable body of ideas that have their origins in popular belief or in folklore thus finds a place in Aristotle's zoological investigations. For him – as for so many other Greek writers from Homer onwards – the wild boar is ferocious, the lion noble, the deer timid, the fox mischievous, the snake mean. Moreover this attribution of character and of intelligence to animals is all the more remarkable in that it contrasts, even if it does not actually conflict, with aspects of the analysis he offers in his moral philosophical treatises. As he makes clear in the ethics, courage, strictly speaking, implies moral choice and deliberation – which no animal has – and so too do all the other

discussed by Joly 1962. The story is told that when the physiognomist Zopyrus diagnosed faults in Socrates's character from his appearance, Socrates himself agreed but claimed that they had been overcome by reason: see Cicero, *De Fato* 5.10, *Tusc.* IV 37.80, Alexander, *De Fato* 6.

[51] The fortunes of physiognomy fluctuated after Aristotle, but some endorsement of the practice is given by a large number of authors. Förster 1893, I and II, contains not only the principal complete texts devoted to the topic but also a representative selection of shorter passages from a wide variety of Greek and Latin authors, including not only such writers as Pliny and Plutarch, but also and especially Galen; see, e.g., Evans 1941, Pack 1941, pp. 330ff, Armstrong 1958. On the practice and associated beliefs as they are found in other societies and later in Europe – including both the naturalising representation of man and the humanising representation of animals – see Lévi-Strauss (1962a) 1966, pp. 115ff, and plates III and IV especially.

[52] Thus both *HA* 491 b 12 and *Phgn.* 811 b 29f suggest a correlation between large foreheads and sluggishness (the term is βραδύτεροι in *HA*, νωθροί in *Phgn.*) and *Phgn.* adds that oxen are referred to as an example (cf. n. 48 above). *Phgn.* also shares with *HA* a preference for qualities that correspond to a mean between two extremes, see, e.g., *Phgn.* 811 b 21f, 24f, and cf. *HA* 492 a 8ff, 10ff, b 30f.

moral excellences and φρόνησις, practical intelligence.[53] According to the ethics, then, we can only speak of animals as courageous or as φρόνιμος, intelligent, in a metaphorical or at least extended sense. Yet in the zoology he frequently uses these terms in relation to animals with no hint of any reservation – without, that is, calling attention to the point that these are at most 'natural' not 'moral' excellences.

Of course what is happening here is that characteristic human differentiae (differences in character and moral disposition or behaviour generally) are being used to map differences between animals – the exact converse of using animal types to map the differences between human natures: but it is only because of the deeply ingrained assumption of the parallelism of the two series that Aristotle evidently feels that he has to consider and assimilate differentiae of this kind alongside differences in, for example, methods of reproduction in his zoological account.

There was every reason, we might say, from the point of view of his analysis of human character and intelligence, for Aristotle to have insisted on a hard and fast contrast between animals and humans in these respects. In the zoological works some distinctions are maintained – such as that man alone is capable of deliberation[54] – and he certainly holds that character differences are more marked in man than in animals.[55] Yet in other contexts the boundaries set up in the ethics tend to be eroded. That assumption of the parallelism between the human and the animal series, which is such a feature of Greek popular belief, still finds an echo in Aristotle's inquiries, both in the particular characterisations of animal species that he offers, and in the fact that he offers such characterisations (in terms of *character* and *disposition*) at all.

Neither the attribution of constant characters to animal species, nor the idea that certain resemblances to animals can indicate character in humans, is ruled out by Aristotle. On the contrary, the effect of his discussion is rather to provide these ideas with some kind of rational basis, while at the same time limiting them and restricting their range of application. Physiognomical inferences depend on a strict correlation between sign and affection. Since the soul and the body often change together, such correlations can occur, although in

---

[53] See, e.g., *EN* 1111b4ff, 1144b1ff and the comparisons with animals in the accounts of courage and temperance, e.g. 1116b24f, 30ff, 1118a23ff: cf. Fortenbaugh 1971. The references to the 'political' organisations of animals are similarly, and more obviously, metaphorical or extended: see, e.g., *HA* 488a7ff, 589a1ff, and in the account of bees, especially, at *HA* 553a17ff, 623b8ff.

[54] See, e.g., *HA* I ch. 1, 488b24f.

[55] *HA* VIII ch. 1, 588a18ff (see above, p. 19) and cf. IX ch. 1, 608a11ff.

practice the range of examples in the *Historia Animalium* is not very extensive. Equally the correlation of character traits with certain physical qualities – for example the qualities of the blood – entitles the zoologist to investigate, up to a point even commits him to investigate, the characters of animal species, although again, in practice, Aristotle pays far less attention to such matters as the jealousy of the peacock and the meanness of the snake, than to their anatomy, physiology and methods of reproduction or mode of locomotion. In both these areas there is, we may say, a limited acceptance of ideas that stem from popular or folk beliefs, although Aristotle is largely successful in avoiding their more excessive and more arbitrary manifestations. More importantly, in both cases, what is taken over is incorporated within the framework of his zoological theories. Some of the underlying assumptions, at least, are made explicit, and the pursuit of parallelisms between the animal and the human series is provided with some justification or rationalisation within his account of the proper subject-matter of zoology.

3. MAN AS MODEL IN ARISTOTLE'S ZOOLOGY

No one who reads the zoological treatises is likely to fail to register that man is allotted a special place in Aristotle's account of the animal kingdom, although, since this feature corresponds to certain deep-seated assumptions widely shared today, it may occasion little surprise.[56] We are all familiar with representations of the animal kingdom as a single many-branched tree. Since Darwin, such trees have been interpreted in evolutionary terms. But long before Darwin the tree idea and tree diagrams were common devices for structuring the interrelations of the main groups of animals – with man regularly appearing at the top, as the supreme animal. Aristotle is quite explicit both about the uniqueness of man and about his position as model or paradigm. He has, to be sure, a psychological theory that grounds the claim that man is the supreme animal, for – despite the evidence we have considered above that shows that Aristotle is willing to talk about animals as intelligent, φρόνιμος – man alone has the power of reasoning, νοῦς. But the claim that man is exceptional or unique takes

---

[56] Most discussions of Aristotle's zoology deal with aspects of this question, though sometimes without attaching great importance to it. See, however, e.g., Le Blond 1945, pp. 44f, Bourgey 1955, pp. 122ff, Joly 1968, pp. 231ff, Dierauer 1977, pp. 100ff, 151ff, Vegetti 1979, pp. 50ff, 104ff, Byl 1980, pp. 304ff, and especially Clark 1975, pp. 28ff. On many particular points the notes in Ogle 1882 are instructive, as also are some of the observations in Lewes 1864 (though some are inaccurate). Among studies that discuss aspects of later developments Lovejoy 1936 and Foucault (1966) 1970 must be mentioned especially.

many other forms. My aim here is first (I) to review such claims,[57] and then (II) to examine the influence of what we may call the anthropocentric perspective on Aristotle's zoology more generally. How did it affect the way he formulated the questions to be studied? What light does it throw on the tension between the descriptive and the normative aspects of the concept of nature in his work?

I

As a matter of mere organisation, man regularly comes either at the beginning or at the end of Aristotle's discussion of the other species of animal. At *HA* I ch. 6, 491 a 19ff, discussing the order in which the parts of animals should be considered, he writes: 'First the parts of man must be grasped. For just as everyone reckons currency by the standard that is most familiar to themselves, so indeed we proceed in other matters also. Man is necessarily the animal most familiar to us.'[58] Yet immediately we confront a paradox. Although man's *external* parts are, to be sure, most familiar to us, the same is certainly not true, for Aristotle, of his *internal* parts. Quite the reverse. Indeed when Aristotle turns to consider the internal parts a little later, at *HA* I ch. 16, 494 b 21ff, he points out that 'those of man are, on the contrary, for the most part unknown, and so we must refer to the parts of other animals which those of man resemble and examine them'. Although some scholars have argued that Aristotle may have carried out dissections on the human embryo,[59] it is sufficiently clear that in general neither Aristotle nor any of his contemporaries entertained the possibility of dissecting adult human subjects *post mortem*.[60] Nevertheless Aristotle evidently has man principally in mind throughout his preliminary account of the external and internal parts in *HA* I chh. 7ff. Here as elsewhere man provides a standard of comparison for the other animals.[61]

To this first, epistemic, reason for man's priority, Aristotle elsewhere adds others derived from his doctrine of man's essential

[57] I am most grateful to my colleague Professor Gabriel Horn for the opportunity to consult him on a number of anatomical and zoological points. He bears, however, no responsibility for the accuracy of my statements.

[58] Aristotle does not here imply his usual contrast between what is more familiar 'to us' and what is more familiar 'by nature' (e.g. *APo.* 71 b 33ff, cf. *Ph.* 184 a 16ff), for other animals are not more familiar 'by nature'.

[59] See Ogle 1882, p. 149, Shaw 1972, pp. 366ff. However at *HA* 583 b 14ff, where he purports to describe a human embryo aborted on the fortieth day from conception, he records what happens when the embryo is put into water and its external membrane is removed to reveal the embryo inside, but there is no suggestion that he then proceeded to a dissection.

[60] This is suggested not only by *HA* 494 b 21ff, but also, e.g., by *HA* 511 b 13ff and 513 a 12ff.

[61] Cf. further below, p. 41 and nn. 165–7.

nature. Introducing his account of the anhomoeomerous parts at *PA*
656a3ff, he writes that their variety is greater in animals than in
plants, and particularly so in animals that share not just in life, but in
the good life, as man does. 'For of the animals familiar to us he alone
shares in the divine, or does so most of all. So for this reason, and
because the shape of the external parts is especially familiar, we must
speak of him first.' To these considerations he adds another to which
we shall return later: 'the natural parts are according to nature in him
alone, and his upper part is directed to the upper part of the
universe.[62] For man alone of the animals is upright.'

In a variety of passages in the psychological and zoological works[63]
Aristotle engages in quite detailed discussions of such questions as
which animals possess which senses (though, to be animals, they must
all have the sense of touch[64]), and he acknowledges that many
animals have φαντασία, imagination,[65] and μνήμη, memory,[66] and
that some have some kind of practical intelligence, φρόνησις, and
capacities that are analogous to skill, τέχνη, and sagacity, σοφία.[67]
But although there are certain fluctuations in his statements concerning the relationship between νοῦς and φαντασία,[68] his view of the
major distinction between man and the rest of the animal kingdom is

---

[62] Yet in the *De Caelo* II ch. 2, especially 285b14ff, when he considers the sense in which up and
down, right and left, front and back can be applied to the spherical universe, he concludes
that the visible northern celestial pole is the lowest part of the universe – that is that the
sphere is 'upside down' – basing this on the principle that movement starts from the right
and is 'to the right' and on the observed rotation of the outermost heaven from east to west.

[63] Apart from the *De Sensu*, see especially *De Anima* II chh. 7ff, 418a26ff, *HA* IV ch. 8, 532b29ff,
PA II chh. 10ff, 656b26ff. I use the terms 'psychological' and 'zoological' for the treatises we
conventionally distinguish as such, although for Aristotle there is an important sense in
which the latter works engage in an inquiry that is continuous with that of the former: see,
e.g., *Sens.* 436a1–11.

[64] E.g. *PA* 666a34. The difficult question of which living beings are animals and which plants
is to be resolved primarily in terms of the presence or absence of perception, although in
practice Aristotle recognises that there may be disagreement on such cases as the sponges
(contrast *HA* 487b9f and 548b10ff with *HA* 588b20f, *PA* 681a9ff and 15ff) and he states
that nature passes in a continuous gradation from lifeless things to animals (*HA* 588b4ff, *PA*
681a12ff, cf. further below, p. 51).

[65] At *de An.* 413b21ff Aristotle suggests that imagination and desire follow on perception,
though at *de An.* 428a8ff he says that not all animals have imagination, instancing ants and
bees. There are subtle analyses of Aristotle's doctrine of φαντασία in Schofield 1978 and
Nussbaum 1978.

[66] See, e.g., *Metaph.* 980a27ff, b25ff, cf. *EN* 1147b5. At *Mem.* 453a6ff and *HA* 488b25f he
points out, further, that while many animals have the power of memory, the faculty of
recollection, ἀναμιμνήσκεσθαι, belongs 'virtually' to man alone.

[67] See, e.g., *HA* 588a23ff, 29ff (which adds σύνεσις), 608a15, 612b18ff, 616b27, *PA* 648a5ff,
GA 753a11ff, *Metaph.* 980b21ff, *EN* 1141a26ff, and cf. above, pp. 20ff and 24.

[68] While νοῦς is sometimes contrasted with φαντασία (as for example at *de An.* 428a16ff, cf.
433a10ff) he states at *de An.* 431a16f that the soul does not think without φάντασμα, and he
canvasses the possibilities at 433a10ff that φαντασία is a kind of thinking, νόησίς τις, and at
403a8f that thinking, νοεῖν, is a kind of φαντασία or 'not without' φαντασία.

not in doubt. Man alone, as we said, has reason, and it is evidently primarily on this account that man 'alone or supremely' may be said to share in the divine.[69]

This conception of the essential distinction between the psychological faculties of man and those of other animals provides the general background against which Aristotle's frequent remarks about the exceptional anatomical or physiological characteristics of the human species must be viewed, although the occasions for those remarks extend far beyond contexts directly related to the doctrine of ψυχή. The accuracy of the claims that Aristotle advances is very variable, and the diversity of topics they relate to is remarkable.

One such claim that is both readily comprehensible and quite unexceptionable is that man alone is capable of speech, διάλεκτος, although many species have voice, φωνή.[70] However, ignoring the role of the vocal chords, Aristotle sets about explaining this, in part, by referring to differences in such parts as the tongue, lips and teeth. Thus at *PA* 659b30ff he describes men's lips as soft and fleshy and able to be separated both for the sake of protecting the teeth and to make speech possible. At *PA* 661b13f he says that the incisors are as many as they are, and have the character they have, for the sake of speech, though he does not specify this further. Yet the general correlation that Aristotle suggests between the level of vocal articulation and the looseness and flexibility of the tongue is, in certain respects, problematic. At *PA* 660a30ff he suggests that the blooded viviparous quadrupeds have a limited vocal articulation because they have a hard and thick tongue and one that is not loose or free, ἀπολελυμένη, and at 660b3ff he says that blooded oviparous land-animals have tongues that are useless for voice because they are 'fastened down', προσδεδεμένη, and hard. Man's tongue, on the other hand, is said to be especially free and soft and broad (*PA* 660a17ff) and at *PA* 660a29ff he claims that 'among birds the most articulate talkers are those with the broadest tongues'.[71] However compared with such creatures as the lizard or the snake that catch food with their tongues, man can hardly be said to have a more flexible or 'freer' tongue.[72]

---

[69] See *PA* 686a27ff, cf. *GA* 736b27ff, 737a10. Yet Aristotle is prepared to acknowledge that other species of animals have something of the divine, θεῖον, for example that bees do, *GA* 761a4f, cf. *Div. Somn.* 463b12ff.

[70] See *HA* 535a27ff, 536a32ff, cf. *GA* 786b18ff.

[71] Cf. also *HA* 536a20ff.

[72] The tongues of snakes and lizards are described as long and forked, *HA* 508a23ff, *PA* 660b5ff, 691a5ff, and they are not explicitly excepted from the generalisation, at *PA* 660b3ff, that the tongues of blooded oviparous animals are useless for voice because 'fastened down' and hard.

A rapid survey of some of the other claims that are made for the uniqueness or exceptional character of man will indicate their variety. Man, we are told, alone has a face, πρόσωπον;[73] alone has hair on both eyelids;[74] blinks most and has eyes with the greatest variety of colours.[75] Man alone cannot move his ears,[76] and alone has no teeth when born.[77] He alone is erect,[78] has breasts in front,[79] has hands,[80] can alone become ambidextrous,[81] and has the smallest nails.[82] Humans alone have a variable period of gestation,[83] and can produce either one or a few or many offspring at a single parturition.[84] In proportion to their size women have the greatest quantity of menses,[85] and men of sperm,[86] and man has, proportionately, the largest and moistest brain[87] – the bregma being especially soft in the young[88] – and he is more liable to baldness than any other animal.[89] He has, too, the largest feet in proportion to his size,[90] and he is the only animal to have fleshy legs and buttocks.[91]

To these instances can be added others where he introduces certain qualifications to the claims he makes. Thus on the question of the length of life of different species of animals he expresses himself with some caution. Man is the longest-lived animal 'at least of those of which we have reliable experience', with the exception of the elephant.[92] This is, to be sure, open to correction: of the species of animals well known to Aristotle, the tortoises at least often live longer than man. But his awareness of the complexity of this issue comes out

---

[73] See *HA* 491 b9ff, *PA* 662 b17ff: yet contrast, e.g., *HA* 579a2 and 631 a5f, where πρόσωπον is used in relation to other animals.

[74] *PA* 658a14f, 24f, *HA* 498b21ff: the remark is qualified at *HA* 498b24f, however, and cf. *PA* 658a25f.

[75] *HA* 492a5f, *PA* 657a35ff, *GA* 779a26ff, which refers both to differences in eye-colour and to changes in the colour of the eye during early infancy.

[76] *HA* 492a22f, 28. Aristotle is speaking of the external appendage rather than the auditory duct or πόρος.

[77] *GA* 745b9ff, *HA* 587b13ff.

[78] A much repeated statement, e.g. *PA* 653a30f, 656a12f, 662b20ff, 669b5ff, 686a27ff, 687a4ff, 689b11ff, 690a28f, *IA* 710b9ff.

[79] *HA* 497b34ff, cf. 500a15ff, *PA* 688a18ff.

[80] *PA* 687a5ff.

[81] *HA* 497b31, cf. *EN* 1134b33ff, *MM* 1194b33ff.

[82] *GA* 745b17f.

[83] *HA* 584a33ff, *GA* 772b7ff.

[84] *HA* 584b26ff, *GA* 772a37ff.

[85] *HA* 521a26f, 572b29ff, 582b28ff, *GA* 727a22f, 728b14f, 738b4ff, 775b2ff.

[86] *HA* 523a15, 583a4ff, *GA* 728b15f.

[87] *HA* 494b27ff, *PA* 653a27f, 658b7ff, *GA* 744a26ff, *Sens.* 444a28ff.

[88] *HA* 587b11ff, *PA* 653a33ff, *GA* 744a24ff.

[89] *GA* 783b8ff.   [90] *PA* 690a27f.

[91] *HA* 499a31ff, *PA* 689b5ff, 14ff.

[92] *GA* 777b3ff, cf. *Long.* 466a11ff. At *Long.* 466a9f he says that the longest lived living things are certain plants, such as the date-palm.

in his more detailed discussion of the problem in *De Longaevitate*. There he explicitly rejects a series of correlations as not holding universally. It is not the case, straightforwardly, that it is the largest animals that are longest lived, nor that it is the small ones:[93] nor is it the blooded kinds, nor the bloodless ones; nor does habitat determine the matter, for it is not always those that live in the sea, nor again always the land-animals and plants, that live longest.[94] Again when he considers the individual senses, he claims that man has the most accurate sense of touch and taste, but he is well aware that some of man's other senses are less exact than those of certain other species of animals.[95]

But if Aristotle thus shows a certain caution in some of his pronouncements concerning the exceptional physical characteristics of the human race, many more of his statements are exaggerated or even grossly inaccurate. It is particularly striking that several of his generalisations conflict with other remarks to be found in the zoological treatises in the detailed accounts of other species of animals.[96] His statement that in man alone there is a variable period of gestation (above, n. 83) contrasts with what we read elsewhere. In *HA* v and vi a number of species are said to have periods of gestation that vary to some degree, for example dogs,[97] while other texts note that the period of gestation of other species is disputed.[98] Again his statement that man is exceptional in producing either one or a few or many offspring at a single parturition (above n. 84) should be read in the light of other texts that refer to other species of which the same is true, for example the bear and the pig.[99]

Several of his claims are particularly difficult to reconcile not just with what is true of the anthropoid primates, but with what passages in the zoological treatises themselves tell us about them. The discussion of the ape, monkey and baboon in *HA* ii chh. 8–9 is brief,

---

[93] *Long.* 466a1ff. 'For the most part', however, larger animals are longer lived than smaller ones: 466a13ff.

[94] *Long.* 466a4–9. 466b7ff suggests that salacious animals and those that abound in seed age quickly, which appears to conflict with his view that man is both long-lived and abundant in seed (above, n. 86).

[95] See *HA* 494b16–18, *PA* 660a11ff (where Aristotle claims that man's flesh is the softest: cf. also his view that man's skin is the thinnest, *GA* 781b21f, 785b8f, and that man is most naked, *GA* 745b15ff, cf. *HA* 582b34ff), *GA* 781b17ff (where he distinguishes perception at a distance from the ability to discriminate differences), cf. *de An.* 421a18ff, *Sens.* 440b31ff (where he even says that man's sense of smell is worse than that of any other animal).

[96] It is, of course, possible that some such discrepancies reflect the inauthenticity of isolated texts, or of extended sections, of the zoological treatises.

[97] See *HA* 545b6ff, 574a20ff.

[98] See *HA* 578a17ff on the elephant, and cf. 575a25ff on the cow.

[99] *HA* 579a20ff, *GA* 774b17ff, 23ff, and cf. *HA* 575b33ff on the mare.

but includes a number of points that conflict with claims made elsewhere about man's peculiar characteristics. Among the features that the ape, for example, shares with man are that it has hair on both eyelids (cf. above n. 74) though the lashes on the lower lid are fine and small;[100] that it has breasts on its chest (cf. above, n. 79);[101] that it has a face, πρόσωπον, that resembles that of man in many respects (cf. above n. 73),[102] and indeed that it has arms, hands, fingers and nails like those of man (cf. n. 80) although the arms are hairy and the other parts 'more beastlike'.[103] The ape bends its arms and legs in the same way as man,[104] and as a biped it has no tail, or only a very small one.[105] On the other hand it shares certain characteristics with the quadrupeds,[106] and it is said to spend more time on all fours than upright.[107] In view of the special importance that Aristotle attaches to man's possession of hands,[108] it is particularly remarkable that he allows that the ape too has hands and even uses its feet as both feet and hands.[109]

In many other instances the problem is not that Aristotle is verifiably wrong nor that he appears to be inconsistent, but rather that his statements are so imprecise that they are very hard or even impossible to evaluate. This applies especially to some of his physiological doctrines, for example his account of the differences in the quality of the blood in different species. As we saw before (p. 22), it is, in part, in terms of these differences that various physical and psychological characteristics, including strength, intelligence and character, are to be explained. At *PA* 647 b 29ff he identifies the chief differentiae of the blood as being thickness and thinness, purity and turbidity, coldness and heat, and he remarks that such differences within the homoeomerous parts serve a good purpose. The thicker

---

[100] *HA* 502 a 31ff.

[101] *HA* 502 a 34ff. 502 a 22ff points out that the ape has hair on the front/underside of the body, like men, though the hair is coarse.

[102] *HA* 502 a 27ff, cf. 502 a 20f on baboons and 503 a 18f on the χοιροπίθηκος, pig-faced baboon.

[103] *HA* 502 a 35ff, b 3ff.

[104] *HA* 502 b 1ff, a point that is not taken up again when Aristotle considers the various flexions of the limbs in *IA* chh. 12f, 711 a 8ff.

[105] *HA* 502 b 22f, cf. *PA* 689 b 33f. On the other hand it shares with the quadrupeds that it has no buttocks, *HA* 502 b 21f, *PA* 689 b 33f.

[106] For example it has hair on its back (*HA* 502 a 23) and the upper portion of its body is greater than the lower (*HA* 502 b 14ff – the 'upper' parts of quadrupeds being their fore parts, cf. below, n. 158).

[107] *HA* 502 b 20f.

[108] In a famous passage in *PA*, 687 a 9ff, Aristotle argues that man was endowed with hands because of his superior intelligence, not (as Anaxagoras had held) that he has superior intelligence because he possesses hands.

[109] *HA* 502 b 3ff, 10ff, 16ff. The claim (above, n. 90) that man has the largest feet in proportion to his size also seems to overlook the ape (see *HA* 502 b 5ff).

and warmer the blood is, he continues (*PA* 648a2ff), the more conducive it is to strength, while the thinner and colder it is, the more it contributes to perception and intelligence. The differentiae apply also to what is analogous to blood in the bloodless animals, and so it is that bees are more intelligent than some blooded creatures. Best of all, he concludes at *PA* 648a9ff, are those animals whose blood is hot and at the same time thin and pure, for that is good both for courage and for intelligence. That he has humans in mind is obvious and is confirmed by, for example, the statement at *HA* 521a2f that men have the thinnest and purest blood.

Yet how precisely the 'purity' and the 'thinness' of the blood are to be determined is not explained. As for 'heat', he points out the ambiguity of the term and recognises how difficult it is to decide which animals, and which parts, are hotter or colder than others.[110] One of the outcomes of his treatment of the topic is to insist that superficial appearances – whether something appears hot to the touch – may be misleading.[111] Although he occasionally remarks on, for example, the particular thickness of bull's blood,[112] and the poor coagulation of the blood of the deer,[113] we may have doubts about how far his general doctrines are based on detailed empirical observations. Two factors especially must be thought to call in question the extent, or at least the quality, of such observations. First, while Aristotle engages in the long-standing controversy on the question of whether males or females are hotter,[114] there is no sign that he had noticed – any more than his predecessors did – that the temperature of women varies at different parts of the menstrual cycle. The issue of the temperature of the two sexes still continues to be discussed without reference to such variations, although it must be

---

[110] *PA* 648a33–649b8 and 649b20ff.

[111] Thus the heat may be acquired, not innate, or it may be accidental, not essential (*PA* 648b35ff). At *PA* 649a17, b23f, he implies that in the case of blood the substratum is not hot, but blood owes its heat to another factor, the vital heat from the heart. It is the temperature of the heart that determines the heat of the blood (cf. *PA* 670a23ff), but of course determining the temperature of the heart is no easy matter, even though Aristotle asserts (*PA* 666b35ff) that of the three vessels of the heart the right has the most blood and the hottest, the left the least and the coldest. Elsewhere (*GA* 732b32ff) the possession of lungs is said to be an indicator of heat (the role of the lungs in respiration being to cool the heat round the heart), and Aristotle further suggests correlations between the heat of a species and its method of reproduction (*GA* 733a32ff, cf. above, p. 18 n. 35).

[112] *HA* 521a3f, mentioning also its blackness and the similar qualities of asses' blood, cf. *HA* 520b26f, *PA* 651a2ff, on its particular coagulability.

[113] See *HA* 515b33ff, 520b23ff, *Mete.* 384a26f, *PA* 650b14ff (where Ogle notes, ad loc., 1882, p. 161 n. 2, that the blood of hunted animals coagulates imperfectly: cf. D'Arcy Thompson on *HA* 515b33ff, and Lewes 1864, pp. 283f).

[114] *PA* II ch. 2, 648a28ff, and for an account of the dispute in Aristotle's predecessors, see Lesky 1951, pp. 31ff, Lloyd 1966, pp. 17, 58f.

added that Aristotle might well have considered them irrelevant to the question of the essential heat of males and females.

Secondly, although he suggests that blood in the upper parts of the body is superior to that in the lower in the characteristics he is interested in (purity, thinness and heat) and again that blood on the right side is similarly superior to that on the left,[115] at no stage does he draw attention to – even if only to dismiss as irrelevant to his concerns – the far more obvious apparent differences in colour and pressure between the blood in the venous, and that in the arterial, system.[116] Thus while certain partly imaginary differences provide the framework of his theoretical distinctions, other directly observable differences are ignored.

Similarly the evidential basis for his repeated remark that the male human emits more seed than any other animal (above, n. 86) is problematic. It is true that some quantitative data are given in his discussion of the analogous question of the extent of the catamenia in different species, where he evidently treats bloody discharges in female vivipara in heat as strictly comparable to the menses in humans, and where he also repeatedly claims that the quantity of the discharge is greater in women, in proportion to their size, than in any other female animal (above, n. 85). Thus at *HA* 573a5ff he remarks that cows in heat discharge 'about half a cotyle or a little less'. Yet not even that statement shows clearly that he had in fact undertaken any *precise* quantitative investigations in support of his general view and it is a good deal more likely that that view was based, rather simply, on a general impression. As for his statement that the male human emits more seed for his size than any other animal, it is not certain, first, whether this means in total or at each coitus.[117] But again this generalisation is not supported by any precise data. If it was not based solely on the analogy of the great abundance of the menses in women,[118] it may be that its chief justification lay in the – correct – observation that unlike many, though not all, other species, humans are fertile and have intercourse at any season of the year.[119]

Three main conclusions emerge from this first part of our inquiry.

---

[115] *PA* 647b34f, 667a1f, 670b18ff.

[116] A general distinction between the blood-vessels connected with the aorta and those with the vena cava is drawn at *PA* 667b15ff, and at *HA* 513b7ff he contrasts the sinewy texture of the aorta with the membranous nature of the vena cava.

[117] In the three texts mentioned in n. 86 Aristotle uses terms that mean discharge or emit or emission (προίεσθαι, ἀφίεναι, πρόεσις) but this is not conclusive.

[118] Semen and menses are, in his view, strict analogues, *GA* 727a2ff, 25ff, and cf. below, pp. 97ff.

[119] This is, however, true also of the horse, as is remarked at *HA* 576b20f, and of some other animals, cf. 546a20ff, 567a3ff, 572a5ff.

First, it would not be true to represent *all* of Aristotle's statements concerning the unique or exceptional characteristics of the human species as fictitious or as the product of his theoretical preconceptions, for some of his claims have solid, and others at least some, empirical support, and several are qualified by Aristotle himself. Secondly, and on the other hand, at other points the influence of those preconceptions on his generalisations, and on what he presents as the results of his investigations, is apparent. Thirdly and most importantly, the frequency of the theme clearly indicates his preoccupation with the question. While he is interested in the problem of the differentiae of animals and their parts in general, he is *especially* interested in the differences that mark man out from the other animals.

II

Our second more intricate problem concerns the possible influences of anthropocentric presuppositions on the general framework of Aristotle's zoological investigations. This is not, or not just, a matter of style, of the order of presentation of his material, where, as we have seen, he often either begins with man as the most familiar animal or ends with him as the most important and interesting.[120] Rather, we are concerned with certain basic assumptions that appear to guide Aristotle's inquiry and that influence the very questions he chose to investigate.

Although there is no exact explicit statement, in the zoological works, of the doctrine that later came to be known as the *Scala Naturae*,[121] there is no doubt that Aristotle thought of the main groups of animals as a *hierarchy*. The division by methods of reproduction in *GA* II is a division according to the degree of *perfection* of the offspring produced.[122] First come the viviparous animals that produce a living creature. Second come the ovoviviparous animals that produce live offspring, but only after first producing an egg internally. Next come animals that produce not a perfect living creature, but a perfect egg, and after these come other ovipara that bear imperfect eggs, that is eggs that reach perfection only outside the parent (e.g. *GA* 733b7ff). Fifthly there are creatures that do not produce an egg, but a larva which develops and becomes 'egg-like'.[123]

---

[120] Apart from *HA* 491a19ff and *PA* 656a3ff, mentioned above, pp. 27f, cf. *GA* 737b25ff (man first) and contrast pp. 37f below on *HA* 539a6ff, *PA* 682a31ff (man last).

[121] The hierarchy and continuity of living things are, however, expressed at *HA* VIII ch. 1, 588b4ff (cf. *PA* 681a12ff) especially.

[122] *GA* 732b28ff, see above, p. 18 n. 35.

[123] *GA* 733b13ff. Aristotle says that the 'so-called chrysallis' has the δύναμις of an egg.

The notion of the relative perfection of the *offspring* is intelligible in terms of the criteria that Aristotle uses, that is the various transformations that the young undergo as they develop towards a state where they can survive independently. But the *mature creatures* themselves are also graded according to their relative perfection, for, as he says, the perfect offspring are produced by the more perfect parents.[124] Nor is this by any means the only context in which Aristotle suggests degrees of perfection in the animal kingdom. On a variety of occasions he represents the imperfect or lower animals as approximating to or striving towards the state found in the perfect or higher ones. He does so, for instance, in connection with his belief that it is *better* for right and left, up and down and front and back to be differentiated.[125] Thus the crabs, he says at *IA* 714b16ff,[126] show only a feeble differentiation betwen right and left, but they do so in that the right claw is bigger and stronger than the left 'as if right and left wished to be differentiated'.[127] Again since nature would – if she could – assign the most honourable position to the most honourable part, the controlling part should be in the middle of the animal,[128] and moreover it should be single, though when nature is unable to achieve this – as happens with certain insects that can live when cut up – she makes it multiple.[129] Similarly it is *better* for male and female to be differentiated, though it is only in man that the full range of differentiations, including those of character, is clearly marked.[130] Thus Aristotle treats it as a mark of the inferiority of certain testacea and of the plants that in them the distinction between male and female does not appear 'except metaphorically'[131] – an example where, for once, the strength of the positive analogy that Aristotle's comparative zoology suggested was *under*estimated.[132]

---

[124] See *GA* 732b28ff, 733a2ff, 33ff.

[125] See, e.g., *IA* 706a20ff.

[126] Cf. also *HA* 527b4ff and *PA* 684a26ff. At *IA* 705b25ff he notes the lack of clear right/left differentiation in some other creatures, while at 706a10ff he uses his definition of 'right' as the side from which movement begins to decide which is the 'right' side of stromboid testaceans: cf. *PA* 680a24ff, with Ogle's note, ad loc., 1882, p. 224 n. 43.

[127] Cf. *PA* 669b20ff, where he says that the brain and each of the sense-organs 'wishes' to be double.

[128] E.g. *PA* 665b20ff. Yet Aristotle knows that in man the heart is on the left of the body, and he explains this as being due to the need to counteract the particular cold of the left side: see Lloyd 1966, pp. 52f, cf. Byl 1980, pp. 238ff. Characteristically Aristotle mentions the heart being on the left in relation to man alone (e.g. *PA* 666b6ff), though this is not uncommon in a number of other species as well.

[129] *PA* 682a6ff.

[130] See *HA* 608a21ff, b4ff, especially, cf. above, p. 25 n. 55 and below, pp. 94ff and 98ff.

[131] See *GA* 715a18ff, b19ff, 731a24ff, b8ff.

[132] It was, no doubt, difficult for Aristotle to accept true sex differentiation in plants when it was less marked or not evident at all in some animals.

Similar hierarchical assumptions are, no doubt, so common in the taxonomies of so many other zoologists[133] besides Aristotle, that it is easy to miss or play down their significance. In Aristotle's case in particular some of the ways in which such beliefs influence the account of animals that he offers have gone comparatively unremarked. Two fundamental points are worth underlining. First the amount of attention he devotes to the various main groups of animals broadly reflects his view of their degree of perfection. It is true that he insists, in a famous passage in *PA* I ch. 5,[134] that the natural scientist should study every kind of animal, noble and ignoble alike. Yet in a less-well-known passage in *PA* IV ch. 5, when he turns back from considering the internal parts to the study of the external ones, he has this to say: 'We had better begin with the creatures we have just been discussing [i.e. the bloodless groups] and not with those where we left off [on the external parts] in order that, starting from those that need less discussion, our account will have more time to deal with the perfect, blooded animals' (*PA* 682 a 31–4). Similarly at *HA* v ch. 1, 539 a 6ff, when he embarks on the study of methods of reproduction, he warns that man will be taken last as he requires most discussion. Moreover in practice, as the figures given by such authorities as Meyer show,[135] Aristotle identifies proportionately far fewer of the species of the lower kinds of animals than he does those of the higher, and while some of the brevity of his accounts of the former may be put down to the difficulties of observing very small creatures without optical aids, we may believe, as *PA* 682 a 31ff suggests, that value-judgements have also played their part.

My second point concerns the manner in which Aristotle's interpretations of the role and function of various of the parts of the lower species of animals are influenced or even determined by doctrines derived from his study of the higher animals. To represent the animal world as forming a systematic whole requires a formidable effort of synthesis. Apart from his overarching psychological doctrines, the key concept used by Aristotle in establishing links *across* the

---

[133] This is, however, much less true of botanical taxonomies: see further below, p. 43.

[134] Especially at *PA* 645 a 6ff, 15ff and 26ff. It should be noted that the argument of this passage is not to deny that there are differences in τιμή between different animals (and between the sublunary and the superlunary world, *PA* 644 b 24ff). On the contrary, in suggesting that the investigation should, as far as possible, not omit even the 'least honourable' kinds, the passage positively endorses such differences.

[135] Meyer 1855, p. 144, basing his comparisons on the species identified in Bronn's *Allgemeine Zoologie* of 1850, remarked that Aristotle identified a mere 81 of Bronn's 74,030 insects, and some 37 compared with 5,000 crustacea and testacea. The corresponding figures for mammals, birds, reptiles and fish are 75 to 2,067, 160 to 7,000, 20 to 1,055 and 117 to 8,000. The general point is clear, even though exact figures of the species that Aristotle might have identified without the use of optical aids cannot be given.

main groups of animals is that of similarity 'by analogy'.[136] Yet it is remarkable that a substantial group of the proportional analogies that he proposes work, as it were, *in the same direction*: the part of the lower species is understood or explained as performing the same function, or having the same capacity,[137] as one in a higher species.

A prime example of this, which illustrates the heuristic value of the idea, is the doctrine of what is analogous to the blood in the bloodless groups – even though this is another instance where it can be argued that in important respects Aristotle failed to recognise the full strength of the positive analogy that he had himself proposed.[138] In his view blood is essential to the animal's life,[139] it is the material that goes to form the other parts of the body,[140] and as we have seen differences in the blood are held to account for a wide range of physical and psychological characteristics.[141] But in animals that do not have blood *another liquid performs analogous functions*.[142] Similarly Aristotle speaks of what is analogous to flesh,[143] to the brain,[144] and, most importantly, to the heart, in the lower, bloodless groups. Thus what is analogous to the heart exists in the lower groups not only as the receptacle for what is analogous to blood,[145] but also as the centre of perception, of imagination and locomotion in those animals that have them, and indeed of life in general.[146]

One of the most important doctrines that guides Aristotle's investigations of the lower groups is that of the principal parts of the living creature. At *PA* 655b29ff and *Juv.* 468a13ff he identifies the three main essential parts of animals as (1) that by which food is taken in, (2) that by which residues are discharged and (3) what is

---

[136] Such passages as *Metaph.* 1016b31ff and 1018a12ff set out the canonical schema of grades of unity and sameness or difference, namely (*a*) in number, (*b*) in species, (*c*) in genus and (*d*) by analogy.

[137] At *PA* 645b6ff 'by analogy' is explained as 'having the same δύναμις' (function or capacity), and at *HA* 519b26ff it is glossed as 'having a similar nature' (cf. *PA* 648a19ff).

[138] Aristotle only recognises red blood as blood: cf. Peck, note to *PA* 645b9, 1937, pp. 102f.

[139] E.g. *HA* 489a20ff, 520b10ff, *PA* 665b11ff.

[140] E.g. *PA* 647a35ff, 651a14f, 652a6f, 665b5f, 668a19ff, 678a31ff. Semen, in particular, is derived from blood according to *GA* 726b3ff, 728a2of.

[141] See above, pp. 22f and 32f.

[142] See especially *HA* 489a20ff (where this liquid is compared with ἰχώρ, serum), *PA* 645b8ff, 648a1ff, 19ff, 678a8f, *GA* 728a2of.

[143] E.g. *HA* 511b4ff, 519b26ff, *PA* 653b20ff. Flesh being the organ of touch – the primary perception that all animals must possess to be animals – in creatures that have no flesh the analogous part must perform this function, e.g. *HA* 489a23ff.

[144] E.g. *Somn. Vig.* 457b29ff, *PA* 653a10ff. In Aristotle's view the role of the brain is to help to cool the heat in the region round the heart. In these passages he argues that it is the brain or its analogue that brings about sleep by its cooling effect.

[145] E.g. *PA* 665b11ff.

[146] E.g. *Juv.* 469b3ff, *PA* 647a30f, 678b1ff, *MA* 703a14ff, *GA* 735a22ff, 738b16f, 741b15ff, 742b35ff, 781a20ff.

intermediate between them, where the ἀρχή or controlling principle is located: in addition animals capable of locomotion also have organs for that purpose, and elsewhere he adds reproductive organs where male and female are distinguished.[147] In his detailed accounts of the internal and external parts of the bloodless animals in *HA* IV chh. 1–7, this doctrine both stimulates and limits what he looks for, and it influences the interpretations he offers for what he finds. The anatomy of the mouth – the presence or absence of teeth and tongue or analogous organs – is regularly discussed, and so too is the rest of the alimentary canal. Thus several texts suggest that he actively considered whether or not certain lower groups produced residue and that he attempted to identify and trace the excretory vent. In the hermit-crab, he says at *HA* 530 a 2f, a passage for the residue is hard to make out. At 531 a 12ff he remarks on the difficulty of seeing the two passages, for admitting and discharging water, in the ascidians, and in his account of the sea-anemones he observes that in their case (as in the plants) no residue at all is apparent.

On the other hand what is not included in his doctrine of the main essential parts of animals receives little attention. While the external organs of locomotion of the bloodless groups are carefully identified and classified, the internal musculature is almost entirely ignored.[148] Although he recognises that an analogue to the brain may exist in bloodless animals, he argues that in general the lower animals do not require one since – as they lack blood – they have little heat[149] – the main function of the brain being, in his view, to counteract the heat of the heart. For similar reasons he has little to say about lungs or their equivalent or other parts of the respiratory – or as he would say refrigeratory – system.[150]

His doctrine of the role of the heart, especially, leads him to look for the animal's controlling principle, and to look for it in the centre of its body. This is indeed stated as a general rule at *PA* 681 b 33ff. Thus in his remarks about the crustacea and cephalopods in particular he was clearly concerned to identify an organ analogous to the heart, but missing the actual heart, he identified the analogue, in the cephalopods, as the μύτις – in fact the liver.[151] The doctrine of the heart as

---

[147] See *HA* 488 b 29ff, 489 a 8ff, and cf. also *PA* 650 a 2ff.

[148] Similarly, although he describes the principal limbs, his osteology is otherwise crude.

[149] *PA* 652 b 23ff, cf. *HA* 494 b 27ff. In *HA* IV chh. 1–7 the brain is mentioned only at 524 b 4 and in a probably corrupt passage, 524 b 32.

[150] In *Resp.* 475 b 7ff, however, he says that the crustacea and octopuses need little refrigeration and at 476 b 30ff that the cephalopods and crustacea effect this by admitting water, which the crustacea expel through certain opercula, that is the gills (cf. also *HA* 524 b 20ff).

[151] See *PA* 681 b 12ff, 26ff. He identifies the μύτις with the analogue to the heart partly because of its central position and partly because of the concocted, bloodlike character of the fluid it

the seat of perception and locomotion stems in part from philosophical considerations, but it acted both as a stimulus to look for an equivalent control centre in the lower animals and also as an obstacle to the recognition of the possibility of a decentralised or acephalous nervous system: Aristotle had, to be sure, no understanding of the role of the nerves themselves,[152] but more importantly he was evidently predisposed to identify a single centre of control, even though he does recognise that some animals can continue to live when cut in two.[153] While we must acknowledge that the doctrine of the principal parts of the living creature is not derived from his reflections on man alone, it provides an excellent illustration of the degree to which his study of the lower animals was guided by ideas and theories stemming from his observations of the higher groups.

My final topic concerns another area where value-judgements are much in evidence. On a variety of occasions groups as a whole or individual characteristics of a particular species that are clearly recognised to be natural in the sense of normal or regular are nevertheless described in terms that assimilate them to the abnormal, the irregular or even the monstrous. Some animals are said to be 'deformed' (πεπηρωμένος or ἀνάπηρος) or 'warped' (διεστραμμένος) in respect of a particular organ or part. The mole is, for example, since it is said to have no sight, although it has residual eyes beneath the skin;[154] the lobsters too are said to be deformed in that it is a matter of chance which claw is bigger;[155] and flat-fish, which swim as one-eyed man walk, are said to be warped.[156] Here in each case closely related groups provide the standard by which a particular species is judged to be defective, and a similar idea figures prominently, as we shall see,[157] in the accounts that Aristotle offers of 'intermediate' groups.

In his discussion of the organs and methods of locomotion, especially, Aristotle repeatedly uses the higher animals – the viviparous quadrupeds and man – explicitly or implicitly as his standard of comparison to arrive at conclusions in which he suggests that the

---

contains. Cf. Ogle 1882, p. 227 n. 64, who remarked: 'The mytis, which in cephalopods is traversed by the oesophagus, is the liver . . . not the heart. The real heart of cephalopods, as of all other Invertebrata, escaped Aristotle.'

[152] The nervous system was discovered by the Hellenistic anatomists, Herophilus and Erasistratus: see Solmsen 1961.

[153] E.g. de An. 409a9ff, 411b19ff, 413b16ff, Long. 467a18ff, Juv. 468a26ff, Resp. 479a3ff, HA 531b30ff, IA 707a27ff.

[154] HA 533a2ff, but cf. 491b27ff and de An. 425a10ff.

[155] They have claws, but do not use them for their natural purpose (prehension) but for locomotion, PA 684a32ff. Evidently the lobster's claws are here implicitly compared with hands, not with the forefeet of quadrupeds.

[156] IA 714a6ff.

[157] Cf. below, pp. 45ff.

lower animals are defective. Quadrupeds themselves are said to be 'weighed down' by the excess of the bodily part – compared with men, that is – and in them 'upper' and 'front' coincide.[158] Moreover none of the bipeds, with the exception of man, is erect. As we have seen (above, n. 107) he says that the ape spends more time on all fours than upright, but he also describes the birds as bipeds that are unable to stand erect,[159] and he says that they are like quadrupeds, except that they have wings instead of forefeet.[160] When he comes to fish, he remarks that their external parts are 'even more stunted' (μᾶλλον κεκολόβωται) (than the birds) for they have neither legs nor hands nor wings.[161] As for the testacea, having their head downwards they are said to be 'upside down'[162] – as also are the plants, as they take in food through their roots.[163] He entertains the possibility that the whole group of testacea is 'maimed' (ἀνάπηρον) and puts it that while they move, they move *contrary to nature* (παρὰ φύσιν) explaining this by remarking: 'for they are not mobile creatures: but on the one hand considered as stationary beings and as attached by growth, they are mobile, while on the other considered as mobile, they are stationary'.[164]

Thus he even claims that, compared with man, *all* other animals are 'dwarf-like', in that they have the higher parts, or those near the head, larger than the lower ones.[165] Just as he maintains, notoriously, that females are a 'natural deformity', taking the male as the yard-stick,[166] so he takes man's unique erect stance as grounds for the assertion that 'in man alone the natural parts are in their natural positions': εὐθὺς γὰρ καὶ τὰ φύσει μόρια κατὰ φύσιν ἔχει τούτῳ μόνῳ.[167] Here, while the first use of 'natural', φύσει, is (in part) descriptive, the second, in the phrase κατὰ φύσιν, is clearly normative

---

[158] *PA* 686a31ff, cf. 657a12ff, *IA* 706a29ff: man's front is divided into upper and lower; in quadrupeds, the forelegs are both 'upper' (defined functionally in relation to the distribution of food) and 'front'. The idea of quadrupeds being 'weighed down' may be compared with Plato, *Ti.* 91e.

[159] *PA* 695a3ff, *IA* 710b17ff, 30ff, 712b30ff.

[160] *PA* 693b2–15, *IA* 712b22ff. Birds are biped because (1) they are blooded animals, (2) they have wings, and (3) the greatest number of motion-points that any blooded creature can have is four.

[161] *PA* 695b2ff.

[162] *PA* 683b18ff.

[163] *PA* 683b18ff, 686b31ff, *IA* 705b2ff, 706b5ff.

[164] *IA* 714b8ff, 10ff, 14ff.

[165] See *PA* 686b2ff, 20ff, 689b25ff, 695a8ff. At *IA* 710b12ff infants are said to be dwarf-like in comparison with adults.

[166] Cf. below, pp. 94ff.

[167] *PA* 656a10ff, cf. *HA* 494a26ff, 33ff, *IA* 706a16ff (most of all the animals man has his parts in accordance with nature), 706a20ff (the right side is 'most right-sided' in man), 706b9f (man is the biped most in accordance with nature).

and evaluative. What he represents as 'natural' is, in this case, quite exceptional, in that the vast majority of living creatures are considered to deviate from the norm provided by man. 'Nature' is here equated not with what happens always or for the most part in the animal kingdom, but with what applies exclusively to man, and the whole of the animal kingdom is, in a way, a decline from man, though not in the sense that animals are thought of as evolving from degenerate men (as in Plato's *Timaeus* 90e ff (see above, p. 15)), only in the sense that animals are judged inferior to man.

While the terminology of mutilations and deformities has its primary sphere of application in connection with ways in which an individual member of a species may fall short of the norm provided by the species as a whole, Aristotle employs similar terminology also to advance comparative judgements between one species or group and another, and in comparing every other animal with man. The evaluative function of such judgements is obvious: at the same time they may also play an important heuristic role. The search for and reflection on points of comparison between different species provides Aristotle with one of the main means of organising the vast body of data he had collected in his inquiry concerning animals.

The pervasive theme of man as model or as supreme, paradigmatic animal, is not an idea that Aristotle can be said to have taken over from previous popular beliefs or folklore. Yet that theme translates, into his own terms, a preoccupation that had been a preoccupation of popular beliefs, namely the concern with animals as related to man. Aristotle now offers a complex psychological doctrine to ground his particular view of the similarities and contrasts between man and the other animals. But the anthropocentricity of his zoology may be said to correspond to the deep-seated preoccupation with the question of where man stands in relation to animals that runs through so many Greek (like so many non-Greek) myths. Man must, to be sure, be included somewhere in a zoological taxonomy – once it is recognised, as it clearly is by Aristotle, that man *is* an *animal*. Moreover so far from being alone in putting man at the top of the scale of nature Aristotle conforms to a general rule to which one would be hard put to find many exceptions.[168] The point remains, however, that so to locate man is not just a response to the particular biological characteristics of the species, not just a response to a type of upright stance, the use of speech, or even a particularly developed social life, but also an answer

---

[168] That is among animal taxonomists. More generally the idea that animals are often physically superior to man is expressed in the context of what Lovejoy and Boas 1935, p. 19 and ch. 13, have called 'animalitarianism'.

to or at least a comment on the fundamental question of man's place in nature.

The importance of this notion of a hierarchy within the animal kingdom can be underlined, finally, by a comparison and a contrast with the sister discipline of botany. The similarity is that here too, as in zoology, the taxonomist is confronted with the problem of organising or structuring a vast body of material. The more important contrast lies in the fact that in botany hierarchical assumptions have never been very prominent. From the ancient world, although we do not have Aristotle's own treatise *On Plants*,[169] Theophrastus's major works *The Inquiry into Plants* and *The Causes of Plants* are extant, and these make the point clearly enough. In botany there is no clear-cut supreme species, and correspondingly no tightly ordered hierarchy into which the main groups are to be put, only at most a very loose structure, where the ordering of most of the entries was, and for long continued to be, largely conventional, not to say haphazard.[170] The interest is not in stratifying plants, nor in establishing their taxonomic distance from some fixed point. The result is, or was in the ancient world,[171] some degree of taxonomical anarchy or at least conventionalism, but also much less rigidity than that imposed on the zoological series from the position of man at the top of the hierarchy.

[169] The treatise with that title which figures in the Aristotelian Corpus is a late fabrication.

[170] Theophrastus has four main groups of plants, (1) δένδρον – tree – springing from the root with a single stem, (2) θάμνος – shrub springing from the root with many branches, (3) φρύγανον – 'under-shrub' springing from the root with many stems and with many branches, and (4) πόα – herb – coming up from the root with its leaves and with no main stem and with the seed borne of the stem (*HP* I 3.1). He is still influenced by the analogy of zoology to the extent that he suggests that the most perfect plants should be used as a standard (*HP* I 1.5) and he proposes using trees as the group to act as such (*HP* I 1.11, cf. *CP* II 19.6). Even so trees do not act as the models by which the other groups are assessed to anything like the extent that man does in the animal series in Aristotle. Theophrastus explicitly states that his four main definitions must be taken as 'applying generally and on the whole. For in the case of some plants it might seem that our definitions overlap; and some under cultivation appear to become different and depart from their essential nature' (*HP* I 3.2). Moreover nature does not 'possess necessity': 'our distinctions therefore and the study of plants in general must be understood accordingly' (*HP* I 4.3). Below the level of the four main groups the differentiae deployed are even less systematic than in zoology, though it is largely because of expectations generated by the pattern in that field that the absence of hierarchy in botany is often taken as a sign of backwardness (cf., e.g., Strömberg 1937, p. 155). Although the subdivisions of the plant families are not arrived at on any systematic basis, a considerable body of information is conveyed and has been analysed. Thus in his discussion of the kinds of ivy, for example, (*HP* III 18.6–8), Theophrastus first distinguishes ivy that grows on the ground from types that grow high; the latter are then said to fall into three main groups, white, black and spiral; the white is subdivided into a kind with white fruit only and one with white leaves also, and the varieties of the spiral kind are discussed at some length.

[171] Far more than in zoology, botanical taxonomy in the ancient world – as also in the Middle Ages and Renaissance – was influenced by the contrasting and conflicting interests of on the

4. DUALISERS IN ARISTOTLE'S ZOOLOGY

My third case-study takes us back to topics that are more directly related to issues at the centre of the anthropological debate that I outlined in the opening section. One item much discussed in that debate is the special role that marginal or intermediate kinds often have as a means of conveying and reinforcing ideas of the separateness of particular social groups and of the importance of separations and boundaries themselves. It is striking that Aristotle's zoology has a quasi-technical expression that appears exactly suited to the discussion of the phenomenon of boundary-crossing. Aristotle frequently uses the term ἐπαμφοτερίζειν, to 'dualise',[172] for intermediates and boundary-crossers – especially but not exclusively species of animals – that share in two or more normally distinct characters. Peck, who is one of the few classical scholars to have paid much attention to the use of the term, noted that it 'expresses something distinctive in Aristotle's thought'.[173] That is certainly the case: but the further question that we may raise is whether or to what extent Aristotle's zoology here reflects popular or pre-scientific interests in marginal species or boundary-crossers. Where he appears to owe something to earlier ideas and motifs, he is certainly reworking them, and the

one hand the pharmacologists and collectors of, and commentators on, *materia medica*, and on the other the agriculturalists and horticulturalists. Although efforts towards systematisation were made, for example, by Cesalpino. it was not until Linnaeus (1707–1778) that a comprehensive and reasonably coherent hierarchical botanical taxonomy was proposed, with far-reaching consequences not just for the requirements of organisation set for such taxonomies, but also in the elision of much information that resisted systematisation. Moreover Linnaeus's taxonomy depended crucially on the elaboration of the *sexual* differences in plants, an idea that depended on the recognition of the analogy between plants and animals – for although sexual differences are noted in some ancient authors (who sometimes mistakenly interpret two different species as male and female specimens of the same species), this had not been made the basis of systematic classification. The background to Linnaeus's work has been studied by, for instance, Cain 1956, 1958, and Stearn 1959: on the general issue, apart from the classic hand-books such as von Sachs 1890 and Daudin 1926, see Sloan 1972.

[172] ἐπαμφοτερίζειν is not an Aristotelian coinage, but is used before him of playing a double game (Pherecr. fr. 19, Th. VIII 85), of wavering between two opinions (Plato, *Phdr.* 257b) and of equivocating (Plato, *R.* 479b 11 and c 3, Isocrates XII 240): the passage in the *Republic* is especially interesting in that in it Plato illustrates a general point about the world of becoming with, among other things, an allusion to the riddle of the bat (see below, n. 184). Aristotle also uses ἐπαλλάττειν in some similar contexts in zoology when speaking of the 'overlapping' between normally distinct groups, e.g. *HA* 501a21ff (of the seal, cf. below, p. 45), *GA* 774b17ff (of swine, cf. below, n. 189), *GA* 733a27ff (there is overlapping between the larva-producing animals and those that produce imperfect eggs: the eggs of the latter are larva-like, while the larvae of the former become egg-like as they develop), *GA* 770b5ff, cf. also *Long.* 464b26ff and ἐπάλλαξις at *GA* 732b15 (cf. below, p. 51 and n. 206).

[173] Peck 1965, pp. lxxiii ff. Peck gives a convenient short account of the main contexts in which Aristotle uses this notion.

nature of the modifications he introduces enables us to analyse the relationship between his zoology and a set of often highly-charged pre-scientific concerns.

Three different types of cases must be distinguished. (1) First it is noticeable that certain species of animals that in earlier or popular belief were regularly treated as boundary-crossers are accommodated straightforwardly as *normal* groups within Aristotle's classification system. Thus the various kinds of octopus or cuttlefish (for example πολύπους, σηπία, τευθίς) had often been marked out as anomalous creatures, both for their supposed guile and deceitfulness, and as animals that are at once fish and not fish.[174] Now in Aristotle's taxonomy they are all included in one of the four main groups of bloodless animals he identifies, namely the μαλάκια or cephalopods. He certainly calls attention to some striking features both of particular species and of the group as a whole, for instance in their methods of reproduction[175] and in the way in which the octopus uses its tentacles both as feet and as hands.[176] But in his various careful discussions of the different kinds of octopus and cuttlefish he is quite clear that they form well-established natural groups within the cephalopods.[177]

(2) A second and larger group consists of cases where animals that were popularly thought of as boundary-crossers are explicitly stated by Aristotle to 'dualise'. In the great majority of instances Aristotle gives his reasons, and these generally lie in fairly obvious features of the morphology or the ecology of the species. In such cases he may be represented as following – or mirroring – popular assumptions in treating the species as anomalous, but as providing a rational basis for such a judgement within the framework of the regular differentiae he appeals to in advancing towards a zoological taxonomy.

Thus the seal, φώκη, already treated as a marvellous or monstrous creature of the deep in Homer,[178] is said at *PA* 697b1ff to 'dualise' between the land-animals (πεζά)[179] and the water-animals (ἔνυδρα),

---

[174] See, for example, Detienne and Vernant (1974) 1978, pp. 29ff, cf. D'A.W. Thompson 1947, pp. 206f, 232, 260f.

[175] See, for instance, *GA* 720b15ff, *HA* 541b1ff. Aristotle several times mentions the belief that the octopus uses one of its tentacles as a penis in copulation (the phenomenon known as the hectocotylisation of the tentacle), but he expresses his doubts that this is the true function: see *GA* 720b32ff, cf. *HA* 524a8f, 541b8ff, 544a12f.

[176] *HA* 524a2ff. Aristotle does not, however, use the term ἐπαμφοτερίζειν in this context.

[177] The principal general accounts of the cephalopods and of their main kinds are at *HA* 523b1ff, 21ff, *PA* 684b6ff, cf. also *HA* 534b12ff, *PA* 654a9ff, 678b24ff, *GA* 720b15ff, 757b31ff.

[178] *Od.* 4.404ff.

[179] The contrasts between πεζά (land-animals, walkers) and ἔνυδρα (water-animals) on the one hand, and πτηνά (winged animals, fliers) on the other, are complex: see below, n. 196.

sharing in the characters of both and of neither. Considered as water-animals they are anomalous in having feet: considered as land-animals they are anomalous in having fins,[180] for their hind-feet are exactly like those of fish, and moreover their teeth are saw-like.[181] At *HA* 566b27ff it is again said to be a dualiser. It belongs to the land-animals in that it does not take in sea-water, and it breathes and sleeps and brings forth its young on the land. Yet as it spends most of its time in the sea and gets its food from the sea it has to be considered with the water-animals. In this case, then, Aristotle takes into account (1) diet, (2) habitat, (3) anatomy and (4) mode of reproduction. The last-named criterion leads him to place the seal generally with the viviparous quadrupeds.[182] Yet even though he is evidently proceeding along the usual lines of his discussion and keeps rigorously to his usual biological differentiae, a certain embarrassment – or at least his sense of the anomalous character of the animal – can be detected in his repeated statements that the seal is a *deformed* creature.[183]

Similarly, the positions of bats, apes and other creatures that are said to dualise are gone into with some care. The bat, a proverbially ambivalent creature,[184] is said by Aristotle to dualise between the πεζά (land-animals) and the πτηνά (winged animals), a view that he justifies on purely morphological grounds at *PA* 697b1–13. Considered as winged animals, bats are anomalous in having feet (that is, of a kind that birds do not have – on their wings), but as quadrupeds they do not (that is, they do not have feet of the kind quadrupeds have). Again they have neither a quadruped's tail (κέρκος) – because they are winged – nor a bird's rump (οὐροπύγιον) – because they are land-animals.[185]

The apes, said by Aristotle himself to be a caricature of man,[186] dualise in that, as we have seen (above, p. 32), they share some of the

---

[180] Reading πτερύγια at *PA* 697b5 with Ogle against πτέρυγας with Bekker.
[181] Cf. also *HA* 501a21ff.
[182] See, e.g., *HA* 506a21ff, *GA* 781b22ff.
[183] See *HA* 487b23f, 498a31ff, *PA* 657a22ff, *IA* 714b12f. At *GA* 781b22ff, however, the fact that the seal has ear-passages, but not ears, is spoken of as an example of the admirable workmanship of nature, for the ear-appendage itself would have been of no use and indeed a positive disadvantage to the animal since it would have acted as a receptacle for a large volume of water.
[184] As in the well-known γρῖφος or riddle alluded to at Plato, *R.* 479c, and recorded by the Scholiast to that passage and by Athenaeus, 452 cd. Three different versions are recorded but in all three a 'man who is not a man' (viz a eunuch) hits a 'bird that is not a bird' (viz a bat) as it sits on a 'twig that is not a twig' (viz a reed) with a 'stone that is not a stone' (viz pumice).
[185] Aristotle adds that as creatures with membranous (skin-like) wings they necessarily have no οὐροπύγιον, for no animal has one unless it has barbed feathers, *PA* 697b10ff.
[186] *Top.* 117b17ff, cf., e.g., Semonides 7.71ff.

characteristics of man, others of quadrupeds.[187] Like quadrupeds they have hairy backs; their upper/fore parts are larger than the lower/hind; they have no buttocks and they spend more time on all fours than upright. But they are man-like in having hair on their fronts (except that the hair is coarse), in having eyelashes (though fine and small ones) on the lower lid, in having nostrils, ears, teeth, arms, hands, fingers and nails like man's, and in having no tail or only a very small one.

The ostrich, too, is another dualiser, for it has some of the parts of a bird, and some of a quadruped.[188] As not being a quadruped, it has feathers. As not being a bird, it cannot fly and has feathers that are like hairs and useless for flight. As a quadruped, it has upper eyelashes, but as a bird, it is feathered on its lower parts. As a bird, it has two feet, but as a quadruped it has (according to Aristotle) cloven hoofs (having hoofs and not toes).[189]

Among the lower creatures two of the most notable dualisers are the hermit-crabs and the sea-anemones. The hermit-crab, καρκίνιον, is said to be like the crayfish in its nature, but in that it lives in the vacated shells of other creatures it is like the testacea and so appears to dualise between that group and the crustacea.[190] The sea-anemones or sea-nettles known as κνίδαι or ἀκαλῆφαι fall outside the groups reached by division and 'dualise in their nature between plants and animals'.[191] They are like the latter because some of them can detach themselves and fasten on their food, because they are sensible of objects that come up against them, and because they use the 'roughness' of their bodies – more accurately their stinging pow-ers[192] – for the purposes of self-preservation. But they are like plants in that they are imperfect or incomplete (ἀτελές), in that they quickly attach themselves to rocks and in that, although they have a mouth, they produce no visible residue. Although we have no clear evidence that the hermit-crab itself had been thought of as a boundary-crosser

---

[187] *HA* 502 a 16 – b 26. Most of this account is devoted to the ape, πίθηκος, but the chapter opens with a remark that implies that Aristotle also treats monkeys, κῆβοι, and baboons, κυνοκέφαλοι, as similar dualisers. Cf. also *PA* 689 b 31ff. The dualising of the ape continues to be discussed in similar terms and using the expression ἐπαμφοτερίζειν in Galen, see *UP* xiii 11, ii 273.8ff H, K iv 126.1ff, and xv 8, ii 366.26ff H, K iv 251.7ff.
[188] *PA* 697 b 13ff. For Greek folk-lore concerning the ostrich or 'Libyan sparrow', see D'A.W. Thompson 1936, pp. 270ff.
[189] Swine too are described as dualisers, but this is not because all swine share in certain ambivalent characteristics, but because the group is said to contain both cloven-hoofed and solid-hoofed members, *HA* 499 b 11ff, *GA* 774 b 17ff.
[190] *HA* 529 b 19ff, cf. 548 a 14ff.
[191] *PA* 681 a 35ff, cf. *HA* 487 a 23ff, 588 b 16ff. Cf. *GA* 731 b 8ff, 761 a 15ff, where the testacea as a whole are said to be intermediate between plants and animals.
[192] See *HA* 621 a 10f.

before Aristotle, the folklore about crabs in general is rich,[193] and the
sea-anemones are mentioned as the subject of a food taboo in our
sources for Pythagoreanism.[194]

An examination of this second group of cases shows that Aristotle
sometimes explicitly labels as 'dualisers' species of animals that
already had some reputation – either popularly or within certain
circles such as the Pythagoreans – as anomalies. In several instances
such a reputation may have acted or probably did act as one stimulus
to Aristotle's analysis. Yet even where he was influenced by such
popular beliefs, he was evidently not just repeating or recording
them. What Aristotle provides – much as a modern anthropologist
might provide – is a discussion of the grounds on which the animal
may be said to dualise, that is why it cannot straightforwardly be
located in one group but straddles two. These grounds never, in
Aristotle's case, include an appeal to any supposed magical, mystical
or sacred properties the animals were popularly held to possess. On
the contrary, the criteria employed all fall within the scope of the
normal differentiae he appeals to in his zoology, concerning morphology, habitat,[195] behaviour, modes of reproduction and so on. In the
case of land- and water-animals especially he engages in an intricate
and quite sophisticated discussion of the complex and sometimes
conflicting criteria to be used in the application of the differentiae.[196]
At the same time, although the arguments may sometimes be
different – and it is important that they are now made explicit – the
conclusions are occasionally the same or similar, in that what folklore
marked out specially as animals to revere or to avoid, Aristotle in turn
treated as anomalies or as natural deformities.

(3) My third group of texts is more heterogeneous. Although the
principal field of application of the notion is in zoology, Aristotle also
speaks of dualising in some other contexts, for example in physics and
in ethics. Thus at *Ph.* 259a23ff when he rejects both the idea that
everything is at rest and the idea that everything is in motion, he refers
to things that 'dualise' in that they have the capacity of sometimes
moving and sometimes being at rest. At *Ph.* 205a25ff he says that,
unlike fire and earth, both of which have a determinate natural place,

---

[193] See D'A.W. Thompson 1947, pp. 105f, Detienne and Vernant (1974) 1978, pp. 269ff.

[194] See Aulus Gellius iv 11.12–13 (purporting to quote Plutarch quoting Aristotle), Porphyry,
VP 45, and cf. Burkert 1972, p. 172.

[195] A clear example of animals said to dualise in respect of habitat is the fish that are said to do so
as being found both in shallow waters and in the deep sea, see *HA* 598a13ff, 602a15ff.

[196] The distinction between land- and water-animals depends in part on where an animal lives
and feeds, in part on whether it takes in and emits water or air: see especially *HA* viii ch. 2,
589a10ff, 20f, 590a8f, 13ff, and *PA* 669a6ff. There is a detailed discussion of the problem in
Peck 1965, pp. lxxvii-lxxxix.

air and water 'dualise' between 'up' and 'down', and when he discusses mixture, κρᾶσις, in *GC* I ch. 10, distinguishing it from, among other things, the imposition of form on matter, he speaks of certain physical substances that 'hesitate' towards each other and 'dualise' in that they show a slight propensity to combine and yet one tends to act as receptive and the other as form (*GC* 328 b 8ff).

As these and other texts show,[197] the term 'dualise' may be applied in a variety of contexts where two normally distinct properties, qualities or characteristics are combined in some way either at once or successively. Furthermore within zoology itself some of its uses depart quite radically from the patterns of those we have so far discussed. Aristotle sometimes speaks not just of species of animals dualising, but of particular parts doing so. Thus in his account of whether the viscera naturally form pairs he says that some appear to dualise as between being single (like the heart) and double (like the kidneys). His example is the liver and the spleen, which can either be considered as each a single organ, or as forming a pair, since in some creatures (those that have a spleen 'of necessity') the spleen may be thought of as a 'kind of bastard liver', while in others (those that do not) the spleen is very small, but the liver is patently double.[198] Again in one of his discussions of how the legs of different species of animals bend when they move, at *HA* 498 a 16ff, he remarks that in the many-footed animals the legs in between the extreme ends 'dualise', that is they move in a way that is intermediate between them, bending sideways rather than forwards or backwards.[199]

But the most striking evidence of a use of the notion of 'dualising' that is independent of the associations of earlier beliefs and free from any pejorative undertones comes from some of Aristotle's remarks about humans. As we have seen in our previous study, man frequently serves, in Aristotle, as the model by which other animals are to be judged. Man is exceptional, indeed, but only because he is supreme. Yet in two contexts man is said to dualise. First at *HA* 488 a 7, in an admittedly problematic passage, he does so in that he is both a gregarious and a solitary creature.[200] Then at *HA* 584 b 26ff and *GA*

---

[197] Cf. *Pol.* 1332 b 1ff (some habits are said to dualise in that they may turn either towards good or towards evil), 1337 b 21ff (some established branches of education dualise between being liberal and illiberal). The verb is also used at *MM* 1197 a 31 in the sense 'be in doubt'.

[198] *PA* 669 b 13ff, 26ff. On the belief that the spleen is the left homologue of the liver, see Ogle 1882, p. 206 n. 1 to *PA* III ch. 7. At p. 207 n. 4 Ogle further remarks that 'there is some foundation for the statement that the size of the spleen and the distinctness with which the liver is divided into lobes are inversely related to each other'.

[199] Cf. *IA* 713 a 26ff.

[200] At *HA* 488 a 2 καὶ τῶν μοναδικῶν must presumably be deleted, with Schneider, D'A.W. Thompson, Peck. However Thompson 1945, pp. 54–5, conjectured that in this and several

772 a 37ff he dualises in the number of offspring produced at one birth. Whereas some species produce a single offspring, others few, and others many, man sometimes produces one, sometimes a few and sometimes many children at one parturition.[201] 'Dualising' may evidently be asserted not merely of creatures that Aristotle thought of as natural deformities or as boundary-crossers, but also, in certain respects, of man, where there can be no question of pejorative undertones.

Dualising thus provides a remarkable case of an interaction – within Aristotle's zoology – of traditional beliefs and his own independent theorising. Implicit popular notions concerning anomalous species seem to provide the background to many of the cases where Aristotle speaks explicitly of dualising, and it can hardly be doubted that he was to some extent influenced by such beliefs both in general (in that they acted as a stimulus to investigate boundary cases) and in particular (in some of the particular views he expresses about certain such species). The question of whether a species is a boundary-crosser, combining normally distinct characteristics or belonging to normally distinct groups, is one that is often present in his mind and one that comes to the fore in his discussion.

His task of determining the principal differentiae of the main groups of animals is made easier by his acceptance – at least his provisional acceptance – of such combinations. In some cases, to be sure, dualising may be a matter of a mere appearance,[202] or it may occur in respect of some evidently non-essential attribute,[203] or the characteristic in question may belong to some members of a group but not to others, suggesting a possible subdivision within the group.[204] But even when these cases have been resolved there remain the substantial difficulties presented by the instances where a species straddles two well-established groups or where the differentiae in question (which 'belong' and yet 'do not belong' to the species) are ones that will still presumably need to figure in a complete account of the species' nature. Here, where we might have expected him – if not

other passages in *HA* ἄνθρωπος in the MSS is a corruption, via the abbreviation ἀνος, for ὄνος, and in this case Thompson suggested that it is the fish ὄνος, not the ass, that was originally intended. As we have it, however, the text apparently claims that – despite the fact that man is a πολιτικὸν ζῷον – he may be either gregarious or solitary.

[201] Cf. above, pp. 30f and nn. 84 and 99.

[202] As in the case of the hermit-crab, *HA* 529 b 19ff, above, p. 47 and n. 190, which seems to dualise (ἔοικεν) because of a contrast between its nature and where it lives.

[203] As with the fish that are found in both shallow waters and the open sea, cf. above, n. 195.

[204] As with swine where the group contains both cloven-hoofed and solid-hoofed members, cf. above, n. 189.

to abandon the idea that the particular species is a single kind – then to have concluded that the evidence of dualising indicates that the differentia in question should be rejected, he shows no clear signs of doing so. Thus he continues to treat the seal, the bat, the ape, the ostrich as each a single kind: but there appears to be no question of his completely discarding 'quadruped', 'biped', 'winged' and so on as relevant differentiae,[205] even though in a famous passage, *GA* 732 b 15ff, he shows the lack of correlation between such differentiae and differences in the modes of reproduction.[206] In the case of plants and animals alone he is driven to remark that intermediate instances suggest a blurring of the boundaries of the groups themselves – nature passes imperceptibly, in a continuous gradation, from plant to animal – and he explicitly calls attention to the problematic nature of the creatures in between and to doubts about how the problems are to be resolved.[207] Nevertheless it is notable that the issues here – concerning such species as the sea-anemones and the ascidians – are still posed in terms of the question of *whether* they belong to the plants *or* to the animals.[208] The assumption is that, despite the difficulties presented by particular species and despite the references to the continuity between 'plants' and 'animals', these two still form two mutually exclusive categories.

The dualisers are thus often allowed to stand despite the threat that they might otherwise be thought to pose to the principle that normally a species should not figure on both sides of a division either by manifesting opposing essential qualities or by having some claim to belong to opposing superordinate groups.[209] Rather than make his account altogether more complex *either* by breaking down the large 'natural' groups (such as 'birds' and 'fish', or even 'plants' and 'animals') and introducing new ones,[210] *or* by re-examining the

---

[205] Even πεζόν and ἔνυδρον remain in play in his account, though these differentiae are, to be sure, refined by his explicit discussion of the complex of factors involved, e.g. *HA* 487a 15ff, 590a 13ff, and cf. above, n. 196.

[206] Bipeds are not all viviparous, nor all oviparous. The same is true also of quadrupeds, and not only of these footed kinds but also of footless animals. A differentiation between the ways in which 'biped' attaches to birds, and to men, is suggested at *PA* 643a 3f, 693b 2ff. In *IA*, however, e.g. 707a 16ff, Aristotle points out certain correlations between the way an animal moves and whether it is blooded or bloodless: thus blooded animals move on no more than four 'points' (even the way in which footless animals move is analysed in terms of four points of motion) and bloodless animals that have legs are all many-footed, πολύποδα (moreover πολύποδα had been used as an example of a group that should not be broken up at *PA* 642b 18ff in the criticism of dichotomous division).

[207] See especially *HA* 588b 4ff and *PA* 681 a 12ff.

[208] *HA* 588b 12ff, *PA* 681 a 25ff.

[209] See *PA* 642b 31ff, 643a 13ff, passages which make it clear that Aristotle seeks an exclusive system of classification, not merely a description of non-exclusive groupings.

[210] As he had done for the cephalopods, see above, p. 45. Compare also the recognition of the ovoviviparous animals as a group, above p. 17.

criteria of their differentiation, he is prepared to countenance cases of intermediates treated as anomalies, and in so doing he may be said to have the tacit support of a powerful, if unformalised, set of popular assumptions.

At the same time, the distance between Aristotle and folk belief is considerable. This is in part a matter of greater explicitness. In Greece, as often, even usually, elsewhere,[211] the grounds on which a species is popularly thought of as a boundary-crosser are frequently left unexpressed. Aristotle states not only *that* certain species are dualisers, but also *why*, and the differentiae he appeals to are all ones that he regularly deploys in his zoology. Even when antecedent popular beliefs lie in the background, Aristotle aims to provide his view with a rational justification. Moreover dualising, in Aristotle, is both more extensive, and narrower, than earlier folk beliefs. It is more extensive, because we find the notion applied in other contexts outside the domain of zoology and of popular taxonomy of any kind, and indeed within zoology to certain cases where there is no reason to suspect the influence of prior popular assumptions and where the residual pejorative undertones of dualising have disappeared completely. But it is also narrower, because in some notable instances of creatures previously considered with special interest or respect as boundary-crossers, Aristotle's zoological conclusion is to treat them as well-established natural groups.[212]

Yet if he is, on this as on other questions, often implicitly or explicitly critical of earlier assumptions, Aristotle still exhibits their influence. The debts of his zoological taxonomy to previous thought have usually been discussed in terms of his use and modification of groupings that are already present in earlier writers, from Homer to the Hippocratics and Plato. In the case of dualising, it is not so much earlier literature, as certain deep-seated popular beliefs, whose influence is still apparent not only in the frequency with which the issue of dualising is raised in Aristotle's discussions, but also when Aristotle reacts to the anomalous character of some dualising species by passing judgement on them as 'natural deformities'. As we said before (above, p. 41), judged from the point of view of man, the whole

---

[211] It should be stressed that popular taxonomies reported by anthropologists in their field-work often represent the anthropologists' own systematisations of their data, rather than the actors' own categories: see Goody 1977, ch. 4.

[212] One context where we might have expected the notion of dualising to have been brought into play is in the discussion of cross-breeding or hybridisation. But although Aristotle occasionally refers to the breeding of hunting dogs, and discusses the breeding and sterility of mules, he shows comparatively little interest in the question. The idea that new fertile strains or even species of animals might be produced conflicted with his fundamental principle of the fixity of natural kinds.

of the rest of the animal kingdom is a decline. But if from that point of view all animals are natural deformities (as failed human beings, as it were), it is still the case that some are more so than others, and among those that are more so, intermediate creatures figure prominently. Aristotle does not lay down rules for avoidance behaviour in respect of the seal and the bat: but he certainly says that they are deformed creatures, quadrupeds, but not proper quadrupeds.[213]

5. CONCLUSION

In ancient Greece, as in so many other cultures, animal species provided a rich storehouse for the expression of fundamental moral, social, religious and cosmological ideas. The animal series was the language in which many such ideas were conveyed. We may think of them as metaphors, only we should not suppose that the metaphors were translatable back, without remainder, into any single univocal literal message. It would be better to think of them as an alternative language, radically indeterminate in its translation into literal terms.

But to think your morality *with* animals is one thing. To try to get clear *about* animals is another. Here the framework provided by popular assumptions may so easily become a straightjacket. In reworking traditional ideas zoological taxonomy can certainly take over and use a good deal that had been implicit before. It may, for example, rationalise the grounds on which avoidance behaviour or special interest or respect had been based, and that there are such implicit rational grounds emerges as an impressive fact about many apparently random or bizarre notions concerning anomalous creatures. The anomalies presuppose, indeed, a firm and intelligible, if implicit, classificatory system.

But if much of the traditional material can be reworked, the earlier questions are not the questions that anyone interested in establishing a classification of animals for its own sake must ask. The concerns of Hesiod in the *Theogony* are reflected in the extent of the scale of beings he deals with, which includes not just men and animals, but also and more especially a whole range of divine, semi-divine and hybrid figures. The philosopher Empedocles too still deals extensively with monstrous and imaginary creatures, ox-faced men and man-faced

---

[213] See the passages cited above, n. 183, on the seal, and, e.g., *HA* 589b29ff, where he discusses natural deformities in connection with land- and water-animals and draws a comparison with masculine females and feminine males.

oxen, the products of different phases in the cycle of the struggle for
power between Love and Strife.[214] In the fourth century, a view of
the main kinds of animals is firmly linked by Plato, in the *Timaeus* at
least, to the doctrine of transmigration,[215] and the author of the
Epinomis[216] speaks of five principal types of creatures associated with
the five elements, the visible gods (the stars) associated with fire, the
creatures of the earth (men and many-footed animals and footless
ones and those 'rooted' to the earth) and between these two three
further kinds, the *daimones* of the aither, a race of airy beings and a
race of watery ones – presumably the nymphs.[217]

Long after the first hesitant attempts at zoological taxonomy, real
or imaginary animals continued to serve as the mediators of moral
and religious messages, and such a use is manifestly never *supplanted* by
scientific investigations. But the more deeply ingrained such preoccupations are, the more difficult it is for zoological taxonomy to define
its own distinct and proper domain of study.

Aristotle's work marks a watershed. He was recognisably doing
animal taxonomy – among other things – more clearly so, indeed,
than many later writers in antiquity and through the Middle Ages.
First he works with clear definitions of the various vital faculties that
settle the outer boundary of the study of animals.[218] There is no
question of his failing to provide a demarcation between zoology and
mythology or religion. The focus of attention is explicitly on animals:
the imaginary, the mythical, the poetic are excluded. He has a role for
the conception of monsters, τέρατα, individual aberrant natures
where the form does not master the matter, as well as for whole species
of 'natural deformities'. But both monsters and naturally deformed
species are there to be seen: they are closer to what is given in what is
observed, not purely imagined.

Secondly, while he adopts many of the classes embedded in his own
natural language, he does not do so uncritically, but modifies existing
usages and introduces substantial new coinages where he sees a need.
He approaches his inquiry with many preconceptions, to be sure, and
he allows common beliefs, the ἔνδοξα and the φαινόμενα, a key place

---

[214] Fr. 61 (DK), cf. Frr. 57–60 and 62. The interpretation of the phases of the cosmic cycle with
which different imaginary creatures are associated is disputed. While Empedocles is
certainly not attempting a taxonomy he uses ideas about past generations of living creatures
to reinforce messages concerning the interaction of Love and Strife.

[215] See above, p. 15 on *Ti.* 91d ff.

[216] Although this work is not now generally thought to be by Plato himself, it is usually dated to
the fourth century.

[217] *Epin.* 980c ff, especially 981b–e, 984b–d.

[218] Even so, the gods, in Aristotle's view, are linked to men (though to man alone of the animals)
in that the gods possess reason – though this alone of the faculties of the soul.

in his methodology.[219] Yet while he usually respects what is generally held to be the case, that is sometimes where his *problems* begin. The common beliefs are not sacrosanct, but explicitly open to scrutiny and revision, and at points they will have to be abandoned.[220]

Thirdly and more generally, he engages in a massive task of collecting and evaluating information, both expanding and sifting the data base. His attempts to separate the true from the false in his information are, naturally, far from all successful. But he repeatedly shows himself at pains to reject not just some of the wilder stories about fabulous creatures,[221] but also much of what he has read in such earlier authorities as Ctesias and Herodotus.[222] He is aware, too, of the problem of verifying what his other informants – fishermen, hunters, bee-keepers and the like – tell him, frequently expressing his doubts about the reports he has received, and even more often stressing that further investigations need to be undertaken to check particular points.[223]

At the same time his work was anything but value-neutral – and not just in the way that no science is or can be *ultimately* value-neutral. In including animals' characters in his investigations into their differentiae, he still thinks about animals in human terms, assuming a parallelism between the animal series and the moral one. The anthropocentricity of his system illustrates – if it needs illustration – how he uses taxonomy to convey value-judgements about man's place in nature and to express a strongly value-laden concept of nature itself. His use of the notion of dualising, especially, shows him reworking a common motif, modifying and purifying it, to be sure, but allowing it to provide some too easy solutions to problems concerning the position of certain species in relation to neighbouring groups. In each of these three areas the influence of earlier patterns of thought – not so much on particular points of detail as on the fundamental presuppositions with which taxonomy is undertaken – is stronger and more persistent than might be supposed.

While zoology is in principle, and on the whole indeed in practice, divorced from mythology, it is still for Aristotle strongly bound up

---

[219] See Owen (1961) 1975.

[220] This point does not receive quite the emphasis it deserves in the otherwise perceptive study of Nussbaum 1982.

[221] Among the occasions when Aristotle explicitly rejects a story as 'mythical' or 'fabulous' are *HA* 578b23ff, 579b2ff, 16ff, cf. also 580 a 14ff, 21f. It is possible that such a rationalising tendency was continued, in Aristotle's school, in the treatise περὶ τῶν μυθολογουμένων ζῴων, attributed to Strato, though we have no direct information concerning the contents of that work which would enable us to confirm this.

[222] See, for example, *HA* 523 a 17ff, 26f, 606 a 8ff, *GA* 736 a 2ff, 10ff, 756 b 5ff.

[223] Cf. Lloyd 1979, pp. 211f.

with morality through the notion of teleology. Every aspect of the animal kingdom has something to teach the natural philosopher – and, we may add, the philosopher in general. Animal species provide, after all, some of the very best examples to establish and illustrate Aristotle's central metaphysical doctrine of form. The notion that certain individuals share certain definable characteristics or fall into clearly demarcated groups is often introduced primarily with reference either to artefacts or to animal, or less frequently plant, species – then to be applied also to other more difficult cases such as moral dispositions or political constitutions.

More particularly he remarks that 'every kind of animal possesses the natural and the beautiful' to some degree (*PA* 645 a 21 ff) and it is important that they do so in *varying* degrees. Both the perfections and the imperfections convey lessons, the perfections manifesting the beauty of nature, its form and finality, the imperfections just as surely illustrating that nature is a hierarchy, a notion with direct implications for the human and social sphere since it underpins not just his idea that animals are, in a sense, for the benefit of man,[224] but also and more importantly his notion that human beings themselves, while sharing in a common humanity, differ nevertheless in their capacities and in their excellences. At this point zoological taxonomy relates not just to notions of value and to morality, but to fundamental ideological convictions and we shall be returning to reconsider these more fully in our final chapter.

As a coda to this inquiry, however, we may remark briefly on the continuity of certain of the themes and problems we have been discussing with later zoological taxonomy. With Aristotle, we said, zoological taxonomy is, for the first time in our extant sources, marked out as a clearly defined inquiry. But Aristotle's work is also, from many points of view, the high-water-mark of zoology in antiquity.[225] Most of the extant Greek and Latin texts that tackle different aspects of the subject of animals after him revert to the anecdotal – a trend especially pronounced in such writers as Pliny and Aelian. Few followed Aristotle's lead in attempting first to set out clear definitions of the problems to be pursued, with a clear methodology of how to pursue them. They often preferred to devote more attention to the strange and the marvellous[226] than to emulate

---

[224] This idea is most fully worked out in *Pol.* I, e.g. 1256 b 15ff.

[225] We shall be returning, in Part III, to other aspects of the life sciences in late antiquity.

[226] Certainly stories about animals figure prominently in the tradition of writers of mirabilia, from the pseudo-Aristotelian *Mirabilium Auscultationes*, through the books of *Mirabilia* of Antigonus of Carystus (third century B.C.) and of Apollonius Paradoxographus (second century B.C.) to Phlegon in the second century A.D. See Westermann 1839 and Keller 1877.

Aristotle's careful and detailed investigations of 'noble' and 'ignoble' creatures alike. In the Middle Ages and Renaissance a similar predilection for the marvellous or the anecdotal only gradually yielded once again to attempts at more systematic zoological taxonomies, now often serving a different morality, and exhibiting different theological preconceptions, but still usually strongly moralising in tone.[227] Only with evolutionary theory, and with modern genetics, do the patterns of explanation alter radically: nor has evolutionary theory necessarily meant the end of all assumptions concerning the privileged position of man and the hierarchical structure of the animal kingdom. This serves to remind us that in many of the features of Aristotle's zoology we have drawn attention to he is far from unique: and that is another way of pointing up the deep-seated preconceptions often at work in zoological taxonomy and its frequent more or less covert moralising aims.

[227] On the importance of the exclusion of 'animal semantics' in the development of 17th-century biology, and on competing models of classification, see Foucault (1966) 1970, and on the latter point Sloan 1972.

PART II

THE FEMALE SEX: MEDICAL TREATMENT AND BIOLOGICAL THEORIES IN THE FIFTH AND FOURTH CENTURIES B.C.

1. INTRODUCTION

Whereas serious critical studies of one massively exploited group in ancient society – the slaves – go back to the late eighteenth century,[1] it took the social and political developments of the last twenty years, and especially the new self-consciousness of the women's movement, to focus attention explicitly on the neglect of many aspects of the study of the position of women in the ancient world. Some isolated earlier exceptions stand out as just that,[2] and commentators have not failed to diagnose the neglect as due as much to the male domination of the classical profession as to the male domination of ancient society itself. The first number of *Arethusa* devoted to women studies[3] certainly revealed a thinness of coverage that cannot be put down solely to problems relating to the thinness of the evidence, though those problems are in many cases an undeniable factor.

In the domain of the history of medicine, for instance, we have quite extensive discussions of aspects of the medical treatment of women by doctors in the fifth and fourth centuries B.C. in the important series of gynaecological treatises in the Hippocratic Corpus. Yet several of the treatises in question have still, in 1983, never been translated into English, and many have no critical modern edition and commentary in any language. Admittedly the authors of these treatises are all *male*: I shall come back to that problem of bias in the evidence shortly. Yet that is not why these works have been so neglected. Rather that neglect would be explained, in some quarters, no doubt, in terms of their inferior quality, when set besides what pass as the acknowledged masterpieces of Hippocratic medicine. The gynaecological treatises have never been in the forefront of the discussion of the Hippocratic question. Since antiquity,[4] few who did not adopt the catholic view that

---

[1] Finley 1980 provides a full, authoritative and subtle analysis of this development.
[2] As for example, in the history of science, Diepgen's monograph, 1937.
[3] *Arethusa* 1973, with Pomeroy's bibliography, 1973, pp. 125ff.
[4] In antiquity itself, however, Soranus, for example, ascribed to Hippocrates views that

58

virtually the whole Corpus is authentic have claimed them as the work of the great Hippocrates himself – and whether a treatise was believed to be by his hand has been, and still in places is today, a sensitive indicator of how highly the work is rated. But leaving aside the question of the ideological component in such evaluations, we cannot discount a further factor in this neglect, a tendency among scholars, if not also among doctors, to relegate gynaecology to second place, an assumption that there is nothing of special or particular interest either in the question of the differentials in the medical treatment of the two sexes or in gynaecological pathology and therapeutics in general. The simple fact remains that it would be difficult to find any other field of Hippocratic studies where such rich sources of evidence have been, for so long, so unexploited.

My aim in this part is not to investigate the inferior status of women in Greek culture as a whole: that status, and the attitudes that went with it, are to be taken, broadly, as given. Rather my subject is aspects of the repercussions of such prejudices and assumptions on the developing life sciences, on medicine and on biology. Certain general remarks about the degree of penetration of the prevailing ideology in ancient society, and about the problem of biased evidence, must, however, be made before I identify the particular questions on which I shall concentrate.

The ideology of the inherent superiority of the male and of the priority of the values he stood for was, without a doubt, enormously pervasive. Yet it would be wrong to assume that it was never contested. It was, no doubt, bitterly resented by many women who nevertheless did not confront males much or at all with their feelings. But the existence of a Sappho or of other women poets shows that – here as on most other aspects of even deep-seated Greek beliefs – alternatives to the dominant views were put forward at least in certain restricted contexts. Male-oriented values were not the only ones that found articulate expression. But the very fact that very little of Sappho and even less of most other women poets[5] survives serves to illustrate the vulnerability of heterodox view-points when the control of, or at least the responsibility for, the transmission of literature was in the hands of those who normally represented or shared the

correspond to some we find expressed in the gynaecological treatises, though that is not to say that Soranus necessarily had those works specifically or exclusively in mind when he did so (cf. below, p. 173 n. 208). We may, however, certainly conclude that for Soranus Hippocrates held some detailed theories on a variety of gynaecological questions.

[5] The total extant remains of the poetesses Erinna (if indeed she is not a pseudepigraphon, see West 1977 and cf. Pomeroy 1978b), Praxilla, Corinna, Cleobulina, Telesilla, Anyte, Nossis and Moero amount to a very few pages – in no one case to more than one hundred complete verses.

dominant values. But there were clever and sophisticated women who formulated independent views, and their work was not totally suppressed, nor completely forgotten.

Sappho can, in however fragmentary a form, speak for herself. But when we turn to the history of science in the periods we are chiefly concerned with here – the fifth and fourth centuries B.C. – there is no Hippocratic author, and no prominent biologist, who is a woman, just as there is no astronomer, mathematician or physicist.[6] The fact that our evidence comes exclusively from male sources represents a massive bias. Yet it does not altogether negate an ambition to study the interactions of ideology and the emerging life sciences in this field. In biological theory, for instance, we can still investigate what happened when the difference between the sexes and their roles in procreation came to be the objects of would-be scientific inquiry, that is when attempts began to be made to describe and explain in some detail those differences not just in humans but also in other animals. In particular we can still examine how far in male authors common assumptions were questioned, modified or rejected, whether alternative views were put forward, and to what extent exceptions or counter-evidence were acknowledged as such or what the response to them was.

We have no woman writing on the subject in the fifth and fourth centuries, and that itself is symptomatic of the ideology in question. But we can study in some detail how male writers who were, in some cases, explicitly committed to the principles of research (ἱστορία) and to the critical examination of common opinions, handled the topic. Aristotle, who is one of our chief sources, is, of course, so committed, and as is well known, he does not simply agree with, but develops an elaborate theory to support and justify, the common assumption of the inherent superiority of the male sex. The principal question here is

---

[6] Cf. however below, p. 63 n. 11, on certain female authorities, Salpe, Lais, Elephantis, Olympias, Sotira, and Antiochis, cited by Pliny and by Galen. (Of these Salpe and Sotira are called 'midwives', *obstetrices*, in Pliny, though Olympias is several times included in the list of 'medici' cited as authorities in *HN* I for the contents of Books xx ff). Pliny appears to be drawing on written, rather than oral, material and if so, this would indicate that by the first century A.D. at least not all the literature dealing with medical topics was the work of male authors: yet even this evidence is, of course, mediated for us by the male author, Pliny – and Salpe and Sotira themselves did not survive. The only two Greek medical texts ascribed to female authors that have been preserved, at least according to Diels's list of the manuscripts, 1905–6, are a work on affections of the womb by Metrodora (still unedited) and a work on women's diseases by Cleopatra (extant in a Latin version: the author may well be the same Cleopatra as the one referred to, for example, by Galen, e.g. K XII 403.16, 446.1, as the writer of a work on cosmetics). Outside the life sciences, the most prominent woman is the mathematician Hypatia, the daughter of Theon of Alexandria and the author of a commentary on Diophantus in the early fifth century A.D. See further on the issue in general, Pomeroy 1977.

the relationship between that theory and his detailed zoological investigations, the extent to which the latter were skewed to fit the former, or how, in short, he squared his empirical findings with his preconceptions.

But Aristotle is not the only, even if he is the most important, biologist whose work we can examine. On the problem of the role of the sexes in reproduction, especially, there is evidence of an extensive and protracted debate that starts well before Aristotle, in the fifth century – and that continues after him. Moreover in this exclusively masculine debate theories were proposed that offer alternatives to the prevailing assumptions concerning the inherent superiority of the male, and we may examine the evidence and arguments adduced to support these theories and consider how far they represented a challenge to aspects of the dominant ideology.

In medicine, where the treatment of women patients is our chief problem, we shall see that some of the male authors on whom we rely were themselves aware of some, at least, of the difficulties presented by the barriers to communication that existed between men and women. What these men have to say about their own relationships both with their women patients and with women healers of various kinds represents, to be sure, just one side of those questions: we have no direct access to the women patients and women healers themselves. Yet the evidence can, with discretion, be used to provide the basis of some observations on what the authors themselves sometimes recognise to be complex issues. How far were women, when sick, treated differently from men? To what extent did the diagnosis and treatment of gynaecological conditions in particular reflect assumptions concerning the inferiority of women? As in biological theory, we may ask how far the doctors who discuss these questions merely mirrored the dominant ideology, or how far and on what grounds they criticised or broke away from it.

Where, as in beliefs about the female sex, common prejudices are particularly deep-seated, held with particularly dogmatic conviction, and sanctioned in a multitude of ways – outside the purely intellectual domain – in firmly entrenched patterns of social and cultural behaviour, the obstacles that this represented to the emergence of critical and rational investigation are evidently especially formidable. The fact that our evidence comes from the half of the population that is especially likely to display or to be influenced by such prejudices introduces a systematic bias that we must acknowledge. At the same time the bias in our sources can be said to make the confrontation between the common assumptions and the claims to be scientific or to proceed according to rational methods all the more pointed.

2. THE TREATMENT OF WOMEN IN THE HIPPOCRATIC CORPUS

Although in the recent increase of interest in the role and position of women in the ancient world some notice has begun to be taken of aspects of the relationship between doctors and their female patients, many issues have still not been dealt with as thoroughly and as carefully as they merit. Diepgen's classic monograph, published in 1937, admirable as it was in many ways, missed many of the important problems. So too do several of the principal handbooks on Greek medicine.[7] As for the most recent work, the two latest specialised articles on Hippocratic gynaecology, those of Manuli and Rousselle (both 1980), come, interestingly enough, to radically divergent, indeed almost diametrically opposed, conclusions on one central topic, namely who undertook the internal examination of female patients – each scholar tending to underline a different part of the evidence, Rousselle stressing that most of the information about women's diseases came from women, including the patients themselves, Manuli emphasising the part played by male doctors in the examination of women.[8]

Yet the material available for this study is, comparatively speaking, very rich. A group of treatises specialising in the diseases of women forms an important portion of the Hippocratic Corpus: *On the Diseases of Women* I and II, *On Sterile Women, On the Diseases of Young Girls, On Superfetation, On the Excision of the Foetus, On the Nature of Woman, On the Seventh Month Child* and *On the Eighth Month Child*.[9] In addition,

---

[7] The brief sections in both Bourgey 1953, pp. 168–78, and Phillips 1973, pp. 108–14, raise, without being extended enough fully to discuss, some of the fundamental questions. Abortion and contraception both within the Hippocratic Corpus and more generally have been extensively studied: see, e.g., Hopkins 1965–6, Nardi 1971, Dickison 1973. Some passages in *Mul.* I are analysed by Hanson 1975 and the relation between the doctor and the female patient is briefly discussed in Koelbing 1977. See also Pomeroy 1975 and 1978a and Arthur 1976.

[8] See Rousselle 1980 and Manuli 1980, especially p. 396 and n. 2.

[9] Cross-references within *Mul.* I, *Mul.* II and *Steril.* suggest that these works were either originally planned as a group or were subjected to later editorial revision to form one together with the embryological treatises *Genit., Nat. Puer.* and *Morb.* IV, cf. Lonie 1981, pp. 51ff. An editorial hand is clearly at work in labelling some of the later sections of *Mul.* I as spurious (νόθα: see Littré VIII 220.20ff, with his remarks on pp. 221 and 223). *Nat. Mul.* and *Superf.* are clearly composite works, incorporating, often in an abbreviated form, material that appears in other treatises in the group (see Trapp 1967, pp. 24ff for *Nat. Mul.* and Lienau in *CMG* I 2,2 pp. 45ff for *Superf.*) and the possibility that *Mul.* I, *Mul.* II and *Steril.* are also composite, indeed multi-author, works cannot be ruled out, even though we find the first person singular used both in some of the cross-references and in some reports of personal observations (see next note).

general works such as the *Epidemics* and the aphoristic treatises provide us with valuable further evidence on how women were treated, on how far the differences between women's and men's pathological conditions and physiology were recognised and allowed for, and on the relative importance of women in the clientèle of the Hippocratic doctors.

As we said, there is nothing to suggest that any of the authors[10] responsible for either the gynaecological or any other of the extant Hippocratic treatises was a woman.[11] However the major questions that the references to the treatment of women in the Hippocratic Corpus pose, and that we can hope to go some way towards answering, concern the interactions of tradition and critical innovation. How far was this department of Hippocratic medical thought and practice still bound by traditional or popular beliefs or by schemata that reflect male-oriented ideas and assumptions – that is, either ideas and assumptions that reflect the dominant position of the male in Greek society, or those that may stem from the predominance of males among literate medical practitioners? How far, on the other hand, are there signs of the breaking down of the barriers imposed by traditional constraints, and of the development of a critical and innovatory approach to gynaecological questions, in the Hippocratic Corpus? I shall begin with some general observations concerning the evidence available from the other Hippocratic works before turning to the gynaecological treatises themselves.

First there are several works that are directed primarily, though no doubt not exclusively, to consideration of the *male* patient. This is true particularly of the main surgical treatises, *On Fractures*, *On Joints*, *Instruments of Reduction* and *On Wounds in the Head*. Here the patient is throughout referred to in the masculine. No doubt this is natural enough, given the usual gender of ἄνθρωπος – and it is this term, rather than ἀνήρ, that is generally used to designate the patient. But

---

[10] It should be remembered that many Hippocratic treatises were, in all probability, the work of several hands: they are not carefully composed literary unities, but practical handbooks and as such they were subject to extensive additions and modifications before they reached the form in which they have come down to us (see Lloyd 1975*b*, especially pp. 180ff). In view of this exact conclusions on date have usually to be renounced. Most of the material in the gynaecological treatises can be dated no more precisely than to the late fifth or the fourth century B.C.

[11] Pliny, however, refers to some women authorities on medical topics, the midwife Salpe (xxviii 38, 66, 82, 262, xxxii 135, 140), Lais (xxviii 81–2), Elephantis (xxviii 81, cf. also in Galen, K xii 416.3ff), Olympias (xx 226, xxviii 246, 253) and Sotira (xxviii 83), and from Galen we can add, for example, Antiochis (K xiii 250.3 and 341.2). But there is no indication that any of these was active as early as the fourth century B.C. nor that any was responsible for any known extant writing.

there is more to it than that. It is, for example, striking that although very great attention is paid to the differences between young and old patients from the point of view both of diagnosis and of treatment,[12] and a good deal to those between fat and thin, or fleshy and emaciated,[13] and even to bilious and non-bilious,[14] subjects, as also to the distinction between congenital and acquired abnormalities,[15] the differences between male and female patients are generally ignored.

In part the explanation of the predominant interest in male patients in these works lies simply in the contexts in which the lesions described were sustained. Wounds and lesions sustained in battle or in the palaestra form an important proportion of those discussed in *On Wounds in the Head* and *On Joints* especially.[16] Moreover specifically female surgical operations connected with childbirth, miscarriage, female sterility and the like are dealt with in the gynaecological treatises themselves. Nevertheless many Greek women, we may presume, dislocated their shoulders, twisted their ankles, suffered from fractures of the leg or arm and were afflicted by congenital club-foot or hump-back, and the absence of any specific recognition that their treatment and diagnosis may need to differ from those of men is remarkable.[17] There is, for instance, no indication in these works that women patients might find some of the more violent treatments, such as succussion on the ladder or the reduction of extensions on the Hippocratic bench, hard to endure,[18] and it is also surprising that, although both *On Fractures* and *On Joints* allude to the problem of the *shame* ensuing from lesions or from their unsuccessful treatment,[19] neither work recognises or mentions the

---

[12] See, e.g., *Art.* ch. 29, L iv 140.4, ch. 41, 180.15ff, ch. 52, 230.9ff, ch. 53, 232.12ff, ch. 55, 238.21ff, 240.19ff, 242.12ff, ch. 58, 248.4, 252.17ff, ch. 60, 256.10ff, 258.13ff, *Mochl.* ch. 5, L iv 350.15ff, ch. 18, 360.2f, ch. 20, 360.21ff, ch. 21, 364.10, ch. 23, 366.8ff, ch. 24, 368.3ff, ch. 37, 380.15ff, *Fract.* ch. 4, L iii 428.9ff.

[13] See, e.g., *Art.* ch. 8, L iv 94.10ff, 98.8f and 13f, *Mochl.* ch. 5, L. iv 350.1.

[14] See, e.g., *Fract.* ch. 36, L iii 538.14ff.

[15] See, e.g., *Art.* ch. 56, L iv 242.19ff, ch. 58, 252.17ff, ch. 62, 262.10ff, ch.85, 324.1f, *Mochl.* ch. 5, L iv 350.9ff, ch. 11, 356.1, ch. 18, 360.1f, ch. 19, 360.7, ch. 20, 360.16, ch. 21, 364.6, ch. 23, 366.13, ch. 24, 368.7, ch. 29, 372.2f, ch. 40, 388.6ff.

[16] See, e.g., *VC* ch. 2, L iii 188.12ff, ch. 3, 192.16ff, *Art.* ch. 4, L iv 86.9f, ch. 11, 104.17f, 18f.

[17] When, as in *Art.* ch. 8, L iv 94.2ff, and ch. 71, 292.5ff, the writer points out that the surgeon has to take into account the differences in the 'natures' (φύσιες) of different individuals, those differences no doubt include those that relate to sex: these are not, however, specifically mentioned.

[18] At *Epid.* v ch. 103 (L v 258.9ff) and *Epid.* vii ch. 49 (L v 418.1ff) the case of a woman (the wife of Simos) who had been succussed in childbirth ends fatally (contrast *Epid.* vi sec. 8 ch. 28, L v 354.4f). References in the gynaecological treatises to such treatments as succussion are given below, pp. 73f and 81.

[19] See, e.g., *Fract.* ch. 19, L iii 482.9ff, and *Art.* ch. 37, L iv 166.12ff.

different modalities of such feelings as they would affect men and women.

In another group of treatises, the aphoristic works, there is a fairly sharp distinction between the generally quite short section devoted to the diseases of women and the rest of the treatise where, for the most part, as in the surgical works, it is male patients that are in view. This is the pattern found both in the *Aphorisms* itself and in *Coan Prognoses* where, in both cases, little attention is paid to differences between men and women until we reach the section devoted to women's complaints.[20] These sections themselves concentrate almost exclusively on questions concerning menstruation, conception, pregnancy, childbirth and miscarriage, and present an amalgam of the products of sensible, though no doubt often not original, observations and rationalised popular beliefs. Thus we may compare many of the signs that are supposed to indicate, and many of the tests that purport to reveal, whether a woman can conceive, or whether she is pregnant with a boy or a girl, with folk beliefs extensively reported in medical anthropological literature.[21]

On the other side there are occasional references, both in these and in other treatises, to the differences between men and women either in the incidence of diseases, or in their outcome, or in the treatments to be used. Thus *Aph.* III 11 (L IV 490.2ff) is one passage that notes a difference in the incidence of certain complaints as between males and females under certain circumstances. *Aph.* III 14 (L IV 492.3ff) and *Coac.* IV 163 (L V 618.17ff) notice similar differences in the reactions to climatic conditions and in what certain signs indicate. The different responses among men and women to climatic and other factors, and the different incidences of diseases, are noted repeatedly in *On Airs Waters Places*,[22] and although *On Diseases* II is a work that generally

---

[20] See *Aph.* v 28–62, L IV 542.5–556.2, *Coac.* XXXII 503–44, L V 700.13–708.8.

[21] See, e.g., *Aph.* v 38, 41, 42, 48, 59, VII 43, L IV 544.11ff, 546.1ff, 4f, 550.1f, 554.3ff, 588.14 (cf. below, n. 93 for similar passages from the gynaecological treatises) and cf. Aristotle, *GA* 747a7ff. See Joly 1966, pp. 59f and cf. Saunders 1963, pp. 16ff, who notes parallels in ancient Egyptian medical papyri and suggests an Egyptian origin for some Greek practices. Thus Pap. Carlsberg, as reconstructed by Iversen 1939, pp. 20ff, 22ff, 26ff, at least, contains (1) a version of the garlic test for whether a woman can conceive (garlic or onion is left in the womb overnight: if her mouth smells in the morning she will conceive) found also in *Steril.* ch. 214, L VIII 416.2ff, and also versions (2) of a fumigation test (for ability to conceive) and (3) of a drink test (for pregnancy) (cf. *Aph.* v 41 and 59, L IV 546.1ff, 554.3ff), though in both the latter cases the parallelisms are not exact. See further Lefebure 1956, pp. 101ff, on Pap. Kahun 19 and 26–32 (Griffith 1898, pp. 9f) and Pap. Berlin 193–9, and cf. Labat 1951, Appendix pp. xxxv ff and pp. 200ff, on the similarities and divergences between Greek and Babylonian prognostic, including predictions concerning childbirth.

[22] See, e.g., *Aër.* ch. 3, *CMG* I, 1,2 28.8ff, ch. 4, 30.22ff, ch. 5, 32.24, ch. 7, 36.13f, 16f, 20ff, ch. 10, 48.11, 15, 19, 21, 52.4, ch. 17, 64.11ff, ch. 18, 66.10ff, ch. 21, 72.1ff.

envisages the male patient,[23] ch. 70 remarks that a particular phlegmatic complaint attacks women more than men.[24]

Differences in the treatments to be used, or in the effects of certain treatments, are occasionally mentioned in such works as *On Regimen in Health* and *On the Use of Liquids*,[25] and when the treatise *Prognosis* remarks that a certain development in the course of a disease affected both males and females,[26] or observes, after setting out certain general rules concerning the crises in fevers, that these also apply to women suffering from fever after childbirth,[27] these passages too are evidence that the question of possible differentiations between the sexes in pathology and therapeutics was being attended to. *On Diseases* I especially several times records points concerning the illnesses and the treatment of women in particular,[28] and in ch. 22 (L VI 182.22ff) observes as a general rule that the outcome of diseases may differ according to the sex as well as to the age of the patient.

Meanwhile there is undoubted concern with the differentiation of males and females in theoretical and speculative, rather than practical, contexts in treatises such as *On the Nature of Man* and *On Regimen* that set up what are admittedly often highly fanciful general physiological and pathological doctrines. Thus *On the Nature of Man* ch. 9 writes of diseases that attack both sexes equally in an analysis of one of the two main genres of illness, namely those that are attributable to the air we breathe rather than to diet,[29] and as we shall be studying in detail later, in contrast to the common view that held that the male parent alone provides the seed for the offspring, the mother supplying merely the place for its development, *On Regimen* I and the embryological treatises *On the Seed, On the Nature of the Child* and *On Diseases* IV offer explanations of the sex of the embryo in which either the male or the female parent may be the determining factor.[30]

The treatises we have considered so far show that, as we might expect from the dominant position of the male in Greek society as a whole, in some of the Hippocratic works the focus of attention is very much on the male patient. This is not just a matter of conventionally

[23] This is suggested by such features as the prescription of gymnastics in therapy, ch. 13, L VII 24.12, ch. 49, 76.5, ch. 66, 100.22ff, ch. 73, 112.9, and precautions concerning intercourse, using the term λαγνεύειν, ch. 73, 112.8 (both features that recur also, for example, in *Int.*, e.g. ch. 25, L VII 232.5ff, ch. 28, 240.21, ch. 30, 246.14ff).

[24] *Morb.* II ch. 70, L VII 106.10f. Cf. *Haem.* ch. 9, L VI 444.1ff, where haemorrhoids as they affect women are dealt with in a separate chapter.

[25] See, e.g., *Salubr.* ch. 6, L VI 82.2ff, *Liqu.* ch. 4, *CMG* I,1 88.14f, ch. 6, 89.3.

[26] *Prog.* ch. 24, L II 184.8ff (cf. also, e.g., *Aph.* v 69, L IV 560.6ff).

[27] *Prog.* ch. 20, L II 172.2ff.

[28] See, e.g., *Morb.* I ch. 3, L VI 144.6 and 19, ch. 5, 146.19, ch. 7, 152.20 and 22, ch. 8 154.7f.

[29] *Nat. Hom.* ch. 9, *CMG* I 1,3 188.10ff at 17f.

[30] See below, pp. 89ff.

referring to the patient in the masculine, but also, on occasions, a question of the conditions investigated, of the treatments prescribed, and of a certain neglect of differences between the sexes where such differences might have been thought relevant.[31] Yet the Hippocratic doctors did not attend male patients exclusively, and indeed the deontological treatises show special concern on the topic of how the doctor should behave in relation to the female members of the households he enters, some of whom are no doubt envisaged as his patients.[32] The evidence available in the seven books of the *Epidemics* – both the records of individual case-histories and the more general accounts of the outbreaks of types of diseases – throws valuable light both on the clientèle of the doctors in question and on the issue of how far they made any distinction, in their medical practice, between male and female patients.

Two points may be made straight away. First the progress of female patients' illnesses is recorded, in general, with just as much care and attention to detail as that of male patients. This is true both of the references to female patients in the general descriptions of the 'constitutions' and in the series of individual case-histories. Secondly women patients form a considerable proportion both of the cases mentioned incidentally in the course of the general descriptions and of the case-histories that receive full and detailed documentation.

However that second generalisation can and should be refined. In not one of the seven books of the *Epidemics* taken as a whole are female patients in a majority. Although exact percentages cannot, in some cases, be given (the sex of some of the infants is not specified), the approximate proportion of females among the individuals whose cases are either set out in detail or at least clearly alluded to varies from 45% to 24%.[33] In general their social status varies as does that of the males: they include both slave and free. But only a very small proportion of the women are named, the great majority being identified by their relationship to a named male or – less frequently – by where they lived. Although in some books the fatalities among the women are higher than among the men in the cases whose

---

[31] In the long list of factors to be taken into consideration in diagnosis in *Epid.* I ch. 10, L II 668.14ff, while the customs, mode of life, practices and age of the patient are all explicitly mentioned, sex is not. See also *Epid.* III ch. 16, L III 102.2ff, *Aph.* I 2, L IV 458.9f, II 34, 480.7ff: cf. however references to women, e.g. at *Epid.* I ch. 8, L II 646.9, ch. 9, 656.6ff and *Epid.* III ch. 14, L III 98.1.

[32] See, e.g., *Jusj.* ch. 6, *CMG* I, 1 5.3f, *Medic.* ch 1, *CMG* I, 1 20.20ff.

[33] The appropriate figures for females as a percentage of the total cases mentioned in the several books of *Epid.* are as follows: *Epid.* I 27.3% (though females account for 35.7% of the cases in the series of detailed case-histories), *Epid.* II 44.7%, *Epid.* III 42.8%, *Epid.* IV 36.7%, *Epid.* V 26.5%, *Epid.* VI 23.5% and *Epid.* VII 25%.

outcome is clearly recorded, this is not invariably so.[34] The dangers that faced women in childbirth and from complications arising from it emerge very clearly in these books, as do the hazards not just from war but also from what we may call occupational accidents for the men.[35] But there is nothing in the *Epidemics* to suggest that in general women were more prone or less resistant to disease than men, or that – once they became the doctor's patients – they were less well cared for, even though their chances of becoming patients may have been rather lower than those of males and that certainly appears to be true of their having their cases recorded.

All of this goes to confirm that, so far as the doctors represented in the seven books of the *Epidemics* are concerned, there was no question of their being inhibited by assumptions of the superiority of the male sex from taking the problem of the study of their female patients' conditions very seriously indeed. The *Epidemics* do, however, from time to time provide evidence of some of the problems that might arise in the relationship between the doctor and the female patient. Thus on one occasion in *Epidemics* IV a woman patient's report is glossed by the remark that the doctor did not know whether she was speaking the truth,[36] and in two other passages which both concern women patients the addition of the phrase 'so she said' marks a distinction between the patient's own account and what the doctor himself can vouch for.[37] Finally in what appears to be one of the comparatively uncommon references to treatment contained in these treatises it is in relation to a woman patient that *Epidemics* III sees fit to record that 'she would not obey instructions'.[38]

---

[34] In *Epid.* II, IV and VI the outcome of the diseases of individual patients is often not specified. But in the other books, if we take those cases where the outcome is clearly recorded, the figures for the women who died as a percentage of the total number of women patients are as follows: *Epid.* I 40%, *Epid.* III 75%, *Epid.* V 57.7%, *Epid.* VII 57%, compared with figures for male fatalities, expressed as a percentage of the male patients, of 55.6%, 56.2%, 54.2% and 62% respectively.

[35] Of the seventeen female patients whose cases are recorded in detail in *Epid.* I and III, childbirth, miscarriage or pregnancy is mentioned in the description of nine (i.e. over 50%) and the onset of menstruation in a further two. The 'occupational' cases among the men include such instances as that of a man whose finger was crushed by an anchor, *Epid.* V ch. 74 (L V 246.21ff), cf. VII ch. 36 (L V 404.14ff): see also, e.g., *Epid.* V chh. 32 and 45, L V 230.1ff, 234.4ff. [36] *Epid.* IV ch. 6, L V 146.11f. Cf. Aristotle, *HA* x ch. 7, 638a5ff.

[37] *Epid.* IV ch. 20, L V 160.6, ch. 22, 162.5 (in both cases the patient's report concerns an abortion or miscarriage), and cf. *Decent.* ch. 14, *CMG* I, I 29.3ff.

[38] *Epid.* III second series case 14, L III 140.18. Several features of this case indicate that the patient was considered mentally disturbed, see 140.22, 142.3. Littré took a passage in *Mul.* II ch. 171, L VIII 352.5, in a similar way, translating καὶ ἐσακούειν οὐκ ἐθέλει 'la malade ne prête pas l'oreille'. But this interpretation is rendered unlikely in view of the general use of ἐσακούειν and ἐνακούειν in the gynaecological treatises to refer not to the reluctance of the patient to follow the doctor's orders, but to a failure of the disease to respond to treatment, cf. *Mul.* I ch. 29, L VIII 74.3, *Mul.* II ch. 145, L VIII 320.20, ch. 153, 328.6f.

On the question of the relation between the doctor and the female patient – as on the other related topics we are concerned with – by far the most important and extensive evidence is contained in the specialised gynaecological treatises and it is to this that we must now turn. Many of the concerns expressed in these treatises conform to general patterns found in other Hippocratic works. Such themes as the emphasis on the prediction of the outcome of a complaint – prognosis – and the criticism of faulty treatments and diagnoses (including some for which the responsibility lay with other doctors) are, as is well known, common throughout the Hippocratic Corpus. The doctors who composed the gynaecological treatises, who never refer to themselves by any special term, corresponding to our 'gynaecologist',[39] were in a similar competitive situation, and faced similar delicate problems of winning and retaining the confidence of their prospective clients, as other Hippocratic doctors. Certain features of the relationship between doctors and women patients are, however, exceptional.

We may begin by broadly categorising the other healers with whom these doctors were directly or indirectly in competition. There is no doubt that they included, first, a variety of types of religious healer. These ranged from those who tended the sick in the well-established shrines of Asclepius[40] to the kind of itinerant charlatans mentioned by Plato[41] and the 'purifiers' criticised extensively by the writer of *On the Sacred Disease*.[42] We have direct evidence in *On the Diseases of Young Girls* that there were seers, μάντιες, who persuaded young girls suffering from certain kinds of diseases to dedicate costly garments to Artemis.[43] The writer's own recommendation[44] is that the girls should have intercourse, for pregnancy will cure them. Here it may be that girls were particularly vulnerable to exploitation, but of course such vulnerability, and maybe a certain gullibility concerning religious healing, were far from being confined to the young or to the female sex.[45]

[39] Though the term γυναικεῖοι ἰατροί appears, for example, in Soranus, *Gyn.* III 3, *CMG* IV 95.7.

[40] The chief evidence relates to the shrine of Asclepius at Epidaurus, where we have detailed inscriptions from the later part of the fourth century B.C., see Herzog 1931, and Edelstein and Edelstein 1945. Women patients or inquirers account for 17 out of the 70 cases recorded on the four main inscriptions.   [41] See Plato, *R.* 364b ff, *Lg.* 909a ff, 933a ff, especially.

[42] See *Morb. Sacr.* ch. 1, L VI 352.1ff and passim: cf. Lloyd 1979, ch. 1.

[43] See *Virg.* L. VIII 466.4ff, 468.17ff (the first text shows that the writer is dealing with a wide range of conditions, including, but not limited to, the sacred disease).

[44] Indeed he uses the same term κελεύειν of his own recommendation (κελεύω δ' ἔγωγε, L VIII 468.21) as he had of the seers' telling the girls to dedicate their garments to Artemis (κελευόντων τῶν μάντεων, 468.19), in part no doubt to point up the *contrast* in the context of the recommendations, but also implying that *he too* issues orders.

[45] It is clear, at least, that the shrine at Epidaurus aimed to cater for clients of all kinds.

A more distinctive feature of the position of male doctors who treated female patients is that among those who also attended women were women healers of various kinds, especially but not exclusively those who practised primarily as midwives. Several texts in the gynaecological treatises and elsewhere[46] refer to such women healers under various descriptions and the question of their relationship with the Hippocratic writers themselves is an intricate one. How far did the women offer an alternative, rival, service?[47] When they cooperated with male physicians, what was the division of responsibility between them? While our answer to the first question is bound to be impressionistic, we have a good deal of evidence in the gynaecological treatises that throws light on the second.

Several texts make it quite clear that the internal examination of the patient was sometimes undertaken in whole or in part by someone other than the male doctor himself. We may distinguish between two types of case, first where the male doctor instructs the patient herself to examine the inside of her vagina or womb, for example, and secondly where he asks a female attendant to do so, although in a number of passages the text leaves it indeterminate which of these two types of case we are dealing with,[48] while making it clear that it was not the doctor himself who was to perform the examination.

In *Mul.* 1 ch. 40 (L viii 96.16ff, 98.1) a female patient who is, exceptionally, named as Phrontis is said to have discovered an obstruction in her genital passage by feeling herself.[49] Here there is no

---

[46] See, e.g., *Carn.* ch. 19, L viii 614.8ff, which refers to ἀκεστρίδες present at births, and cf. the reference to ἡ ὀμφαλητόμος at *Mul.* 1 ch. 46, L viii 106.7, and to the criticism of the way 'women' treat cases of ulceration of the womb at *Mul.* 1 ch. 67, 140.15f, where, however, it is not specified whether the patients or women healers or both are involved.

[47] The story of Hagnodice recorded in Hyginus, *Fab.* 274, pp. 171–2, Bunte, would imply both that originally the Athenians did not allow women to learn medicine and that after her exploits the law was changed to permit this (she dressed herself as a man, revealing her real sex only to her female patients when they were ashamed to receive treatment from a man). We may well believe that women were, and continued to be, inhibited at being treated by men (see below, pp. 78f and n. 76 on *Mul.* 1 ch. 62). But we have no other evidence to suggest either that women were once forbidden by law at Athens or anywhere else to learn medicine, or that the law was changed to permit this, and the gradations between different types of healer (which we can document from the Hippocratic treatises) and the general lack of a formal legal framework for medical practice make both suggestions rather unlikely. Meanwhile in *Republic* v, when Plato discusses the education of his Guardian rulers and argues for equal treatment for both sexes in this content, he states the view that a woman is potentially just as able to become a doctor as a man is (455e f). There is, however, no firm indication in this passage either that this happened *regularly* or that it *never* happened.

[48] Moreover in several cases that we shall consider Littré's text is open to question. For *Nat. Mul.* I use the text of Trapp 1967. I have had the benefit of consultations with Professor Ann Hanson on the text of *Mul.* 1.

[49] Reading ψηλαφῶσα with Littré rather than ψηλαφωθεῖσα with D.

mention of the male doctor instructing Phrontis to examine herself, but elsewhere that is evidently what happened. At *Mul.* ii ch. 133 (L viii 286.16f) the doctor is told to tell the patient, during treatment by fumigation, to feel the orifice of the womb if she can.[50] The aim of this treatment, as the fuller description of a fumigation at L viii 294.7ff shows, is partly to open and soften the orifice of the womb and partly to bring the womb itself down towards the vagina – as the Hippocratic writers put it – and the patient is instructed to examine herself no doubt in order to report on the progress of the treatment. At *Mul.* ii ch. 146 (L viii 322.15ff) it again appears to be the woman patient herself who is asked to examine herself and report on her condition the morning after the application of a pessary. It is if *she* says that the orifice of the womb has become more straight that the next stage in the treatment is to be undertaken. In *Mul.* ii ch. 157 (L viii 332.16ff) the patient apparently touches the orifice of the womb to see if it seems soft,[51] and this may well be what lies behind another text, *Mul.* ii ch.119 (L viii 260.10f), where the doctor is told what to do if the patient, on being asked, says that the orifice of the womb is hard and painful. We find other similar passages outside the gynaecological works also: at *Epid.* v ch. 25 (L v 224.10f) the patient herself reports what she feels at the orifice of the womb.

Elsewhere, however, it is evidently not the patient herself, but another woman who is asked to conduct part of the examination. In *Mul.* i ch. 21 there is a discussion of the signs and causes of miscarriages in the third or fourth month, and one of the causes is said to be that the womb is – either naturally or because of lesions – excessively smooth. One can find out, the writer says, about some aspects of such cases – for example about disturbances in the belly, weakness, fever and loss of appetite – by asking exact questions. But on the question of the womb's smoothness, the doctor will find out 'if another woman were to touch the womb when it is empty: for otherwise it [the smooth condition] does not become manifest' (L. viii 60.15ff). In several other passages it is as likely to be some such 'other woman', as to be the patient herself, who is asked to carry out the investigation. Thus in the opening chapter of *On Sterile Women*, where several causes of sterility are discussed, there are a number of references to diagnosing these by touching or palpating (ψηλάφησις) the womb. Some of these leave it quite indefinite who is to undertake the

---

[50] Cf. also *Mul.* ii ch. 133, L viii 288.8, where, however, the instruction does not specify who it is who is to try to touch the orifice of the womb.

[51] Reading ψαυούσῃ αὐτῇ with Littré: the αὐτῇ is not specified, but it seems more natural to take it to refer to the patient herself, not to a female attendant, though the latter cannot be ruled out.

examination,[52] but at L VIII 408.17 it is certainly a woman who is to
do so,[53] and at 410.3f it is again a woman who does so and who also
asks the patient certain questions about whether she has ever suffered
from lesions in the womb.[54]

Yet it is not the case that the male doctor never undertakes the
internal examination of the female patient himself. Although there
are many passages in the gynaecological works that – in the characteristic style of the Hippocratic writings – refer to such examinations
quite impersonally, without specifying who was to perform them,
there are enough texts that point unambiguously to the personal
intervention of the male doctor to establish that female internal
examinations were not carried out solely by females – whether by the
patient herself or by a woman attendant. The audience or readership
to which these treatises are principally addressed consists of
the writers' own male colleagues and pupils, and the writers
frequently give them explicit instructions on how they are to conduct
an examination and on what they should expect to find when they do
so.

At *Mul.* I ch. 20 (L VIII 58.16f) the writer claims that, if the woman
does not receive the seed even though the menstrual discharge is
normal, there will be a 'membrane' in the way, though there may be
other causes, and he proceeds: 'you will discover this with your finger
if you touch the obstruction'. In *Mul.* I ch. 60 (L VIII 120.7ff) the
reader is told how he will recognise a case of dropsy of the womb:
'feeling (ἀφάσσων) with the finger, you will recognise that the orifice
[of the womb] is withered and full of liquid'. In the second book,
chapters 155 and 156 deal with two types of induration of the womb.
The first is marked by the suppression of the menses and by their
appearance like rough sand if they do come. 'And if one touches with
the finger, you will find the orifice of the womb to be hard like a callus'
(L VIII 330.13f). In the following chapter, in a similar case, the writer
says: 'if you touch, it seems to be like a stone there, and the orifice is
rough and fibrous and not smooth in appearance and it does not
admit the finger examining it' (L VIII 330.21f), and similar passages
where the male doctors addressed are instructed to ascertain facts

[52] See *Steril.* ch. 213, L VIII 410.13, 20f, 23, and cf. also from outside the Hippocratic writers,
Aristotle, *HA* 583a17f.

[53] Cf. also *Mul.* I ch. 59, L VIII 118.3, *Mul.* II ch. 141, L VIII 314.16, *Steril.* ch. 230, L VIII 438.11
and *Nat. Mul.* ch. 21, L VII 340.10f, and ch. 96, 412.20 (in Trapp's text).

[54] Reading ψηλαφώση γυναικί at 408.17 and ψηλαφώση καί εἰρομένη at 410.3, with Littré. In
later writers, too, it is often the midwife who is charged with the internal examination of the
patient: see, for example, Galen K VIII 425.1f, 433.15ff, and cf. Oribasius XXII 3 (Bussemaker
and Daremberg III, 1858, 53ff at 54.15f).

for themselves by internal examination of their patients can be multiplied both from *On the Diseases of Women* and *On the Nature of Woman*.[55]

We are then faced with something of a paradox. It is not that the male doctor refrained in principle and under all circumstances from a personal internal examination of his female patients.[56] Yet, as we have seen, he sometimes entrusts to the patient herself or to a female attendant the verification of certain points that are crucial to his understanding of the case, and he relies on their reports on occasions where it would have been possible – and one would have thought desirable – to establish the facts directly for himself. A wish to avoid any but the most necessary personal examinations would be readily understandable: yet it is not that any such principle is explicitly formulated, nor even clearly implied, and we can do no more than guess the precise factors that weighed with these doctors in deciding when to examine personally and when to delegate this to others.[57]

A similar situation also obtains in connection with aspects of the treatment of women patients. Even though many of the instructions contained in these treatises are, no doubt, not intended for the addressees personally, it is often clear enough that it is the male doctor who is envisaged as carrying out certain treatments. This is true particularly of some of the difficult and dangerous surgical interventions recommended, such as some of the passages describing how to deal with faulty presentation,[58] with prolapse of the womb,[59] or with

[55] See also *Mul.* II ch. 160, L VIII 338.5, ch. 163, 342.13f, ch. 167, 346.1, ch. 168, 346.20, *Nat. Mul.* ch. 8, L VII 322.13, ch. 13, 330.14, ch. 35, 376.23f, ch. 36, 378.22ff, ch. 37, 380.6ff (these three last passages parallel *Mul.* I ch. 60, *Mul.* II chh. 155 and 156 respectively), ch. 39, 382.15f, ch. 42, 386.8, ch. 45, 390.4f, ch. 46, 390.17f, and ch. 67, 402.8 (cf. *Mul.* I ch. 20). Although some of the instructions given to the addressees or readers of the treatises were, no doubt, not meant to be carried out by them personally in their medical practice, in these cases – where the addressee is told to examine the patient by feeling or touching her – this was presumably the expectation.

[56] We may contrast the practice reported from China up to recent times, that the female patient indicated to the male doctor that part of her anatomy in which she felt pain on a *model* of a female body, and was not examined directly at all: see Veith 1979–80, pp. 255ff. On the other hand post-mortem examination and dissection was sometimes carried out for forensic purposes, see O'Neill and Chan 1976.

[57] There is, for example, no indication that the gynaecological writers modified their procedures according to the social status of the patient, nor that the differences in the method of examination correspond to the personal preferences of different writers responsible for different sections of these treatises (we are not, in any case, in a position to establish individual authorship either of particular chapters or of groups of chapters).

[58] Thus in *Superf.* chh. 4–6 the second person singulars (CMG I 2,2 74.7 and 24, L VIII 478.5 and 24) and masculine participles (*CMG* I 2,2 74.14, 20ff, 25ff, L VIII 478.13, 19ff, 25ff) suggest that the male doctor himself is envisaged as operating.

[59] See *Mul.* II ch. 144, L VIII 316.13ff, *Steril.* ch. 248, L VIII 460.14ff, *Nat. Mul.* ch. 5, L VII 316.20ff.

the excision or removal of a dead foetus from the womb.[60] Some of the more drastic surgical procedures involve the use of assistants, either men or women. Where *On the Diseases of Women* I ch. 68 (L VIII 144.13) refers to two male assistants who are to hold the patient's legs while succussion on the ladder is performed, in a similar case in *On the Excision of the Foetus* ch. 4 (L VIII 514.17f) the writer recommends the use of four women, two for the arms and two for the legs. In this instance, where the assistants had to be both strong and skillful, it was presumably in part for psychological reasons that *On the Excision of the Foetus* proposes the use of women, who would be more reassuring or less frightening to the female patient undergoing the operation.[61]

Yet again, as with internal diagnostic examination, the patient herself or other women are also brought into action, just as, in the general surgical treatises, the patient is sometimes involved in his own treatment.[62] In the gynaecological works the doctor evidently relies on the patient herself, or on another woman, at many points where simple and straightforward procedures, such as, for example, the application or removal of a pessary,[63] are concerned. Several texts leave it indeterminate whether the woman who is to follow the doctor's orders is indeed the patient herself or another woman in attendance. Thus *Mul.* II ch. 134 deals with a case where the womb becomes attached to the hip-joint and an induration forms. The patient is fumigated 'until she says her sight is dim and she feels faint' (L VIII 302.22f). The patient is bathed, and then 'she touches with her finger and draws the orifice of the womb towards the healthy hip'. At night emollients are applied and then 'when she says that the orifice is straight', the doctor administers an aromatic fumigation, more emollients and lead pessaries on three successive days (304.1–6). Here the subject of the first 'she says' (302.22) is evidently the patient herself, but neither this text nor the passages describing similar procedures in other works[64] resolve the question of who it is that undertakes the straightening of the orifice of the womb and reports on

---

[60] *Foet. Exsect.* ch. 1, L VIII 512.1ff (note the instruction to cover the patient's head so that she does not see what you do, 512.3f), cf. *Mul.* I ch. 70, L VIII 146.19ff, *Superf.* ch. 7, *CMG* I 2,2 74.28ff, L VIII 480.3ff, *Steril.* ch. 249, L VIII 462.16ff.

[61] Cf. Soranus, *Gyn.* II 5, *CMG* IV 53.12ff. Cf. *Art.* ch. 37, L IV 166.7, where, in dealing with the reduction of a fractured nose, the writer specifies that a boy's or a woman's hands should be used to apply pressure, because they are soft.

[62] See, e.g., *Art.* ch. 37, L IV 166.1ff, ch. 52, 228.6ff, *Mochl.* ch. 5, L IV 352.6f.

[63] See, e.g., *Mul.* I ch. 37, L VIII 92.6f, ch. 66, 138.14f, ch. 88, 212.11f, *Steril.* ch. 221, L VIII 428.8ff, ch. 227, 436.11ff (with μίξας at 13 and 16 contrast μίσγουσα at 14), *Nat. Mul.* ch. 32, L VII 348.20, ch. 109, 430.4, and cf. also *Mul.* I ch. 13, L VIII 52.1.

[64] Cf. *Steril.* ch. 217, L VIII 418.23ff, *Nat. Mul.* ch. 6, L VII 320.7ff, ch. 40, 384.10ff.

this (304.1–6, cf. above on such passages as L VIII 286.16f and 60.15ff). The fact that no change of subject is signalled is not conclusive, for abrupt and unannounced changes of subject are common in these works: they pay little attention to style or even syntax and they often rely on their readers being familiar, in general terms, with the kinds of procedure described.[65]

We can, however, set against the indeterminacy of some passages the more definite information contained in others. At *Steril.* ch. 222 (L VIII 428.25ff) instructions are given for drenching the womb using a clyster which is described in some detail. The top of the tube should be smooth, like a probe, and there should be a hole near the top and other narrow ones along the length. To the tube a sow's bladder is to be attached: the holes are plugged and the bladder is filled with mare's milk. Then the doctor is told to give the device 'to the woman you intend to drench' (430.11f): she will take the plug out and insert it in her womb – 'she will know herself where it should be put' – whereupon the doctor pumps the milk into the womb until he sees that there is no more pus coming out with the milk.

While *Steril.* ch. 222 clearly involves the patient herself in her own treatment, there is an equally unambiguous reference to the intervention of a woman healer who is present at the difficult operation described in *Mul.* I ch. 68 (L VIII 142.13ff). This chapter ends with an account of the removal of a dead foetus from the womb after succussion, and it is a woman referred to as ἡ ἰητρεύουσα who is to open the orifice of the womb gently to remove the foetus together with the umbilical cord (144.22ff). Outside the gynaecological treatises, too, we find that in the case in *Epid.* v (ch. 25, L v 224.6ff) where a woman felt something hard at the orifice of her womb, it is 'another woman', ἑτέρη γυνή, who inserts her hand and presses out a 'stone like the whorl of a spindle' (224.11ff).

The evidence relating to examinations and treatments already suggests on the one hand a certain distance or reserve between the male doctor and the female patient, and on the other a certain desire on the part of the doctor to enlist the assistance both of the patient herself and of the women who attend her (though none of the latter is

---

[65] See, e.g., the switch from masculine to feminine nominative participles in *Steril.* ch. 227 (above, n. 63). Again at *Nat. Mul.* ch. 6, L VII 320.9ff, where the patient herself is the subject of πινέτω at 9, and of κατακείσθω at 11, our MSS have a masculine nominative participle, συμμίσγων at 10. In some cases, no doubt, we may suspect corruption in our manuscripts (cf. Trapp 1967, p. 172, on the possible substitution of masculine for feminine participles when it is assumed that only a male doctor would undertake certain investigations). But the frequency of abrupt changes of subject suggests that the authors themselves were often unconcerned to mark them with care.

graced with the title of doctor – ἰατρός[66] – the nearest we come to that is the reference in *Mul.* I ch. 68 to ἡ ἰητρεύουσα). But we can go further. A certain ambivalence in the relationship between the male doctor and the female patient – the need for the former to rely on the latter, and yet the distrust he might feel or had to overcome – comes out even more clearly when we consider the evidence relating to the interviews the doctors conducted with their patients.

Like many other Hippocratic works, the gynaecological treatises set great store by the proper conduct of the questioning of the patient, although none goes quite so far as the elaborate advice provided in *On Diseases* I concerning how the doctor should formulate his questions, how he should deal with objections and how he should answer the questions put to him in return.[67] One text in *Mul.* I (ch. 62 L VIII 126.11f) suggests in general terms that the doctor learns the nature of the disease from the patient herself, and references to his questioning the patient punctuate the gynaecological works.[68] However, we have already cited evidence from the *Epidemics* that shows that the veracity of women patients' reports (particularly where they related to childbirth and miscarriage) was sometimes doubted.[69] In most cases, to be sure, no such reservations are expressed or implied. Yet two extended texts in particular highlight the problems that might arise.

In *On the Eighth Month Child* ch. 6 (Grensemann = *Septim.* ch. 3, Littré) (*CMG* I 2, I 92.4ff, L VII 438.21ff) the author notes that women are unanimous on the difficulties they experience in the eighth month of pregnancy, and they are correct about this. However the period of difficulty is not just the eighth month, for one has to include some of the days of the seventh and of the ninth as well. 'But women neither state nor recognise the days uniformly. For they are misled because it does not always happen in the same way: for sometimes more days are added from the seventh month, sometimes from the ninth, to arrive at the forty days. . . But the eighth month is undisputed.'[70] Here the

---

[66] ἰατρός – and μαῖα – are, however, the terms used about a certain Phanostrate in the inscription dated to around the middle of the fourth century, on her tomb, *IG* II² 6873. Cf., e.g., the first-century B.C. inscription from Tlos in Kalinka 1920, II no. 595, and Robert's discussion of the use of the term ἰατρείνη on a second- or first-century B.C. inscription at Byzantium, Firatli and Robert 1964, pp. 175ff; cf. also Galen, e.g. K VIII 414.6ff, 425.1f. See now Nickel 1979.

[67] *Morb.* I ch. I, L VI 140.1ff and passim, on which see Lloyd 1979, pp. 91f.

[68] See, e.g., *Mul.* I ch. 6, L VIII 30.12f, ch. 10, 40.12ff, ch.21, 60.15f, ch. 62, 126.17ff, *Mul.* II ch. 119, L VIII 260.10f, ch. 133, 298.3f, *Steril.* ch. 213, L VIII 412.17, 414.11ff, *Nat. Mul.* ch. 10, L VII 326.3ff.

[69] See above, p. 68 and nn. 36–7.

[70] *CMG* I 2,I 92.7ff (L VII 440.4ff), reading ἀναμφισβήτητος with Grensemann, Joly, Littré at 92.12, where one MS has ἀμφισβητήσιμος. The reference to the forty days is to the period of difficulty as the writer himself calculates it.

writer expresses general agreement – though with some reservations – with what he represents as the unanimous opinion of women
on the difficulties of the eighth month of pregnancy. Chapter 7,
however, shows that the situation is more complex. It opens with the
statement that 'one should not disbelieve what women say about
childbirth' (*CMG* I 2,1, 92.15, L VII 440.13). The tendency for the
male doctor to do just that was, as we have seen, there, and this writer
resists it. Yet the effect of his support for the women's own reports is
rather lessened by what follows.

For they say what they know[71] and they will always continue to do so. For they could
not be persuaded either by fact or by argument that they know anything better[72]
than what goes on in their own bodies. Anyone who wishes to assert otherwise is at
liberty to do so, but the women who decide the contest and give the prizes[73]
concerning this argument will always say and assert that they bear seven and eight
and nine and ten and eleven month children, and that of these the eighth month
children do not survive.[74]

The general endorsement that this writer gives to the proposition
that women are authoritative on matters concerning childbirth does
not stop him from introducing his own modifications on the question
of the exact calculation of the critical periods, nor from alluding,
wrily, to the women's tendency to dogmatise.[75] There were, no
doubt, conflicting opinions among women themselves on these
problems, and the male doctors, for their part, were in considerable
doubt – and confusion – about what to believe, a doubt that is
reflected in the fluctuating views expressed on the topic in other
treatises. Thus the writer of *On Fleshes* ch. 19 (L VIII 610.3ff)
confidently asserts that public *hetairai* know when they have conceived and he gives details of how conception is to be recognised
(610.10ff), adding that he himself knows this on the basis of what
experienced women have indicated to him. *On the Seed* ch. 5 (L VII
476.23ff) puts it that experienced women know when they have
conceived from the fact that the seed remains in the body, a view also

---

[71] Reading ἅπερ ἂν εἰδέωσι with Grensemann and Joly. Littré has λέγουσι γὰρ πάντα καὶ αἰεὶ
λέγουσι, that is, perhaps, 'they say all kinds of things and always say them'.

[72] Reading μᾶλλόν τι γνῶναι ἢ τὸ . . . γινόμενον with Joly (cf. Grensemann's ἄλλο τι γνῶναι ἢ
τὸ . . . γινόμενον and Littré's ἀλλ' ὅτι – 'et rien, ni fait ni parole, ne pourrait les persuader
qu'elles ne savent pas ce qui se passe dans leurs corps').

[73] Littré and Joly both take τὰ νικητήρια here to mean 'victorious proofs', as does LSJ. But LSJ
gives no parallel for this sense, and it seems more likely (with Grensemann) that the word
has its usual meaning 'prizes'.

[74] *CMG* I 2,1 92.16–21, L VII 440.13–442.4. On the slender chances of survival of the eighth
month child, see also Aristotle, *GA* 772 b 8ff.

[75] Cf. also ch. 9, *CMG* I 2,1 94.15ff (ch. 5, L VII 444.1ff) where he notes that when they are
delivered of a malformed child, they will report that they had a difficult eighth month, and
where he goes on to offer an explanation of why this indeed happens.

found in the companion embryological treatise *On the Nature of the Child* (ch. 13, L VII 490.5ff). Yet later on in the latter work the writer argues that it is impossible for a pregnancy to last more than, at most, ten months, giving the reason that by the end of that period the mother is unable to supply the nourishment the embryo needs and this brings on the birth, and here he rejects the notion that some women have – which he says he has often heard – namely that they have been pregnant for more than ten months: he explains that the women in question are mistaken concerning the time of conception (ch. 30, 532.14ff, 534.8ff).

Our second major text on this problem is in *On the Diseases of Women* I ch. 62. Here after observing that many women's diseases are difficult to understand (L VIII 126.6), the writer complains that women do not realise they are suffering from an illness until 'time and necessity' teach them what is responsible for their diseases. Sometimes the disease becomes incurable before the doctor has been correctly instructed by the patient on her condition. The writer then proceeds to identify the source of the trouble: 'for women are ashamed to speak even when they know; they think the disease to be shameful through inexperience and lack of knowledge' (126.12ff). But the problem is not just one that arises from the patients being inhibited.[76] The writer goes on to point out that doctors too make mistakes by not carefully investigating the cause of the disease and by *treating them as if they were the diseases of males*. He for his part claims that the treatment of women's diseases is very different from that of men's and he asserts that he has seen many women perish through a failure to understand this and to examine them exactly (126.14–19).

These two texts in *On the Eighth Month Child* and *On the Diseases of Women* I both indicate the nature of the problem and show that some writers, at least, were concerned to overcome it. They suggest both that women could be inhibited about talking about their complaints to the doctors, and that they could be dogmatic on such topics as the time of conception or on the viability of eighth month children. The question of what to believe in the patient's own report about his or her condition – a tricky one in any case – was particularly difficult where

---

[76] Cf., from outside the medical writers, the indication at Euripides, *Hipp.* 293–6, that women might be inhibited from speaking about some complaints to males, while being prepared to talk about them to other women. From much later, in the second century A.D., Galen's story about the wife of Boethus (*De Praecognitione* ch. 8, *CMG* v 8,1 110.13ff, K XIV 641.5ff) suggests that even ladies of rank continued to be affected by inhibitions in speaking about their symptoms to a male doctor and preferred to entrust themselves in the first instance to midwives. Similar inhibitions would, however, also be felt by men in certain contexts. Thus Plutarch, *De curiositate* 7, 518cd illustrates the point with two examples, (1) that of an abscess in the anus, and (2) that of a woman speaking about cancer of the womb.

the patient was a woman. *On the Diseases of Women* I ch. 62 further suggests that there were doctors who assimilated gynaecological cases to men's diseases without due reflection. This text is eloquent testimony to the author's realisation of the problem. Yet when we recall the evidence we considered earlier concerning the examination and treatment of women patients in the gynaecological treatises – where the male doctors evidently sought to involve the patient herself, but where they present uncertain and fluctuating guidelines on the question of when and where to rely entirely on her – we may be sceptical about just how far the authors of these works were successful in overcoming the difficulties pointed to so clearly in *Mul.* I ch. 62.

We may, in conclusion, broaden the scope of our discussion somewhat and attempt an overview of the strengths and weaknesses of Hippocratic gynaecology. A rounded appraisal is all the more difficult to secure as the evidence about how women were generally otherwise treated is largely inferential. What we know from other writers,[77] as well as the references we have considered from the Hippocratic treatises themselves, suggest, however, that the norm was that women were not only delivered, but when sick were attended, by other women. There were, no doubt, many gradations on the scale, from receiving the ministrations of someone in your own household,[78] through calling in some neighbour thought to have some special skill in the matter of healing, to having recourse to someone with a more than merely local reputation. When outside help was sought, this could be a matter of the patient going to Epidaurus or to another shrine of Asclepius or of some other healing god or hero, or of her consulting one or other of the types of women healers referred to in the Hippocratic works: we are in no position to evaluate the probability of her calling in – or rather of her male relatives calling in – a male doctor such as those represented by the authors of the Hippocratic treatises themselves.

Faced with a bewildering amalgam of more or less well-founded folk or popular beliefs and practices, and with competition from a variety of more or less exploitative rival healers, the doctors responsible for many or most of the Hippocratic treatises unite, at least, in their desire to turn the practice of healing into a τέχνη, even

---

[77] See, e.g., Soranus, *Gyn.* I 4 and III 3, *CMG* IV 5.10ff and 95.6ff, Galen K XI 187.1ff, 188.5ff, and cf. the discussions in Diepgen 1937, pp. 306–8, and Nickel 1979, pp. 515ff.

[78] Xenophon, *Oec.* 7.37, suggests that the housewife's duties included making sure that the sick in her household were cared for, and (Ps.-)Demosthenes LIX 55ff further illustrates a case where women care for the sick when no doctor is available.

though they were far from agreeing on just how that was to be achieved. Just as in other areas of Hippocratic medicine the claims are often made, or the ideals expressed, that medicine has tried and tested methods of procedure, that progress can be and has been made, that theories and practices must be, and are, subject to scrutiny, so similar principles are stated or implied in the gynaecological works. Here, where the world of woman-to-woman relationships no doubt seemed to the men private and enclosed – and vice versa – and where, moreover, we have direct evidence in our texts concerning the inhibitions some women felt in talking to the men about their complaints, the problems of evaluating traditional, or new, beliefs were as difficult as in any area of medicine. Yet what we may broadly call a critical approach was evidently what these writers were – at least in certain aspects of their work – striving to adopt.

As we have seen, not only do they reject interferences in medical cases from priests or prophets, they also criticise many current practices and assumptions. These included some which they represent as common among the women, as for example when in *Mul.* I ch. 67 (L VIII 140.14ff) the writer draws attention to the harmful effects of acrid pessaries and other treatments which women, he says, adopt. But they also attack many others for which other male doctors themselves were responsible. Thus, to mention just some of the instances from *Mul.* I alone, we there find criticised (1) doctors who do not recognise that tumours above the groin may be due to the suppression of the menses and who put their patients at risk by carrying out excision (ch. 2, L VIII 20.14ff), (2) doctors who use astringent drugs in cases where the womb is swollen after childbirth (ch. 34, 80.20ff), (3) those who prescribe milk for headache and water for swooning, when – in the writer's opinion – it is the converse treatment that should be adopted (ch. 63, 128.19ff) and (4) doctors who mistake the swelling associated with acute ulceration of the womb for dropsy and treat it as such (ch. 65, 134.9ff). Moreover positively and constructively, the importance not just of gaining the patient's confidence, but of entering into dialogue with her, is often clearly recognised. Not only do these writers suggest engaging in the usual Hippocratic practice of questioning their patients carefully in order to learn as much as possible from them about their complaints: they also involve their patients – and their women attendants – in both their own diagnostic examinations and their own treatment.

But alongside these signs suggesting the growth of a critical approach to the treatment of women, other factors must also be given due weight. Indeed each of the positive points we have identified has potentially – and in some cases actually – a negative side. The criticism of other doctors' ideas or of current practices could be engaged in merely in a spirit of rivalry. The questioning of the patient was, in part, a deliberate psychological device and could be used sometimes not so much in the hope of eliciting genuine information as simply in order to win the patient's trust and cooperation and to provide the doctor with an opportunity to display his knowledge. The enlisting of the patient herself in her own internal examination could mean that sometimes instead of checking for himself, the doctor relied on what may have been a very inexperienced report.

Although the gynaecological writers do, from time to time, show signs of recognising that they were, on occasions, very much in the dark about the cases they were treating[79] – at a loss for a diagnosis or for an effective remedy or for both – this feature is not so prominent as in some other Hippocratic works,[80] and the elements of dogmatism and even pure bluff are correspondingly more pronounced. The difficulty, danger and painfulness of some of the treatments prescribed are occasionally mentioned,[81] but – as elsewhere in Hippocratic medicine – recourse to drastic remedies is common. Among the more violent surgical interventions were succussion of the patient strapped upright or even upside down on a bed or on a ladder, used for prolapse of the womb and in certain cases of difficult delivery,[82]

---

[79] Apart from *Mul.* I ch. 62, L VIII 126.5ff, which (as noted before) points out the difficulty of understanding women's diseases, there are occasional passages that recognise, for example, that none of the treatments used was effective (e.g. *Steril.* ch. 232, L VIII 446.1f) and more frequent references to the slim chances of survival from certain complaints (e.g. *Mul.* ch. 41, L VIII 100.12ff, ch. 61, 126.1ff, *Mul.* II ch. 115, L VIII 248.9, ch. 118, 258.1ff, ch. 119, 260.21f, ch. 121, 264.19f, ch. 129, 278.4ff, ch. 133, 282.21ff, ch. 169, 350.9f, ch. 171, 352.8f, ch. 174bis, 356.16f, *Nat Mul.* ch. 38, L VII 382.12ff). As elsewhere in the Hippocratic Corpus, in some of the cases described as incurable, the writer warns the doctor not to undertake treatment, e.g. *Mul.* I ch. 71, L VIII 150.12 (but cf. the continuation). Some passages encourage the doctor to try out remedies and modify their treatment according to the patient's response, e.g. *Mul.* I ch. 60, L VIII 120.16, *Mul.* II ch. 110, L VIII 236.5ff, ch. 113, 244.4f, ch. 139, 312.19f, ch. 141, 314.17f, ch. 149, 324.20f, *Nat. Mul.* ch. 40, L VIII 384.12f, ch. 44, 388.18f, cf. also *Steril.* ch. 230, L VIII 444.2ff. Yet there are many occasions when aetiologies or accounts of the course that a disease will take are stated dogmatically: see, e.g., *Mul.* I ch. 25, L VIII 64.13ff, ch. 34, 78.11ff, *Steril.* ch. 222, L VIII 428.17, ch. 223, 432.4f, ch. 244, 458.4ff.

[80] Contrast, especially, the surgical treatises and the *Epidemics*.

[81] See, e.g., *Mul.* I ch. 2, L VIII 20.14ff, ch. 66, 138.6ff, ch. 78, 196.12ff, *Mul.* II ch. 206, L VIII 398.9ff, ch. 209, 404.1ff, *Steril.* ch. 230, L VIII 442.19ff, 22 and 24ff. The injunction to take into account the patient's strength and how much she can withstand is common: e.g. *Mul.* II ch. 133, L VIII 288.8ff, 296.12ff, ch. 181, 364.3f, *Steril.* ch. 230, L VIII 444.1ff, ch. 241, 454.23ff.

[82] See *Mul.* I ch. 68, L VIII 142.20ff, *Mul.* II ch. 144, L VIII 318.5ff, *Foet. Exsect.* ch. 4, L VIII 514.14ff, *Nat. Mul.* ch. 5, L VII 318.11ff.

the forcible mechanical straightening or widening of the orifice of the womb,[83] and the scraping of its internal surface.[84] Fumigation and bleeding were evidently sometimes carried on until the patient was exhausted or even lost consciousness.[85] To the usual list of potent and possibly dangerous drugs (such as hellebore) commonly prescribed by the Hippocratic writers, the gynaecological treatises add some for which they show their own particular predilection, notably canthar-ides.[86] No doubt in some cases, such as the excision of a dead foetus, drastic remedies were unavoidable.[87] But in others it is likely that they were favoured in part in order to impress.[88] Certainly the prescription of some of the more elaborate, exotic and expensive drugs – such as those prepared from Egyptian myrrh, Ethiopian cummin, Zakynthos asphalt, seal's rennet and many other rare animal products[89] – seems designed partly to add to the doctor's prestige, not to mention to the cost of the treatment.

Although many popular beliefs were rejected in these treatises, others were endorsed, either straightforwardly or by being rationa-lised or otherwise incorporated in some theoretical schema. The common association of right and male, the idea that the production of male offspring is somehow connected with the right side of the body, figures in one form in *On Superfetation*.[90] The notions that the

[83] See, e.g., *Mul.* I ch. 11, L VIII 46.10ff, ch. 13, 50.14ff, *Mul.* II ch. 133, L VIII 288.12ff, ch. 156, 332.5ff, ch. 158, 334.17ff, *Steril.* ch. 217, L VIII 418.23ff, ch. 221, 426.9ff, *Nat. Mul.* ch. 37, L VII 380.12ff, ch. 39, 382.22f, ch. 40, 384.10ff.

[84] See *Mul.* II ch. 144, L VIII 318.4f, *Steril.* ch. 248, L VIII 462.2, *Foet. Exsect.* ch. 5, L VIII 516.12ff, *Nat. Mul.* ch. 5, L VII 318.10ff (and cf. also ch. 42; 386.15f) with Littré's comments, L VIII pp. 522f.

[85] See, e.g., *Mul.* II ch. 110, L VIII 236.21ff, ch. 133, 286.15f, 288.8ff, ch. 134, 302.22ff.

[86] See, e.g., *Mul.* I ch. 59, L VIII 118.9f, *Mul.* II ch. 125, L VIII 270.4f, ch. 135, 306.17ff, ch. 175, 358.4f, *Nat. Mul.* ch. 8, L VII 324.1ff, ch. 32, 346.14ff, 348.19f, ch. 109, 428.2ff. Some of the painful effects of cantharides are recognised at *Mul.* I ch. 84, L VIII 208.17ff, 210. 1ff.

[87] *Mul.* I ch. 70, L VIII 146.19ff, *Superf.* ch. 7, *CMG* I 2,2 74.28ff (L VIII 480.3ff) and *Foet. Exsect.* ch. 1, L. VIII 512.1ff, give detailed instructions for operating on the dead foetus to remove it from the womb.

[88] Cf. *Art.* ch. 42, L IV 182.14ff, which criticises doctors who use succussion for effect, 'to make the vulgar herd gape, for to such it seems marvellous to see a man suspended or shaken or treated in such ways; and they always applaud these performances, never troubling themselves about the result of the operation, whether bad or good'.

[89] See, e.g., *Mul.* I ch. 74, L VIII 160.1, ch. 78, 182.7f and 24, *Mul.* II ch. 203, L VIII 390.8f, ch. 206, 402.1f, *Nat. Mul.* ch. 32, L VII 364.10, ch. 68, 402.14, and cf. also the use of the 'so-called Indian drug', *Mul.* II ch. 185, L VIII 366.19f, and of the 'Ethiopian root', *Nat. Mul.* ch. 101, L VII 416.7f. In interpreting the use of the rennet of the seal, it is relevant to recall its status as a marvellous creature of the deep, see above, pp. 45f.

[90] *Superf.* ch. 31, *CMG* I 2,2 90.12ff (L VIII 500.5ff), cf. the theory attributed to Leophanes and others by Aristotle, *GA* 765 a 21ff, and, among other Hippocratic texts, *Epid.* VI sec. 4 ch. 21, L V 312.10f: see Lesky 1951, pp. 39ff.

periodicities of the moon affect the female body,[91] and that conception occurs most often in the middle of the lunar month,[92] appear in the gynaecological works as well as elsewhere in Greek literature. As in aphoristic works, so too in the gynaecological treatises, the tests represented as methods of determining whether a woman is pregnant or not, and if so, whether with a boy or a girl, no doubt generally stem from popular practices,[93] and the writer of *On Superfetation* endorses the idea of a connection between what the pregnant mother says she wants to eat and marks on the head of the child she will bear.[94] Such substances as bull's blood or bile or urine, stag's horns or marrow or genitals, goat's horns, snakes, and a woman's own chorion, figure repeatedly in the prescriptions suggested,[95] and this clearly owes more to the symbolic associations of the substances in question than to their objective efficacy.[96]

Although the gynaecological writers are sometimes quick to criticise the ideas and practices of other doctors or theorists, they could accept – and may sometimes themselves have invented – some highly fantastical doctrines. Like many other Hippocratic authors, they had only the vaguest notions on some points of internal anatomy, for example concerning the course of the 'veins', φλέβες or φλέβια, which they supposed to carry not just blood and air but also a variety of other substances round the body.[97] Some of the tests for pregnancy imply a belief in the direct connection between the mouth and the womb or the vagina.[98] The general doctrine that the womb is in sympathetic communication with several parts of the body – the bregma, the stomach and the intelligence – is stated in one chapter in

[91] *Oct.* ch. 1, *CMG* I 2,1 78.16ff (= *Septim.* ch. 9, L vii 448.4ff), and cf. Aristotle, *HA* 582a34ff, *GA* 738a16ff, 767a1ff, see Préaux 1973, pp. 88f.

[92] *Oct.* ch. 4, *CMG* I 2,1 88.11ff (ch. 13, L vii 460.4ff), and cf. Aristotle, *HA* 582b2f, contrast *Superf.* ch. 31, *CMG* I 2,2 90.12ff (L viii 500.5ff), *Mul.* I ch. 17, L viii 56.15ff, ch. 24, 62.19ff.

[93] See, e.g., *Superf.* ch. 25, *CMG* I 2,2 80.28ff (L viii 488.12ff), *Steril.* chh. 214–16 and 219, L viii 414.17ff, 416.8ff, 18ff, 422.23ff, *Nat. Mul.* ch. 96, L vii 412.19ff, and cf. above, n. 21.

[94] *Superf.* ch. 18, *CMG* I 2,2 80.8ff (L viii 486.7ff).

[95] See, e.g., *Mul.* I ch. 74, L viii 156.9, ch. 75, 166.15, ch. 81, 202.10, ch. 84, 206.2ff, ch. 91, 220.1, *Steril.* ch. 223, L viii 432.6, ch. 224, 434.11, ch. 225, 434.15f, ch. 230, 442.9, *Nat. Mul.* ch. 32, L vii 362.16ff, ch. 75, 404.18, ch. 103, 418.4, ch. 109, 424.11ff, 426.17. Cf. Leach 1964, p. 38, on the use of excreta in medicines.

[96] Such 'efficacy' as they had was a matter of their being generally accepted or assumed to be fitting or appropriate. Their efficacy depended (as in the case of placebos) on their being believed to work – though, in contrast to what is true of placebos, it was not that the doctors themselves were aware that the substances contained no active therapeutic ingredients. On the contrary, the Hippocratic doctors in question too – like their patients – were presumably persuaded that the substances were specifics for the complaints for which they were used.

[97] See, e.g., *Mul.* I ch. 17, L viii 56.21, ch. 24, 64.3f, ch. 29, 72.7, ch. 61, 122.17.

[98] See, e.g., *Steril.* ch. 214, L viii 414.20ff, 416.2ff, ch. 219, 422.23ff, *Superf.* ch. 25, *CMG* I 2,2 80.28ff (L viii 488.12ff), and cf. *Aph.* v 59, L iv 554.3ff, *Mul.* ii ch. 146, L viii 322.12ff.

On the Diseases of Women I.[99] Most strikingly of all, several of the
gynaecological treatises develop elaborate theories about how the
womb wanders all round the body and thereby causes diseases.[100]

A male orientation of interest may be detected in the heavy
concentration, in these works, on the woman's reproductive role – on
questions relating to how to overcome sterility, on determining
whether a woman could conceive or had done so, and whether the
child was going to be male or female – not that these questions were
not also concerns (and not just for reasons that reflect their position in
society) of Greek women as well as of Greek men. A more distinct
masculine bias is, however, present in the explanations offered of
sterility. Although as we have noted, some theorists held that the
contribution of the female parent is on a par with that of the male,
there is, on the whole, little recognition, in the gynaecological works,
that failure to conceive may be due to the male as much as to the
female.[101]

Yet there is another side to the question. Take the issue of the
frequent recommendation of intercourse or pregnancy for certain
complaints.[102] At first sight this might look straightforwardly
exploitative – male chauvinism at its worst. Yet given that elsewhere
(though admittedly less often[103]) the advice is to *avoid* intercourse

[99] See *Mul.* I ch. 38, L VIII 94.7–10.

[100] See especially *Mul.* II chh. 123–31, L VIII 266.11–280.3, ch. 201, 384.1ff, ch. 203, 386.21ff,
Nat. Mul. ch. 44, L VII 388.4ff, chh. 48f, 392.9ff, 15ff, ch. 58, 398.1 ff, ch. 62, 400.3ff, and
compare from outside the gynaecological works, *Loc. Hom.* ch. 47, L VI 344.3ff. Cf., e.g.,
Plato, *Ti.* 91c (and cf. also *Ti.* 70d ff which compares the whole of the appetitive,
ἐπιθυμητικόν, part of the soul to a wild beast). Several Egyptian medical texts suggest that
the ideas that the womb wanders around the body and that it is alive were present at an
early stage in Egyptian medicine (see Papyrus Ebers, XCIII, Ebbell 1937, p. 109, and Pap.
Kahun prescription 6, Griffith 1898, p. 7), though that is not to say that that was necessarily
the source of the Greek medical theory (contrast Veith 1965, p. 7). Among later Greek
medical writers, Soranus especially criticises the belief in no uncertain terms, see below, pp.
171f.

[101] This is generally true not only in *Steril.* but also in *Mul.* I chh. 10–20 (especially ch. 17, L VIII
56.1ff) and chh. 22–4, where failure to conceive is treated usually as a problem of remedying
a defect in the woman. Occasionally, however, the gynaecological writers make remarks
about, for example, the regimen the man should adopt, e.g. *Mul.* I ch. 75, L VIII 164.22ff,
Steril. chh. 218 and 220, L VIII 422.18ff, 424.14ff, *Superf.* chh. 26 and 30, *CMG* I 2,2 82.12ff,
90.8ff (L VIII 490.3ff, 498.23ff), and cf. *Oct.* ch. 4, *CMG* I 2,1 88.4ff (= ch. 13, L VII 458.17ff).

[102] See, e.g., *Mul.* I ch. 37, L VIII 92.6ff, ch. 59, 118.18, ch. 63, 130.16f, *Mul.* II ch. 127, L VIII
274.4f, ch. 128, 276.8, ch. 131, 280.1ff, ch. 139, 312.20f, ch. 141, 314.19f, ch. 169, 350.9f,
Virg. L VIII 468.21ff, *Nat. Mul.* ch. 2, L VII 314.13, ch. 3, 316.5ff, ch. 8, 324.9, and cf. Diepgen
1937, pp. 255f. From outside the gynaecological treatises, see, e.g., *Genit.* ch. 4, L VII 476.8ff,
and cf. the reference to the beneficial effect of a pregnancy at *Epid.* v ch. 12, L v 212.5ff.

[103] See, e.g., *Mul.* II ch. 149, L VIII 324.21ff, *Steril.* ch. 230, L VIII 444.17f, and cf. *Mul.* II ch. 143,
L VIII 316.12 (≈*Nat. Mul.* ch. 4, L VII 316.19) where, however, the text is disputed. *Nat. Mul.*
ch. 12, L VII 330.1 is one case where a condition combined with pregnancy is said to be fatal.
At *Mul.* II ch. 144, L VIII 316.17f (cf. also *Mul.* II ch. 143, 316.3f) there is a case where
intercourse during the period of the lochial discharge is a possible cause of a complaint (cf.

and there is some recognition of the dangers of becoming pregnant in certain illnesses, we should rather acknowledge that sometimes at least these doctors are attempting a medical evaluation of different types of case, not just using their position to try to insure the maximum exploitation of the reproductive capabilities of the females in the population.

Despite their tendency to prescribe what must have been very frightening treatments, these writers do not ignore the psychological state of their patients: on the contrary frequent reference is made to the psychological symptoms that the patients show along with their physical condition,[104] and some writers go out of their way to try to alleviate their patients' fears and anxieties.[105] In particular they insist that women should not be alarmed at not becoming pregnant, for example, or at miscarrying.[106]

When we take into account the lack of effective remedies available to these doctors, as well as their lack of basic anatomical and physiological knowledge, and when we add that several common surgical procedures, and many of the drugs prescribed, would today be thought hazardous in the extreme, it may be doubted whether, on balance, Hippocratic gynaecological medicine was, in practice, superior to folk medicine or to no doctoring at all.[107] Yet we can hardly fail to feel some admiration for the ideals that these writers set before themselves, and the stated principles that guided them,[108] for their attempts to overcome the problems presented by the barriers between men and women in Greek social life, and for their

Nat. Mul. ch. 5, L vii 318.1ff). The prescriptions to procure conception far outnumber those to prevent it. But there are some examples of the latter, e.g. *Mul.* i ch. 76, L viii 170.7f ($\approx$ *Nat. Mul.* ch. 98, L vii 414.20f) cf. Aristotle, *HA* 583 a 21ff. It is evident, for example, from Soranus that the questions of whether permanent virginity is healthy, and whether pregnancy is, were actively debated: see Soranus *Gyn.* i 30–2, *CMG* iv 20.1ff, and 142, 29.16ff (Soranus himself concluded that permanent virginity is healthy and that pregnancy is natural but not healthy).

[104] See, e.g., *Mul.* i ch. 8, L viii 36.4ff, ch. 11, 44.15, *Mul.* ii ch. 174bis, L viii 356.2, ch. 182, 364.12ff.

[105] See, e.g., *Foet. Exsect.* ch. 1, L viii 512.4.

[106] See *Steril.* ch. 213, L viii 414.15f, *Mul.* i ch. 25, L viii 68.14ff.

[107] No doubt some of the simple surgical procedures, adopted, for example, to correct faulty presentation, were effective. Yet we should not underestimate what may have been achieved in cases of such a type long before Hippocratic medicine: see Diepgen 1937, pp. 36ff. The comparative data suggest that the range of possibilities is very wide: the evidence relating to trepanning, especially, shows that intricate and dangerous surgical operations were sometimes undertaken already in the stone age (though not always for therapeutic motives): see Sigerist 1951–61, 1 pp. 110 ff, Lisowski 1967, Margetts 1967, Ackerknecht 1971, pp. 104ff.

[108] Thus *Steril.* ch. 230, L viii 442.27ff, urges the doctor to be φυσικός in his approach to the problem of treatment, to consider the force and disposition (ἕξις) of the patient, and not to expect a single standard or measure (σταθμός) for cures. Such sentiments can be paralleled, and are more fully developed, in other Hippocratic works such as *VM*.

determination both not to ignore what is distinctive about women's complaints, and at the same time to bring gynaecology within the ambit of the medical art.

3. ALTERNATIVE THEORIES OF THE FEMALE SEED

In line with assumptions concerning the superiority of the male sex in the dominant ideology it was commonly supposed that the essential or more important contribution to reproduction and to heredity was that of the male parent. As is well known, the notion that the father alone makes or creates the child and that the mother provides merely the place for its development occurs already in a context innocent of pretensions to biological investigation (though one heavy with social and political implications) in Aeschylus's *Eumenides*.[109] Aristotle, in time, was to provide, as we shall see, massive support for the view that the male's contribution to reproduction is the formative one. His particular definition of the female in terms of an incapacity, his idea of the relationship between male and female as not just analogous to, but an example of, that between form and matter, and his development of the idea that the male is an efficient cause in reproduction all involve or incorporate new conceptions. They represent his own solutions to the problems and are supported by new empirical considerations and arguments.[110] But the broad agreement between his position and the common general assumption of the superiority of the male role is clear.

Yet beginning already in the mid-fifth century B.C. there was a good deal of speculation on the problems of reproduction and heredity on the part of both philosophers and medical writers. The interactions between different types of theory, some focusing on the role of the blood, others associating the difference between the sexes with differences between the two sides of the body, and their subsequent history and influence not just in antiquity but right down to the seventeenth and eighteenth centuries, have been discussed authoritatively by Erna Lesky, and there is no need to repeat her findings here.[111] The particular aspect of this controversy that concerns us – and that Lesky herself did not bring into sharp focus – is the problem of the implications of the various types of theory proposed for the evaluation of the position of women. The question may be put the other way round: if we take as our starting-point the

---

[109] A. *Eu.* 658ff, on which see Lesky 1951, p. 54.
[110] See below, pp. 94ff.   [111] Lesky 1951.

all too evident prevailing assumptions of the inherent inferiority of the female sex, we may ask to what extent and on what basis early Greek biologists suggested theories of reproduction or heredity that broke away from, ran counter to, or directly challenged, the dominant norms. Our problem is, as before, the confrontation between ideology and biological theory. If, on this occasion, those theories are highly speculative in character, and their empirical support at best meagre and selective, the confrontation is none the less interesting on that account, for the question must still be pressed, on what grounds alternative views – dissenting from the assumption of the determining role of the male and allotting equal importance to the female – were put forward.

A number of Presocratic philosophers are reported in our secondary sources as having held that the woman provides seed as well as the man. In Censorinus[112] the list of those who did so includes Parmenides, Empedocles, Anaxagoras as well as Alcmaeon (who is otherwise attested as having a special interest not just in physiological but also in pathological questions and who represents a bridge between the work of the natural philosophers and that of the medical writers). This is the barest of reports[113] of the positions adopted on what continued to be a controversial topic among philosophers as well as among doctors. Our other sources enable us to add a little to the picture,[114] and Aristotle, especially, sometimes supplies details of some of the different versions of the theory that he attacks. Thus in connection with one objection that he raises – that if both parents produce seed, then the result should be *two* animals – he reports an interesting view of Empedocles that each parent provides as it were a tally – σύμβολον – and that the new living creature is produced by both halves together (a view that Aristotle rejects on the grounds that

---

[112] *De Die Nat.* ch. 5,4 p. 10.4ff, which refers also to Epicurus. The contrary view is attributed by Censorinus to Diogenes, to Hippon and to the Stoics. Yet according to Aetius (v 5.3) Hippon held that females emit seed no less than males, though female seed does not contribute to reproduction: this report continues, however, with the suggestion that the bones come from the male, the flesh from the female, parent.

[113] Whether Censorinus's report is accurate may also be questioned, first in relation to Hippon (see last note) and then on Anaxagoras. While Aristotle reports (*GA* 763b30ff) that Anaxagoras held that sex differentiation exists already in the seed, he also suggests that Anaxagoras thought that the 'seed comes from the male and the female provides the place' – which conflicts with Censorinus's account: contrast Lesky 1951, pp. 52ff, with Joly 1960, pp. 78ff.

[114] Thus Caelius Aurelianus paraphrases Parmenides b 18 (DK). Aetius, v 5.1, further reports that Pythagoras, as well as Democritus and Epicurus, held that the female emits seed, and v 11.1 refers to Empedocles's views on the similarities between parents and offspring. Cf. also D.L. viii 28 which may suggest that some of the Pythagoreans held that the male alone produces seed.

parts of a living creature cannot be imagined as capable of surviving on their own in any form).[115]

By far the fullest information concerning a fifth-century theory of reproduction ascribed to a philosopher relates to the doctrine according to which the seed is drawn from every part of the body (usually dubbed the 'pangenesis' doctrine after the Darwinian theory that it resembles) which is discussed at length by Aristotle and which Aetius attributes to Democritus.[116] We have every reason to suppose that this doctrine was applied generally to the body of the female parent, as well as to that of the male, since one of the objections that Aristotle brought against it was that the offspring does not, in fact, have parts corresponding to *every* part of *both* parents (not both female and male genitalia).[117] It may be inferred, therefore, that the doctrine allotted at least *broadly similar* roles to the male and female parent in reproduction. It may even be that those roles were *precisely* equal, though we have no explicit evidence to corroborate this. 'Pangenesis' is compatible with the view that the female's contributions are inferior – in one respect or another – to the male's, and while it is possible that this was denied or ruled out by Democritus, we cannot directly confirm this.

These reports are interesting and important in that they show that the topic of reproduction, and in particular the question of the female's role in it, were already much discussed in Presocratic speculative thought. Yet the detailed evaluation of the theories put forward can scarcely be undertaken in the absence of substantial original texts. Similar theories are, however, proposed, whether independently or (as is far more likely) under the influence of earlier philosophical speculation, in Hippocratic treatises of the late fifth and fourth centuries. Several works allude briefly to aspects of the problems of reproduction and heredity,[118] but the treatise *On Regimen*, and the group of embryological works consisting of *On the Seed*, *On the Nature of the Child* and *On Diseases* IV, discuss these questions at considerable length and provide the best opportunity to assess both the character of the theories proposed and their grounds and motivation.

---

[115] *GA* 722b6ff (mentioned below, p. 97), cf. 764b15ff, and cf. also Galen's objections, *De Semine* II ch. 3, K IV 616.5ff, 11ff, 617.13ff.

[116] See especially Aristotle, *GA* 721b11ff, cf. 764a6ff, cf. Aetius v 3.6, 5.1, Censorinus, *De Die Nat.* ch. 6,5 p. 11.7ff. On the difficulty of establishing who precisely originated the pangenesis theory, and on the question of the possible role of Anaxagoras, see the cautious remarks of Lonie 1981, pp. 62ff, 115 and n. 101.

[117] Aristotle, *GA* 722b3ff: see further below, pp. 96f.

[118] See, e.g., *Aph.* v 59, 62 and 63, L IV 554.3ff, 12ff, 556.3ff, *Aër.* ch. 14, *CMG* I, 1,2 58.20ff, *Morb. Sacr.* ch. 2, L VI 364.19ff, *Mul.* I chh. 8, 17, 24, L VIII 34.9f, 56.21f, 62.20f.

We may begin by setting out the texts. In the embryological treatises[119] the writer of *On the Seed* states in ch. 4 that – in addition to the male, whose seed had been said in ch. 1, L vii 470.1ff, to come from 'all the humour [that is fluid] in the body' – the female too 'emits something from her body' (474.16f).[120] Chapter 5 refers to the seed 'from both partners' (476.18), and ch. 6 (478.1ff) suggests that 'what the woman emits is sometimes stronger, and sometimes weaker; and this applies also to what the man emits. In fact both partners alike contain both male and female sperm (the male creature being stronger than the female must of course originate from a stronger sperm).' This leads to a discussion of the possible combinations of male and of female seed from the two parents:

> Here is a further point: if both partners (*a*) produce a stronger sperm, then a male is the result, whereas if (*b*) they both produce a weak form, then a female is the result. But if (*c*) one partner produces one kind of sperm, and the other another, then the resultant sex is determined by whichever sperm prevails in quantity. For suppose that the weak sperm is much greater in quantity than the stronger sperm: then the stronger sperm is overwhelmed and, being mixed with the weak, results in a female. If on the contrary the strong sperm is greater in quantity than the weak, and the weak is overwhelmed, it results in a male. (478.5–11)

Clearly it is not just the 'strength' or the 'weakness' of the seed that has to be considered, but also the quantity of each kind – although the writer is not too coherent about how these factors interact.[121]

Chapter 7 (478.16ff) returns to the problem with an argument for the thesis that both male and female parents have both male and female seed:

> Now that both male and female sperm exist in both partners is an inference which can be drawn from observation. Many women have borne daughters to their husbands and then, going with other men, have produced sons. And the original husbands – those, that is, to whom their wives bore daughters – have as the result of intercourse with other women produced male offspring; whereas the second group of men, who produced male offspring, have with yet again other women produced female offspring. Now this consideration shows that both the man and the woman have male and female sperm. For in the partnership in which the women produced daughters, the stronger sperm was overwhelmed by the larger quantity of the weaker sperm, and females were produced; while in the partnership in which these same women produced sons, it was the weak which was overwhelmed, and males were produced. Hence the same man does not invariably emit the strong variety of sperm,

---

[119] I use the translation of Lonie 1981. Cf. the discussions of these theories in Joly 1966, pp. 111–16, Preus 1977, pp. 71ff, Morsink 1979, pp. 91ff, as well as in Lonie's own commentary.

[120] *Genit.* ch. 4 also stresses the pleasure the female takes in intercourse, which suggests an active rather than a passive role, see Manuli 1980, pp. 394 and 405ff.

[121] He does not make clear to what extent the 'strength' of the 'strong' seed may compensate for its small quantity. In the case where the weak is overwhelmed, the strong seed is said to be 'greater in quantity' than the weak, though not '*much* greater in quantity' (πολλῷ πλέον), the expression used in the converse case (478.8).

nor the weak invariably, but sometimes the one and sometimes the other; the same is
true in the woman's case. There is therefore nothing anomalous about the fact that
the same women and the same men produce both male and female sperm: indeed,
these facts about male and female sperm are also true in the case of animals.

The rest of this treatise and *On the Nature of the Child* and *On Diseases*
IV do not add to our understanding of the principal thesis,[122] but offer
further supplementary arguments and considerations, notably concerning the resemblances that children may show to their parents. *On
the Seed* ch. 8, 480.10ff, argues that 'if from any part of the father's
body a greater quantity of sperm is derived than from the corresponding part of the mother's body the child will, in that part, bear a closer
resemblance to its father; and vice versa', and it rules out the
possibilities (*a*) that the child resembles its mother in all respects and
its father in none, (*b*) that it resembles its father in all respects and its
mother in none, and (*c*) that it resembles neither parent in any
respect. The principle that 'the child will resemble in the majority of
its characteristics that parent who has contributed a greater quantity
of sperm to the resemblance – that is, sperm from a greater number of
bodily parts' (480.16ff) is used to account for such cases as a girl
bearing a closer resemblance in the majority of her characteristics to
her father than to her mother. The next chapter, 9, 482.3ff, produces an
explanation of why weak children are sometimes borne to parents who
are both strong, introducing two other considerations besides the
strength/weakness and the quantity of the parents' seed, namely (1) the
nutriment supplied by the mother in the womb, and (2) the space
available, in the womb, for the embryo's growth, and the latter
consideration is also adduced, among others, to account for deformities.

The discussion of similar problems in *On Regimen* forms part of that
author's wide-ranging speculations on physiological questions. In ch.
3, L VI 472.12ff, he puts it that every kind of animal, including human
beings, is constituted of fire and water. Fire is hot and dry (though it
has some of the wet) and is able to move and change everything:
water is cold and wet (though with some of the dry) and is able to
nourish everything. Chapter 9, 482.13ff, promises a discussion of how
males and females are produced, and chh. 27ff, 500.1ff, duly deliver
on this promise. Chapter 27 first associates females with the cold and
wet, males with the hot and dry, and then suggests (500.5ff) in line
with this, that if it is desired to produce a female child, a watery
regimen should be adopted, whereas for a male child, the regimen
should be fiery. 'And not only the man should do this, but also the

---

[122] Both *Nat. Puer.* and *Morb.* IV clearly presuppose the thesis that both parents produce seed:
see *Nat. Puer.* ch. 12, L VII 486.1ff, ch. 31, 540.16ff, *Morb.* IV ch. 32, L VII 542.3ff.

woman. For it is not only what is secreted by the man that contributes to growth, but also what is secreted by the woman.'

Chapter 28, 500.23ff, then produces an elaborate theory of three kinds of men constituted by different combinations of male and female seed from the male or female parent, and ch. 29, 502.24ff, does the same for three kinds of women. Male seed from the male parent together with male seed from the female parent produces men who are 'brilliant in soul and strong in body, unless they are harmed by their subsequent regimen'. When male seed from the male encounters but proves stronger than female seed from the female, the men are less brilliant, but still 'manly', ἀνδρεῖοι, and rightly called such. But when female seed from the male is overpowered by male seed from the female, ἀνδρόγυνοι result who are correctly called such ('androgynous'). In the corresponding combinations giving rise to the three types of women, female seed from both the male and the female parent produces women that are most female and εὐφυέστατοι – very well-endowed. When male seed from the male is overcome by female seed from the female, the women are bolder but still graceful, κόσμιαι.[123] But when female seed from the male overcomes male seed from the female, the women are more brazen and are called 'manly', ἀνδρεῖαι.

Chapter 32, 506.14ff, analyses further combinations of different kinds of fire and water, though not in relation to the sex of the offspring, but ch. 34, 512.13ff, remarks generally that males are hotter and drier, females wetter and colder, not only because of their original natural constitutions, but also because, once born, males tend to have more laborious regimens that heat and dry them, while females have wetter and idler regimens and purge the heat from their bodies every month.

What differentiates these two discussions is as remarkable as what they have in common. Both theories insist that the female parent emits seed just as much as the male does. Both also maintain that both parents produce both male-generating and female-generating seed, and both generalise their theories as applying not merely to humans but also to other animals. *On the Seed* still thinks of the male-producing seed as strong, the female-producing seed as weak: to that extent the author still appears influenced by notions of the inequality of the sexes,[124] even though he holds both that the contribution of the

---

[123] κόσμιαι may mean – alternatively or in addition – well-behaved, orderly.

[124] There are other indications of his taking over popular ideas with similar associations, for example the belief that the male embryo moves earlier than the female, and takes less time for its development than the female: e.g. *Nat. Puer.* ch. 18, L vii 498.27ff, ch. 21, 510.22ff and cf. Lonie 1981, pp. 190ff.

female parent may sometimes overcome that of the male, and, in general, that a greater quantity of 'weak' seed may overcome a smaller quantity of 'strong'. *On Regimen*, however, adopting, on this question, not a strong/weak, but a male/female differentiation of the two kinds of seed that both parents have, risks thereby circularity (explaining male offspring in terms of 'male' seed),[125] but is not committed to the associations of the former pair of terms.

Both treatises maintain that there is, overall, not just a general similarity, but a precise equality in the contributions of each of the two parents: cases where the male parent's contribution is dominant are exactly balanced by cases where the female parent's is. The authors of both works also seem to recognise that it is their views about the role of the female parent that may occasion surprise or are less straightforwardly acceptable. *On the Seed* starts with the less controversial case of the male parent's seed in ch. 1, and turns to the female's in ch. 4. Similarly *On Regimen* ch. 27 first remarks that if children of a particular sex are desired, then the father's regimen should be modified accordingly,[126] and then adds that this is also true of the mother's.

Yet in general *On Regimen* provides much less by way of evidence and argument for its position than does *On the Seed*. *On the Seed* not only implicitly recognises that the idea of the female seed is controversial, but undertakes to *establish* this thesis. Elsewhere in the embryological treatises, the comparison of the development of the human egg with that of a hen in *On the Nature of the Child* ch. 29, L vii 530.3ff, where the writer suggests hatching a batch of twenty eggs to observe the day by day growth of the embryo chick, shows a quite sophisticated grasp, at least in principle, of the deployment of empirical methods of research. But on the question of the female seed, the data adduced in *On the Seed* are quite inconclusive. That some fathers, and some mothers, can and do produce both male and female children is perfectly compatible with *both* the thesis that the male parent alone determines the sex of the child *and* the thesis that the female parent alone does. His data, correct enough in themselves, precisely do *not* show what he wants to prove, namely that *both* parents produce both kinds of seed.[127]

---

[125] The treatise does, however, advance a theory correlating 'male' and 'female' with hot and dry, and cold and wet, respectively, see above, pp. 90f on chh. 27 and 34, L vi 500.1ff, 512.13ff.

[126] καὶ οὐ μόνον τὸν ἄνδρα δεῖ τοῦτο διαπρήσσεσθαι, ἀλλὰ καὶ τὴν γύναικα, 500.7f. For other Hippocratic works that make a similar point, see above, p. 84 n. 101.

[127] Thus Aristotle, with his very different view of reproduction, is able to accommodate the point that those who produce female children may later or also produce male ones, *GA* 723a26ff.

Otherwise the writer supports his views by appealing to analogies, which illustrate the point he wishes to make, but do not establish it.[128]

By comparison the writer of *On Regimen* relies far more on mere assertion. What may have led him to his view of the general balance between the roles of the father and mother is a difficult question to answer. In that he does not employ a strong/weak analysis of the male/female dichotomy he may in that respect be further from traditional notions of the disparity between the sexes than the author of *On the Seed*, even though *On Regimen* does hold, as we have seen, that the sexes have different natural constitutions, one fiery, the other watery.[129] The less detailed evidence he brings for his overall views, the more he might perhaps be thought to be directly concerned to break away from or react against aspects of the traditional attitudes. That may be the case, but we should remark on the context in which he develops his six-fold schema. His explanandum is in part provided by the 'facts' of androgynous men and of masculine women. His thesis concerning the various combinations of male and female seed from male and female parents enables him to offer an account of these more ambivalent cases, and it must therefore be acknowledged that this – rather than any reaction against traditional value-judgements – may have provided the initial or the main stimulus to his speculations.

Nevertheless the implications of the notion, in both treatises, of the general balance between the contributions of the two parents are there to be drawn. Against those who represented those contributions as, in one way or another, radically different in kind – the female providing merely the place, or merely the matter as opposed to the form, of the developing child – both these authors assert that those contributions are strictly equal, and that the mother's contribution may be the dominant one just as much as the father's may. Both treatises develop the view that goes back at least to Democritus, that the seed is drawn from all the parts of the body. But by itself, we said, that theory did not necessarily imply the precise equality of the contributions made by the two sexes.[130] What *On the Seed* and *On*

---

[128] Thus he compares the mixture of the two kinds of seed with a mixture of wax and fat, ch. 6, L VII 478.11ff. When different quantities of these are melted together, then so long as the mixture remains liquid, the predominant constituent will not be apparent, but it becomes visible when the mixture solidifies. The use of analogies in the embryological treatises is discussed in Lloyd 1966, pp. 346ff, and by Lonie 1981, pp. 77–86.

[129] This is the implication of the passages from chh. 27 and 34, referred to above, n. 125.

[130] Thus it is not certain whether Democritus, like the writers of *Genit.* and *Vict* I, held that both parents produce both male-generating and female-generating seed.

Regimen add is a clear statement to that effect. Neither treatise produces very impressive grounds for their particular views: they represent, nevertheless, important dissenting voices against the notion of the essential disparity between the contributions of the two parents. This is certainly not to challenge the whole prevailing ideology in relation to the female sex: yet it does provide alternatives to one type of biological theory that – of set purpose or otherwise – underpinned that ideology.

Aristotle had little difficulty in showing that the evidence that had been used to establish that both male and female parents produce seed is inconclusive. Yet the type of theory put forward by *On the Seed* and *On Regimen* continued to find influential support. We must next consider the Aristotelian position not just on the question of reproduction but on the differences between the sexes in general, before turning to review briefly the post-Aristotelian debate. Meanwhile the material we have so far discussed shows that already before the end of the fourth century B.C. the opinions of theorists on the role of women in reproduction were divided. In the face of widespread negative attitudes in society, shared and sometimes actively endorsed by some writers, others were evidently able to offer and develop an alternative thesis. The grounds on which they did so were not – so far as we can tell – themselves *primarily* ideological. They reflected, rather, a response to the biological problems, even if the biological data adduced for them were generally inconclusive and subject to arbitrary interpretation. Yet they are evidence of the possibility of alternative view-points even in areas of biological theorising where the dominant ideology was deeply implicated.

4. ARISTOTLE ON THE DIFFERENCE BETWEEN THE SEXES

It is notorious that Aristotle considers the male sex inherently superior to the female.[131] His general prejudices in this area reflect – we said – certain deep-seated attitudes that were widespread – among men – in Greek society and that found expression in a long line of writers from Hesiod, through Semonides to Plato and beyond. In the Pandora myth in Hesiod the first woman is represented as the source of all evils, toils and diseases for men. In this myth women have a separate origin from men (Pandora is created by

---

[131] See among the most recent literature, Joly 1968, pp. 224, 226, 228ff, Clark 1975, Appendix B, pp. 206ff, Preus 1975a, pp. 52ff, Horowitz 1976, Morsink 1979, Byl 1980, pp. 210–22.

Zeus when he takes revenge on Prometheus for giving men the gift of fire[132]) and the idea that women are a distinct γένος – race or family – is also common.[133] Despite the views expressed on the equal potentiality of the sexes in the *Republic*[134] when Plato runs through the various main types of animals in the context of his account of the degenerate transformations of men (male humans) in the *Timaeus*, he begins with women. They are the δευτέρα γένεσις, the second generation, that arise from cowardly males and those that spent their life in wrong-doing, birds being the third, wild land-animals the fourth, and water-animals the fifth race.[135] Yet Plato is not attempting a comprehensive zoology and his hierarchy of animals is patently normative in aim, being directly linked to his ideas concerning transmigration and the rewards and punishments that are to be expected after death.[136]

Aristotle, by contrast, has no such eschatological preoccupations in his zoology,[137] which is directed towards establishing the differentiae of animals and their causes and which is clearly based on much detailed and often careful research, his own and that of his associates. But if, as is fairly evidently the case, his account of women in particular and of the female sex in general provides some kind of rationalisation or accommodation of widespread Greek social attitudes, the question that this raises is what price has he paid? How painstaking is his research in this area and how accurate is it? To what extent was he aware of exceptions that run counter to his general rules and how does he deal with them? What lessons, in short, can be learned from the study of this confrontation between a well-entrenched preconception and his detailed investigations in comparative zoology?

In his analysis of the various methods of reproduction among animals he claims that it is *better* for the two sexes to be differentiated.[138] Nevertheless females are defined by their incapacity – as males by their capacity – to concoct the blood, and he calls the female sex a 'natural deformity'.[139] He is no more convinced by the view

132 *Th.* 585ff, *Op.* 6off.
133 See especially Semonides 7, and Loraux (1978) 1981, cf. Vegetti 1979, pp. 122ff.
134 We shall be considering these later: cf. below, p. 107.
135 *Ti.* 90e ff, on which see above, p. 15.
136 *Ti.* 90e6ff, cf. also *R.* 619b ff, *Phdr.* 248e ff, *Lg.* 903d.
137 We have discussed in Part I the value-laden character of parts of Aristotle's zoological investigations.
138 See especially *GA* II ch. 1, 731 b 18ff.
139 See, e.g., *GA* 716 a 17ff, 728 a 18ff, 765 b 8ff, 766 a 30ff. The production of female rather than male offspring is associated with a series of different types of failure or weakness, see *HA* 582 a 29ff, 585 b 14ff, 24ff, *GA* 766 b 29ff, 31ff, 767 a 33ff, b 10ff, cf. Byl 1980, p. 219.

that females produce seed[140] than he is by the theory that the seed comes from every part of the body. Indeed he associates these two positions together, outlining the main arguments adduced in their favour and undertaking to refute them jointly in *GA* I chh. 17 and 18.

Neither the argument from the resemblances of children to their parents, nor that from mutilated parents having mutilated offspring, impresses him.[141] On resemblances, he develops a dilemma (*GA* 722 a 16ff): the seed must be drawn either (*a*) only from the uniform parts (such as flesh, blood, sinew) or (*b*) only from the non-uniform parts (such as face, hand) or (*c*) from both. Against (*a*) he objects that the resemblances that children bear to their parents lie rather in such features as their faces and hands, than in their flesh and bones as such. But if the resemblances in the non-uniform parts are not due to the seed being drawn from *them*, why must the resemblances in the uniform parts be explained in that way? Against (*b*) he points out that the non-uniform parts are composed of the uniform ones.[142] He tackles (*c*) too by considering what must be said about the non-uniform parts. Resemblances in these must be due either to the material (that is the uniform parts) or to the way in which the material is arranged or combined. But on the latter view, nothing can be said to be drawn from the *arrangement* to the seed, since the arrangement is not itself a material factor. Indeed a similar argument can be applied to the uniform parts themselves, since they consist of the elements or simple bodies (earth, water, air, fire) combined in a particular way. Yet the resemblance in the parts is due to their arrangement or combination, and has therefore to be explained in terms of what brings this about,[143] and not by the seed being drawn from every individual part of the body.

As for mutilations, they are to be explained in the same way as other resemblances and they are not, in any case, always transmitted from one generation to another (*GA* 724 a 3ff). More generally,

---

[140] That is properly concocted seed, but, as we shall see, he acknowledges and even insists that the menses are analogous to seed and sometimes says that they are seed, though 'not pure' and 'in need of elaboration' (*GA* 728 a 26ff, 737 a 27ff). (In *HA* x, generally thought to be spurious – see Rudberg 1911, but cf. Balme unpublished – the female is said to emit seed without qualification, e.g. 636 b 15ff, 637 a 35ff, b 30ff, but this account diverges from that in the other zoological works in other respects also, notably in the role assigned to the menses.)

[141] The other two arguments for pangenesis that he mentions at *GA* 721 b 13ff are the pleasure experienced by females in intercourse (an obviously inconclusive consideration) and the suggestion that it seems reasonable that just as there is something from which a whole comes, so there should be also for each of the parts (an analogy that does not impress Aristotle): cf. Preus 1977, pp. 74ff, Morsink 1979, pp. 94ff.

[142] Moreover this option, like (*a*), would suggest that the seed is not drawn from *all* the parts.

[143] The semen has just such a function of supplying the efficient cause in Aristotle's own theory.

Aristotle argues that if the seed comes from every part of both parents, that should produce two whole animals (*GA* 722b6ff), and why does the female then need the male to reproduce at all? Empedocles' suggestion that a 'tally' is torn off each parent will not do, since the parts cannot remain sound when thus torn off.[144]

It is essential to his own view that male semen and female menses are analogous to each other: both are 'residues' from the 'useful nourishment' (where his opponents had said that semen is drawn *from* the whole body, he wants to propose that it is distributed *to* the whole body, *GA* 725a21ff). Blood is the final form of the nourishment and that from which all the parts of the body are formed. The menses are both greater in quantity and more bloodlike than the semen – signs, Aristotle takes it, that the menses are less concocted, as you would expect, he says, in the weaker and colder sex, for, being colder, women are less able to concoct the useful residue. As he puts it at *GA* 726b30ff, 'the weaker creatures must necessarily produce more residue and less concocted residue, and this, if such is its character, must necessarily be a quantity of bloodlike fluid. But what has a smaller share of heat is weaker and the female is just like that [i.e. colder].' It follows that the menses are a residue, and as it is the case that no creature produces two different seminal secretions at the same time (*GA* 727a25ff), it follows further that females do not contribute any seed – only an unconcocted residue – to generation.

What women do contribute, however, is not just the place, but also the matter for the offspring. Indeed the role of the male's semen is confined to supplying the form and the efficient cause (*GA* 729a34ff). He develops a series of analogies with the work of a craftsman and with the action of rennet in curdling milk in order to support this conclusion,[145] and it is apparent that he is influenced by the fact that at a single coitus the semen of the male parent can generate several offspring, for example it can fertilise several eggs.[146] Certainly he cites

---

[144] *GA* 722b17ff (cf. above, pp. 87f and n. 115). Aristotle also believes that his opponents will find it difficult to explain how it is that twins of different sexes will be born (*GA* 764b1ff) and how a female child can resemble her father or a male child his mother (*GA* 769a15ff). Yet we have seen that the writer of *On the Seed* had a theory that appealed to the possibility that the seed that dominates in one part of the body may be different from the seed that does so in another: sometimes the father's seed may predominate, sometimes the mother's (ch. 8, L VII 480.10ff, cf. above, p. 90).

[145] See *GA* 729a9ff, 28ff, b12ff, 22ff, 730b5ff, 737a12ff, 739b20ff, 771b18ff: on these analogies see Lloyd 1966, pp. 368–70.

[146] E.g. *GA* 723b9ff, 729a4ff. At 729b33ff, he cites as the 'strongest indication' (μέγιστον σημεῖον) that the male does not emit any material part that will remain in the foetus, what he believes to be the facts about hens and oviparous fish, for example that when a hen that is producing an egg is trodden by a second cock, the chick will resemble the second cock (cf. also *HA* 542a1ff, 556a27f).

this consideration as a difficulty for pangenesis: for 'we cannot
suppose that at the moment of discharge the seed contains a number
of separate portions from one and the same part of the body' 'nor that
these portions are separated out as soon as they enter the womb' (*GA*
729a6ff).

Although Aristotle has some powerful arguments against the
theory that the seed is drawn from the whole of the body, he appeals
to a number of patently *a priori* considerations to support his own
thesis. To define the female in terms of an incapacity is to assume that
the male provides the model and the norm. Females fail to produce
semen: but males are not said to fail to produce menses. The menses
are bloodlike: but he explains the fact that they resemble the useful
nourishment (blood itself) more closely than the male semen does as a
sign not of their greater perfection, but of the failure of the female to
turn them into something else. When he says that it is better for there
to be sexual differentiation, he is explicit that this is because it is better
for the superior to be separated from the inferior (*GA* 732a3ff).

His conception of the essential difference between the sexes is
reflected in a whole series of comparative judgements concerning the
psychological, physiological and morphological characteristics of
males and females across a wide range of animal species, and these
must now be analysed in some detail. The fullest text in the zoological
writings on the subject of the natural differences in the characters and
dispositions of males and females comes in *HA* ix ch. 1. Even though,
as we noted before (p. 21), there are doubts about the authenticity of
this book, at least in the form in which we have it, it usually represents
views that are close to Aristotle's, and the chief passage we are
concerned with merely provides a more detailed statement of a
general thesis that can be illustrated in many other texts.[147]

In all the kinds in which male and female are found, nature makes more or less a
similar differentiation in the character of the females as compared with the males.
This is especially evident in man, in the larger animals and in viviparous quadrupeds.
For the character of the females is softer, they are more quickly tamed, admit
caressing more readily, and are more apt to learn, as for example in Laconian hounds
the females are cleverer than the males. . . . In all cases except the bear and the
leopard the females are less spirited than the males: in those two kinds the female is
recognised as more courageous. In the other kinds the females are softer, more
mischievous, less simple, more impulsive, and more considerate in rearing the young.
The males on the other hand are more spirited, wilder, more simple and less
scheming. Traces[148] of these characters occur more or less everywhere, but they are
especially evident in those whose character is more developed and most of all in man.
For he has the most perfected nature, and so these dispositions are more evident in

[147] Cf, e.g., *PA* 661b26ff (cf. below, p. 101), *Pol.* 1254b13ff, 1259b1ff.
[148] On the metaphorical use of ἴχνος see Dirlmeier 1937, pp. 55ff.

humans. Hence woman is more compassionate than man, more tearful, and again more envious and more querulous, more given to railing and to striking out. The female is more dispirited than the male, more despondent, more shameless and lying, more given to deceit, more retentive in memory, more wakeful, more shrinking, and in general more difficult to rouse to action than the male, and she needs less nourishment. The male is, as was said, more ready to help and more courageous than the female, for even in the case of cephalopods when the cuttlefish is struck by the trident the male helps the female, but when the male is struck the female makes her escape. (*HA* 608a21–28, 33 – b18.)

Several characteristic features of the handling of this topic in Aristotle's zoology emerge from this passage. First it is acknowledged that the generalisations proposed apply to varying degrees to different species of animals. On the whole the greater the differentiation between the sexes the better, that is the more perfect the species, human beings, as usual, providing the model to which other animals approximate, the ideal from which they fall short.[149] But in addition particular exceptions are also noted. The female bear and the female leopard or panther, πάρδαλις, are singled out as particularly courageous, though whether this reflects direct or reported observations of their behaviour or stems merely from the popular reputations these creatures had is an open question.[150]

These exceptions do not, however, prevent the expression of some very sweeping generalisations indeed. In *all* other animals the females are softer, more mischievous and so on. Many of the statements in question are imprecise, even grossly impressionistic, and correspondingly more difficult to substantiate and less liable to refutation. Remarkably enough, however, some of the generalisations conflict, rather, with points made in the detailed accounts of particular species. Thus although *HA* ix ch. 1 asserts that 'in [all] the other kinds the females are ... more considerate in rearing the young' (608a35 – b2), ch. 37, 621a20ff, of the same book contains the famous description of the way in which, in the river-fish *Glanis*, it is the male that stands guard over the young, while the female, after parturition, goes away.[151] It is particularly striking that Aristotle is sufficiently confident of the general validity of the principle that males do not tend their young to use this as one of several considerations in favour of his conclusion that the worker-bees are neither male nor female.[152] Again the general characterisation of females as 'softer'

---

[149] Cf. above, pp. 26ff.

[150] Thus the leopard, in particular, appears as an anti-lion in some texts, and the feminine qualities of the species as a whole are emphasised as for example in *Phgn.* 809b36ff: see especially Detienne (1977) 1979, pp. 20ff.

[151] Cf. above, pp. 20f.

[152] *GA* 759b5ff, cf. below, p. 102 and n. 162.

contrasts with the observation in *HA* ix ch. 39, 623 a 23f, that in the spiders it is the female that does the hunting, while the male takes a share in the catch, and *HA* v ch. 27, 555 b 14f, reports that in one species of spider the male shares in the incubation of the larvae.

The psychological differentiae of the two sexes can be related, in Aristotle's view, to differences in what we should term their physiological constitution. As we have seen before, one of the key factors is the quality of the blood, though here too many of Aristotle's formulations are imprecise and very difficult to assess. Thus on a number of occasions he insists on the greater 'thinness' and 'purity' of the blood in males, who have moreover hotter blood than females, though the latter have blacker blood and more of it in the inner parts of their bodies than males, though less on the surface.[153]

Various suggestions might be made about what Aristotle has in mind and what he has seen or thinks he has seen. The idea that females have a special abundance of blood in their inner parts is probably to be associated straightforwardly with menstruation, mentioned prominently in this context,[154] as also perhaps is the idea of the blackness of their blood. Yet as we have remarked before,[155] the striking point about these generalisations is that Aristotle pays no attention to other differences which are, in some cases, a good deal more readily observable, as, for instance, to those between arterial and venous blood in *both* males and females. Like his predecessors, whose theories on the subject he mentions and discusses,[156] Aristotle is looking, on the whole, for a *simple* correlation between a series of pairs of opposites, male and female, thin and thick, pure and impure, hot and cold. When we remark that these correlations also correspond, in some cases, to some of his claims concerning the differences between humans in general and other animals,[157] and that other pairs can also be brought into the schema, up and down,[158] and right and left (where he asserts, what he can certainly not have verified, that the blood in the right side of the heart is hotter than in the left[159]), it becomes clear that he is more influenced, in these generalisations, by his expectation that there will be such correlations

---

[153] See especially *HA* 521 a 21ff, *PA* 648 a 9ff, *GA* 765 b 17ff.

[154] See *HA* 521 a 26f, *GA* 765 b 18ff.   [155] Cf. above, pp. 33f.

[156] See especially *PA* 648 a 25ff.

[157] Compare, e.g., *HA* 521 a 2ff and 21ff, and cf. above, pp. 32ff.

[158] See especially *PA* 647 b 34f, 648 a 11f, *Sens.* 444 a 10ff, *Somn. Vig.* 458 a 13ff, *HA* 521 a 4ff.

[159] *PA* 666 b 35ff, cf. 648 a 12f. Ogle 1882, p. 200 n. 27, noted: 'According to Bernard, though the correctness of his statement is not universally accepted, the blood in the left cavity is really somewhat colder than in the right. But, even if it be so, Aristotle can only be right by accident; for he had no possible means of measuring the difference, which is but a fraction of a degree.'

than by any direct empirical evidence. We have seen that at *GA* 726b30ff he uses the notion that females are colder in his argument for the conclusion that the menses are analogous to the semen, only less concocted. Yet elsewhere, in one of the principal texts that discusses the question of the comparative heat of males and females, the view that males are hotter is said to follow *necessarily* from the essential difference between the sexes represented by their ability or inability to concoct the blood. Given the two principles, (1) that males and females differ in respect of that capability and (2) that concoction is effected by heat, it can be *deduced* that males are hotter.[160]

The *a priori* elements in some of Aristotle's more imprecise statements are evident. Yet it would be premature to conclude that there is nothing more to it than that. Physiology was, in any event, bound to be a good deal more speculative than anatomy, where he can and does refer to some directly verifiable data to support some of his assertions. Thus the claim that males are stronger and more spirited than females is associated at *PA* 661b26ff with the general principle that nature allots defensive and offensive organs only to those creatures that can use them – or allots them to a greater degree to such.

'This applies to stings, spurs, horns, tusks and suchlike. For since males are stronger and more spirited [than females], sometimes the males alone have such parts, sometimes they have them to a greater degree.' Females have the necessary parts, for example for nutrition, though even these 'in a less degree', but not the non-necessary parts. 'Thus stags have horns, but does do not. Cows' horns differ from bulls' and similarly also in sheep. In many species the males have spurs but the females do not. And likewise with the other such parts.' (*PA* 661b31–34, b36 – 662a6.)

Other features are added in a similar passage describing the anatomical and other differences between the sexes at *HA* IV ch. 11.

In all animals the upper and front parts in the males are superior, stronger and better equipped than in the females, and in some females the back and lower parts are similarly. This applies to man and to all other viviparous land-animals. Also the female is less sinewy and less articulated, and has finer hair in species that have hair, or the equivalent in species that have no hair. The females also have flabbier flesh than the males, are more knock-kneed, have thinner calves and more delicate feet, in species that have these parts. With regard to voice, in those that have it, all females have a slighter and higher-pitched voice, except for the cow, whose lowing is deeper than that of the bull.[161] (*HA* 538b2–15.)

[160] *GA* 765b8ff, 16ff, cf. *Long.* 466b14ff.
[161] On voice cf. also *HA* 545a14ff, *GA* 786b17ff.

Although some of these generalisations are too sweeping, many obviously have substantial evidence in their support. Common, often large, animals provide most of Aristotle's examples – cattle, deer, the barnyard cock – and it is to them that the generalisations are particularly applied. Problems arise, however, even in this area, when Aristotle appeals to his general principles to make inferences in doubtful cases. Like the doctrine that males do not, as a general rule, tend their young, the principle that nature does not assign defensive weapons to females is cited in his unfortunate discussion of the sex of bees and is one of the grounds on which he rejects the idea that the worker bees (which have stings) are female.[162]

The correlations he expects lead him, also, to a number of superficial and some quite inaccurate statements on anatomical points which it should not have been too hard to check. At *HA* 501 b 19ff, for example, he says: 'males have more teeth than females in men and also in sheep, goats and pigs. But in other species observations have not yet been made.'[163] Yet his investigations of the four species he names cannot have been very careful, and it is possible that he allowed himself to be misled by the doctrine that males have the parts necessary for nutrition 'to a greater degree' than females.[164] Again it would not have been impossible for him to have carried out the observations that would have revealed the incorrectness of his assertion that men have more sutures on the skull than women. He represents the latter as having a single circular suture[165] – a doctrine that corresponds to the view that males are hotter than females, for the sutures have the function of cooling the brain and providing it with ventilation.[166] That view is again what underlies his further claim that, just as humans have a larger brain in proportion to their size than any other animal, so males do than females, although this would, to be sure, have been much more difficult to check.[167]

[162] *GA* 759b1ff, but cf. 760b27ff.

[163] Harig and Kollesch 1977, p. 125, have, however, suggested that what may lie behind this remark is a comparison between animals of different ages or with women who lacked wisdom teeth. Even so it is remarkable that the passage contrasts what Aristotle claims to be the case with humans, sheep, goats and pigs with other species where *observations have not yet been made.*   [164] *PA* 661 b34ff.

[165] *HA* 491 b2ff, 516a 18ff, *PA* 653 a37ff. D'A.W. Thompson 1910, notes to *HA* ad loc., suggests that Aristotle may have imagined that the sutures correspond to partings in the hair. Ogle 1882, p. 168 n. 26, notes that 'the opportunities of seeing a female skull would be much fewer than of seeing a male skull; for battle-fields would no longer be of service.' Compare the account of the different configurations of the sutures in *VC* ch. 1, L iii 182.1ff, and cf. Galen *UP* ix 17, ii 49.26ff H, K iii 751.7ff.   [166] *PA* 653b2f.

[167] *PA* 653a27ff. Ogle 1882, p. 167 n. 18, reviews the inconclusive modern data, the calculation being complicated by the fact that Aristotle's statement concerns not absolute size, but size in proportion to the body as a whole. *PA* 655 a 12ff further claims that the bones in males are harder than in females.

The complex discussion of the issue of the relative longevity and sizes of the two sexes illustrates Aristotle's readiness to acknowledge exceptions to his general rules but also throws light on how he deals with these. At *Long.* 466 b 9ff, after noting that in salacious species females are longer-lived than males, he remarks that 'naturally and to state the general rule males are longer-lived than females', the reason being that males are hotter. At *HA* 538 a 22ff, however, this statement is qualified further. 'In blooded, non-oviparous land-animals as a general rule the male is larger and longer-lived than the female. . . . But in oviparous and larva-producing animals, such as fish and insects, the females are larger than the males.' He instances snakes, certain spiders, the gecko and the frog and adds that the longevity of female fish is shown by the fact that females are caught older than males.[168] Yet he recognises that there are exceptions to these generalisations too. At *HA* 574 b 29ff he notes that the Laconian bitch lives longer than the dog, the male being less long-lived because of the greater work he is made to do.[169] Elsewhere he remarks that the mare is longer-lived than the stallion[170] and so too are female mules than male ones.[171]

Mules are, however, deformed creatures and a major factor in Aristotle's tolerance of exceptions to the general rules that he states may be that such exceptions are usually to be found in deviant or deformed creatures[172] or in species that are low in the hierarchy of animals. He is confident that in humans the male is longer-lived than the female and in his day (though not in ours in many countries) the life expectancy of females was indeed less than that of males.[173] This then legitimates the claim that *naturally* – and to state the general

[168] The greater size of the females of certain species is noted at *HA* 540 b 15ff (cartilaginous and other fish), 582 b 32ff (some non-viviparous animals generally) and *GA* 721 a 17ff (oviparous fish and oviparous quadrupeds – where the reason is offered that the females' greater size is an advantage when a great bulk is produced inside the body by the eggs at breeding time).

[169] Cf. *Long.* 466 b 12ff. At *HA* 575 a 3ff Aristotle notes that in other breeds of dogs it is not very clear which sex is longer-lived – though males necessarily tend to be so.

[170] *HA* 545 b 18ff, cf. 576 a 26ff.

[171] *Long.* 466 b 9ff (which adds the rider 'if the males are salacious') and *HA* 577 b 4ff. On the question of the longevity of the two sexes in oviparous animals, compare *HA* 613 a 25ff and 32ff on various birds.

[172] Although the mare is not said to be a deformed creature, she is exceptional, even proverbial, for her salaciousness (*HA* 572 a 8ff, 575 b 30ff) and at *GA* 773 b 29ff mares are compared with barren women.

[173] See, e.g., Angel 1975, which sets out in Table 1 (facing p. 182) comparative figures for the longevity of male and female adults (aged 15 years and over) from ancient to modern times: in the classical period, from 650 B.C., the figures are, for males 45 years, for females 36.2 years, and for the Hellenistic period, from 300 B.C., 42.4 for males and 36.5 for females: there are slightly different figures in Angel 1972–3, Table 28.

rule – males are longer-lived than females.[174] The reversal of that
rule in some species and even in whole groups – the ovipara and the
larva-producing animals – is, implicitly, a sign of their degeneracy
(even though that is not explicitly asserted in this connection), and
that reversal does not shake Aristotle's conviction in the validity of the
norm he believes he has established. Thanks to the saving clause that
it is in deviant or inferior species that the chief exceptions occur, what
might otherwise be thought of as evidence threatening the validity of
the general principle that males are longer-lived does not do so.
Rather, the general principle stands and exceptions are understood
implicitly as indications of degeneracy.

The quality of Aristotle's research on the differences between the
sexes is uneven and in the confrontation between theory and
observational data the complexity of the latter is not allowed seriously
to undermine the former. There are some signs of caution in his
approach to certain aspects of the problem. At *HA* 538a 10ff he notes
in the context of his discussion of the sex of eels that people can
mistake a diversity of species for a difference of sex. At *HA* 613a 16ff he
remarks that the sex of certain birds is difficult to determine without
an internal examination. He has collected a good deal of information
about such matters as secondary sexual characteristics and the age to
which males and females live, and he writes, on certain occasions, of
the need for further research.

   At the same time he makes some fairly elementary blunders – as in
his statements concerning the number of teeth and the sutures of the
skull in women, where, in both cases, the expectations generated by
his general principles help to lead him astray. Many of his
generalisations are highly impressionistic and difficult to refute, but
by the same token they go beyond the hard evidence available to him
to justify them. Above all while he frequently remarks on exceptions
to his general rules concerning the greater strength, courage, heat,
size and longevity of males, these exceptions are themselves often
explained or understood in terms of the degenerate or deviant
character of the species in question. That principle allows counter-
evidence to be accommodated with all too great facility. The general
views he holds encourage him both to investigate the question of the
differences between the sexes and to admit that the data may be
complex. Yet even if his research had been more comprehensive,
careful and exact, his preconception of the superiority of the male sex
would have survived intact – at least so long as he accepted the

[174] *Long.* 466b9ff, above, p. 103.

ideological presuppositions of his contemporaries concerning the differences between men and women. The firmer the evidence for aspects of the superiority of females among other animals, the greater would have been his commitment to the view that in this, as in other respects, man is the only truly natural creature. Meanwhile those ideological presuppositions acquired some ostensible colour – and reinforcement – from the biological arguments that Aristotle mounted in their support.[175]

5. THE POST-ARISTOTELIAN DEBATE AND CONCLUSIONS

The shortcomings of the ancient discussions of reproduction – the inadequacy of the data available, the weakness of many of the arguments – emerge clearly from the debate between Aristotle and his opponents. Nor are these shortcomings confined to antiquity, for they remain features of the speculations that continued through the Middle Ages and the Renaissance.[176] Although in the practical domain, ancient horticulturalists and stock-rearers were often on the look-out for ways to improve plant strains and animal breeds, it was not until the nineteenth century that systematic investigations on hybridisation were carried out with a view to applying the data so obtained to the theoretical debate concerning heredity. There were no *practical* obstacles to conducting experiments such as Mendel's on the pea (undertaken between 1856 and 1865, but only brought to bear decisively in the theoretical debate at the very end of the century).[177] Both Aristotle and Galen refer, on occasion, to examples

---

[175] Cf. Horowitz 1976 on Aristotle's influence in this regard.

[176] Much of this later debate is conveniently summarised in Lesky 1951. Cf. also Diepgen 1949, Adelmann 1966, II pp. 749ff, Maclean 1980.

[177] Mendel's work, its initial reception and its 'rediscovery', have been the subject of extensive recent discussion, see Gasking 1959, Olby 1966 and 1979, Orel 1973, Weinstein 1977 and Brannigan 1981 especially. On the background to Mendel, see for example Roberts 1929, Zirkle 1951, Provine 1971. It is remarkable that before the 'rediscovery' of Mendel in 1899–1900, William Bateson called for the study and analysis of hybridisation and cross-breeding in the following terms: 'At this time we need no more *general* ideas about evolution. We need *particular* knowledge of the evolution of *particular* forms. What we first require is to know what happens when a variety is crossed with its *nearest allies*. If the result is to have a scientific value, it is almost absolutely necessary that the offspring of such crossing should then be examined *statistically*. It must be recorded how many of the offspring resembled each parent and how many showed characters intermediate between those of the parents. If the parents differ in several characters, the offspring must be examined statistically, and marshalled, as it is called, in respect of each of those characters separately.' The continuation shows, however, that Bateson's expectations of results were, at that stage, modest: 'Even very rough statistics may be of value. If it can only be noticed that the offspring came, say, half like one parent and half like the other, or that the whole showed a mixture of parental characters, a few brief notes of this kind may be a most useful guide to the student of evolution' (Bateson (1899) 1900, p. 63).

of the cross-breeding of animals,[178] and yet neither undertakes any
systematic research into this to increase the data available on the
topic of the likenesses between parents and offspring. First
the common assumption of the *fixity* of natural species inhibited the
development of an interest in the idea that new species might be
formed by hybridisation: though it was recognised that, rarely, some
hybrids are fertile, most were treated as sports. Secondly and more
generally, what was lacking was the idea of the statistical analysis of
complex bodies of data.[179]

In the fifth and fourth centuries B.C., as we have seen, some
empirical evidence is brought to bear on the problems, but much of
what passed as such was anecdotal or was accepted uncritically. Even
Aristotle implicitly accepts that mutilated parents sometimes have
mutilated offspring, and that the resemblances between parents and
offspring included acquired as well as congenital characteristics.[180] It
is just that he insists that this does not *always* happen. The occasional
striking instance of resemblance – such as the case of a black child
born to white parents when one of the grandparents was
black[181] – receives a good deal of attention. But there is little or no
systematic collection and evaluation of data in this field, though there
was a greater effort to do so in the comparative anatomy of male and
female animals.

The physiological theories proposed – such as that appealing to
differences between 'strong' and 'weak' seed – were, understandably,
usually purely speculative, and most of the arguments deployed on
either side were inconclusive. Where the writer of *On the Seed* proposed
one analogy – comparing the interaction of male and female seed to
the mixture of two different substances – Aristotle put forward
another, or rather two main others, first the analogy of the fig-juice or
rennet which does not (he claims) become part of the milk it curdles,
and then the more general analogy of the craftsman who does not
himself become part of the object he produces.

Undoubtedly the strongest parts of Aristotle's discussion are the
negative and destructive arguments he brings against his opponents,
especially the dilemma argument he develops against the inference of
pangenesis from the resemblances of offspring to their parents. Yet

---

[178] See, e.g., Aristotle, *GA* 738b27ff, 746a29ff, Galen, *De Semine* II 1, K IV 604.4ff.
[179] On the conceptual shortcomings of the ancients' analysis of bodies of discrepant data and
the lack of the notion of statistical probability, see Lloyd 1982. It is this, as much as or more
than any simple failure to deploy *testing* procedures, that is relevant to the case of breeding
plants deliberately in order to explore the inheritance of characteristics.
[180] *GA* 721b17ff, 29ff, 724a3ff.
[181] E.g. *GA* 722a8ff, *HA* 586a2ff.

constructively the case he makes out for his own solution depends at certain points on a quite arbitrary appeal to abstract metaphysical principles. The consistency and coherence of his theories are impressive, but this has been bought at a price. He moves all too swiftly to the conclusions that the female is colder than the male and that the menses are analogous to the male semen – conclusions that correspond all too neatly to his prior expectations concerning the female as a deficient male.

In these circumstances much of the ancient debate has the air of shadow-boxing. Yet the underlying issues were sensitive and highly charged. Since nothing like conclusive evidence was forthcoming on this topic, one might have expected *all* ancient theorists simply to have endorsed one or other version of the view that corresponded to the prevailing ideology. That this is not the case – that a sequence of philosophers and doctors dissented from the view that the female provides just the matter or just the place for the offspring[182] – testifies to the extent to which Greek thinkers were able to challenge deep-seated assumptions, even if, as we said, the grounds on which they did so were not themselves primarily ideological, that is they do not appear to have arisen directly from a dissatisfaction with or a wish to challenge preconceptions concerning the inequality of the sexes.

Yet even if the challenge was a challenge, initially, only at the level of physiological theory, it had possible general implications for the equality of the sexes. Just how far the full implications were in the minds of Democritus or of the Hippocratic authors we cannot tell. However, outside the physiological debate the thesis of the equal potentiality of the sexes was developed, though not by Hippocratic authors nor, so far as we know, by Democritus, but by Plato, and then only in the specific context of his consideration of the education of the Guardian rulers of his ideal state. In famous passages in *Republic* book v[183] he insists that difference in sex is just as irrelevant to the question of education as whether a person has hair or is bald. What matters is not sex, but what kind of *psyche* a person has. Provided you have the right *psyche*, there is no reason why you should not become a musician or a doctor or a Guardian, whether you are a man or a woman.[184] It should, however, be remarked that even this passage still talks of the female sex as the weaker.[185] Nor should we forget that when Plato

---

[182] If anything, the doctrine propounded by Aristotle is the *minority* view among those attributed to *named* theorists from the period down to his death, although, as we have seen (p. 87 n. 112), Censorinus reports that Diogenes of Apollonia and Hippon also denied that the female produces seed.

[183] *R.* 451c ff, 454b ff.   [184] *R.* 455e f.

[185] *R.* 455e 1f, 456a 11, cf. 451e 1f.

comes to write about the relation between men and women and the various kinds of animals in the *Timaeus,* he reverts to the more conventional male Greek view of women as degenerate men.

Although much of the theoretical debate in physiology down to the latter part of the fourth century B.C. looks, as we said, like shadow-boxing, certain developments take place in the generation after Aristotle. The most important of these was the discovery of the ovaries by Herophilus.[186] It is clear from the evidence in Galen, especially,[187] that Herophilus both identified the ovaries and explained their general function correctly – representing them as the analogues of the male testes and indeed rather exaggerating the positive analogy between them and the testes.[188]

After Herophilus any physiologist who was familiar with his work was unlikely to be under any illusions concerning the fact that females produce seed. Yet the effect of his discovery was a limited one. First it is likely that some of the philosophers continued to debate the question of reproduction either in ignorance of, or deliberately ignoring, Herophilus's anatomical researches.[189] Just as some Stoics continued to adhere to the Aristotelian view that the heart is the controlling centre of the body despite the discovery of the nervous system and the identification of the brain as the source of many of the nerves,[190] so similarly on the question of the female's contribution to

---

[186] Yet some time before Herophilus described the ovaries, the excision of certain parts of female animals – whether or not these parts were clearly recognised as analogous to the testes – was an established practice in animal husbandry. The ovaries of sows were excised to fatten them and those of camels to prevent them conceiving (as reported in Aristotle, *HA* IX ch. 50, 632a21ff, 27ff, and cf. Galen, *De Semine* I 15, K IV 570.1ff, II 4, 622.7ff, *AA* XII (D 109), who suggests that the former practice was common among others besides Greeks).

[187] Galen quotes at length from the third book of Herophilus' *Anatomy* at *De Semine* II 1, K IV 596.4ff (cf. also *UP* XIV 11, II 323.18ff H, K IV 193.2ff). All the relevant texts have now been collected and evaluated by von Staden, forthcoming.

[188] In particular Herophilus apparently took the ovaries to communicate with the bladder, a view evidently influenced by the analogy with the male which is expressly invoked both here and elsewhere in his account, see Galen, *De Semine* II 1, K IV 597.9ff, and cf. 596.8ff, 17, 597.7–8, and see von Staden, forthcoming, ch. VI. Contrast, however, Potter 1976, pp. 55ff, who believes that Galen has misinterpreted Herophilus and that Herophilus's analogy between female and male seminal ducts was restricted merely to their both *emptying into* some other organ.

[189] Thus it is doubtful how far the ongoing debate between Stoics and Epicureans of different generations on this subject took account of Herophilus's anatomical discoveries. Our evidence is limited and, at points, inconsistent. The Epicureans evidently maintained a version of the pangenesis theory: see Lucretius IV 1209ff, Aet. V 5.1, and cf. Lesky 1951, pp. 92f. Most of our sources for individual Stoics or for the school as a whole suggest that they held that the female produces no seed (Censorinus, *De Die Nat.* ch. 5,4 p. 10.3f) or at least no fertile seed (D.L. VII 159, Aet. V 5.2). On the one apparent exception, Aet. V. 11.4, if taken together with V 11.3, where a positive role is ascribed to the female seed, see, for example, the reservations of Lesky 1951, pp. 167ff. None of these texts makes any reference to the ovaries.

[190] Chrysippus's view is bitterly attacked by Galen on this score in a sustained polemic that takes up most of the first five books of *PHP*.

reproduction there may well have been similar barriers or obstacles to communication between at least some philosophers and some medical writers as well as within each of those two broad groups.[191]

Secondly, even those who admitted that females produce seed did not necessarily accept that the female role in generation is equal to that of the male. A knowledge of the function of the ovaries could be, and sometimes was, combined with an unqualified adherence to the belief in the innate superiority of the male sex.

The position of Galen is instructive. On the one hand he is critical, to the point of being contemptuous, of many of Aristotle's mistakes on questions of anatomy and physiology. First where Aristotle had argued that the testes do not produce sperm but merely serve to keep the seminal passages taut – like weights on a loom – Galen is clear that this is an error.[192] Secondly, he insists that Aristotle is wrong in his belief that the role of the male semen is merely to provide the efficient cause in reproduction.[193] Thirdly and most importantly, Galen contradicts Aristotle on aspects of the role of the female. In his view it was 'Hippocrates' who first discovered that females produce seed, and *On the Nature of the Child* is quoted to support this.[194] Herophilus himself is also quoted at some length for his description of the structure and function of the ovaries – though Galen corrects Herophilus in turn, particularly on the communications between the ovaries and the womb.[195] Finally in Galen's view the Aristotelian doctrine that the menses are the matter of the embryo is seriously mistaken – for the menses are not the principal material for the foetus and they are indeed unsuitable for that role.[196]

On the other hand Galen positively endorses several other

---

[191] Galen reports the views of a number of other theorists besides Herophilus on this subject in the *De Semine*. He criticises Athenaeus, for instance, for arguing that women have non-functional, rudimentary seed-producing parts on the basis of the analogy of breasts in males (*De Semine* II 1, K IV 599.11ff, and cf. II 2, 612.3ff, which ascribes to him the Aristotelian view that the menses are the matter and the male semen supplies the form). The continued debate on the contribution of the female to reproduction can also be followed in the opposing arguments in Dionysius of Aegae, see Photius in Migne, *PG* 103, 1860, codices 185 and 211, cols. 541 and 692.

[192] See Aristotle, *GA* 729a34ff, cf. 717a34ff, 787b19ff, 788a3ff, and cf. Galen, *De Semine* I 13, K IV 558.11ff, I 15, 573.14ff, 574.13ff.

[193] Galen, *De Semine* II 2, K IV 613.8ff, cf. I 3, 516.5ff, 518.7ff, discussing *GA* 737a7ff.

[194] *De Semine* II 1, K IV 595.13ff.

[195] *De Semine* II 1, K IV 596.4ff, 598.5ff. Against the view he ascribes to Herophilus, Galen denies that the ovaries communicate with the bladder and asserts that there are visible spermatic ducts (i.e. the Fallopian tubes) between the ovaries and the womb, *De Uteri Dissectione* 9, *CMG* V 2,1 48.17ff, K II 900.8ff, cf. *UP* XIV 10, II 318.8ff H, K IV 186.6ff.

[196] Galen, *UP* XIV 3, II 288.9ff H, K IV 147.9ff, *De Semine* I 5, K IV 527.17ff, 529.15ff, II 2, 613.8ff, II 4, 623.3ff. On Galen's criticisms of Aristotle's theories of reproduction, see further Preus 1977, pp. 8off.

fundamental Aristotelian theses, notably the notions (1) that the woman is less perfect than the man,[197] (2) that the female is colder and wetter than the male,[198] and (3) that while she produces seed, she produces imperfect seed, seed that is scantier, colder and wetter than the male's and that could not, by itself, generate an animal.[199] Galen even repeats Aristotle's view that the female is like a deformed creature – οἷον ἀνάπηρον[200] – and he holds that females are the product of weaker and as it were sickly seed.[201] The overall thesis for which he argues not just in *On the Use of Parts* but repeatedly elsewhere throughout his work is that the *whole* of the animal kingdom and *all* the parts of animals testify to the supreme craftsmanship of nature. But contemplating the difference between the sexes, he revealingly comments that the creator would not have made half the race mutilated unless there was some use in that mutilation.[202] His ambivalence is manifest. Nature's work is good: indeed all of it is good.[203] Yet that does not mean that the female is *as good as* the male. On the contrary, it is assumed that she is not and is indeed some kind of deformity. So Galen construes his problem as being to explain how it is that nature made half the human race imperfect, finding the main part of his answer, readily enough, in the needs that have to be served for the purposes of reproduction.

At first sight it may seem paradoxical that the most powerful statements of the thesis of female deficiency, even deformity, come from teleologists such as Aristotle and Galen who were firmly committed to the proposition that nature does nothing in vain – while the, or a, more egalitarian view of the female's role in reproduction was sometimes proposed by anti-teleologists.[204] Yet the view that 'nature does nothing in vain' did not usually mean that the products of her workmanship are all equally good. Rather it corresponded to the belief that some good is to be found in all or most of her works, and that was compatible with a very strong conception of the different degrees of perfection attained by different natural

---

[197] Galen, *UP* xiv 5, ii 295.27ff H, K iv 157.12ff. On other aspects of the male's greater perfection, see, e.g., *UP* xi 14, ii 154.20ff H, K iii 900.10ff.

[198] *UP* xiv 6, ii 299.5ff H, K iv 161.13ff, cf. ii 301.3ff H, K iv 164.1ff.

[199] *De Semine* i 7, K iv 536.16ff, i 10, 548.6ff, *UP* xiv 6, ii 301.3ff H, K iv 164.1ff, xiv 10, ii 317.5ff, 318.1ff, H, K iv 184.16ff, 185.18ff.

[200] *UP* xiv 6, ii 299.19ff H, K iv 162.10ff.

[201] *UP* xiv 7, ii 308.19ff H, K iv 173.18ff.

[202] *UP* xiv 6, ii 299.19ff H, K iv 162.10ff.

[203] Whereas Aristotle explicitly recognises the limits of final causation in nature, where what happens is the outcome of 'necessity' rather than 'for the good', Galen more rarely qualifies his statements implying the universal applicability of the principle that all of the products of nature are good.

[204] This is true, in the period after Aristotle, of the Epicureans especially.

species or by different natural products of any kind. Teleology was thus often combined with hierarchical beliefs, and in the case of attitudes towards the sexes that meant a conviction of the superiority of the male. With the advance of anatomy and physiology *some* aspects of the original assumptions concerning the female's role in reproduction were criticised and undermined. Yet many of those assumptions were immune to refutation, even though they were occasionally challenged quite openly in certain specific contexts.

PART III

DEVELOPMENTS IN PHARMACOLOGY, ANATOMY AND GYNAECOLOGY

1. INTRODUCTION

Our third group of studies ranges over a wider set of fields than hitherto – pharmacology and anatomy as well as gynaecology – and takes us beyond the period of the initial emergence of the life sciences in Greece in the fifth and fourth centuries, to which we have largely restricted our inquiries so far. The chief problems to be investigated stem in part from reflections on the situation in the life sciences towards the end of the fourth century B.C., and in part from points in modern controversy though more often points from outside the specialist field of classical scholarship than from within it.

Many of the most fertile ideas, especially the most fertile methodological ideas, in Greek science as a whole are the product of the fifth and fourth centuries B.C. This is true, for example, of the key notions (1) of an axiomatic, deductive system, (2) of the application of mathematics to the explanation of physical phenomena, and (3) of empirical research. In some cases the elaboration and application of those ideas in the mature sciences of the Hellenistic and Roman periods follows an expected pattern. Certainly the development of astronomical theory depended not just on advances in mathematics (for example, trigonometry) but also on the collection of a considerable body of empirical data. While quantitative astronomical models were already proposed in the fourth century B.C., they still fall very far short of the fully elaborated and, in the main, confident and successful *Syntaxis*, Ptolemy's great work of synthesis in the second century A.D., the production of which presupposes first a series of advances in theory (Apollonius, Hipparchus) and secondly improvements in the observational data (Timocharis, Aristyllus, Hipparchus and others). But if the main stream of the development of astronomical theory[1] follows a clear-cut pattern and might tend to confirm a thesis of the

---

[1] How far the more complex astronomical models were generally accepted or understood is, to be sure, another matter. The more or less popular and elementary accounts of astronomy in such writers as Geminus, Cleomedes and Theon of Smyrna all elide – when they do not garble – many of the more sophisticated astronomical notions developed by theorists from Eudoxus onwards: see, e.g., Neugebauer 1975, II pp. 578ff, 652, 949f.

reasonably steady and sustained advance of inquiry, in other fields of science, and notably in some branches of the life sciences, no such pattern emerges. On first impression it may appear that, even though the methodological ideas were well established, or at least clearly set out, in the fifth or the fourth century (especially the importance of thorough, and critical, research), little opportunity was taken to apply them in practice – that the promise of the classical period was not fulfilled either in the Hellenistic period or later. An exception could certainly be made of anatomy, where – despite the difficulties in the standardisation of anatomical terminology which we shall be studying in section 4 – advances were undoubtedly made and they were, or at least could on occasion be, cumulative. The work of Herophilus and Erasistratus represented one massive step forward on that of Aristotle, that of Galen another: even though the method of dissection remained controversial, and human dissection positively declined, Galen was certainly able not just to use, but often to improve on, the work of his predecessors.[2]

Yet in other fields, in zoology and botany, and in pharmacology, the situation appears noticeably different. The masterpieces of Aristotle and Theophrastus in zoology and botany took those subjects to a high level of achievement. Yet both Aristotle and Theophrastus themselves repeatedly insist on how much work still remains to be done. Such demands may take one or other of two forms. Most commonly in Aristotle the point is that observations have yet to be undertaken or are not yet complete. But both he and Theophrastus also quite frequently identify difficulties where there is a problem not just of inadequate data, but of inadequate theories or explanations. Theophrastus, for instance, enters a notable plea for the investigation of the whole question of spontaneous generation at the end of a discussion in which he points out that many cases that passed as such must be excluded.[3]

But if we turn to the work of the successors of Aristotle and

[2] While Galen often concentrates on the work of Herophilus and Erasistratus, he provides extensive evidence also of that of many other later anatomists. He thought highly both of Marinus and of his pupil Quintus in particular. Marinus, he tells us, wrote an *Anatomy* in twenty books: his description of the muscles is praised by Galen (*AA* II 1–2, K II 280.1ff, 283.7ff) even though he also speaks of shortcomings in the work. Quintus wrote nothing, but was the teacher of a number of prominent anatomists of the generation before Galen, including Satyrus, Numisianus and Lycus. Galen himself studied under Numisianus and Pelops, described as among the best of the pupils of Numisianus (*CMG* v 9,1 70.10ff, K xv 136.10ff, and see more generally *CMG* v 9,1 69.29ff, K xv 135.14ff, *AA* xiv 1, 183–4, Duckworth and K xviii B 926.1ff). On the other hand he attacked Lycus repeatedly, telling us that Lycus's book, published posthumously, enjoyed wide circulation but was full of errors.

[3] See *CP* I 5.5 and cf. also *HP* III 1.1–6.

Theophrastus in zoology and botany with the hope that they will follow up not just topics where notice had been given of the need for further research, but many others as well, we are often disappointed. As always there is the problem of the source material available to us. Some works that may well have been outstanding representatives of their discipline or at least of their type are lost, as are, for example, the botanical treatises of Crateuas.[4] What we can reconstruct of these from our indirect information suggests that original work continued in certain areas,[5] and a similar point can be confirmed with reference to treatises that we do have, such as Dioscorides's *De Materia Medica*, which – whatever their own degree of originality may have been – at least certainly carry aspects of their subject further than their extant predecessors.[6] On the other hand we have other works that align themselves broadly with the methodological principles formulated by Aristotle and Theophrastus, and yet where the actual delivery on that implied promise is meagre. To explain this, as has often been done, merely in terms of the mediocre quality of their authors is too swift: while to do so in terms of the general decline of ancient science is, of course, merely to restate the problem.

A first set of questions concerns the relationship between the stated methodological principles, and the actual practice, in certain areas of the life sciences. How far was critical research sustained? Where it was not, or not too successfully, can we identify the difficulties and constraints in the way of fulfilling the methodological promise, or otherwise account for the shortfall? We can investigate these topics first of all with regard to Pliny's work, especially in botany and pharmacology (section 3). There is no question of attempting to generalise our results from that study to apply straightforwardly to the *whole* of later Greco-Roman science. As already noted, the history of anatomy presents a different pattern of more sustained development. The constraints there were of a different kind and relate in part – as we shall see in section 4 – to the transmission of results as

---

[4] According to Pliny, *HN* xxv 8, Crateuas, followed by Dionysius and Metrodorus, instituted the practice of illustrating their botanical treatises with paintings of the plants discussed. Wellmann 1897, and others, have even suggested that Crateuas's own illustrations may lie behind those that appear in the Constantinopolitanus MS for Dioscorides (cf. also on this problem, Bonnet 1903, pp. 169ff, 1909, pp. 294ff, Johnson 1912–13, Buberl 1936, Gerstinger 1970, pp. 8 and 20f).

[5] One interesting development relating to the instruments of research available in botany is the collection of plants made by Antonius Castor. What we know of his interests suggests that this was partly for the purposes of study: it was then a proto-botanical garden. It is mentioned, and was visited, by Pliny (*HN* xxv 9, see below, pp. 139f).

[6] The range of Dioscorides's work, which mentions an estimated 600 types of plants, is considerably wider than that of any earlier – or later – extant ancient source. For a summary assessment, see Riddle 1971.

much as to sustaining the impetus of research. In gynaecology, too, where Soranus, especially, offers opportunities to draw comparisons between methodological theory and practice, and between classical and post-classical work, we may test not just how far critical research was sustained, but also how successful he was in squaring a sophisticated anti-speculative, even anti-theoretical methodology with actual gynaecological practice (sections 5 and 6). Every allowance must be made for these and other divergences in the history of different aspects of later Greco-Roman medicine and biology. Yet certain features of one fundamental and recurrent problem, that of the application, in practice, of the principles of critical scrutiny, can be illustrated through our particular case-studies.

Two further major types of problem arise from aspects of modern discussion and controversies. A crucial question that has been much debated in connection with the rise of science is the development and implications of literacy. Goody and Watt first stressed the importance of literacy for understanding developments that take place both in the ancient Near Eastern civilisations and in ancient Greece,[7] and Goody has subsequently refined and modified his thesis.[8] First he has qualified his account of the developments that take place in Greece in particular, expressing reservations about aspects of the 'Greek miracle', or at least of the uniqueness of the Greek case, that he had earlier been inclined to accept. Secondly he has insisted that the dichotomy pre-literacy/literacy needs to be viewed with greater caution and to be refined by taking more account of the stages in the *transitions* between the two and by recognising the lack of clear-cut cases of totally non-literate societies or at any rate of societies with no recording or mnemonic devices whatsoever. At the same time he sees literacy as either *the*, or at least *the most important*,[9] cause in the rise of the kind of critical and rational approach that is prominent in aspects of Greek thought and that is a *sine qua non* of the development of science in Greece.

The aspects of this question that relate to the origins of Greek science need not concern us at this point.[10] But the problem of literacy is relevant not just to the emergence of science, but also to its growth and transmission, and this in two quite distinct, indeed opposite, ways. Although we cannot quantify either the numbers of

[7] Goody and Watt 1968.
[8] Goody 1977 and unpublished.
[9] Thus although Goody unpublished begins by explicitly ruling out monocausal explanations, the thrust of his argument is that other factors are effectively to be discounted.
[10] The new arguments and evidence adduced in Goody unpublished do not lead me to modify the view I expressed in Lloyd 1979, ch. 4.

copies of important scientific texts that were produced at any period in antiquity or – more important – the numbers of people who could read them, there can be no doubt that the availability of books enormously facilitated the publication, preservation and accumulation of the results of scientific investigations – and the study of those results was no longer limited to occasions of oral performance. Again there can be no doubt that literacy was a crucial factor in scientific education at all levels from the elementary up, not that Greek education ever focused on science as such in particular. The development of the scientific text book can, however, be followed broadly both in mathematics (where Euclid came to occupy the dominant position) and in medicine (where Galen, for instance, composed a series of special works designed as introductions 'for beginners').

At the same time two factors in the spread of literacy were potentially negative in their effects.[11] (1) The prestige of written documents could inhibit critical scrutiny. The deadening effect of authority on later Greek science is in general well known, and that authority was almost always mediated by the written text, even if that text was subject to the oral glosses and explanations of the lecturer or commentator. But one lesson to be learned from our particular case-studies of Pliny (section 3), of anatomical writers (section 4) and of Soranus (in section 5) is that the reverence accorded to the great figures of the past was very variable.

(2) More importantly, the production of a literate elite could present obstacles to communication particularly in fields of inquiry that depended, or drew heavily, on practical experience. These were, to be sure, not the only such obstacles – as our study of Hippocratic gynaecology has already illustrated and as our examination of Soranus will again go to confirm. But our case-studies in fourth-century and in later pharmacology (sections 2 and 3) will be concerned with the barriers that existed (and are explicitly acknowledged by Pliny to exist) not just between literate authors of different types but also between these and other largely, if not exclusively, non-literate groups, the root-cutters, the drug-sellers and more generally – to use Pliny's own expression – the 'illiterate country-folk'.[12] This aspect of

---

[11] Cf. the sophisticated and critical discussion in the studies of Derrida (1967a), 1976 and (1967b) 1978 especially, of theses he associates with writers ranging from Rousseau to Lévi-Strauss.

[12] To cite just two examples among many from later periods: Paracelsus is quoted by Debus 1978, p. 10, as follows: 'not all things the physician must know are taught in the academies. Now and then he must turn to old women, to Tartars who are called gypsies, to itinerant magicians, to elderly country folk and many others who are frequently held in contempt.

the interrelations of 'science' and traditional belief will lead us to consider some of the negative as well as the positive effects of the growth of book-learning.

This last point takes us to a third area of current controversy relevant to our studies. This concerns the social organisation and groupings of those who contribute to natural scientific inquiry. The idea of a scientific community – that investigators working in a particular field and with shared methods and assumptions constitute in important ways their own society within a society – is familiar in a variety of contexts from the work of Kuhn and many other sociologists of science.[13] The consensus of the group may be one and the most important factor in legitimating particular research programmes and in inhibiting or even banning deviant ideas or theories. In 'normal' science – in Kuhn's terminology – work is concentrated on elaborating and supporting an existing set of agreed and unchallenged models or paradigms:[14] only in rare periods of crisis will the paradigms themselves be in question and then generally from outside the group, by individuals who – consciously or not, and voluntarily or not – come to be excluded from the existing scientific community and who, if their challenge is successful, come in time to form their own self-legitimating community.

The thesis of the role of the consensus of the scientific group is connected by some interpreters (including Kuhn himself)[15] with a relativist view according to which there is no other standard or criterion – apart from the opinions of a particular group or groups – by which the validity of a scientific theory can be tested – so that all judgements concerning truth must be relativised to the group or groups in question. Yet this is not a necessary or integral part of the thesis concerning the importance of the scientific consensus. The points concerning the influence of the scientific community in forming and controlling opinions, in inhibiting some inquiries, in stimulating others and in evaluating their results, can be accepted and used without any commitment to epistemological relativism.

From them he will gather his knowledge since these people have more understanding of such things than all the high colleges.' Secondly there was the use made by Jenner, in the development of vaccination, of what was common knowledge among dairy workers in England, namely that those who had suffered from cow pox were not subject to small pox: see Jenner (1798) 1801, case II p. 11 and cf. case VI, p. 15.

[13] See Kuhn (1962) 1970a and 1970c, cf. Berger and Luckmann 1967, S.B. Barnes 1969, 1972, 1973, 1974, Mulkay 1972, Lukes 1973, Skorupski 1976, as well as others writing in a different, continental, tradition, or rather traditions, notably Habermas and Althusser.

[14] On this see Kuhn 1974, Shapere 1964, Scheffler 1967, Masterman 1970.

[15] See especially Kuhn 1970c, e.g. p. 266: 'If I am right, then "truth" may, like "proof", be a term with only intra-theoretic applications.'

In the modern world, with the intense specialisation of science, the thesis has widespread implications. Though sometimes neglected by commentators on ancient science, there can be no doubt of its relevance, though on a far smaller scale, at all periods in the ancient world. It is true that the institutional organisation of science in the ancient world was minimal. Science as such lacked an institutional framework such as is provided by modern research foundations and universities – and we shall see the relevance of this in one context in our study of aspects of the development of anatomy in section 4. All the greater, then, is the role of such frameworks as did exist, that is of the communities of co-workers in particular fields.

If there was no place for the scientist as such, there was one for the natural philosopher, one for the practising physician – and one too for the 'mathematician' (a term that for the ancients regularly included the practising astrologer). Members of the first two of these loosely-knit groups often shared certain assumptions, including not just theories and explanations, but also the methodological principles or protocols underpinning their inquiries. At the same time the fundamental motivation of their investigations could differ profoundly in this respect, that the natural philosophers (as such) always lacked what was a central concern of the physician, the practical orientation to questions of healing the sick. In competition *within* each of these two communities, questions of reputation, at least, and, in differing degrees, questions of livelihood, were at stake. Controversy *between* the two groups was often a matter of boundary-marking. Yet the two groups were sufficiently distinct for it to be possible for them to develop alternative approaches to the same or related problems without coming into confrontation. While that possibility evidently had positive advantages in providing alternative sources of critical evaluation, it had its negative effect where there was not only no explicit controversy between competing approaches but a positive failure to take rival points of view into account.

Two of our studies illustrate different aspects of this complex situation. In Soranus (in section 6) we can see how philosophical ideas could, up to a point, be accommodated to medical practice. But the question here will be up to what point, and with what success, this accommodation was achieved. In our study of aspects of the discussion of pharmacological questions in Theophrastus and certain Hippocratic writers (section 2) we are faced with a very different phenomenon – of fairly marked differences in focus between the natural philosopher on the one hand and the doctors on the other. These differences, it may be suggested, relate to features of the doctors' position as healers competing with others to treat the sick, that is with the distance that some of the medical writers wished to set between their practice and that of some of their rivals.

Our case-studies in this Part will explore examples of the different use of, and reaction to, the stock of traditional beliefs and of ideas sanctioned by structures of authority of different kinds. We shall investigate the acknowledged and unacknowledged borrowings from and adaptations of some items and the explicit or implicit criticisms and rejection of others, and thereby illustrate both the barriers to communication that existed between the different groups of those who might lay claims to special knowledge and the partial successes that were achieved in overcoming those barriers. Our final study will return to the question of the differing basic motivations of ancient scientists and to aspects of the relationship between them and the values of the society within which they worked.

2. THEOPHRASTUS, THE HIPPOCRATICS AND THE ROOT-CUTTERS: SCIENCE AND THE FOLKLORE OF PLANTS AND THEIR USE

The uses and properties of plants, real or imagined, were the subject of intense interest from the earliest times. Already in our earliest Greek literary source, Homer, certain plants are marked out for their special qualities and for the special way they need handling. Many passages in the *Iliad* speak generally of, for example, pain-removing drugs – often plants – applied to battle wounds:[16] the action of one at *Il.* 5.900ff is compared to rennet curdling milk, and at *Il.* 11.844ff a 'bitter root' is applied to a thigh wound with both pain-killing and styptic effects: 'it dried the wound and stopped the bleeding'. In a famous passage in the *Odyssey* (*Od.* 10.302ff), where Hermes gives Odysseus a φάρμακον as an antidote to those Circe used to turn men into beasts, he digs up a plant: 'it had a black root, but the flower was like milk. The gods call it μῶλυ. It is difficult for mortal men to dig up, but the gods can do anything.'

Alongside what was commonly known or believed, much esoteric lore grew up, and the boundaries between the two, never clearly defined, were subject to constant fluctuation and negotiation. Thus much of what Hesiod recommends in the sections on agriculture in the *Works and Days* was, no doubt, common practice: but some of his injunctions, especially concerning the particular days of the month suitable or to be avoided for particular activities, are – on his own claim – more 'learned'. He remarks, for instance, that sowing should

[16] E.g. *Il.* 4.191 and 218.

not be begun on the thirteenth day of the month, but that day is best for planting (*Op.* 780–1). The section on the 'days' ends with the comment that few people know about which days are good, which harmful – 'one man praises one day, another another' (*Op.* 824) – a passage that suggests both that many of the rules he has referred to were not universally recognised and, by implication, that Hesiod himself possesses special knowledge.

By the fifth century, if not before, the term ῥιζοτόμοι, 'root-cutters', comes to be used of those who concerned themselves especially with the collection of plants. Sophocles even wrote a play with that title: only fragments survive and little is known of the plot, but it is clear that the play belonged to the Medea legend,[17] and it is possible that it underlined the marginal status of such people.[18] As in numerous other societies, those with claims to special knowledge about wild plants were often viewed with some distrust as well as with a certain admiration or even awe. The 'root-cutters' are often associated with the 'drug-sellers', φαρμακοπῶλαι, and although there were plenty of other drugs in common use beside plant products, the latter always constituted by far the most important element in Greek pharmacology. Although the two activities are distinct, the same individuals sometimes evidently engaged in both the collecting and the selling of plant-medicines, as also in their administration.[19] Moreover the relationship between those who defined themselves or were defined by others as 'root-cutters', and those who saw themselves as doctors – ἰατροί – is also a delicate one, for while some might choose to emphasise the distinction and the contrast between the two, there was also a possible overlap: among the notable fourth-century medical writers (and practising physicians) who also composed a work he entitled ῥιζοτομικόν is Diocles.[20]

By the middle of the fourth century a variety of different types of writer had already begun to attempt to verify, systematise and extend the knowledge of plants and their uses, or what passed as such. We have two very rich and largely independent sources for these

---

[17] The evidence is collected by Pearson 1917, II pp. 172–7.

[18] In Diogenes Laertius I 112 there is some indication of a tradition according to which Epimenides – the legendary purifier of Athens – withdrew into solitude (ἐκπατεῖν) and engaged in collecting roots, ῥιζοτομία.

[19] On the other hand laymen sometimes bought medicines and administered them for themselves, as is clear, for example, from ps. Demosthenes LIX 55ff.

[20] The evidence for the contents of Diocles's ῥιζοτομικόν is meagre: see Wellmann 1901, pp. 191f. Many of the ῥιζοτόμοι were, no doubt, illiterate: but that there could be literate authors who were known as such is suggested by the case of Crateuas, the writer of botanical treatises in the first century B.C. who is referred to by Dioscorides as a ῥιζοτόμος, Proem 1, W I 1.12f.

developments, first a number of Hippocratic treatises that deal with *materia medica*, and secondly the botanical works of Theophrastus.[21] The view-points from which they write are substantially different. Theophrastus is not concerned primarily with the medicinal uses of plants, though that is certainly one of his interests and a particularly prominent one in book IX of the *Inquiry concerning Plants*.[22] Conversely, none of the Hippocratic writers attempts a systematic study of the kinds of plants, let alone even a sketch of their taxonomy, and indeed most of their comments on plants are strictly limited to their use as food or drugs.

Nevertheless there is an area of overlap between these two types of works. Both may be seen as reacting to common opinions and to such special lore as may be associated with the 'root-cutters' and 'drug-sellers'. Both take over and use much from that complex background. At the same time both implicitly or explicitly criticise aspects of previous and contemporary beliefs and practices. Furthermore there are interesting contrasts in the nature of the criticisms developed or implied by Theophrastus on the one hand and by the Hippocratic writers on the other – as well as further divergences between different Hippocratic authors amongst themselves.[23] Both sources bear witness to the attempts made, in this field of inquiry, to bring order and reason into a bewildering mass of more or less well grounded, more or less fantastical, popular ideas. By studying the tensions that this created, and in particular the divergences in the response of different writers, we shall aim to throw light on more general issues relating to the accommodation of traditional ideas within ancient science, to the obstacles to the development of scientific inquiry and to the varying success with which these obstacles were overcome.

Theophrastus is at once more systematic and more self-conscious in his approach to the inquiry concerning plants than the Hippocratic writers and we may begin by setting out the evidence relating to his

---

[21] Theophrastus is also our best source for the interest shown by such philosophers as Democritus in various problems concerning plants, see, e.g., *CP* I 8.2, II 11.7ff, VI 6.1, 17.11.

[22] Although the authenticity of book IX or of parts of it has sometimes been challenged, in part precisely because of the 'folk-lore' it contains (see, e.g., Singer 1927, pp. 2f), the style and framework of the discussion are broadly similar to the rest of *HP*. Cross-references to *HP* IX in, for example, *CP* (e.g. at *CP* II 6.4 to *HP* IX 18.10, a passage excluded by Hort) do not prove the authenticity of the texts referred to, but suggest at least that they were incorporated in *HP* at an early stage (even if *HP* may have undergone, or even probably underwent, several editorial revisions). On the whole issue, see Regenbogen 1940, cols. 1450ff, with full references to the earlier literature, and cf. Senn 1956, pp. 16ff.

[23] *Vict.* II, for instance, deals primarily with plants as foods (rather than as medicines) and develops its own complex analysis of these in terms of an elaborate schema of opposites.

awareness of some of the problems. Like the fishermen, hunters, bee-keepers and so on whom Aristotle cites in his zoological treatises, the root-cutters and drug-sellers are not unimportant sources used by Theophrastus both in the *Causes of Plants* and in the *Inquiry*, especially though not exclusively in book IX. Certain particularly famous or remarkable individuals are named, Thrasyas of Mantinea (*HP* IX 16.8, 17.1f), his pupil Alexias (*HP* IX 16.8), two men named Eudemus (*HP* IX 17.2f) and Aristophilus from Plataea (*HP* IX 18.4), and in some cases what they said or did is recounted with a certain amount of circumstantial detail. *HP* IX 16.8 records certain details about the φάρμακον that Thrasyas claimed gave an 'easy and painless end', including where he gathered the hemlock which was one ingredient, and IX 17 tells various stories about how little effect drugs have on those who have become habituated to them, including the feat of a shepherd who ruined the reputation of one drug-seller who had been held in some awe for eating one or two hellebore roots: the shepherd ate a whole bunch of them and survived.

But the occasions when a particular source is named are far fewer than those on which Theophrastus is less definite in his identification. We are told what the Tyrrhenians of Heraclea do (*HP* IX 16.6), for example, or the people of Ceos (IX 16.9) or those of Anticyra (IX 14.4), and far more often still a report is introduced with the anonymous 'they say' or simply recorded in *oratio obliqua*.

Whenever the fact of quotation is signalled in one of these ways this already establishes a certain distance between the author or authors of some view and Theophrastus himself, and it opens the question of whether the authors are to be believed or how far Theophrastus endorsed their report. True to the traditions of ἱστορίη he inherited,[24] Theophrastus sometimes reports alternative accounts and points out the discrepancies or contradictions between them, as he does, for instance, in his unhappy chapter on the origins of frankincense, myrrh and balsam in *HP* IX 4.[25] Whether or not he had to adjudicate between competing views, and whether he was dealing with some common belief or with special lore, the problem of sorting out fact from fantasy is one that recurs on page after page of the botanical works. He is well aware that as a whole the drug-sellers and the root-cutters are far from totally reliable. At *HP* IX 8.5 he says: 'further we may add statements made by drug-sellers and root-cutters

---

[24] These extend, of course, beyond natural scientific inquiry and include what we call history, where the presentation of alternative versions of a story is already a prominent feature in Herodotus.

[25] See *HP* IX 4.8.

which in some cases may be to the point, but in others contain exaggeration'. Again at *HP* ix 19.2–3 he discounts a series of stories about amulets and charms with the remark that their authors were trying to 'glorify their own crafts'.[26]

That shows him to be on his guard: but the question that that raises is what the principles or grounds were on which he rejected what he had been told. In some cases he has little hesitation at arriving at a verdict. Having given one account about cinnamon and cassia in *HP* ix 5.1, he goes on with what others say in ix 5.2 as follows:

Others say that cinnamon is shrubby or rather like an under-shrub; and that there are two kinds, one black, the other white. And there is also a tale (μῦθος) told about it; they say that it grows in deep glens, and that in these there are numerous snakes which have a deadly bite; against these they protect their hands and feet before they go down into the glens, and then, when they have brought up the cinnamon, they divide it in three parts and draw lots for it with the sun; and whatever portion falls to the lot of the sun they leave behind; and they say that, as soon as they leave the spot, they see this take fire. Now this is sheer fable (τῷ ὄντι μῦθος) (trans. Hort).[27]

The features of this story that roused Theophrastus's suspicions are not explicitly identified, but they no doubt included the notion that the sun would cause spontaneous combustion of the portion left behind as soon as the gatherers had left.

On several occasions, however, Theophrastus shows himself much more hesitant and cautious in reaching a judgement. One text that illustrates this vividly is the continuation of *HP* ix 8.5ff, the passage which opens with the remark quoted above that some of what the drug-sellers and root-cutters say may be to the point whereas other stories are exaggerated. He first notes some of their injunctions about how plants are to be gathered. In cutting the plant called θαψία, for instance, one should stand to windward and also anoint oneself with oil – for one's body will swell up if one stands to leeward. There are dangers, too, to the eyes unless one stands to windward in gathering the fruit of the wild rose, and some plants must be gathered at night, others by day. This paragraph elicits the comment: 'these and similar remarks may well be thought not to be off the point (ἀλλοτρίως)', and he gives as a general reason 'for the powers of some plants are dangerous'. He goes on, however, with a number of other recommendations which he describes as ὥσπερ ἐπίθετα καὶ πόρρωθεν – adventitious and far-fetched. These include the need to dig up the plant

---

[26] Contrast *HP* ix 14.1, where Theophrastus records what he has been told by a doctor said to be no charlatan nor liar (οὐκ ἀλαζὼν οὐδὲ ψεύστης).

[27] Cf. Herodotus iii 111. For a structuralist analysis of this fable, see Detienne (1972a) 1977, ch. 1. In the last sentence I have quoted (which is not included in Detienne's discussion), the addition of the expression τῷ ὄντι, 'really', shows that μῦθος must here have the pejorative sense of fable, not just the neutral sense of story.

called γλυκυσίδη at night: 'for if a man does it in the day-time and is
observed by the woodpecker while he is gathering the fruit, he risks
the loss of his eyesight, and if he is cutting the root at the time, he gets
prolapse of the anus'. Other stories follow about κενταυρίς, πάνακες,
ξίρις, μανδραγόρας, κύμινον and hellebore. In a spirit of restrained
piety he is prepared to acknowledge that 'there is perhaps nothing
absurd in offering a prayer when cutting a plant' (IX 8.7), but he ends
his discussion by repeating that these stories 'appear adventitious',
even though he adds that 'there are no other methods of cutting roots
except those we have specified', a remark which seems to imply that
the practices he has described were widespread if not universal.

Theophrastus evidently displays a considerable respect for the
potentially powerful properties of plants. The subject was one on
which, as he knew, exaggeration was rife. Yet it was, in his view, as
well not to reject stories about the potent effects of drugs too quickly.
Among those that he records without critical comment are one
relating to the 'deadly root' with which they smear their arrows in
Ethiopia (*HP* IX 15.2) and another about a styptic plant that grows in
Thrace that stops the flow of blood (IX 15.3). The Indian plants that
are said to disperse the blood or, in other cases, to collect it are,
however, described as 'most extraordinary' (περιττότατα), and he
adds 'if they tell the truth' (IX 15.2). Again the story about the
so-called 'scorpion-plant' which kills that animal if it is sprinkled on
him (though sprinkled with white hellebore he comes to life again) is
not dismissed out of hand. 'If these and suchlike are true, then other
similar stories are not incredible' (IX 18.2). Nor is Theophrastus being
entirely ironical, for he proceeds: 'even fabulous stories (τὰ μυθώδη)
are not composed without some reason'. The statement of that
principle suggests that Theophrastus's starting-point is to see if there
is not something in a story however unlikely it may seem. He is
prepared to believe that even fables and myths may contain a grain of
truth, even if much has to be rejected as 'adventitious', 'far-fetched' or
'absurd'.

The difficulties he faced in evaluating his sources were clearly
severe. If someone reported stories of the marvellous properties of
plants found in Ethiopia or India or Scythia, verifying these
presented formidable problems. How far afield Theophrastus himself
had travelled is not clear,[28] but even if he was able to check some
accounts from foreign lands by personal observation, there must have
been many other occasions when the best he could do was to check

---

[28] With Kirchner 1874a, pp. 462ff, Bretzl 1903, and Hort 1916, 1 pp. xix ff, compare
Regenbogen 1940, cols. 1358 and 1468.

one informant against another and use his judgement about their reliability. Even if he could discount stories of the woodpecker attacking those who collected a particular plant or of the sun selecting part of a crop to burn up as irrational, that did not get him very far.

Even with plants that were familiar enough in Greece, ascertaining their precise properties without any equivalent to chemical or biochemical analysis was highly problematic. The known powers of plants – of those used as poisons or common drugs especially – were sufficiently impressive to make it inadvisable to dismiss *all* the stories of the root-cutters and drug-sellers as exaggerated, even if many of them were and even if their possible motives for exaggeration were obvious enough. In particular Theophrastus was well aware that the effects of drugs depended upon a large number of factors. Even though it might well make no difference whether or not the person who collected a root left an offering for what he had taken, the season in which a root was lifted or fruit picked could evidently be as important as the correct time for sowing seed or harvesting corn. On what he realised to be a tricky issue, Theophrastus appreciated that different individuals may react differently to the same drug. Commenting on the phenomenon of individuals becoming immune to certain drugs in *HP* IX 17.1ff, he remarks that both their nature or constitution (φύσις) and the extent of their habituation (ἔθος) clearly contributed to the effect. At *HP* IX 19 he observes more generally that plants may have many different powers or properties and yet produce the same effect. The problem is a general one – to know whether what produces a particular effect is the same cause in each case or whether the same effect may result from a variety of different causes (IX 19.4). Yet having identified the difficulty, Theophrastus comments no further on it: nor is it clear how in practice he coped with it in his evaluation of particular plants.

In a field as obscure and difficult as the analysis of plant properties 'common sense' would not take one far. Theophrastus appeals from time to time to what he asserts is 'absurd' or 'foolish'. It may be that the main reason why he rejects stories about amulets (περίαπτα) and charms (ἀλεξιφάρμακα) for bodies and for houses (*HP* IX 19.2–3) is that he is convinced on general grounds that wearing a plant or attaching it to a house can have no such effect as is claimed: 'fair fame', εὐδοξία, is not the sort of thing that can be obtained by such a method. Yet as is well known,[29] scepticism about the efficacy of amulets was far from universal among Theophrastus's contempor-

---

[29] See, e.g., Deubner 1910, Stemplinger 1919, and cf. the brief discussion in Lloyd 1979, pp. 42ff. Cf. further below, p. 177.

aries or Greeks at any period: it was far from being the unanimous opinion even of those who prided themselves on being leading representatives of the medical art, including some highly literate individuals whose writings have come down to us. What is 'common sense', or as the Greeks more often put it what is 'likely' εἰκός, was, in general, subject to constant modification and negotiation, and what Theophrastus took to be such sometimes reflected merely the views of a comparatively small circle of his associates.

But if commonly accepted assumptions about what was plausible offered, in this domain, a very insecure basis for judgement, and if the general theoretical understanding of the properties of plants was of little use either (for neither talk of the hot, the cold, the wet and the dry, nor references to the main juices or humours, provided a very adequate foundation for the analysis of those properties), the main guide had, of course, to be experience. It was not so much what the root-cutters or drug-sellers said about their plants, as what happened when they were used in medical practice, that counted. But while Theophrastus was clearly in touch with individuals who claimed first-hand experience, including some who called themselves – and whom he called – doctors, ἰατροί, as well as with the root-cutters,[30] he was not himself a medical practitioner. Nor is there any evidence of his attempting to obtain direct evidence of the effects of drugs by carrying out tests on either men or animals,[31] although such tests were, from time to time, undertaken, usually on human subjects, in the ancient world.[32] Yet by referring to Hippocratic treatises, many of which were written not long before Theophrastus's own time or were even contemporary with him, we can see what some doctors, at least, believed on some aspects of this subject.

As we should expect, there is a very considerable overlap between the plant-drugs mentioned in Theophrastus and those referred to in our principal medical texts.[33] This is a question not just of the commonest drugs, such as hellebore, but of quite a number of other, rarer ones, even though Theophrastus includes many plants not mentioned in the Hippocratic Corpus, nor indeed in any other extant text before him. But two major, even fundamental, differences in the accounts of our two types of source stand out.

First Theophrastus – as is natural enough in view of his overall

---

[30] Though these were not necessarily exclusive categories: see above, p. 120.
[31] References to the alleged effects of drugs on animals are, however, not uncommon, see, e.g., *HP* IX 16.1.
[32] As is reported, for example, by Galen, K XIV 2.3ff, in relation to Mithridates.
[33] The chief studies of Hippocratic pharmacopoeia are those of Dierbach (1824) 1969, von Grot 1889, Stannard 1961, Goltz 1974 and Harig 1980.

concerns with the similarities and differences of plants – usually takes considerable trouble to specify precisely the plant he is referring to, describing it with some care, and noting, where necessary, both that the same name may be applied to different plants, and conversely that the same plant may be known by different names. The Hippocratic writers, by contrast, regularly *assume* that the plants they name will be well known to their audience or readers. Thus in his discussion of dittany in *HP* IX 16.1ff Theophrastus identifies three different kinds. True dittany, which is peculiar to Crete, is a rare plant: Theophrastus describes its leaf as like βληχώ ('pennyroyal', according to Hort[34]) though the twigs are slenderer. False dittany (ψευδοδίκταμνον) is like it in leaf but has smaller twigs and is far inferior to it in power, δύναμις. Some say, he goes on, that dittany and false dittany are the same plant, and that the false variety is simply the inferior form produced by being grown in richer soil. He does not himself pronounce on this, but he is confident that a third plant, again called dittany, has 'nothing in common with dittany except the name. It has neither the same appearance nor the same δύναμις [power or property]: it has a leaf like σισύμβριον ['bergamot-mint', Hort] and its twigs are larger.' Yet in the various references to the use of dittany in such treatises as *On the Nature of Woman, On the Diseases of Women* I, *On Sterile Women* and *On the Excision of the Foetus*,[35] there is never any description of the plant. 'False dittany' is mentioned once along with 'dittany',[36] and 'Cretan' dittany is specified several times:[37] but no attempt is made to distinguish the third of the varieties that Theophrastus mentions from the first two.

On such occasions it may be that the professional colleagues to whom the Hippocratic treatises are addressed knew exactly what was meant by 'dittany'. Certainly in the many references to hellebore in the Hippocratic Corpus there was often no need to specify when the black variety was intended or when the white. Yet it would clearly be rash to assume that the doctors always knew precisely which plant they were dealing with. Of the two main kinds of χαμαιλέων – where

---

[34] I include the identifications made by Hort, though many of these must be considered doubtful, and the confidence that – following Thiselton-Dyer – he showed in our ability to equate ancient plant-names with in many cases narrowly defined modern equivalents was, in general, misplaced (a point stressed by J.E. Raven in his unpublished 1976 Cambridge J.H. Gray lectures): compare the identifications suggested, for example, by Scarborough 1978.

[35] *Nat. Mul.* ch. 32, L VII 348.17 and 358.2, *Mul.* I ch. 46, L VIII 106.1, ch. 71, 150.18f, ch. 77, 170.11, 14, 172.9, ch. 78, 180.15f, 184.15, *Steril.* ch. 233, L VIII 448.3f, *Foet. Exsect.* ch. 4, L VIII 516.7f.

[36] *Nat. Mul.* ch. 32, L VII 358.2.

[37] *Nat. Mul.* ch. 32, L VII 348.17, *Mul.* I ch. 71, L VIII 150.18f, ch. 77, 172.9, ch. 78, 180.15f, *Steril.* ch. 233, L VIII 448.3f, *Foet. Exsect.* ch. 4, L VIII 516.7f.

Theophrastus, *HP* IX 12.1, notes that the appearance and the 'powers' of the roots are different – the author of *Wounds* specifies the black type,[38] but in *On the Nature of Woman* a prescription refers without further specification to the root of χαμαιλέων.[39] Where Theophrastus discusses at some length the different kinds of στρύχνος and of τιθύμαλλος,[40] prescriptions involving these two are common in the Hippocratic treatises, but with one exception they all leave the variety unspecified:[41] the exception is a text in *Fistulae* that refers to the 'big' τιθύμαλλος[42] (though that is not a term used of any of the three main kinds Theophrastus speaks of). Again where Theophrastus says that μηκώνιον is an alternative name for τιθύμαλλος (*HP* IX 8.2), some Hippocratic writers at least appear to refer to two different plants by these names.[43]

It is particularly striking that whereas according to Theophrastus two drachms, by weight, of the kind of στρύχνος he calls μανικός are enough to give a man delusions, three drachms drive him permanently insane, and a dose of four drachms kills him outright, the writer of the Hippocratic work *On Internal Affections* prescribes no less than half a cotyle (a cotyle being 0.226 of a litre or nearly half a pint) of the juice of στρύχνος, with a quarter of a cotyle of the honey and milk mixture called μελίκρητον, in water, with the yolk of a boiled chicken's egg, as a pain-killer to be taken daily.[44] If we base ourselves on Theophrastus's figures, even though a direct comparison between a liquid and a dry measure is difficult, it would seem that if the stronger kind of στρύχνος was used a dose of the size the Hippocratic writer specifies would be enough to kill more than just the pain.

Due allowances must be made for the different concerns of our two types of source. Theophrastus, as we have noted, has as one of his principal interests the varieties of plants: the Hippocratic writers concentrate exclusively on their medicinal use. Yet the problems of the confusion in the identification of plants that the text of Theophrastus reveals are almost entirely ignored by the Hippocratic authors. How much that reflects legitimate professional confidence in

---

[38] *Ulc.* ch. 15, L VI 418.13, ch. 17, 422.8.

[39] *Nat. Mul.* ch. 32, L VII 348.11.

[40] E.g. *HP* VII 15.4 and IX 11.5–9, and cf. VII 7.2.

[41] E.g. στρύχνος at *Ulc.* ch. 11, L VI 410.16, *Fist.* ch. 7, L VI 454.23, *Morb.* III ch. 1, L VII 118.14, *Nat. Mul.* ch. 29, L VII 344.14, ch. 34, 376.8, *Mul.* I ch. 78, L VIII 196.11 and 18, as well as *Int.* ch. 27, L VII 238.4, mentioned below. τιθύμαλ(λ)ος at *Acut. Sp.* ch. 38, L II 526.3f, *Aff.* ch. 38, L VI 248.5, *Nat. Mul.* ch. 32, L VII 364.5, ch. 33, 370.9f, *Mul.* I ch. 74, L VIII 160.17, ch. 81, 202.18, *Superf.* ch. 32, *CMG* I 2,2 90.28 (L VIII 500.21), cf. τιθυμαλλίς at *Int.* ch. 1, L VII 168.14, ch. 10, 190.17, *Superf.* ch. 28, *CMG* I 2,2 84.19 (L VIII 492.18).

[42] *Fist.* ch. 3, L VI 448.22.

[43] E.g. *Nat. Mul.* ch. 33, L VII 370.9 and 10, cf. 'white' μηκώνιον at *Fist.* ch. 7, L VI 456.2f.

[44] *Int.* ch. 27, L VII 238.3ff.

what they were doing, or how much it is a sign of an uncritical reliance on popular lore and terminology, we cannot know for sure: but there is obviously a distinct possibility that the Hippocratic authors sometimes seriously underestimated the problems or were even themselves misled, failing to distinguish sufficiently species that passed by the same name.

The second major difference between the accounts of plants in Theophrastus and in the Hippocratic writers concerns the inclusion of details of their use as charms, amulets and the like. As we have seen, Theophrastus provides us with a good deal of information about this as well as about popular practices in collecting plants aimed at insuring their effectiveness, and his attitude varies from the dismissive through the neutral to a cautious or limited acceptance. Although many of the same plants are mentioned quite frequently in Hippocratic pharmacological texts, these never mention, let alone recommend, their use as amulets.

Thus κυκλάμινος is an ingredient in a wide variety of prescriptions in *On the Diseases of Women* I and II, *On Superfetation* and *On the Nature of Woman*. In different texts it is recommended as a pessary for dropsy of the womb in pregnant women,[45] to draw down the menstrual blood,[46] to promote the lochial discharge,[47] and as an ingredient in an infusion for peripneumonia.[48] Theophrastus, for his part, notes the use in pessaries (*HP* IX 9.3), adds that the root is applied to suppurating inflammations, but then goes on to mention the view that the root is also good as an amulet (περίαπτον) to promote delivery and for 'potions', φίλτρα, presumably primarily love-potions. Theophrastus does not comment on these uses himself, but so far as our Hippocratic texts go, we would never have known that there were such beliefs at all.

The peony known as γλυκυσίδη is recommended to be taken internally, usually in wine or water, and either on its own or with other ingredients, in a further set of texts in the gynaecological works,[49] where there is no mention of the popular belief recorded by Theophrastus (which we have quoted above, p. 124) that it should be dug up at night – lest the woodpecker see you.

---

[45] *Mul.* I ch. 60, L VIII 120.17f, cf. also ch. 81, 202.11ff, ch. 84, 206.16, and cf. *Mul.* II ch. 175, L VIII 358.3.

[46] *Mul.* I ch. 74, L VIII 154.19.

[47] *Nat. Mul.* ch. 9, L VII 324.15, cf. also ch. 6, 320.16, ch. 32, 362.16f, ch. 35, 378.11, ch. 36, 380.1, ch. 42, 386.10, ch. 92, 410.7.

[48] *Morb.* II ch. 47, L VII 68.2. For other uses cf., e.g., *Mul.* II ch. 155, L VIII 330.15, ch. 157, 334.3, ch. 162, 340.5, ch. 165, 344.7, ch. 205, 396.13f, ch. 207, 402.11, ch. 208, 406.3.

[49] E.g. *Nat. Mul.* ch. 6, L VII 320.9, ch. 8, 324.2, ch. 25, 342.14, ch. 32, 350.6, 352.7, 10, 17–18, 358.7, 10, 18, 360.1, and from outside the gynaecological works, e.g. *Int.* ch. 40, L VII 266.9.

The stories concerning γλυκυσίδη are included in the group that Theophrastus considers 'far-fetched', but those about θαψία – about standing to windward and anointing your body with oil before cutting the plant, *HP* IX 8.5f, above, p. 123, cf. also *HP* IX 9.1 and 5f, and IX 20.3 – are thought possibly to be 'not off the point'. Θαψίη too frequently figures in Hippocratic recipes for evacuants, clysters and emetics, without any reference to the dangers involved in collecting it.[50] An even more famous case is that of μανδραγόρας, for this too is recommended both as a pessary and as a clyster in the gynaecological works[51] and in more general therapeutics. Thus in *On Diseases* II ch. 43 (L VII 60.10f) there is a prescription for the treatment of quartan fever involving ὑοσκύαμος, an equal quantity of mandragora, and other ingredients, to be taken in neat wine. More startlingly, *On the Places in Man* ch. 39 (L VI 328.17 and 19) describes a treatment for those who are 'in pain and sick and wanting to strangle themselves' as follows: 'make them drink early in the morning the root of mandragora in a dose less than is enough to send them mad'. The author repeats this prescription, along with a recommendation to light a fire on either side of the patient's bed, to cure spasm. On the other hand no Hippocratic text says that to cut the plant one should draw three circles round it with a sword, face the west, and at the cutting of the second piece dance round the plant and say as much as possible about τὰ ἀφροδίσια (HP IX 8.8, among the 'adventitious' stories). At *HP* IX 9.1 Theophrastus further records views concerning the medicinal uses of the plant, including several for which no parallel can be given in the Hippocratic Corpus, and adds that the root was applied πρὸς φίλτρα, in love potions.

My final example can be used to illustrate both the main differences I have referred to between Theophrastus and the Hippocratic writers. A plant called πάνακες figures from time to time in the prescriptions recorded in *On the Nature of Woman* and *On the Diseases of Women* II. In the former, ch. 32, L VII 350.5, it is an ingredient in a recipe to help draw down the menstrual discharge, and at 358.7 it is one of a long list the writer says can be used 'as you like', 'on their own or mixed', 'in water or in wine': they are good for the womb. Again scrapings of πάνακες are included in a recipe for a fumigation in ch. 34, L VII 372.13ff. In *On the Diseases of Women* II πάνακες is used in another prescription for pains in the womb (ch.

---

[50] E.g. *Morb.* III ch. 8, L VII 128.1, ch. 15, 140.22, ch. 16, 146.17, *Int.* ch. 18, L VII 210.21, ch. 42, 272.15, *Nat. Mul.* ch. 33, L VII 368.19, *Mul.* I ch. 78, L VIII 192.6, 194.17f, ch. 92, 222.1, ch. 109, 230.15, *Mul.* II ch. 118, L VIII 256.17, ch. 119, 260.7, *Superf.* chh. 32f, *CMG* I 2,2 90.27, 92.4 (L VIII 500.21, 26), *Epid.* VII ch. 79, L V 436.2f.

[51] *Mul.* I ch. 74, L VIII 160.12 and 15, ch. 80, 202.1, *Mul.* II ch. 199, L VIII 382.6.

206, L VIII 400.17) and again with other plants for 'hysterical' displacement of the womb (ch. 201, 386.1 and 6).[52]

Yet in Theophrastus several different varieties of πάνακες are distinguished. In addition to the variety found in Syria, described in *HP* IX 9.2, there are τὸ Χειρώνειον, τὸ 'Ασκληπίειον and τὸ 'Ηράκλειον, each of which is described in some detail in IX 11.1–3, and the following section, 11.4, adds two further kinds, one with a fine leaf and one without. The properties of these last two kinds are said to be the same (they are good for sores and as pessaries for women), but the others differ quite markedly. It may be that the Hippocratic doctors were in no doubt about which 'all-heal' they were referring to, but it is clearly possible that there was some confusion in their minds, as also in those of their patients. Moreover at *HP* IX 8.7 Theophrastus records the practice of leaving an offering of fruits and a honey-cake when cutting the 'Ασκληπίειον variety of the plant, but there is no hint of this in our Hippocratic authors.

The lack of any references whatsoever in our Hippocratic pharmacological texts to special practices in collecting certain herbs, or to their use in charms or amulets, might be taken at first sight as testimony to the hard-headed rationalism of the authors concerned. Where Theophrastus records a number of folk beliefs and superstitions, criticising some of them as far-fetched, but reserving judgement cautiously about a number of others, the Hippocratic writers do not even deign to mention them. Yet the situation is more complex than that, since even though the Hippocratic writers do not refer to folk beliefs, their existence may well have made a difference to the expectations of their patients and to the popularity of certain drugs.

The omission of references to special rites or prayers when using particular plants is, to be sure, in line with the rationalist tendencies that are prominent in a number of Hippocratic works and that are made explicit in the polemic against superstitious beliefs and practices in *On the Sacred Disease*. Consciously or otherwise, many Hippocratic writers often adopted a stance on these issues that was in certain respects at least in marked contrast to the practice of temple-medicine, let alone to that of itinerant sellers of charms and purifications.[53] Yet that did not prevent there being an important overlap between the competing strands of medicine, both in that temple-medicine used naturalistic[54] methods as well as supernaturalistic ones, and in that the Hippocratic authors, for their part, showed

---

[52] On this belief in the womb wandering around the body, see above, p. 84 and n. 100.

[53] Cf. Lloyd 1979, pp. 37–49.

[54] That is what the Hippocratic authors themselves would have accepted as such.

different degrees of readiness to endorse, for example, the belief in the diagnostic value of dreams. Meanwhile the whole vocabulary of drugs and spells (φάρμακον could refer to both) and that of purges and purifications (κάθαρσις, καθαρμός) were systematically ambiguous and were available for use – in different acceptances – by both the main rival strands of medicine. No doubt some of the clients in view in the Hippocratic pharmacological writings would expect their authors to maintain the hard-headed rationalist stance that some of the polemical treatises adopt. At the same time when we ask why it is that some of these plant substances are used at all, or why used in the particular way recommended, in some cases a full answer will have to include reference to the folklore surrounding them.[55]

There is no evidence to suggest that any of the Hippocratic authors we have been considering deliberately set out to exploit the gullibility of their clientèle. In many cases the plants that were popularly assumed to have special therapeutic properties were indeed effective, that is that over and above any psychological aspects of the treatment (including the workings of suggestion or auto-suggestion)[56], they had a distinct organic action. It is true that the active ingredient among a combination of medicines was not necessarily correctly identified by the ancients: thus it has been suggested that where μανδραγόρας had a reputation of being a pain-killer, that property belongs rather to ὑοσκύαμος with which it was often used.[57] Nor, as we have already noted, did the Hippocratics, Theophrastus or anyone else have any satisfactory framework within which to advance a theoretical explanation of the effects that were observed.

On some occasions, however, the Hippocratic writers appear to persist in treatment that we have no reason to believe had any organic effect at all – certainly not that claimed for it – and, where such treatment corresponds to an already ingrained popular assumption, that may well provide one and the chief factor in its continued use also in the rationalist tradition (even though that use may be purified by the omission of certain ritual embellishments). When the writer of *On*

---

[55] The mystical and mythological associations of plants can be followed up in, for example, Murr 1890.

[56] Any treatment that was thought by those who received it to be *appropriate* might have a comforting or reassuring effect. What 'worked' or what was 'efficacious' from the patients' point of view certainly included what *they* found – for whatever reason, including for whatever symbolic or affective reason – to be reassuring.

[57] The two are used together at *Morb.* II ch. 43, L VII 60.10f, see above, p. 130. On the pain-killing properties of μανδραγόρας see Pliny, *HN* xxv 150 and Dioscorides IV 75, W II 233.11ff, 235.6ff, 237.8ff. I owe this example to J.E. Raven's 1976 Gray lectures, quoting a suggestion made to Mr Raven by Dr Betty Jackson: cf. Randolph 1904–5, Staub 1962, Jackson and Berry 1973.

the Diseases of Women II ch. 201 prescribes 'all-heal' for displacement of the womb, it can hardly be because the wombs of patients so treated did indeed return to their proper position. When 'all-heal' and γλυκυσίδη are named as remedies that are good for the womb, to be used 'as you like', 'on their own or mixed', 'in water or in wine', in *On the Nature of Woman* ch. 32, the indeterminacy of this recommendation may suggest that the author himself is none too confident of how to apply them – in which case the popular reputation of 'all-heal' and the association of γλυκυσίδη with stories that suggested its mystical properties (as in *HP* IX 8.6, above, p. 124) may be what chiefly weighed with the patients, if not also with the doctor who used them. Just as the plant called ἀριστολοχία, 'birth-wort' or more literally 'best-birth', started, as it were, with an automatic advantage as a remedy to facilitate child-birth,[58] so when θαψία, κυκλάμινος and μανδραγόρας figure in Hippocratic prescriptions *some* of those who knew the beliefs and practices associated with them would have registered those associations even in the absence of any references to them by the Hippocratic doctor. While those authors eschew, as we said, any allusion to the sacred or the mystical in this context, they did not entirely forgo the use of plants that were connected with ritual practices, charms and spells (and indeed to have done so would have been to deprive themselves of some powerful remedies). Just as the ambiguity in certain medical terminology is exploited by both religious and rationalist practitioners, so there was a good deal of common ground between them in the *materia medica* they employed, even though the style of that employment varied, the rationalists ignoring – what the temple doctors and the itinerant purifiers would have insisted on – the ritual correctness of the use.

The strengths of the account of plants in Theophrastus and the Hippocratic Corpus differ and each approach has its corresponding weakness. Theophrastus clearly attempts a far more comprehensive study, while insisting on the need for further research, and he is fully aware of the complexities of plant identification. He does not merely record many folk traditions concerning the use of plants, but is prepared to take some of them seriously. But his admirable openness occasionally tips over into uncritical or naive acceptance, and his reserving judgement becomes the expression of a bafflement that he was unlikely to be able to resolve.

---

[58] We may leave open the question of how far the plant acquired the name because it had indeed proved effective as a remedy. The idea was later much elaborated in the medieval doctrine of 'signatures', see, e.g., Arber 1938, ch. 8.

The Hippocratic pharmacologists are rigorously rationalistic, yet unconcerned, even careless, on the problems of plant identification that Theophrastus was to explore and reveal. Theirs was the chief clinical experience that had to be relied on to distinguish fact from fantasy in traditional, or any other, beliefs about plants as medicines.[59] Yet here the quality of their work can be described as at best uneven. Lacking a sound theoretical basis for their pharmacopoeia, they had to depend on observation of what worked. But, within the rationalist framework they adopted, their claims were extraordinarily catholic, even indiscriminate, as well as often highly dogmatic, and in many cases they may well owe more to tradition, including folklore, than to the writer's own direct experience.

The very variety of remedies stated to be effective for particular complaints ends by proving self-defeating, bewildering the doctor or patient at a loss to know which treatment to prefer. Such clinical experience as these writers had – and in some cases it may well have been quite rich and varied[60] – was not organised, or at least it was not recorded, in such a way as to maximise the chances of advancing understanding, by introducing controls or otherwise trying deliberately to determine which substances were effective for what. The preference for compound drugs rather than simple ones exacerbates the problem, making the identification of any active ingredient that much more difficult.[61]

Not engaged in medical practice himself, and not concerned with the problem of a relationship with a clientèle, Theophrastus could afford to pay more attention than the Hippocratic pharmacologists did to certain popular beliefs and practices. They had, while Theophrastus did not, a professional reason to wish to distance themselves from other types of healer. But while the implicit contrasts between the Hippocratic authors and some of the root-cutters referred to by Theophrastus are strongly marked, they are often more a matter of presentation than of substance. The techniques of persuasion that the Hippocratic pharmacologists deploy do not include the mystification with which the root-cutters sometimes surrounded their remedies – though that is not to deny that there are

---

[59] As we have noted in another context, p. 81 n. 79, the Hippocratic authors suggest, from time to time, that a prescription should be chosen or modified in the light of how the particular patient responds.

[60] Many of our pharmacological texts come at the end of gynaecological treatises that elsewhere display considerable knowledge and some originality in the treatment of women: see above, Part II, pp. 62ff.

[61] This is so, even before we take into account the belief that we find in a later writer such as Pliny (*HN* xxii 106), that the 'sympathies' and 'antipathies' of plants must also be taken into account when dealing with compound drugs.

large elements of bluff or wishful thinking in the prescriptions they put forward. Yet the plants they both used were very often the same: nor were the Hippocratic writers necessarily much or at all more methodical or systematic in their research, in this context, than their rivals.

3. PLINY, LEARNING AND RESEARCH

One of the central problems that we raised in relation to work done in the life sciences after the fourth century B.C. concerns the extent to which it was guided by the methodological principles set out by Aristotle and Theophrastus. How far did later writers endorse those principles in theory and to what extent did they implement them in practice? How far were they able to respond positively to the frequent calls for further investigation made by their predecessors or what were the factors inhibiting such a response? One author who affords a particularly good opportunity to consider aspects of this problem is Pliny, whose encyclopedic *Natural History* is one of the fullest sources, after the works of Aristotle and Theophrastus themselves, to deal with a whole range of zoological and botanical subjects. It is true that the *Natural History* has a very mixed reputation: it is well known that it contains a wide, at times wild, assortment of ideas, many of them drawing on or merely reproducing traditional or popular beliefs, even myths or folktales. It is these features of his work that have led to his comparative neglect in modern studies of ancient science.[62] For our purposes, however, in our pursuit of aspects of the interaction of science and folklore in the ancient world, this makes him a more, rather than less, valuable subject of inquiry.

Pliny sets out the purpose of his work and describes his methods in the Preface to book 1. No Greek or Roman writer, he claims (Pref. 12ff) has tackled the whole of the subject, the entire ἐγκύκλιος παιδεία, which he aims to treat. He goes on (Pref. 17) to give the figure of 2,000 volumes that he has read, and observing that when collating authorities he has found that 'even the most professedly reliable and most recent writers have copied the old authors word for word without acknowledgement' (Pref. 22) he proceeds to name the authorities he says he has used for each of the books of his own work that is to follow.[63] The list is a catholic one, with 'Orpheus' and

---

[62] On this point see Stannard 1965 and cf. also Lenoble 1952 and André 1955.

[63] Although Pliny thereby covers himself in general terms with his list of *auctores* in book 1, that does not reveal how closely he has sometimes followed them. Nor is his borrowing always acknowledged other than generally in the listing of his authorities in book 1. See further below, pp. 142–4, on dittany, especially.

'Pythagoras' rubbing shoulders with Aristotle and Theophrastus, and including Homer, Hesiod, Aeschylus, Sophocles and Virgil, and a variety of sometimes merely honorific royal authorities (among them Archelaus, Hiero, Attalus Philometor, Juba, Augustus, Claudius and Agrippina). Other figures too appear, such as some of the earlier Presocratics, Thales, Anaximander and Anaximenes, where Pliny has certainly not had access to an original book, but at most to anthologised excerpts or collections of Physical Opinions.

The overwhelmingly literary character of his investigations is thus clear from the outset. Pliny is indeed explicit that one of his chief tasks is to preserve and publicise the knowledge that had been gained in the past, in his time, he claims, much neglected. In *HN* xxv 1ff, discussing the knowledge of plants in particular, he criticises his contemporaries for being secretive about ancient discoveries, and complains that they try to hide and keep these things to themselves and are unwilling to teach anyone what they have learned (2 and 16).

At the same time, on his own account at least, his research has not been wholly literary in nature. First there is his general allegiance to the value of experience. He repeatedly compares the present unfavourably with the past and one of the respects in which he does so is in the lack of energy, care and industry shown by his contemporaries in finding out useful knowledge. Individuals who made particular discoveries in the past or who were especially comprehensive and diligent in their researches are praised, ranging from Aristotle in zoology (vIII 43f) to Mithridates, who besides discovering how to immunise himself against poisons by habituating his body to them also found out a number of antidotes and is said to have been particularly interested in medicine (*medicinae curiosus*) and to have sought out detailed knowledge from all his subjects (xxv 5ff).

His Greek predecessors are sometimes criticised on moral grounds – for describing harmful plants, including abortifacients for example (xxv 24f) – and he attacks the whole medical profession not just for profiteering but for 'making experiments at the cost of our lives' (xxIx 18). More often, however, his theme is the care and industry of the inquiries that past investigators had carried out. At xIv 2ff the contrast is a general one between the industrious past and the idle present. At xxIII 112 he says it is impossible sufficiently to admire the care and diligence of ancient inquirers who have 'explored everything and left nothing untried'.[64] At xxv 1 in his treatment of

---

[64] Similarly also at xxvII 1 and 4. Admiration of the ancients' research is sometimes combined with the idea that their discoveries are attributable to the gods, to Nature and to Chance, e.g. xxvII 1ff, cf. xxv 16.

plants, the men of old are again praised for their care and diligence and for leaving nothing untried or unattempted, and at XVII 42, in connection with a discussion of soils, the Greeks are complimented in similar terms for leaving nothing untested.

On several occasions a contrast is drawn between mere book-learning and actual experience. At XVIII 205 he mentions the disagreements between on the one hand the countrymen (*rustici*) and on the other the 'literary, not just astronomical, experts' (*litterarum expertes, non modo siderum*) on the question of the proper time of sowing. More impressively, in his account of the early history of medicine in XXVI 10 f, he remarks on the decline that set in when experience (*usus*), the most efficient teacher of all things and especially in medicine,[65] degenerated into words and garrulity: 'for it was more pleasant to sit in schools engaged in listening than to go out into the wilds and search for the different kinds of plants at the different times of the year' (XXVI 11).[66] Nevertheless he also acknowledges elsewhere (II 117) that in his day a person might learn some things about his own region more accurately from the handbooks (*commentaria*) composed by people who had never visited it, than from the actual inhabitants themselves.

Some of this obviously has a rather general ring and the praise of the past in particular is a rhetorical commonplace. But Pliny sometimes provides us with more direct evidence of his own personal involvement in inquiry and research. It is true that when he refers to what he has found – *invenio, reperio* – that is not, or not usually, a matter of his personal observation, but of what he has found in his literary authorities. This becomes clear when the phrase 'apud auctores' is added (as often, e.g. XX 215, XXII 11, XXIII 141, XXVIII 65, 151), even though 'auctor' by itself may, of course, refer to any authority, written or oral. Such an addition does not so much contrast these cases with others, where autopsy is involved, as make explicit what is left implicit elsewhere. On the other hand Pliny sometimes tells us what he has ascertained where he says he has drawn a blank among the 'auctores'. He does so, for example, at XXI 74, where he says that the authorities do not say from what flowers poisonous honey comes, though he does not there specify further what his own

---

[65] Again elsewhere, XXXIV 108, he implies a criticism of doctors who relied on druggists' shops rather than preparing and making up their own drugs (an interesting observation in the light of our study of the relationship between the Hippocratics and the drug-sellers in the fourth century B.C., above, Section 2).

[66] Compare Dioscorides's contrast between αὐτοψία, first-hand observation, and ἡ ἐκ παρακουσμάτων ἱστορία, inquiry based on (inaccurate) hearsay, Proem 3, W 1 2.10f, cf. Proem 4f, 1 2.16ff, 3.6ff.

source of information was: nor is his account more than a brief identification of a single noxious plant which he claims is responsible when the blossoms wither in a rainy spring.[67] In other passages he records what personal informants have told him, for example on his travels, as at xxv 18f where he tells us what he learnt in Spain of what had recently been discovered 'on the land of my host' concerning the plant dracunculus. While his source here is not literary, he is still not reporting his own observations: nor does what he claims about the plant suggest that his informants, in this case, were particularly reliable. They told him that the plant was a remedy for the bites of all creatures, that it grows to a height of about two feet when snakes are about to slough their skins and then buries itself in the ground when the snakes also do so.

From time to time, however, Pliny intervenes in his account of what he has learnt from one or other of his sources with a remark about what he has himself seen. Although when the verb 'video' is used it need not mean more than understand or realise (as at ix 136 or xi 57), it more often suggests a claim to personal inspection.[68] Thus at xxxii 154 'vidi' records the fact that he saw a 'hyena-fish' caught on the island of Aenaria.[69] Elsewhere we are given a rather more circumstantial description, as at xxxi 60 of cases of men whom Pliny says he has seen who had become quite swollen from the quantities of medicinal waters they had drunk (the rings on their fingers had become quite covered with skin) and at xxix 53 where he interrupts his account of the stories that the Druids and the Magi ('clever at wrapping up their frauds') have put about concerning snakes' eggs with a brief description of one which he says he has seen (like a round apple of medium size, pitted with hollows like those on the tentacles of an octopus).

Often what Pliny thereby claims to have observed is some strange or exceptional object or event, as for instance what we call St Elmo's fire, at ii 101, or the bodies of dwarfs which he has seen in their coffins (vii 75) or turnips weighing more than 40 pounds (xviii 128) or

---

[67] Cf. xxxii 154. But in other cases where he remarks that his *auctores* do not help him, he himself is unable to supply the lacuna, e.g. xxiv 177, xxvii 39, 102–3, 141, xxx 103.

[68] At xxvii 99 'vidi' explains the limits of Pliny's observation. The *auctores* say that lithospermon lies over and spreads across the ground: 'I have seen it only when gathered.' Elsewhere, e.g. xiii 83, 'vidi' is used to report Pliny's personal inspection of a written document, cf. his citations of inscriptions and other documentary evidence at, e.g., iii 136, vii 97.

[69] Cf. xxv 98 where he reports what fishermen in Campania have done in his presence – *coram nobis*: they took the root of one kind of aristolochia and scattered it over the sea crushed and mixed with lime. The fish, he goes on to claim, rush to it with extraordinary greed and forthwith die and float to the surface.

napkins made of 'non-inflammable linen' (asbestos) (XIX 19).[70] On
the one hand it is natural that Pliny should feel the need to specify that
he can personally verify the striking phenomenon to which he refers:
but on the other we may contrast the frequency of his claims to
personal observation in the case of *mirabilia* with the comparative
absence of references to sustained or systematic researches into more
mundane problems in natural philosophy.

On several occasions he reports findings or developments of the
quite recent past, sometimes contrasting this with what can or cannot
be found in his authorities – as at XIX 81 on a new type of radish (not
described in his sources) – or specifying the *terminus post quem* of a
development (as at XVIII 317 concerning improvements to wine-
presses made in the last twenty-two years, or at XVIII 55 on a type of
millet introduced into Italy from India within the last ten years). The
two most notable such references are at XVIII 209 and XXVI 5, both
relating to the 'very same year' in which he was composing the work
i.e. the book in question. In the first he says that in that year batches of
newly hatched butterflies had been wiped out three times by cold
weather,[71] and that the hope of spring brought by migratory birds
arriving at the end of January had been dashed by spells of wintry
weather, and in the second he reports with some detail how two men
of consular rank whom he names had died from carbuncles.

In connection with his account of plants in XXV in particular, he
makes a notable general claim for personal inspection. He first
contrasts the different approaches adopted by earlier writers, some of
whom included pictorial representations of plants in their work, while
others gave only a verbal description (XXV 8f). Some were satisfied
with merely naming the plants 'since it seemed sufficient to point out
their powers and strength to those willing to seek them out'. 'Nor', he
continues, 'is this knowledge difficult. We at least have had the good
fortune to examine all but a very few plants thanks to the learned help
of Antonius Castor, the highest authority in this subject of our
time – by visiting his little garden (*hortulo*)[72] in which he grew a great
number of plants' (XXV 9). Several features of this passage are

---

[70] There are further notable claims for personal knowledge at, for example, XVIII 160 (cf. XXV
16) where he says he knows that flights of starlings or sparrows can be driven away from
fields of millet by burying a plant at the four corners of the field – even though he does not
know the name of the plant in question – and at XVI 64 where he reports what he has himself
tried out (*experti prodimus*) that if a snake is near a fire and a ring of ashleaves is put round the
snake, it will go towards the fire rather than towards the leaves.

[71] He mentions this in refutation of the belief that butterflies are a reliable indication of the
beginning of spring.

[72] Jones, ad loc., suggests that the diminutive here does not mean 'little garden', but 'seems to
suggest that the *hortulus* was Castor's favourite hobby'. He translates 'his special garden'.

remarkable. The actual extent of Antonius Castor's collection is left vague,[73] and the claim that Pliny had been able to examine 'all but a very few plants' (*exceptis admodum paucis*) is, no doubt, extravagant. It is notable, too, that Pliny's words suggest that he was given guided tours by Antonius Castor, not that he undertook any independent research himself in this proto-botanical garden. Nevertheless, whatever the exaggerations it contains, the passage shows clearly enough Pliny's adherence to the principle of the need, or at least the value, of personal inspection. In another field of inquiry, his curiosity is one factor mentioned by his nephew in the account of the famous incident of the observation of the eruption of Vesuvius that ended in Pliny's death.[74]

Thus although Pliny's own position is different from that of his great predecessors, in part simply because he feels it to be one of his chief obligations to preserve and transmit what they had discovered, he professes broad support for similar methods and ideals, attaching importance to personal observation and noting, on occasion, the need for further work.[75] But we must now press further our investigation of his actual practice, to try to determine how far he lived up to those ideals or to what extent his claimed adherence to them is a merely conventionalised stance. It does not inspire confidence that on a number of related topics there is a marked disparity between some of his explicit general pronouncements and his detailed discussions. Both 'astrology' and 'magic' are firmly and explicitly rejected in principle, but many astrological beliefs and magical practices are recorded without critical comment and some are actually endorsed by Pliny.[76] Our chief concern here, however, is more generally with

---

[73] Castor is, however, named in book I among the authorities for each of the books xx to xxvII and is further cited on a number of occasions in those books, e.g. xx 174 and 261.

[74] Pliny the Younger, *Ep.* vi 16. According to this account, which is based on what the nephew himself claims to have seen as well as on what he describes as reliable sources (in part, presumably, from among the survivors), Pliny, who happened to be in command of the fleet at nearby Misenum at the beginning of the eruption, was motivated both by curiosity and by a desire to help those who were trapped. His first plan was to sail to the area in a fast vessel (*liburnica*) and it was only when he received word asking for help that he ordered the quadriremes to take him in. His nephew refers not just to Pliny's calm and courage throughout the confused episodes of the next day and night (though the nephew himself was certainly not there to see this) but also to his interest in what he observed and his desire to record it as an eyewitness.

[75] E.g. *HN* xxv 15ff.

[76] Thus at II 28 he rejects the belief that the fate of individual human beings is linked to a star; yet he accepts nevertheless that planets have healthy or unhealthy natures (II 34ff), that each star has its own natural effect (II 105ff) and that there are danger periods in the conjunctions or other positions of the heavenly bodies (e.g. xvIII 280–9). He rejects genethlialogy, but still has a deep-seated positive belief in the influence of the heavenly bodies on what happens on earth, not just on the seasons and tides, but also on detailed and particular physical changes, this influence being interpreted as a 'natural' one. Again the

the character of his contribution to the different branches of the inquiry concerning nature that he discusses at considerable length.

The botanical books provide perhaps our best opportunity to compare his theory and practice, not only because of the claims he makes for his study with Antonius Castor, but also because we are in a good position to compare Pliny's discussion with that of some, at least, of the earlier authorities in this field, notably Theophrastus himself. Theophrastus, to be sure, is a special case. It would have been quite negligent for any later writer on botanical topics to have ignored his work. Pliny duly cites him in book I as one of a large number of authorities he has consulted for the material in books XII to XXVII and he actually names him as his source some fifteen times in those books. Yet these references do not reveal either the extent to which he has drawn on Theophrastus or the character of his debts.

In XXV 26, for instance, he describes the plant moly as follows: *radice rotunda nigraque magnitudine cepae, folio scillae, effodi autem haud[77] difficulter*. This is what Theophrastus had said (*HP* IX 15.7): τὴν μὲν ῥίζαν ἔχον στρογγύλην προσεμφερῆ κρομύῳ, τὸ δὲ φύλλον ὅμοιον σκίλλ . . . οὐ μὴν ὀρύττειν γ᾽ εἶναι χαλεπόν. Now as we have noted before,[78] the identification of individual plants, whether in Greek or in Latin, is often problematic. But we can be pretty sure that *cepa* is Pliny's equivalent to κρόμυον, and that *scilla* is to σκίλλη. There is this difference between the two accounts, that in Pliny the comparison with an onion is in size, whereas in Theophrastus the root of moly as such is compared with the onion. But otherwise the two accounts are practically identical.[79]

Moly is, to be sure, an exceptional case, famous from the reference to it in Homer. Pliny also introduces his account with the term 'tradunt' which shows that he is drawing on an authority or

ways of the Magi are severely condemned in a number of set-piece passages, especially in the account of the development of their ideas in XXX and cf. XXVI 18ff). Yet while Pliny often scoffs at their beliefs and practices (as at other people's superstitions generally, cf. e.g., XVI 251 on the Druids) and is aware of the problem of charlatanry, he reports the views of the Magi extensively, and sometimes without any critical comment, e.g. XX 74, XXI 66, 166, XXII 61, XXIV 72, XXVIII 215, 226, XXXII 34: cf. Green 1954. It is particularly notable that he takes the trouble to record practices that are supposed to 'render the arts of the Magi vain' (XXVIII 85, and cf. also 104) – not something that would be necessary if they were all empty fictions. Moreover as we have already noted (p. 136) it is not only the Magi whom Pliny criticises, but the whole of the medical profession, castigating them especially, though not solely, for their avarice (e.g. XXIX 1ff and 14ff citing Cato).

[77] 'Haud' has, indeed, been restored to the text of Pliny by Sillig on the basis of the parallel passage in Theophrastus.

[78] See above, p. 127 n. 34. The problem of the identification of 'moly' in particular has been the subject of a detailed investigation by Stannard 1962.

[79] Pliny, *HN* XXV 26 also has the point that moly grows around Pheneus and on Cyllene, as at Theophrastus, *HP* IX 15.7.

authorities. But he is equally close to Theophrastus in many other cases too. At *HN* xxv 48 black hellebore is said to kill 'horses, oxen and pigs', who all avoid it, precisely as we had been told by Theophrastus at *HP* ix 10.2. Pliny proceeds 'but they eat the white kind', where Theophrastus says that τὰ πρόβατα do, and Pliny then gives a list of the places where the two kinds grow best, the black at Helicon, the white at Oeta around the place called Pyra, secondly at Pontus, thirdly at Elea and fourthly at Parnassus. Though in Theophrastus, *HP* ix 10.2f, the fourth place for white hellebore is Malea or Massalia,[80] the accounts are otherwise in exact agreement. The detail that in Elea the white hellebore grows in vineyards is in both *HP* ix 10.3 and *HN* xxv 49 (with 'ferunt', they say) and the reference to Parnassus in Pliny, where he says the hellebore is adulterated from the neighbouring country of Aetolia, may be a reminiscence of a different point about the Parnassian and Aetolian hellebore in Theophrastus *HP* ix10.4.[81]

The paragraphs devoted to dittany in Pliny are perhaps an especially clear example. At *HN* xxv 92 Pliny is discussing the plants whose properties have been discovered by animals. Dittany, he appears to say, was pointed out to men by deer: when, wounded, they fed on it, their weapons at once fell out. What Theophrastus had said at *HP* ix 16 was that 'they say that it is true about the weapons, that when the goats who have been shot with arrows eat it [dittany] the arrows fall out'.[82] It is rather in what follows in Pliny that the parallelisms come out. I set out the rest of Pliny's account at *HN* xxv 92–4.

Pliny (*HN* xxv 92)	Theophrastus (*HP* ix 16)
The plant grows nowhere except in Crete	Dittany is peculiar to Crete (16.1)
with branches that are very slender	the twigs are slenderer (than βληχώ)
it resembles *puleium* (Jones: pennyroyal)	it is like βληχώ (Hort: pennyroyal)
and is burning and harsh to the taste	cf. 16.2: taken in the mouth it has a violent heating effect
Only the leaves are employed	They use the leaves, not the twigs nor the fruit
It has no flower, no seed and no stem: its root is slender and without medicinal value	(not in Theophrastus)

[80] μαλιώτης is a conjecture of Hahnemann (for μασσαλιώτης) on the basis of Strabo ix 3.3.

[81] Theophrastus had there said that the hellebore of Parnassus and that of Aetolia (which men buy and sell 'not knowing the difference') are tough and very harsh.

[82] At Pliny, *HN* xxv 92 there appears to be no reference to goats, though the text of the beginning of the chapter is corrupt. At Theophrastus, *HP* ix 16.1 αἴγεσι must, on the text as we have it, be understood with φαγούσαις.

Even in Crete it does not grow widely	It is a scarce plant
and the goats are wonderfully eager to hunt it out	The goats graze it down because they are fond of it
A substitute for it is false dittany	(At 16.2 Theophrastus turns to false dittany)
which grows in many lands	(not in Theophrastus)
like true dittany in leaf, but with smaller branches	False dittany is like it in leaf, but has smaller twigs
and called by some *chondris*	(not in Theophrastus)
It is recognised at once, as its properties are less potent	In potency it is far inferior
for the smallest quantity of true dittany, taken in drink, burns the mouth	The power of dittany is perceived directly it is taken into the mouth: for a small piece of it has a violent heating effect
Those who gather them store them in a piece of fennel-giant or reed	The bunches of it are put in the hollow stem of ferula or a reed
which they tie up at the ends	(not in Theophrastus)
to prevent their power from vanishing	so that it may not exhale its power
There are some who say that both plants grow in many places	(not in Theophrastus, who reports that some say true and false dittany are the same plant)
but that while the inferior kinds are found on rich soils, true dittany is only seen on rough ground	but that the latter [false dittany] is an inferior form produced by growing on places with richer soil ... for [true] dittany loves rough ground
There is also a third plant called dittany	(3) There is another plant called dittany
unlike the others in appearance and properties	This has neither the same appearance nor the same power/property
The leaves are those of *sisymbrium* and the branches are larger	For the leaf is like σισύμβριον and its twigs are larger
Pliny then goes on directly to say that:	Cf. 16.3.
'There is the established conviction that whatever simple grows in Crete is infinitely superior to any of the same kind to be found elsewhere'	'Some say that the plants of Crete are superior in leaves, boughs and in general all the parts above ground to those in other places.
'and that the next best herbs are those to be found on Mount Parnassus'	While those of Parnassus are superior to most of those found elsewhere'
(Trans. based on Jones)	(Trans. based on Hort)

Some four or five phrases in this account have no apparent origin in Theophrastus, and no doubt here as elsewhere Pliny is drawing on other sources besides *HP*. Nevertheless the bulk of the three paragraphs is either a paraphrase or a word-for-word Latin rendering of Theophrastus. Pliny's version sometimes represents a slight modification of what is in Theophrastus, but in some cases what he has done is merely to omit Theophrastus's qualifications and in others he seems to have garbled Theophrastus's account, either not

understanding it or not remembering it correctly.[83] Thus where
Theophrastus reports that some unspecified individuals say that the
story about the goats is true (Theophrastus does not endorse it
himself), Pliny does not similarly qualify his version of the story
(about deer). Where Theophrastus reports that some held that true
and false dittany are the same plant, but growing on different ground,
Pliny has the point about the difference in the habitat, but this follows
the much weaker remark that the two plants grow in many places.
Where Theophrastus's comment about the superiority of Cretan
plants is restricted to the parts above the ground, there is no such
qualification in Pliny.

   This chapter may be exceptional in the degree of derivativeness
from a single source which we happen to have (not that Pliny actually
names Theophrastus here)[84], but many other examples can be given.
Whether we turn to other special plants, such as Egyptian cnecos,[85]
or Sicilian cactos,[86] or to very common ones, such as amaracum
(sweet marjoram, Jones/Hort),[87] thistles,[88] the bur,[89] or asphodel,[90]
or to the accounts that Pliny offers of the order in which plants
bloom,[91] there are close parallelisms with Theophrastus not just in
single phrases, but in whole paragraphs. Instances of what appear to
be inadvertent divergences can be multiplied. Where Pliny *HN* xxi 42
reports a story about ἶρις, *HP* ix 8.7 has the same story about ξίρις
(though Dioscorides implies that this is called a kind of ἶρις);[92] the
remark about plants grown in the rites of Adonis at *HP* vi 7.3 appears
to have been taken by Pliny to refer to a plant called Adonium (*HN*
xxi 60); as Jan pointed out, the very strange remark in *HN* xxi 67,
where having referred to crocus Pliny goes on to two kinds of an
otherwise unknown plant 'orsinus', one with and one without

---

[83] Compare, for example, Kroll 1940, pp. 6ff, for similar apparent misunderstandings of
Aristotle's zoology in Pliny.

[84] *HN* xxv 92–4 is in *oratio recta* throughout: contrast, for example, *oratio obliqua* at xxiv 160–6,
where Pliny explicitly draws on 'Democritus' for a series of points largely about foreign
places.

[85] With *HN* xxi 90 compare *HP* vi 4.5 (Pliny may have misunderstood Theophrastus on
atractylis, cf. *HP* vi 4.6 with what Theophrastus had said about cnecos in 5).

[86] With *HN* xxi 97 compare *HP* vi 4.10–11, though again Pliny may not fully have understood
Theophrastus (see Jones ad loc.).

[87] With *HN* xxi 61 compare *HP* vi 7.4 and 6.

[88] With *HN* xxi 94ff compare *HP* vi 4.3.

[89] With *HN* xxi 104 compare *HP* vii 14.3.

[90] With *HN* xxi 108 compare *HP* vii 13.3. Pliny, like Theophrastus, includes a reference to
Hesiod, but appears to have mistaken Theophrastus's point and not consulted *Op.* 41 itself.

[91] *HN* xxi 64ff and 67f on spring, and summer, flowers respectively are very close to
Theophrastus, *HP* vi 8.1ff, although Pliny does note two items in which the sequence in
which flowers bloom in Italy differs from Theophrastus's reports for Greece.

[92] Dioscorides iv 22, W ii 186.5 (where ξυρίς is glossed first as ξιρίς then as ἶρις ἀγρία).

perfume, seems to represent a misreading of *HP* VI 8.3, where Theophrastus distinguishes between two kinds of κρόκος, the mountain form, ὀρεινός, which is scentless, and the cultivated one.[93]

It is particularly instructive to compare Pliny's account with Theophrastus where the latter, describing some special rite or practice in the collection of a plant used for medicinal or quasi-medicinal purposes, adds his own reservations or critical comments.[94] Where Theophrastus is critical in his account of the way in which mandragora is to be collected (*HP* IX 8.8), Pliny merely repeats this as a description of what the diggers do without casting doubt on such practices (*HN* xxv 148). Pliny notes (*HN* xxv 50) that hellebore is collected in a ritualistic way (*religiosius*),[95] repeating the practices described by Theophrastus at *HP* IX 8.8, but again without Theophrastus' more explicitly dismissive comment. *HN* xxi 145 on polium repeats Theophrastus *HP* IX 19.2 on the use of τριπόλιον to secure 'fair fame', includes a reference to Hesiod and Musaeus (as in Theophrastus) and may even go on to imply a criticism of the use of the plant as an amulet for cataract. But Theophrastus had introduced his account with a more general criticism of the silliness and implausibility of what is said about charms and amulets in general, and his conclusion to this group of stories was that they are invented by men who seek to 'glorify their own crafts'.[96]

The stories about glycyside show, however, that Pliny does not always fail to register a critical comment similar to those he found in Theophrastus about certain practices. The idea that this plant should be dug up at night – for if a woodpecker sees a man collect it, he will attack his eyes – is mentioned twice by Pliny (*HN* xxv 29 and xxvii 85) as what certain people recommend or report. In the second passage, however, he goes on to give the second story about the plant which is included in Theophrastus (*HP* IX 8.6), that when the root is

---

[93] 'orsinus' for ὀρεινός suggests a misreading, not a mishearing (though what we are told by Pliny the Younger, *Ep.* III 5, concerning his uncle's methods of work indicates that he was generally *read to*, and in turn *dictated* his own compositions). But the mistake may, of course, have been in the copy of Theophrastus Pliny consulted.

[94] Compare also *HN* xxi 44 with *HP* IX 19.2, and *HN* xxv 30 with *HP* IX 8.7, and cf. in general, above, pp. 123ff.

[95] While *religio* and *religiosus* are often used by Pliny with distinct pejorative undertones, that is not always necessarily the case. In xxx 13, for example, when he reports ancient British practices, Pliny says he remarks how great the debt to Rome is for removing such monstrous rites (*monstra*), in which to kill a man was a most pious act (*religiosissimum*) and for him to be eaten a most healthy one. Here the term 'monstra' in the first clause conveys *Pliny*'s disapproval, to be sure, but 'religiosissimum', like 'saluberrimum', in the second phrase reports what the *British* were believed to hold to be the *positive* characteristics and benefits of these rites, cf. also, e.g., xxv 30.

[96] Cf. above, p. 123.

cut there is a danger of prolapse of the anus. *Both* stories are given by Theophrastus as examples of 'adventitious and far-fetched' ideas: Pliny's comment about the second is 'magna vanitate ad ostentationem rei fictum arbitror'. Just as Pliny is keen, on occasion, to represent himself as critical and sceptical about the beliefs and practices of the Magi, so here he records an adverse comment on one fantasy, though there is a certain arbitrariness in his condemnation of one story but not the other, nor does he indicate that his source had been critical of both. Indeed he evidently wished to appear to be *more* sceptical and critical than Theophrastus at least in one passage (*HN* xxvi 99) where he remarks that what Theophrastus – an 'otherwise serious authority' (*auctor alioqui gravis*) – tells us about the aphrodisiac effects of certain plants is 'prodigiosa'. The passage in Theophrastus in question is *HP* ix 18.9, excluded by Hort though not by Wimmer (the passage was evidently in the version of *HP* that Pliny knew). Yet after recounting the story Theophrastus proceeded with a remark that indicates that he is far from endorsing it unequivocally: αὕτη μὲν οὖν εἴπερ ἀληθὴς ὑπερβάλλουσά τις δύναμις ('this, *if true*, is then an exceptional power').

The heavy, in places total, dependence on literary sources, the sometimes garbled versions of these, the erratic way in which Pliny may or may not include the reservations and criticisms of the authorities he relies on, all add up to a rather strong indictment of his work in this field. What we can put on the other side of the balance sheet is modest enough. First his industry – in collecting the vast amount of material contained in the botanical books of *HN* – is not in doubt. He shows, too, some awareness of the problem of the identifications of plants: at least he often records different names for the same plant,[97] or notes that the same name is used for different plants, even though his descriptions of plants and their habitats are generally less full than those of Theophrastus. Although there is much uncritical endorsement of what he has read, he also records much simply as what named or unnamed individuals hold or report, often distancing himself from their opinions by using *oratio obliqua*, as well as occasionally inveighing against what he recognises to be nonsense.[98]

Above all, though he sometimes follows Theophrastus blindly, there are occasional, admittedly rare, signs of his reflecting critically on what Theophrastus had written. One notable case in point is *HN* xxi 57, the more remarkable in that he does not name Theophrastus

---

[97] At xxv 29, especially, he explicitly notes as a particular difficulty for the study of plants that the same plant is given different names in different regions.

[98] Among the many examples of this we may cite *HN* xxviii 228–9 and xxix 81.

(as he does in XXVI 99) to claim some kind of superiority for himself. In *HP* VI 2.4 Theophrastus wrote: 'they say that [thyme] cannot be grown or become established where a breeze from the sea does not reach. And for that reason it does not grow in Arcadia', and he went on to note that similarly the olive is believed not to grow more than 300 stades from the sea. At *HN* XXI 57 Pliny records it as an 'ancient opinion' about all sorts of thyme, that they will not survive in the absence of sea breezes, and that for that reason it does not grow in Arcadia, while the olive too – they thought – is only found within 300 stades of the sea. Yet, Pliny goes on, 'thyme, we know, now covers even the stony plains of Gallia Narbonensis'. While this is still no proof of Pliny's personal observations, it shows that he is not entirely incapable of independent judgement.[99]

Pliny was one of the most learned men of his age,[100] and one who was, as we have seen, broadly committed in principle to the importance of personal observation. The indifference of his performance in practice – the lack of significant original contributions to botany, for instance – can be related in part to the very conflict which it may be suggested arose for him between learning and research. The encyclopedic enterprise described in the Preface to book I dictated a certain approach. The energy and attention he could devote to independent research in any one field – if only to differentiate the sound from the unsound in what was commonly believed or retailed – were circumscribed by the very comprehensiveness of the task he set himself. The extent to which he actively sought to engage in such research was further inhibited by the great respect he felt for the work of his predecessors, even while he recognised that *their* results depended on the diligence and carefulness of their first-hand investigations.

Two further passages help to throw some light on the dilemma he faced, even if they are no more than straws in the wind. In *HN* XXV 16 he bewails the comparative ignorance about herbs in his day. The reason why they are not better known is that experience of them is confined to illiterate country-folk – *agrestes, litterarumque ignari* – who alone 'live among them'. Moreover nobody takes the trouble to look

---

[99] Cf. also *HN* XV 1, on olives, where, however, Theophrastus is named.

[100] On certain topics, however, particularly in the field of astronomy, he has either not understood or he rejects advanced opinion. While it is understandable that he rejects speculation about the dimensions of the universe as madness (*HN* II 1ff, 87ff), he believes that the stars and moon may be nourished by moisture from the earth (II 46). His accounts of eclipses (II 56ff) and of planetary motion (II 59ff, 72ff) especially are partly sound, but in part badly garbled versions of Greek astronomical theories: cf. Beaujeu's commentary 1950 ad loc, and Neugebauer 1975, I pp. 319ff, II pp. 666ff, 802ff.

for them, when crowds of medical men are to be met everywhere (offering, presumably, their own accounts on the subject). Again at XXII 94 he exclaims about the dangers of finding out about deadly plants, especially mushrooms. When the mushrooms begin to grow, they can, he believes, absorb foreign material from the substances near them and turn this into poison. Who, he asks, is able to detect this except the country-folk and those who actually gather the plants?[101]

Both passages recognise the value of the direct experience of country people, and the first especially suggests a sharp contrast between them and articulate medical men, with the implied criticism that the latters' claims to knowledge were often unfounded. But even while he acknowledges the fund of information available in the oral, non-literate tradition, Pliny evidently found it difficult to exploit this as systematically as he could the written sources he lists.

The contrast between Pliny's position and that of Aristotle and Theophrastus themselves in the fourth century B.C. is striking in this as no doubt in other important respects. Both Aristotle and Theophrastus refer repeatedly to what they have been told by fishermen, hunters, stock-breeders, root-cutters and the like, most of them, no doubt, just as illiterate, or at least non-literary, as Pliny's 'agrestes litterarumque ignari'. The paradox is that, despite the wealth of popular beliefs and traditions that Pliny records, he refers comparatively speaking less often than Aristotle or Theophrastus to particular groups of experienced informers,[102] and that his sources for those beliefs and traditions are often literary.

The development of knowledge and its recording in books in the intervening period led to the possibility, and the temptation, to rely more and more on the written word, a trend that was, of course, to continue and accelerate in late antiquity. While this facilitated the transmission of knowledge between literate individuals in one generation and those in another, Pliny's texts illustrate how it could

---

[101] Yet if we read 'ne hi quidem' with Müller at XXII 95, Pliny appears to go on to say that even country-folk cannot discover some ways in which mushrooms may become poisonous, specifying that they may do so because they grow near a snake's hole or may have been breathed upon by a snake.

[102] Cf., however, e.g., XI 16 (bee-keepers), XXVIII 67 (midwives, indeed 'obstetricum nobilitas'), XXXI 45 (water-diviners), XXXII 61 (specialists who know about oysters) and XXXIII 90 (a reference to what he calls the 'indocta opificum turba' on the classification of different types of gold solder). Yet at IX 133 he says that those who prepare dyes are ignorant of when shell-fish should be collected, and at IX 151 he discounts some of the stories told by sponge-divers as the product of their fear. The *herbarii*, too, though used, e.g., at XXV 174, are accused of dishonesty (e.g. XXI 144, XXVI 24) and criticised at XXVII 67 for not giving full descriptions of plants that were known to them but not generally familiar to others.

also act as a barrier to communication between different groups of his own contemporaries.

The point requires, to be sure, some qualification. It is not as if everything or even most of what illiterate country-folk of any period claimed to know was reliable: Aristotle had already made the point that such informants as he consulted had practical considerations in view and were not engaging in research for its own sake,[103] and his zoological treatises confirm, if confirmation is needed, that what they told him was a mixture of fact and fantasy. Even so their experience in certain fields was often impressive. Conversely it is not that everyone who wrote on zoological and botanical subjects was necessarily so dependent on the literary tradition as Pliny. That, we suggested, was partly the price he paid for his encyclopedic ambitions. Others of his near contemporaries, such as Celsus and Dioscorides, show that the extent to which the written tradition drove out independent research varied, even though the proportions of these two in both these authors are difficult to determine and a matter of some controversy.[104] Even so, the example of Pliny's botanical discussions illustrates vividly the potential dangers of literacy, or at least of learning, and the inhibiting effects of the weight of past tradition on the active pursuit of problems in this area of the life sciences.

4. THE DEVELOPMENT OF GREEK ANATOMICAL TERMINOLOGY

Our own specialised anatomical terminology – the terminology in Gray's *Anatomy* or any other text-book – is complex, technical and precise. It consists partly of words taken over from Greek and Latin, partly of new coinages (often, until recently, following Latin models) and it incorporates only a comparatively small proportion of colloquial or idiomatic terms from the natural language, English. The specialised terms are – usually rightly – represented as more precise than the colloquial or popular equivalents, though there are

---

[103] See for example *GA* 756a33ff.

[104] Celsus's *De Medicina* is one part of a six-part encyclopedia the rest of which is lost, and it has often been doubted whether Celsus had any direct medical experience himself: see Wellmann 1913 and Ilberg 1913. It should, however, be noted (1) that his account of such surgical operations as the couching of cataract (VII 7) displays a detailed understanding of medical practice – even if it does not prove that he undertook such operations himself, (2) that he engages in his own person in the methodological controversy he outlines in the Proem to the first book (45ff, 50ff, and 74f) and (3) that on other medical matters he expresses his own view (e.g. III 4.3, 11.2, 24.3), describes his own practice in treatment (III 5.6) or refers apparently to his own experience (VII 7.6c, 12.4, cf. IV 26.4). See further Spencer 1935–81 pp. xiff for a brief survey of the arguments for regarding Celsus as a medical practitioner, and cf. Temkin 1935, pp. 255f, 262.

references to the shoulderblade as well as to the scapula, to the collar-bone as well as to the clavicle, in Gray's *Anatomy*, over and above the use of terms for gross structures, such as heart, liver, kidneys, where the popular is also the scientific name. The gradations between popular and specialised terminology are indefinite, but the aim of the latter is to provide a complete and exact vocabulary for the description of anatomical structures throughout the animal kingdom.

The origins and antecedents of modern anatomical terminology can be traced back in many cases beyond the seventeenth and sixteenth centuries to Renaissance and Medieval writers, sometimes even to the ancient Greek and Latin authors themselves. The fact that well into the eighteenth century many anatomical textbooks were written in Latin has left an indelible mark,[105] and the Latin used is heavily indebted to Greek, many terms being either loan words (arteria, urethra) or translations (duodenum, rectum, caecum, sacrum). The question we address here is how Greek anatomical terminology itself developed. This was the first such terminology with pretensions towards being technical and scientific. The question of its relation to popular usage is, then, particularly interesting. How far did popular usage form the basis of such technical vocabulary as the Greeks developed? How did this vocabulary grow or get added to? How far was it inhibited by the popular associations or acceptances of terms? How successful, in fine, were the Greeks in developing a comprehensive, exact and standardised terminology in this area of science? It so happens that we are richly endowed with texts in which to study these questions, notably the extant treatises of the Hippocratic Corpus, the zoological works of Aristotle, the fragmentary remains of Herophilus and Erasistratus, the works of Rufus (late first, early second century A.D.) and those of Galen (second century) – not to mention still later authors. The influence of Galen on subsequent usage was in many cases decisive:[106] but we may concentrate here on

---

[105] Attempts to standardise an international anatomical vocabulary in the late nineteenth and the present centuries have also relied on Latin, first the Basle Nomina Anatomica (1895, revised at Birmingham 1933) and then the Paris Nomina Anatomica of 1955, revised 1960: see, e.g., Zuckerman 1961, p. 4.

[106] Galen often displays a certain impatience with the problems of anatomical nomenclature, dismissing much of what had been written and said on the subject as mere quibbling and repeatedly contrasting disputes over terminology with disagreement on points of substance. He tells us in *Libr. Propr.* ch. 11 (*Scr. Min.* II 120.9f and 15f, ch. 12, K XIX 44.11f, 17f) that he devoted two treatises to the 'correctness of names' and 'against those who understand names insolently', though these are both lost. But his impatience is often apparent in his extant treatises, e.g. *UP* IV 9 (I 213.9ff H, K III 290.16ff), VI 16 (I 356.4ff H, K III 488.15ff), VIII 11 (I 483.4ff H, K III 665.16ff), *AA* VI 13 (K II 581.1ff), x 1 (D 31), 3 (D 42), XII 5 (D 118), XIII 4 (D 154). In some passages his attitude appears positively cavalier: thus at *AA* x 9 (D 65) he remarks; 'I advise you to follow normal practice in the use of names, without investigating

the long formative period leading up to his work. Among the treatises ascribed to Rufus, especially, three deal explicitly with problems of anatomical nomenclature, *On the Naming of the Parts of Man*, *The Anatomy of the Parts of Man* and the short *On Bones*, though as the authenticity of the last two is doubtful,[107] I shall draw most of my material from the *Naming of Parts*.

The major problems that faced early writers dealing with anatomi-

whether they are employed correctly or incorrectly'; at *AA* xii 2 (D 115) 'Since they [anatomists] have given them this name, of necessity we must employ the terms which have become customary, even if they have not been applied in keeping with the true conditions'; and at *AA* xv 1 (D 224) 'We allow free choice in the matter of names, so let everyone use whichever he pleases' (though this comes in a passage where he points out that the term 'marrow' is applied both to the bone marrow and to the spinal cord and cranial marrow, despite the fact that the nature of these substances differs). Yet – despite these expressions of indifference on the subject of exactness in terminology – such was Galen's prestige that his usage was often followed by his successors, for example in the enumeration of the cranial and other nerves. On Galen's anatomical terminology, see Simon 1906, ii pp. viii ff.

[107] Daremberg included both the *Anatomy* and *On Bones* in his edition, though describing them merely as 'attributed to Rufus'. Ruelle, in his introductory notes to the Daremberg edition, conceded that the *Anatomy* may have undergone some reworking in the Byzantine period, but argued for a close link between it and the *Naming*, suggesting that both works were planned as a whole by Rufus (Ruelle 1879, pp. xxviii f). Ruelle's arguments are, however, quite inconclusive. (1) The reference to 'anatomy' at *Syn. Puls.* 222.11f is – as Daremberg thought (e.g. 1879, p. 630) – far more likely to be not to a treatise, but to the practice of dissection, and even if it is taken to be to a work, this can hardly be our *Anat.*, since the point at issue in *Syn. Puls.* (that the pulse occurs when the arteries are full, but when the heart itself is empty) is not one that is discussed in the brief passages on the heart and arteries in *Anat.* (176.14ff, paras. 32f, and 183.12ff, para. 65: the latter text just says that the pulse occurs when the pneuma is driven out of the heart). (2) The argument that the reference to a discussion of the internal parts at *Onom.* 134.9ff anticipates the *Anatomy* is plainly invalid, for the reference is clearly forward to the later section of *Onom.* itself, namely 149.12ff (both *Onom.* and *Anat.* deal with both the external and the internal parts).

The question of the authenticity of *Anat.* remains undecided. At first sight the fact that the opening of the treatise refers back to a work dealing with the external parts, just as the treatise *On Bones* does to a work dealing with internal parts, looks in favour of authenticity. But (*a*) such back-references could easily have been added by someone wanting to pass *Anat.* and *Oss.* off as genuine, and (*b*) – as already noted – it is not as if *Onom.* deals exclusively with external parts. On the other hand these back-references may make it more likely that *Anat.* and *Oss.* are later works than *Onom.*

Meanwhile a comparison of the terminology proposed in *Onom.* and in *Anat.* shows that although the two works are in broad agreement, there are some discrepancies, as for example that *Onom.* (141.5f) restricts σταφυλή to the inflammation of the uvula, while *Anat.* (173.8f) records without criticism that the term is used of the uvula itself (see below, p. 163), and that *Anat.* (181.8f) does not employ the term that *Onom.* (146.12ff) recommends for the ureter. But such similarities and differences as exist between the two treatises are quite inconclusive on the question of the identity or the difference of the author(s).

The degree of overlap between the two main treatises is one particularly remarkable feature of their relationship. Both deal, for example, in great detail with the names of the several membranes of the eye (*Onom.* 154.1ff, *Anat.* 170.9ff) and with the spermatic vessels (*Onom.* 158.15ff, *Anat.* 182.1ff). While one could certainly not account for the *whole* of *Anat.* as we have it as a re-working of material already in *Onom.* – as the summary or abbreviation of *Onom.* in Daremberg–Ruelle 1879, pp. 233ff undoubtedly is – the possibility remains open that *Anat.* is derived in part from such a re-working. Cf. especially Gossen 1914, col. 1209, Ilberg 1931, pp. 9–12.

cal topics – whether for the sake of anatomy itself, or in connection with medical or surgical questions – are fairly obvious. Although beginning already with Homer Greek popular anatomical vocabulary is a rich one,[108] it mostly relates to gross structures and several prominent terms are notably imprecise. This is not just a matter of what happens with a word such as φρένες, whose concrete denotation appears to have shifted. Although it later came to be used of the diaphragm,[109] in Homer the φρένες are almost certainly the lungs: at *Il.* 16.481ff, 502ff, they prolapse when a spear is withdrawn from the thorax (which could never happen to the diaphragm).[110] Other terms too that are already found in Homer or in other early authors are notoriously indeterminate. One of the best known examples is νεῦρον, the word which, after the discovery of the nervous system in the Hellenistic period, came to be used generically of the motor and sensory nerves,[111] but which earlier had been applied to a wide range of structures, tendons, ligaments and sinews,[112] as well as what were later identified as nerves.[113] The author of ch. 40 of the Hippocratic treatise *Instruments of Reduction* distinguishes between the νεῦρα that are in 'mobile and moist parts' which are 'yielding', and those that are not, which are less so, but gets no further than that towards specifying the meaning or the reference of the term.[114]

Again φλέβες is one of several terms (ἀγγεῖον, ὀχετός, πόρος) used of vessels of different kinds in the body. They are evidently most often thought of as carrying blood,[115] but they do not correspond precisely

[108] For the anatomical knowledge displayed in Homer, see, e.g., Daremberg 1865, Buchholz 1871–85, I Part 2, pp. 73ff, Körner 1929. Rufus has occasion to comment on several of the terms used in Homer, φάρυγξ (*Onom.* 141.7ff), λευκανίη (142.5f), ἀστράγαλος (147.12f) and νειαίρη (157.5f).

[109] As at *Morb. Sacr.* ch. 17, L vi 392.5ff, Plato, *Ti.* 70a and Aristotle, *PA* 672b10ff.

[110] See Justesen 1928, pp. 4ff, Onians 1951, pp. 23ff.

[111] See, e.g., Rufus, *Onom.* 153.10ff, *Anat.* 184.15–185.7. The classic study of this discovery is Solmsen 1961. Even after the discovery was made, however, the term νεῦρον was not *restricted* to nerves.

[112] νεῦρον is not, however, the only term used for what we should describe as tendons, sinews and ligaments. Apart from such general words as δεσμός (bond, band), τένων is used fairly clearly of sinew or tendon in several passages in Homer (*Il.* 5.307, *Od.* 3.449) as well as in the Hippocratic *Fractures* (ch. 11, L iii 452.17, cf. *Mul.* ii ch. 110, L viii 236.3) and τόνος is often used similarly, although in the Hippocratic *Joints* ch. 11 (L iv 108.15, 110.3, cf. ch. 50, 218.18) Galen took the term to refer to the nerves (K xviii A 380.6ff), cf. *Epid.* ii sec. 4 ch. 2 (L v 124.9ff). At *AA* xiv 2 (D 185ff) Galen goes into the ambiguities of the terms for 'nerves' 'ligaments' and 'tendons', providing his own quite careful distinctions between these three structures but claiming here that Hippocrates's word for the nerves was τένων. On the hesitant differentiation of these terms in Greek anatomical vocabulary, see, e.g., Potter 1976, p. 50.

[113] As at *Mochl.* ch. 1, L iv 344.12, considered in my text, p. 157.

[114] L iv 390.7f. Cf. also *Loc. Hom.* chh. 4f, L vi 284.1ff, 9ff.

[115] φλέψ is already used in Homer, *Il.* 13.546f, where Aristotle took the reference to be to the vena cava (*HA* 513b26ff).

to 'blood-vessels', let alone to 'veins' as clearly distinguished from 'arteries', for there are many Hippocratic texts in which the φλέβες are spoken of as carrying other substances round the body, including air, various humours, milk and seed.[116] ἀρτηρία, the term that was to come to be used of the arteries as opposed to veins, φλέβες, in those authors who clearly distinguish between those two,[117] was also applied to vessels that carried air.[118] The trachea acquired its name from the adjective (meaning 'rough') added to specify a particular air-carrying ἀρτηρία. The term ἀδήν, generally translated 'gland', is used in the Hippocratic treatise *On Glands* not just of what we might consider glands, but of various lymphatic ganglia among other parts. This work speaks of ἀδένες in the kidneys (ch. 6, L vIII 560.13ff) and even compares the brain with an ἀδήν (ch. 10, 564.8ff).[119]

Most of the terms I have mentioned so far relate to physiological as much as to purely anatomical questions, and their imprecision might be thought to reflect the backward state of physiological speculation in the pre-Hellenistic period. Yet even in some straightforward anatomical contexts too there is a similar indeterminacy – among other weaknesses – in the vocabulary used not just by ordinary writers, but by medical specialists in the fifth and fourth centuries B.C. The difficulties that the authors of the surgical treatises in the Hippocratic Corpus encountered in identifying even the major bones of the arm and leg are characteristic. In *On Fractures*, for instance, the bones of the forearm – radius and ulna – are usually identified *either* by referring to them as the 'upper' and the 'lower' bones respectively

[116] Air and blood especially: *Flat.* ch. 8, *CMG* I, 1 96.23, ch. 10, 97.12ff, 15ff; air and various humours: *Morb. Sacr.* ch. 4, L vI 368.1ff, ch. 6, 370.18ff, ch. 7, 372.10ff, 22ff; seed, milk, blood and other humours: *Genit.* ch. 2, L vII 472.20ff (cf. φλέβια, 16ff), *Nat. Puer.* ch. 15, L vII 494.13ff, 23ff, ch. 21, 512.18ff, *Morb.* IV ch. 38, L vII 554.21ff, ch. 39, 558.6ff. Diogenes of Apollonia also spoke of 'seed-carrying' – σπερματίτιδες – φλέβες, Fr. 6.

[117] Broad distinctions between vessels communicating with the right, and those with the left, side of the heart are made already by Aristotle, *HA* 513b7ff, though he uses the same term, φλέβες, of both. A distinction between the arteries and the veins named as such appears in *Alim.* ch. 31, *CMG* I,1 82.13f, but this is a late work which already shows signs of Stoic influence (see Diller 1936–7, Deichgräber 1973, though cf. Joly 1975). It is clear, however, from Herophilus's coinage of the term ἀρτηριώδης φλέψ, 'artery-like vein', for the pulmonary artery, that he distinguished between the two types of vessel both by character and by which side of the heart they were connected to, the latter being evidently the more important criterion: see Rufus, *Onom.* 162.5ff.

[118] However even after 'arteries' had been distinguished from 'veins', the term ἀρτηρία continued to be used by both Rufus and Galen, for instance, both of what we call arteries and of the trachea. Similarly ἀορτή and ἀορτρα are used both of the aorta and of the windpipe or bronchi: see *Coac.* xx 394, L v 672.5, *Loc. Hom.* ch. 14, L vI 306.13, *Morb.* II ch. 54, L vII 82.14, and cf. Rufus, *Onom.* 155.11 and 163.5ff. There is a careful study of the derivation, early use and development of the terms ἀορτή and ἀρτηρίη in Irigoin 1980, pp. 252ff.

[119] See Littré vIII 550 on the range of reference of the term in this treatise. The author appears *not* to include salivary glands, the pancreas, the testicles or the ovaries in his list of ἀδένες.

(ch. 4, L III 428.2ff) *or* by referring to them as the 'shorter' (or 'thicker') and the 'thinner' bones (ch. 37, 542.3f, cf. ch. 42, 552.1, ch. 44, 544.16). Similarly with the bones of the leg, the tibia and the fibula are identified principally by their different thickness in *On Fractures* ch. 12 (460.1ff, cf. ch. 37, 540.18ff), but in ch. 18 by being contrasted as inner and outer (478.23ff). Although this treatise has the term κνήμη that later came to be used of the tibia, it is used here of the lower leg as a whole (e.g. ch. 37, 540.18ff). Similarly in *Instruments of Reduction* ch. 1 (L IV 340.5ff) κνήμη is used of the lower leg as a whole, and the fibula identified as the 'outer one towards the little toe'.[120]

It is generally clear from such expressions *which* bone the writer refers to, even though their cumbersomeness is apparent. In other cases the paraphrases or descriptions are sufficiently indeterminate to leave the question of identification a problematic one. Thus in *Fractures* ch. 44 (L III 554.17ff), discussing separation of the radius, the writer says that 'the lesion is made clear by palpation at the bend of the elbow about the bifurcation of the blood-vessel (φλέψ) which passes upwards along the muscle'. Although the identifications proposed by Withington, that the blood-vessel concerned is the cephalic vein, and the muscle the biceps, are reasonably secure,[121] they rely on *our* knowledge of anatomy and on the assumption that the author knew what he was talking about, rather than on incontrovertible indications in the text.

The two main problems that the conversion of popular anatomical terminology into a specialised vocabulary posed were first the need for new terms – for structures which, for one reason or another, were not named colloquially – and secondly the requirement that the terms used should be clearly defined. Attempts to begin to meet both needs are made in some Hippocratic texts, in relation to certain areas of anatomy such as osteology in particular. One might suppose that when a Hippocratic writer prefaces one of his terms with the expression the 'so-called' (καλεόμενος/η/ον) this would generally indicate a word that had been introduced deliberately into medical vocabulary.[122] But caution is needed. Even Homer introduces some of the rarer anatomical terms he uses with an equivalent expression, for example at *Il.* 5.305ff where he says 'they' call where the thigh turns in the hip-joint (ἰσχίον) the κοτύλη (literally 'cup'). In some

---

[120] Similarly πῆχυς is used of the forearm as a whole, e.g. at *Fract.* ch. 4, L III 428.1, but of the ulna in particular at *Fract.* ch. 41, 548.1, cf. Rufus, *Onom.* 143.12f, and Galen, *UP* II 2,167.4ff H, K III 92.2ff: Galen especially draws attention to the ambiguity of the term.

[121] Withington 1928, p. 193.

[122] Cf. Festugière 1948, p. 68 n. 89.

Hippocratic texts, too, particularly in treatises addressed to a lay audience, the use of similar expressions may indicate merely that the term is not a common one, not that it is a new 'scientific' coinage. Thus the writer of *On the Art* refers to the 'so-called θώρηξ' (ch. 10, *CMG* I, 1 15.27).[123] While it is true that the original meaning of the word is breastplate, not the part of the trunk covered by it – the thorax – it is used in the latter sense outside medical writers.[124] Here, and when he speaks of the 'so-called muscle' (μῦς),[125] the addition of the expression 'so-called' may be simply to warn his audience that the term is not being used in one of its common senses (μῦς also meant mouse), rather than an apology for a brand-new coinage.

On the other hand some uses of this expression may provide an indication of developments that were already taking place in anatomical terminology in the late fifth and early fourth centuries. Although *Prognostic* ch. 23 (L II 178.9) uses the term γαργαρεών in the plural) for the uvula without apology, *Affections* introduces it with an expression that indicates that its use is specialised (ch. 4, L VI 212.7ff), though it is possible that what the writer had in mind is not the uvula as such, but the morbid condition he describes.[126] Again ὀδούς (literally 'tooth') is introduced in *Epidemics* II sec. 2 ch. 24 (L V 96.2ff), where it appears to refer either to the second cervical vertebra or to its apophysis (still called the odontoid process or the dens),[127] although Rufus took it to name the first cervical vertebra (*Onom.* 154.13f) – an example which illustrates the problems that may arise when a new term is employed without a very clear delineation of its reference.

Other apparently new or more specialised osteological[128] and other terms used in the surgical treatises and elsewhere include κορώνη (apparently of what is still called the coronoid process of the ulna, *Joints* ch. 18, L IV 132.4),[129] κορωνόν (of the coronoid process of the mandible, *Joints* ch. 30, 140.10),[130] ζύγωμα (of the zygomatic

---

123 The term appears in a number of Hippocratic treatises, e.g. *VM* ch. 19, *CMG* I,1 50.22, *Liqu.* ch. 2, *CMG* I,1 87.14 and *Morb.* III 16, L VII 152.5. On its ambiguity, cf. below p. 161 and n. 167.

124 Euripides, *HF* 1095, cf. Aristophanes, *V* 1194f. Plato too uses the expression τῷ καλουμένῳ θώρακι at *Ti.* 69e 4.

125 *de Arte* ch. 10, *CMG* I,1 15.21ff.

126 Note neuter τοῦτο (not ταύτην to agree with σταφυλή) at L VI 212.8, though this is not decisive.

127 See Galen, *UP* XII 7, II 198.16f H, K IV 24.3f, but contrast Pollux II 131 (IX,1 124.1ff, Bethe).

128 The descriptions of the bones in *Fract.* and *Art.* have recently been analysed by Irmer 1980, pp. 265ff.

129 κορώνη is, however, also used of the olecranon: see *Mochl.* ch. 1, L IV 344.11, and cf. Galen, *UP* II 14, I 104.10ff H, K III 142.6ff, who indicates that both the olecranon and the coronoid process were called κορώνας or κορωνά (see further next note).

130 Cf. Galen, *AA* xv 2 (D 229), who notes that κορωνά and κορώνας were used of what other anatomists called the 'mastoid processes'.

bones of the jaw, *Joints* ch. 30, 140.10), and ἐπιμυλίς (cf. ἐπιμύλιον, mill-stone) used of the patella or knee-cap, *Instruments of Reduction* ch. 1, L IV 340.10ff.[131] *Fractures* ch. 2 (L III 420.7f) uses the term τό γιγγλυμοειδές to describe the 'hinge-like' end of the humerus (i.e. the trochlea),[132] *Instruments of Reduction* ch. 1 (L IV 340.11) speaks of the κονδυλῶδες, 'knuckle-shaped', form of the proximal epiphysis of the tibia and fibula,[133] and uses the same adjective, along with βαλβιδῶδες,[134] of the distal, elbow, end of the humerus.[135] *Joints* ch. 79 (316.11f) distinguishes generally between two kinds of cavity, κοτυλοειδής or cup-shaped ones, and γληνοειδής (literally 'eye-ball-shaped') of shallower depressions. τενθρηνιώδης, a term used by Democritus according to Aelian,[136] appears in the fragmentary work *Anatomy* (L VIII 538.6) to describe the 'honey-comb-like' character of the lung, and κλῆθρον is used of the epiglottis in *On Diseases* II ch. 28 (L VII 46.2 and 11).[137]

---

[131] Cf. Rufus's comment on ἐπιμυλίς at *Onom.* 148.11, also Erotian's (Fr. 40, 111.10ff, Nachmanson) and Pollux II 189 (IX,1 141.14f, Bethe).

[132] Cf. Galen's term ἡ τροχιλώδης χώρα, literally the 'pulley-like place', at *UP* II 15, I 108.15ff H, K III 147.18ff.

[133] The writer may well have in mind what are still known as the medial and lateral condyles of the tibia.

[134] This term vividly illustrates the problems of interpretation that may arise with Hippocratic anatomical descriptions. The adjective is translated 'with cavities or grooves' in LSJ. The noun βαλβίς is used, again according to LSJ, of the 'rope drawn across the racecourse at the starting and finishing-point' or of 'the posts to which this rope was attached', although the scholiast to Aristophanes, *Eq.* 1159, describes the βαλβίς as the oblique piece of wood, i.e. the cross-piece, which is released (presumably lowered) at the start of the race. For a reconstruction of how such a starting-gate might work, see Broneer 1958, pp. 14f. Our other ancient references generally use the term of a starting-point, but Philostratus *VA* v 5 speaks of a planed or hewn or polished (ξεστή) βαλβίς, and at *Im.* I ch. 24 the βαλβίς is a small platform on which the discus-thrower stands for his throw. Rope, posts, cross-bar and platform are then all possible candidates for the primary connotation of βαλβίς. What the term βαλβιδώδης means in *Mochl.* ch. 1 was already the subject of dispute in antiquity. Erotian (Fr. 42, 112.2ff, Nachmanson) records three competing interpretations, beginning with Bacchius's suggestion that the term means βαθμῶδες: 'for the βαθμός (step) is a βαλβίς: for the part of the humerus at the elbow [is so called] since the front part of the ulna rests on it as on a step'. Galen himself uses the term βαθμίς for the olecranon fossa and for the coronoid fossae of the humerus (*UP* II 15, I 104.22ff H, K III 142.17ff – with the authority of the Hippocratic *Fract.* ch. 37, L III 540.18; cf. ch. 2, 420.8, where the same term is used of the cavity of the *ulna* which receives the trochlea), but the Galenic lexicon (K XIX 87.15) glosses βαλβίς as κοιλότης παραμήκης – oblique cavity. The olecranon fossa is separately identified at *Mochl.* ch. 1, L IV 344.11 (ἔγκοιλον ὄπισθεν see next note) and although βαλβιδώδης might be used of the step-like appearance of the trochlea and capitulum or perhaps especially of the oblique groove for the ulna nerve, it would be as well to stress that such suggestions are quite conjectural.

[135] L IV 344.10f, where the olecranon fossa is fairly clearly meant when the writer speaks of the hollow at the back (of the humerus), in which the κορώνη (i.e., here, olecranon, cf. above, n. 129) of the ulna is lodged when the arm is extended.

[136] *NA* XII 20, where, however, the reading is an emendation due to Schneider. At *Anat.*, L VIII 538.6, the reading is Foes'.

[137] *Cord.* ch. 2, L IX 80.12, has the term ἐπιγλωσσίς (cf. Rufus, *Onom.* 140.11).

Although the terms νεῦρον and χόνδρος (cartilage) are imprecise, *Instruments of Reduction* combines them in an adjective, χονδρονευρώδης to describe the ligament (δεσμός, literally bond) by which the hip bone is attached to the 'great vertebra next to the sacrum' (i.e. the fifth lumbar) (ch. 1, L IV 340.14f). *Joints* ch. 45 (L IV 190.4) describes what binds the vertebrae together as a 'mucous and ligamentous connection' (δεσμῷ μυξώδει καὶ νευρώδει) 'extending from the cartilages right to the spinal cord', and *Instruments of Reduction* ch. 1 (L IV 344.12) identifies a particular νεῦρον as τὸ ναρκῶδες – 'the cord which stupefies' – apparently referring to the ulnar nerve.

In relation to the muscles, too, certain specialised and more or less technical terms appear in some of the Hippocratic works. *Joints* ch. 30 (L IV 140.12) refers to two sets of muscles, called κροταφῖται (literally 'temporal') and μασητῆρες (literally 'chewers') connected with the lower jaw.[138] Here the addition of the expression 'so-called' probably indicates that the terms were rare, even for the more specialised audience to which the surgical treatises were addressed. In *Joints* ch. 45 (194.8) ψόαι (or ψύαι) is used of certain muscles of the loins,[139] and Rufus (*Onom.* 159.13 – 160.5) quotes a passage from the lost work, *Cnidian Sentences*, where the term ἀλώπεκες (literally 'foxes') is used, apparently also for some of the lumbar muscles. But although such examples show that some attempts had begun to be made to name particular muscles in the body, their small number illustrates how meagre the progress towards a systematic and comprehensive nomenclature of the muscles was. Moreover in each of the Hippocratic texts in question the terms appear without clear indications of their references, let alone precise definitions.

The development of anatomy depended primarily on the greater exploitation of the method of dissection.[140] But the great advances achieved in the Hellenistic period by such men as Praxagoras, Herophilus and Erasistratus called urgently for new terminology to express the new knowledge gained. The ways in which such terminology was developed fall into certain main types. A part might be named from a prominent characteristic. The duodenum – δωδεκαδάκτυλος in Greek – acquired its name from its

---

[138] The modern terms 'masseter' and 'temporal' muscles stem ultimately from the desire of ancient anatomists to identify those so named in the Hippocratic text. See Rufus, *Onom.* 152.2ff, and more especially Galen (*In Hipp. Art.* II 3, K XVIII A 428.7ff, 429.7ff, *AA* IV 2, K II 421.7ff, 422.2ff, *UP* XI 4, II 120.21ff H, K III 853.3ff) who is aware of disagreements on the correct use of these terms. The vagueness of the original references is, however, such that we cannot be confident of any *precise* identification of what the author of *Art.* ch. 30 had in mind.

[139] Cf. also *Nat. Hom.* ch. 11, *CMG* I 1,3 194.9.

[140] See especially L. Edelstein (1932–3) 1967, cf. Lloyd 1975a.

length – twelve-fingers' breadth – one of many coinages for which Herophilus was responsible.[141] Many terms were coined from existing ones, for example by the addition of a prefix. This was the way in which such terms as μετακάρπιον – literally 'after the wrist', καρπός – for the bones of the palm of the hand – came to be developed, although in many cases we do not know precisely when they were introduced.[142]

More frequently, analogies between one anatomical part and another, or with some other object, were the source of new terms. Another of Herophilus's coinages was χοριοειδής – literally 'after-birth-like' – for the choroid, or as they used to be called chorioid, plexuses of the ventricles of the brain.[143] He was also responsible for the comparison with a net, ἀμφίβληστρον, which gave rise to the term ἀμφιβληστροειδής, 'net-like', for what we still call the retina (from Latin *rete*, net),[144] and many other examples could be given.[145]

It is clear from the evidence in Rufus and Galen especially that a massive effort was made to develop anatomical terminology during the Hellenistic period, although Rufus himself is, from time to time, critical of some of the suggestions that were proposed. Thus he complains that some of the terms that had 'recently' been coined for the sutures of the skull were the work of 'Egyptian' (that is, probably, Alexandrian) doctors whose knowledge of Greek was deficient.[146]

Nevertheless problems, some of them major ones, remained. Two in particular must be discussed in relation to Rufus's own work *On the Naming of Parts* especially. First there is an evident unevenness in the development of anatomical terminology, reflecting, in many cases, a similar unevenness in anatomical knowledge itself. Although the

---

[141] See, e.g., Galen, *On the Dissection of the Veins and Arteries* ch. 1, K II 780.13ff, *AA* VI 9, K II 572.13ff, *On the Parts Affected* VI 3, K VIII 396.6f. Yet *UP* V 3, I 253.19ff H, K III 346.1ff, suggests that the term was still not standard in Galen's day, since Galen and other anatomists continued to refer to the duodenum sometimes simply as the ἔκφυσις (cf. also *AA* VI 12, K II 578.2).

[142] For μετακάρπιον see Rufus, *Onom.* 144.1, and cf. Galen, *On Bones for Beginners* ch. 19, K II 771.7ff, on later disagreements concerning the precise reference of the term. Other similar compound terms in Rufus are ὑποσφόνδυλον ('below the vertebrae') for the sacrum (*Onom.* 148.2) and περικάρδιος ('around the heart') of the pericardium (*Onom.* 156.4) though the latter term had been used of the blood around the heart already by Empedocles, Fr. 105.

[143] See Rufus, *Onom.* 153.9f, Galen, *AA* IX 3, K II 719.14ff.

[144] See Rufus, *Onom.* 154.9f. Celsus, *De Medicina* VII 7.13b, further suggests that Herophilus also coined, and used, the term ἀραχνοειδής ('web-like') for the retina.

[145] A full account of Herophilus's anatomical discoveries is now available in von Staden forthcoming ch. 6. Cf. also Potter 1976.

[146] *Onom.* 151.1ff (note νῦν 151.1). However these 'Egyptian' doctors were, he suggests, responsible for a set of terms for the sutures of the skull, including στεφανιαία ('coronal') and λαμβδοειδής ('lambdoid'): their term for the sagittal suture was ἐπιζευγνύουσα, literally the 'joiner'.

vocabulary for some superficial and gross structures was far advanced, and sometimes became extremely elaborate, that for many fine structures, and especially for the muscles, nerves and blood-vascular system, was still, even in Rufus's day, quite undeveloped.[147] It is striking, for example, just how detailed the terminology for the external structure of the ear is in Rufus: he explains the terms λόβος, πτερύγιον, ἕλιξ, ἀνθέλιξ, κόγχη, τράγος and ἀντιλοβίς.[148] Even more surprising – in view of some of the omissions we shall be considering directly – is the inclusion of a paragraph dealing with the quite elaborate terminology for the various kinds of growth of hair on the face: πώγων, ἴουλος, προπωγώνιον, μύστακες, πάππος, ὑπήνη.[149]

In contrast to the attention lavished on these parts, little attempt is made, in Rufus, to give a comprehensive and systematic account of the muscles. Certain muscles are mentioned and named in relation to particular bones, but Rufus introduces only two terms not already found in the rather meagre vocabulary for the muscles in the Hippocratic writers.[150] Again although, following the work of Herophilus and Erasistratus, Rufus both distinguishes the nerves as such from other types of structure – ligaments, tendons – and subdivides the nerves into sensory and motor,[151] individual nerves are neither named nor described in *On the Naming of Parts*.[152] In part, no doubt, the explanation of this lies in the nature of the work, which is essentially a handbook summarising the names of the principal

---

[147] The same remains true also of aspects of Galen's anatomical terminology: thus in the absence of special names for many of the muscles, these have to be identified by at times quite complex descriptions, as, for example, in his accounts of the muscles of the hand, arm, head and hip, *UP* II 2, 165.27ff H, K III 90.8ff, *UP* II 16, 1 113.25ff H, K III 155.4ff, *UP* XII 8f, II 203.9ff H, K IV 30.12ff, *UP* XV 8, II 366.5ff H, K IV 250.6ff, cf. *AA* I 9, K II 263.16ff and II 6, K II 306.1ff. We may, however, contrast the development of terminology concerning the membranes of the eye (see below, p. 161), which would seem to reflect particular surgical interest from Hellenistic times: it is clear from Celsus (*De Medicina* VII 7), among others, that intricate eye operations, for example for cataract and staphyloma, were attempted, and this may have helped to stimulate the development of a more technical nomenclature.

[148] *Onom.* 138.6ff, cf. Pollux II 85f (IX,1 109.17ff, Bethe).

[149] *Onom.* 139.8ff. We may compare also the elaborate terminology for the external surface of the liver used in divination, which Rufus reports at *Onom.* 158.5ff, while remarking that the nomenclature of such parts is not necessary for medical purposes.

[150] The two exceptions are that he takes the term ὑποχόνδρια to be a name for the muscular parts below the false ribs (*Onom.* 145.12ff) and ἐπιγουνίς (already in Homer, e.g. *Od.* 17.225, but used in the Hippocratic *Art.* ch. 70, L IV 288.18, apparently of the knee-cap) to be a name for muscles attached to the knee, *Onom.* 148.10 (cf. Pollux II 189, IX,1 141.21, Bethe).

[151] See Rufus, *Onom.* 163.12ff, cf. *Anat.* 184.15ff.

[152] We may contrast the much more detailed accounts of the nerves in Galen, especially in *AA* III 3f, IX 13, XIV and XV and *UP* IX and XVI, reflecting in many cases his own discoveries, though Galen still has to use many paraphrases and descriptions in default of an accepted nomenclature or to establish how his numbering of the nerves is to be interpreted. Cf., e.g., Savage Smith 1971.

parts.[153] But that is just to say that such topics as the musculature, the nervous system and details of the arterial and venous systems[154] were considered too advanced or too difficult to be included.

But the second and far more serious problem relates to the standardisation of anatomical terminology. As already noted, a number of anatomists contributed, at different periods, to the extension of anatomical vocabulary. But it was one thing to propose a particular term for a particular part: it was another for that term to become generally accepted by other anatomists, let alone to become established popular usage. There are two aspects to the difficulties that arose, the use of alternative names for the same anatomical part, and the use of the same name in two or more different acceptances. Rufus's *On the Naming of Parts* has a wealth of examples of both types, as also has the *Anatomy*. In some instances a variety of terms was already in use in popular terminology. At one point Rufus tells us that παρειαί (side of the face or cheek, as, for example, at *Il.* 3.35) 'are also called σιαγόνες and γνάθοι [more often jaw] and again γένυς, of which there is an upper and a lower. The point of the lower γνάθος is called γένειον and ἀνθερεών. The fleshy part under the lower jaw [i.e. the jowl] is called λευκανία, but some call this part ἀνθερεών, and call the hollow beside the clavicle λευκανία.'[155] All these terms appear – whether or not in the sense Rufus gives them – in Homer, and indeed the use of λευκανίη for the hollow beside the clavicle is expressly attributed to Homer, no doubt on the basis of *Il.* 22.324f, a little later in Rufus, where Homer's use is contrasted with the doctors' name, or rather names, for this part namely ἀντικάρδιον and σφαγή.[156]

But as this last example shows, the problem of a variety of terms being used for the same part extends also into more specialised or technical vocabulary. Thus Rufus records three names for the uvula, κίων, γαργαρεών and Aristotle's σταφυλοφόρον.[157] He gives two words for palate, οὐρανός and ὑπερῷα,[158] two for the sacrum, ἱερὸν ὀστοῦν and ὑποσφόνδυλον,[159] two for the spinal marrow, namely

---

[153] We may compare Galen's treatises addressed 'to beginners'. Rufus himself indicates the summary nature of the instruction contained in *Onom.* at 134.12ff.

[154] Various arteries and veins are mentioned, for example, at *Onom.* 161.2f, 4ff, 163.3ff, 167.6ff, cf. also *Anat.* 183.12ff.   [155] *Onom.* 139.3ff.

[156] *Onom.* 142.5f. σφαγή is defined by Aristotle, *HA* 493 b 7, as the part common to the neck and chest.

[157] *Onom.* 141.3ff, cf. also κιονίς (*Anat.* 173.6f) and σταφυλή (*Anat.* 173.8) though Rufus says that the latter term should be reserved for the inflammation of the uvula (see below, p. 163).

[158] *Onom.* 141.2f.

[159] *Onom.* 148.1ff, which adds that κόκκυξ is used for the end of the sacrum, though that term was also used for the sacrum itself, Pollux II 183 (IX,1 139.20f, Bethe), cf. Galen, *On Bones for Beginners* ch. 12, K II 762.15ff.

μυελὸς νωτιαῖος and ῥαχίτης,[160] and three for the bronchi, βρογχίαι, σήραγγες and ἀορταί.[161]

The terminology for the membranes of the eye provides a particularly remarkable example of the lack of standardisation. So far as the cornea and sclera go, their joint regular name was κερατοειδής, literally 'horn-like':[162] the *Anatomy* says that it was also called the 'first' membrane and the 'white' (λευκός) one, though it may be that that term was more strictly applied to the opaque sclera.[163] But the nomenclature of the other three principal membranes recognised by Greek anatomists was very unstable. Thus the second membrane was called ῥαγοειδής (from ῥάξ grape or berry) or χοριοειδής (like the after-birth, χόριον: cf. the modern 'choroid') or the 'pierced', τετρημένος, membrane, or simply the 'second' one.[164] The third – the retina – was called not only the 'net-like', ἀμφιβληστροειδής – after the comparison for which Herophilus was responsible – but also ἀραχνοειδής (literally 'like a spider's web') and ὑαλοειδής (literally 'glass-like', from the vitreous humour it contained).[165] Finally the fourth membrane, corresponding to the capsular sheath of the crystalline lens, was called φακοειδής (from φακός, lentil, i.e. lentiform) and δισκοειδής (from the word for quoit, discus) from its shape, but also κρυσταλλοειδής (literally 'ice-like') from the humour it enclosed.[166]

The converse problem – of a single term having different acceptances or referents – was the source of equal or even greater embarrassment. Rufus points out, for example, that θώραξ was used not just of the area between the collar-bones and the hypochondria, but also of the whole area between the collar-bones and the genitalia.[167] ὦμος was used both of the head of the humerus – where it joins the shoulder-blade – but also of the whole limb, i.e. the shoulder plus the upper arm.[168] χείρ was used both of the whole arm from the shoulder

[160] *Onom.* 153.13ff, though 164.9ff suggests a distinction between these two terms.
[161] *Onom.* 155.10f.   [162] *Onom.* 154.2f.
[163] *Anat.* 170.9ff.
[164] *Onom.* 154.3ff, *Anat.* 171.1ff (from which it appears that the comparison with a grape may be Herophilus's). The term ἴρις ('rainbow') was used of what we call the iris, for example by Rufus at *Onom.* 136.8f: in Galen, however, the term is applied to a section through the ciliary region defined as 'the place where all the membranes are united', e.g. *Methodus Medendi* XIV 19, K X 1020.10ff, *UP* X 2, II 61.22ff H, K III 768.14ff, otherwise called the στεφάνη, crown, as Galen notes, cf. Rufus, *Anat.* 171.3: see Simon 1906 II pp. 258f n. 112, May 1968, II pp. 467–8 n. 10.
[165] *Onom.* 154.7ff, *Anat.* 171.9ff.   [166] *Onom.* 154.11ff, *Anat.* 172.1ff.
[167] *Onom.* 135.2ff.
[168] *Onom.* 142.8ff, cf. Irmer 1980, p. 274. The word was then applied, by extension, to other parts, for example to the 'shoulders' of the womb, *Onom.* 160.9ff, a use that goes back to Herophilus, according to Galen, who cites the third book of Herophilus's *Anatomy* in *De Semine* II 1, K IV 596.11ff. Similarly terms such as κεφαλή (head), αὐχήν and τράχηλος (neck)

and of what we grasp with – the hand.[169] The term σάρξ was applied to, among other things, (1) the solid part between the viscera, (2) the flesh of the muscles, and (3) coagulated material found in wounds.[170]

With each of these common terms the reference would often be clear from the context. But with two others the variations of reference were such as to give rise to serious problems. The denotation of φάρυγξ was particularly unstable, the term being used not just (1) of what we call the pharynx – sometimes including the oesophagus or gullet – but also (2) of the larynx, and (3) even of the trachea, as opposed to the pharynx.[171] Similarly στόμαχος was used (1) of the oesophagus, (2) of the orifice of the stomach, (3) of the neck of the bladder, (4) of that of the womb and even, it seems, (5) of that of the vagina.[172]

Even rather more technical terms exhibit a similar referential indeterminacy. Thus Rufus records that Praxagoras confined the term 'hollow vein' (κοίλη φλέψ: cf. vena cava) to the vein leading from the liver to the kidneys, but others used it for the whole of the vein leading up to the heart through the diaphragm, i.e. the whole of the vena cava inferior.[173] Again the term παραστάτης (literally 'by-stander' or 'defender') which had been used in non-medical texts of the testicles,[174] and which appears in the Hippocratic *On the Nature of Bones* possibly for the epididymis (ch. 14, L IX 188.5f), was applied by Herophilus both (1) to the hyoid bone, because it 'stands by' the tonsils, and (2) to the spermatic vesicles, where two pairs are distinguished, the 'varix-like' παραστάται (the ductus deferentes and their ampullae) and the 'glandular' ones (the seminal vesicles themselves).[175]

---

and πυθμήν (base) do service time and again as the names of parts of the main viscera, for example of the heart (*Onom.* 155.1ff), liver (157.14ff), bladder (158.11ff) and womb (160.9ff). Cf. similarly Richardson 1976, pp. 52ff, on ἀκρώμιον.

[169] *Onom.* 144.2f. Cf. Galen, *AA* III 2, K II 346.12ff, 347.1ff.

[170] *Onom.* 164.5ff.

[171] For (1) see, e.g., the Hippocratic *Prog.* ch. 23, L II 174.14ff, 176.11ff, Rufus, *Onom.* 139.12f, 141.6ff, and Galen, e.g. *UP* VII 5, I 381.21ff H, K III 525.9ff. For (2) see Aristotle, *PA* 664a16ff, and [Rufus], *Anat.* 174.7ff. For (3) see [Rufus], *Anat.* 174.14ff, and cf. Galen, *UP* VIII 1, I 443.13ff H, K III 611.11ff: cf. Strömberg 1944, p. 57ff.

[172] For (1) see *Il.* 3.292, Aristotle, *HA* 495b19ff, Rufus, *Onom.* 155.7f, *Anat.* 174.10, Galen, *UP* IV 1, I 195.10ff H, K III 267.2ff. For (2) see Galen, *In Hipp. Acut.* I 17, *CMG* V 9,1 137.17ff, K XV 460.7ff. For (3) see *Aër.* ch. 9, *CMG* I 1,2 44.19, 22ff, 28ff. For (4) see *Mul.* I ch. 18, L VIII 58.5, *Steril.* ch. 217, L VIII 418.3, 422.3, 7, 13 and ch. 219, 422.23, Galen, *UP* XIV 3, II 290.17ff H, K IV 150.8ff. For (5) see *Mul.* I ch. 36, L VIII 84.23. At *UP* IV 1, I 195.10ff H, K III 267.2ff, Galen explains the term as 'the general term for any narrow passage or isthmus, so to speak, leading to a cavity' (trans. May). Cf. Chantraine 1975, pp. 37ff.

[173] *Onom.* 161.6ff.

[174] E.g. Plato Comicus, Fr. 174.13, I 648, Kock; cf. Pollux II 174 (IX,1 137.2ff, Bethe).

[175] For (1) see Rufus, *Onom.* 155.4f, cf. Pollux II 202 (IX,1, 145.13f, Bethe). For (2) see Rufus, *Onom.* 158.15ff, 159.4ff, Galen, *De Semine* I 16, K IV 582.12ff, *UP* XIV 11, II 321.6ff H, K IV

In some cases such variations in terminology reflect disagreements on points of theory or interpretation, advances in anatomical knowledge, or simply changes in fashion.[176] Rufus several times draws attention to the differences between the old or earlier name for a part and the one in current use in his own day.[177] He notes, for example, the change in the sense of φλέβες. 'In ancient times they used to call the arteries φλέβες. And when they say that the φλέβες beat, they meant the arteries, for it is the function of the arteries to beat.' For good measure, Rufus adds: 'And they also called them [i.e. the arteries] ἀορταί and πνευματικὰ ἀγγεῖα and σήραγγες and κενώματα and νεῦρα.'[178]

Yet although some of the fluctuations in anatomical terminology have, as it were, a diachronic explanation, that accounts for only a very small proportion of the variations in nomenclature remarked by Rufus alone. The overwhelming impression that those variations leave is of a situation bordering on terminological anarchy. Rufus himself criticises, from time to time, the use of certain terms, and he attempts to lay down what he thinks the correct name for a part should be. σταφυλή, he says, should be used of the inflammation of the uvula, not for the uvula itself:[179] yet in the *Anatomy* σταφυλή is recorded without criticism as a term still used for the uvula.[180] In *On the Naming of Parts* Rufus describes the channel which carries seed and urine in the penis and calls it the οὐρήθρα or the πόρος οὐρητικός: it should not be called the οὐρητήρ, for the ureters are different, namely the vessels that take the urine from the kidneys to the bladder.[181] Nevertheless in the work *On the Diseases of the Kidneys and the Bladder* the term οὐρητήρ is clearly used of the urethra at one point.[182]

Elsewhere in *On the Naming of Parts*, after remarking that the bones near the ear are called λιθοειδής (literally 'stone-like', i.e. 'petrous') because of their hardness, he criticises the use of this term for the mastoid process on the grounds that this is, in fact, σηραγγώδης – full of cavities (the mastoid air-cells).[183] In another text he indicates that

190.1ff. On whether the 'glandular' 'bystanders' include the prostate as well as the seminal vesicles, compare von Staden forthcoming, with May 1968, II pp. 644f, n. 55, and Simon 1906, II p. 120 and pp. 312–14, n. 403.

[176] In some cases, too, Rufus records dialect variations, as for example the term κύβιτον used by the Dorians in Sicily for ὀλέκρανον, *Onom.* 143.10f, and cf. 137.8f and 10 on Athenian usage.

[177] See *Onom.* 147.10f, 151.1ff, 157.7ff, 159.1.

[178] *Onom.* 163.3ff: the literal meaning of the five terms is 'suspenders' (aortas), 'pneumatic vessels' (vessels for the air/breath), 'hollows', 'vacancies' and 'nerves/sinews'.

[179] *Onom.* 141.5f, cf. Aristotle, *HA* 493 a 3f.

[180] *Anat.* 173.8f.

[181] *Onom.* 146.12ff.

[182] *Ren. Ves.* ch. 23, *CMG* III,1, 116.4.

[183] *Onom.* 151.10ff.

he is sometimes aware that the advance of physiological knowledge had made an earlier term inappropriate: he notes that the 'vessels that rise through the neck are called καρωτίδες (carotids, literally 'stupefiers') because when they are pressed men become stupefied and lose their voice. But now this has been observed to be an effect not of the arteries, but of the sensory nerves that lie close by. So that one would not be wrong to want to change the name.'[184]

Finally an even more striking instance of indeterminacy, indeed confusion, is provided by his discussion of the use of τυφλά.[185] After observing that there are many holes in the cranium, he says that none of these has a name, except for two which are called τυφλά, that is, literally, 'blind'. However doctors disagree about which holes to call the 'blind' ones, some using the term for the two holes 'that are on either side of the greatest opening in the cranium through which the spinal cord passes' (i.e. probably either the hypoglossal or the condylar canals either side of the foramen magnum) while others use the term for the holes that are 'close to the ears and a little in front of the articulation of the jaw' (identified by Daremberg as the stylo-mastoid foramina). Rufus expresses his dissatisfaction with both views, for in neither case are the holes *not* pierced right through (so that they are not, strictly speaking, 'blind'): the first pair end in the great cavity of the spinal cord, and the second under the ethmoid, and 'certain nerves are seen to grow out through all of these holes'.[186]

---

[184] *Onom.* 163.9ff. A similar criticism is voiced by Galen, *AA* xiv 7 (D 210–12), *PHP* i 7 *CMG* v 4,1,2 86.24ff, K v 195.4ff. Elsewhere too Galen complains that common terms are used inaccurately, as the word 'covering' in relation to the stomach and intestines, *AA* xii 2 (D 115), cf. xii 7 (D 128) and other passages cited above, n. 106. Like Rufus, Galen occasionally attempts to justify a preference for one term over another, as he does in *UP* viii 7, i 472.25ff H, K iii 652.2ff, for example, where he says that Hippocrates's term σπογγοειδῆ (sponge-like) is more appropriate for what other anatomists called the ἠθμοειδῆ (strainer-like, ethmoid) bones, although Galen continues to use the latter term (e.g. *UP* xi 12, ii 150.14 H, K iii 894.13).

[185] *Onom.* 152.6ff. Cf. Galen, *AA* ix 9 (D 9), according to whom 'Herophilus and his supporters' used the term 'blind' for the foramen that transmits the facial nerve, though Galen, like Rufus, remarks that the foramen is not, in fact, 'blind' and that the 'nerve passes on through it outwards', commenting at *AA* xiv 4 (D 196) that 'the earlier anatomists were firmly of the opinion that it [the canal of the facial nerve] is blind or one-eyed, because it is bored crookedly through the bone'.

[186] Thus the hypoglossal canal carries the hypoglossal nerve (and the condylar canal carries the emissary vein from the sigmoid sinus). If Daremberg's identification of the second pair of holes as the stylo-mastoid foramina is correct, these transmit both the facial nerves and the stylo-mastoid arteries. It should, however, be emphasised that there are other possible candidates for the second pair of holes 'close to the ears and a little in front of the articulation of the jaw', particularly in view of Rufus's further remark that they are located 'towards the ethmoid bones'. These possibilities include (1) the foramina ovalia (through which the mandibular division of the trigeminal nerve passes), (2) the foramina lacera, (3) the foramina spinosa (through which the middle meningeal artery, its accompanying vein, and the nervus spinosus, pass) and (4) the foramina rotunda (carrying the maxillary division of

Rufus concludes that they are called 'blind' not because they are not pierced through, but because they are not pierced through *straight*.

Rufus's *On the Naming of Parts* is excellent evidence of the attention devoted to the question of anatomical terminology. Yet this text also suggests very strongly how unsatisfactory the state of the art still was. It was often not clear, except from the context, how such basic terms as στόμαχος, φάρυγξ, σάρξ, even ἀρτηρία and νεῦρον were being used. These terms all had one or more popular acceptances, but these were overlaid with other more technical and specialised, yet still not fully standardised, uses. Meanwhile many individual nerves, muscles and blood-vessels had no name and had to be described – or sometimes numbered – to be identified. Where, as for the membranes of the eye, special terms had been coined, there was still no uniformity among anatomical writers on which to employ.

The halting development of anatomical terminology reflects the organisational or institutional weakness of ancient medicine very clearly. There was, in the ancient world, no medical profession as such in the full modern sense, for doctors had no legally recognised professional qualifications. There was no central authority that could specify the constituents of basic medical education, control medical qualifications and impose sanctions on deviant practitioners, let alone insist on, or make recommendations concerning, a uniform vocabulary in such areas as anatomy. Those who wanted to become doctors apprenticed themselves to medical practitioners, often but far from always in one of the centres of medical training such as Cos or – later – Alexandria. In the Hellenistic period many doctors belonged to one or other of the main medical sects or schools – the Dogmatists, the Pneumatists, the Empiricists and the Methodists – not that these were schools in the sense that they took responsibility for medical education. Moreover they disagreed fundamentally on the question of the value of anatomical investigation to the doctor. Two of the chief sects or groups, the Empiricists and the Methodists, rejected any inquiry into 'hidden causes', including any internal anatomical investigations involving dissection.[187] Accordingly most of those who contributed to the development of anatomy were among

the trigeminal nerve). My colleague, Dr M. Kaufman, to whom I am greatly indebted for an informative conversation on the anatomical possibilities, has further pointed out to me that there are appreciable variations in the appearance of these canals and foramina as between one subject and another, and as between newly dead corpses and others: in particular in the newly dead subject the hypoglossal and condylar canals might well give the appearance of being blind.

[187] See especially Celsus, *De Medicina* I, Proem 27ff, 57 and 62ff, cf. below, pp. 188f.

those who acquired the name Dogmatists. Yet that did not mean that they formed a closely-knit group, united by doctrine or methodology. On the contrary, the internal polemics within the Hippocratic writers, and the disputes that continued in the Hellenistic age between Praxagoras, Herophilus, Erasistratus and their followers, show that the disagreements among those who were later called Dogmatists were sometimes as basic and as far-reaching as those between them and the adherents of other sects. There was no central Dogmatist tradition, for all that those who were so called shared was a readiness to theorise about hidden causes, including both physiological issues and internal anatomy.

The development of a standard technical vocabulary in anatomy and other fields thus depended on the forging of some degree of consensus among practitioners who were usually – for obvious sociological reasons – highly individualistic and competitive.[188] They were often concerned to display their learning – both to their prospective clients and to their colleagues – and even sometimes to lay claim to esoteric knowledge. There was no strong external pressure to keep to a uniform medical vocabulary, and some incentive to claim to be original. While these were more prominent features of pathology and therapeutics, anatomy too was affected. We learn from Galen that a public dissection was often not the occasion for any research, nor even for any instruction, but simply an exhibition by one man, or even a competition between several rival experts all eager to parade their knowledge. Thus on one occasion (*AA* vii 10, K ii 619.16ff) he refers to the remarkable case of a dissection of an elephant, with many physicians present eager to learn whether the heart had two apexes or one, and two cavities or three, when Galen himself – so he tells us – predicted the structure correctly.[189] On another (*AA* vii 16, K ii 642.3ff) he describes the refutation of an anatomist who 'was always promising to exhibit the great artery empty of blood'.

When some ardent youths brought animals to him and challenged him to the test, he declared he would not make it without a fee. They laid down at once a thousand drachmae for him to pocket should he succeed. In his embarrassment he made many twists and turns, but, under pressure from all present, mustered courage to take a lancet and cut along the left side of the thorax especially at the point where, he

---

[188] Some aspects of this are discussed in Lloyd 1979, pp. 86ff.
[189] 'Before it was dissected', Galen says, ' I maintained that the same structure of the heart would be found in it as in all the animals that breathe air. This was apparent when the heart was opened. Moreover, I and my pupils easily found the bone in it, by fingering it. But our inexpert [colleagues], expecting in a large animal a like finding to that in others, concluded that the heart contains no bone, even in an elephant' (trans. Singer).

thought, the aorta should become visible. He proved so little practised in dissection that he cut on to the bone.[190]

Although some anatomical research was carried out in less unfavourable circumstances, notably in the Alexandrian Museum in the late fourth century B.C., the institutional framework it provided was quite exceptional, and in general both the transmission and the development of anatomical knowledge depended on the hazards of the doctor–apprentice relationship. The instruction that a newcomer would receive would vary appreciably with the teacher or teachers they attended. As for new anatomical research, even those doctors who might not seek to cultivate originality were not necessarily alert to the need to avoid the uncontrolled proliferation of alternative anatomical terms.

Yet Rufus's *On the Naming of Parts*, and the *Anatomy*, show that by the second century A.D. concern was being expressed on the question of variations in anatomical vocabulary. The multiplicity of names for a single part, and the multiplicity of referents for a single name, are recurrent themes in both works. This had the effect, at the least, of equipping the reader with a good deal of information that would be essential if he was to understand both earlier and contemporary usage, and Rufus's work no doubt served many generations of students in just that way. Nevertheless this was only a necessary, not a sufficient, condition for the establishment of a standard vocabulary, and despite the démarche that Rufus's work represents, it did not achieve that end. What eventually brought about a rather higher degree of standardisation in anatomical terminology towards the end of antiquity – and beyond – was not any improvement in the institutional framework, nor attempts to build directly on the comparativist foundations laid down by Rufus, so much as the increase in deference to authority, in particular to the authority of a single individual, Galen. In this field, as in others, it was Galen's practice – imperfect as it might be – that tended to provide the model and to serve as standard for later writers.

---

[190] The passage continues: 'Another of the same gang made his cut on to the bone across the intercostal region, and straightaway severed artery and vein. Thus the fellow incurred the ridicule of the youths who had deposited the stakes with the assembled spectators. The youths themselves now carried out what the last had promised, making their incision as they had seen me, without damaging any vessels. Moreover, they quickly applied two ligatures, one immediately beyond the point where the aorta rises from the heart, the other where it reaches the spine. Thus, as the impudent fellow had promised, after the death of the animal it might be seen whether this stretch of the artery between the ligatures were empty of blood. When it was found far from empty, they said that an irruption had taken place into it when the ligatures were applied . . .' (trans. Singer). Cf. also *AA* VII 14, K II 636.3ff, VIII 4, 669.4ff, VIII 5, 677.1ff, VIII 8, 690.3ff, and XIV 7 (D 212), and on the public dissection as a spectacle, see Vegetti 1981*b*, pp. 54ff.

5. THE CRITIQUE OF TRADITIONAL IDEAS IN SORANUS'S GYNAECOLOGY

The subject dealt with in Soranus's principal extant work – the *Gynaecology* – is one where he could draw on, or react to, a large mass of folklore or popular belief as well as an extensive corpus of earlier literature, the work of medical theorists and natural philosophers of many different kinds. The question we shall pose in this first study is how he used or responded to the various strands in these complex traditions. What does he take over or accept from each? To what extent are his gynaecological theories and practices circumscribed by one or other tradition or how far does he attempt – and manage – to free himself from them? What kinds of criticism does he advance, and on what types of principle or grounds? In an area where symbolic, not to say magical and superstitious, beliefs were rife, how clear is he on what could be endorsed or at least accommodated, and how successful in unmasking what to reject? Criticism of various aspects of folk medicine had begun already in some of the Hippocratic writers in the fifth and fourth centuries B.C. We have already studied features of the continuing interactions of popular belief and a commitment to research in Pliny in the first century A.D. Similar issues can be raised also in relation to Soranus in the next century, though, as we shall see, the impression we gain from him of the strengths of the critical approach is a very different one.

In two separate texts Soranus expressly requires that both the ideal midwife and the wet-nurse should be free from superstition, ἀδεισιδαίμων. Yet when 'superstition' is denounced, the questions that immediately arise are what precisely is being rejected, and why. We have only to recall the way in which Pliny explicitly criticises 'magic' and yet endorses many beliefs and practices that appear to us fairly obviously magical in origin, to appreciate that the denunciation of 'superstition' may, by itself, count for little.[191] What is interesting about Soranus's remarks is that he provides a context for, and an explanation of, his recommendations.

The best midwife, he says at 1 4, *CMG* IV 5.28ff, must be ἀδεισιδαίμων 'so as not to overlook what is expedient (τὸ συμφέρον) on account of a dream or omen or some customary rite (μυστήριον) or popular cult (θρησκεία)'.[192] Again on the wet-nurse in II 19, 68.15ff, he first specifies that she should not be ill-tempered because 'angry

---

[191] See above, section 3, especially p. 140.

[192] This and other translations of the *Gynaecology* are taken, with some adaptations, from Temkin 1956.

women are like maniacs and sometimes when the newborn cries from fear and they are unable to restrain it, they let it drop from their hands or overturn it dangerously', and then goes on: 'For the same reason the wet-nurse should not be superstitious (δεισιδαίμων) and prone to ecstatic states (θεοφόρητος) so that she may not expose the infant to danger when led astray by fallacious reasoning, sometimes even trembling like mad.' There may, perhaps, have been rather less danger of a wet-nurse putting the baby to risk than of a midwife doing so, but even so Soranus is concerned to exclude the followers of ecstatic cults and he repeats the general principle that there should be no interference from the side of religious belief with what the medical circumstances of the case require.

But it is one thing to issue warnings specifying that certain of the women assistants whom the doctor would encounter in his practice should be free from superstition: it is another to succeed in sustaining critical judgement in evaluating the bewildering mass of common, or not so common, beliefs concerning the treatment of women. Here Soranus had to deal not just with ideas and practices that he represents as widespread, but also with those that had been proposed by earlier writers, although there is, as we have seen before, a considerable overlap between the literate and the popular traditions and in some cases the contribution of the medical theorist or natural philosopher is not much more than to provide some rational or rationalising support for a current assumption. From the rich material in the *Gynaecology* we may select some examples to illustrate the different types of critical response that Soranus makes to beliefs of varying origins.[193]

First there are certain practices that he represents as common, at least among certain groups, and that he rejects for reasons that he makes explicit. Thus in II 11, 58.12ff, he discusses the severing of the navel cord.

One must cut off the navel cord at a distance of four finger-breadths from the abdomen, by means of something sharp-edged, that no bruising may arise. And of all material, iron cuts best; but the majority of the women practising midwifery approve of the section by means of glass, a reed, a potsherd, or the thin crust of bread; or by forcefully squeezing it apart with a cord, since during the earliest period, cutting is deemed of ill omen. This is absolutely ridiculous, ⟨for⟩ crying itself is of ill omen, and yet it is with this that the child begins its life. And lest a sympathetic affection[194] and irritation arise, when this part of the body is sawn through or crushed on all sides, it is better to be less superstitious (ἀδεισιδαιμονέστερον) and rather cut the navel cord with a knife.

---

[193] Cf. also Caelius Aurelianus, *Morb. Acut.* I 103, III 137, *Morb. Chron.* I 1, 119f.
[194] Cf. further below, pp. 178ff on 'sympathy'.

The reference to crying is, no doubt, meant to suggest that ill omens are unavoidable: more importantly, Soranus's view is that it is merely superstitious not to employ the best material for the job in hand, and he accordingly rejects the idea that iron should not be used because of its symbolic associations.[195]

The next chapter, II 12, 59.10ff, refers to practices that he describes as common among non-Greek peoples and even among some Greeks too.

After omphalotomy, the majority of the barbarians, as the Germans and Scythians, and even some of the Greeks,[196] put the newborn into cold water in order to make it firm and to let die, as not worth rearing, one that cannot bear the chilling but becomes livid or convulsed. And others wash it with wine mixed with brine, others with pure wine, others with the urine of an uncorrupt child, while others sprinkle it with fine myrtle or with oak gall. We, however, reject all of these. For cold, on account of its strong and sudden condensing action the like of which the child has not experienced, harms all; and though the harm resulting from the cold escapes notice in those more resistant it is, on the other hand, demonstrated by those susceptible to disease when they are seized by convulsions and apoplexies. Certainly, the fact that the child did not withstand the injury does not prove that it was impossible for it to live if unharmed; more resistant children also thrive better if not harmed in any way.[197]

Again Soranus mounts a clear argument to support the rejection of a common practice. Cold is bad for all babies, strong as well as weak. The fact that the weak succumb to harsh treatment is no reason for believing that they would not have survived had they been well cared for, and the fact that the strong survive is no indication that they have not been harmed.

It is not just certain harmful practices, but also some mistaken beliefs that Soranus attacks, again often specifying his grounds for doing do. In I 21, 14.6ff, he criticises the idea that menstruation is governed by the moon, a notion that had some support from medical writers and natural philosophers.

Some women menstruate one day, others, two days, still others, even a week or more, but the majority, three or four days. This occurs monthly, not with precision in all cases, but broadly speaking, for sometimes it is advanced or retarded a few days. For

---

[195] Pliny provides much evidence on the topic: see, e.g., *HN* XXIV 12, 68, 103, 176, XXXIV 138ff, 151ff. Cf. also Hdt. I 34ff (the story of Atys) and perhaps also the Pythagorean prohibition against stirring the fire with a knife, see Porphyry, *VP* 42, Iamblichus, *Protr.* 21.8. A wealth of comparative material was collected by Frazer 1911–15, e.g. I p. 159, III pp. 167, 176, 225ff, XI 65, 78, 80 n. 3, 154. See, most recently, Halleux 1974, Part II ch. 6, pp. 149ff.

[196] In Aristotle, *Pol.* 1336a12ff, a similar custom is described without any apparent disapproval: indeed Aristotle himself positively recommends that children should be accustomed to the cold from their earliest years. Cf., however, also Galen, *CMG* v 4,2 24.21ff, K VI 51.7ff, who objects to the custom.

[197] The passage continues with critical comments on the effects of wine, urine, myrtle and oak gall.

each woman it occurs at a stated time characteristic for her, and it does not ⟨seize⟩ all women at the same ⟨period⟩ as Diocles ⟨said⟩, nor, as Empedocles said, when the light of the moon is waning. For some women menstruate before the twentieth day of the month, others on the twentieth, and again some women menstruate when the light of the moon is waxing, some when it is waning and for the rest they menstruate on such days as is customary for them.

This was no doubt a popular belief, and apart from Diocles and Empedocles, named in Soranus's text, it was endorsed by, among others, Aristotle.[198]

Similarly in I 41, 28.25ff, he rejects the idea of external influences determining the time favourable for conception.

Thus the time of the waxing moon has been considered propitious. For things on the earth are believed to be in sympathy[199] with those up above; and just as most animals living in the sea are said to thrive with the waxing moon, but to waste away with the waning moon, and as in house mice the lobes of the liver are supposed to increase with the waxing moon but to decrease with the waning moon, the generative faculties in ourselves as well as in other animals are said to increase with the waxing moon but to decrease with the waning moon.

Soranus rejects this on the grounds of the evidence from the 'phenomena' themselves.[200] 'For we see conception taking place in all seasons as well as being brought to a successful end' (29.5f). Interestingly enough, however, he does not expressly reject – though he does not expressly endorse – the supposed facts about mice and animals living in the sea, only the conclusions drawn from this analogy so far as humans are concerned. 'And if at the changes of the moon some modification took place also in our bodies, we should in any event have observed it just as in mice and oysters. If, on the other hand, nothing of this kind has been observed to take place in our bodies, all such talk will be plausible but false' (29.10ff).

Beliefs such as that in the influence of the moon were widespread but they were also endorsed by prominent writers.[201] Again, who first suggested that the womb was, or was like, a living creature, it is impossible to establish, though, as we have seen, the idea is expressed in Plato's *Timaeus* and in the Hippocratic gynaecological treatises especially.[202] Soranus rejects this notion, although he is more concerned with the treatments connected with it, than with the

---

[198] See *HA* 582a34ff, *GA* 738a16ff, 767a1ff (the second of these passages notes that the periods are not exact) and cf. also, from the Hippocratic Corpus, *Oct.* ch. 1, *CMG* I 2,1 78.16ff (L vii 448.4ff), mentioned above p. 83 and n. 91.
[199] Cf. further below, pp. 178ff.
[200] Cf. further below, section 6.
[201] Cf. above, p. 83 and nn. 91 and 92.
[202] See the texts referred to above, p. 84 n. 100.

doctrine in itself. In I 8, 7.18ff, he simply says that 'the womb is not an animal – as was thought by some people', although he concedes that it is nevertheless similar in certain respects, in having a sense of touch. In III 29, 112.10ff, 113.3ff, discussing some of the treatments for hysterical suffocation that had been proposed by ancient authors who had assumed that the womb 'flees from evil smells', he writes: 'For the womb does not issue forth like a wild animal from the lair, delighted by fragrant odours and fleeing bad odours; rather it is drawn together because of the stricture caused by the inflammation.' Finally in IV 36, 149.21ff, dealing with treatments for prolapse of the womb, he writes:

> Some people apply a hairy bag to the womb, so that the organ may suffer pain from the sharp hair and contract. They are not aware that paralysed parts do not suffer any pain while parts that feel pain contract for a little while and prolapse again. But the majority administer pleasant aromas to smell, while they apply fumigations to the womb of an opposite character; and they believe that now the womb like an animal flees the bad odours and turns towards the good ones. We also censure Strato . . .

In this as in many other instances[203] the overriding consideration that weighs with Soranus in rejecting particular treatments or practices is that they cause discomfort, pain or even positive harm. Thus in II 16, 63.2ff, he criticises what he describes as a Thracian and Macedonian practice of tying down the new-born infant on a level board 'so that the part around the neck and the back of the head may be flattened'. Soranus comments that the effect of the practice is that the 'bodies are ulcerated and bruised because of the roughness beneath, and the head made ugly', though he adds: 'besides, even if this form were becoming, it could be accomplished without danger or sympathetic involvement[204] by shaping during the bath'. In II 50, 88.29ff, he attacks a treatment for tonsillitis. 'The nurses, however, poultice the throat with roasted cummin mixed with water, rub the tonsils with salt and old olive oil, and, seizing both legs with one hand, they place the child head downwards in the doorway and make the bregma touch the threshold of the house;[205] and this they do seven times.' Again the grounds for Soranus's rejection are the unfortunate consequences. 'The position leads to a congestion of the little head and consequently of the tonsils too, and the rubbing in itself exacerbates inflammation and even more so on account of the pungency of the salt. Cummin, ⟨moreover, by reason of⟩ its powerful effluvia also leads to a congestion of the head.'

In this last example there are fairly clear symbolic factors at work,

---

[203] Cf. especially II 12 (above, p. 170) and the texts referred to in n. 207 below.
[204] Cf. further below, pp. 178ff.
[205] Reading ὁδοῦ with Ermerins and Ilberg.

the threshold – a boundary often marked out by rites and customs – and the repeating of the action seven times. But in others the rationale for the practice criticised by Soranus is more obscure, and the mixture of symbolic or mythical beliefs, practical considerations and rationalisations is hard or impossible to disentangle.[206] We can only guess what lies behind a practice criticised in II 51, 89.23ff, where nurses – especially Syrian ones – are said to treat thrush by 'wrapping hair around a finger, dipping it into olive oil or honey and wiping off the ulcers', a practice to be rejected, in Soranus' view, because 'when the crusts are torn off, the ill-treated ulcers are irritated'. Nevertheless, whatever the provenance of a treatment or practice that Soranus believes to be risky or harmful, or even just unnecessarily pungent, he is emphatic in his rejection. Thus in III 29, 112.14ff, he names five separate authorities, Diocles, Mantias, Xenophon, Asclepiades and Hippocrates himself, who had suggested different treatments of varying severity for hysterical suffocation, and comments: 'we, however, censure all these men who start by hurting the inflamed parts and cause torpor by the effluvia of ill-smelling substances' (113.1ff). Similarly in IV 14–15, 144.21ff, 145.14ff, no fewer than eight earlier writers (again including Hippocrates) are named and their proposals for the treatment for the retention of the afterbirth are rejected, along with other treatments whose authors are not identified. 'All the aforesaid things are bad', says Soranus, and again the chief reasons he gives relate to the risk of harmful effects or side-effects.[207]

A considerable array of texts can be cited to illustrate the cautious and critical approach that Soranus adopts towards received opinions. In striking contrast to the uncritical deference that Pliny, for example, usually shows to the authority of the great names of the past, Soranus repeatedly expresses his doubts about the validity or wisdom of the ideas and practices of earlier medical writers. This is true in particular of the views he ascribes to Hippocrates[208] or his followers,

---

[206] Cf. also, e.g., II 41, 83.29ff, and III 12, 102.9ff.

[207] Cf. the rejection of pungent or painful remedies or practices at II 8, 56.24ff, II 14, 61.4ff, II 47, 87.1ff, II 54, 91.10ff, III 12, 101.28ff, III 33, 115.28ff, III 39, 118.15ff, IV 7, 137.6ff, IV 36, 149.11ff.

[208] The views Soranus ascribes to Hippocrates and to his followers correspond to some we find in passages in *Aph.*, *Jusj.*, *Epid.* II, *Mul.* I and II, *Nat. Puer.*, *Nat. Mul.*, *Superf.* and *Steril.* That is not to say Soranus necessarily had those treatises in mind, though on two occasions in *Gyn.* he cites particular works by name (*Aph.* at *Gyn.* I 65, 48.13ff, and *Nat. Puer.* at *Gyn.* I 60, 45.6ff). Elsewhere, for instance, he ascribes to Euryphon ideas that correspond similarly to some we find in passages in *Mul.* I and II, *Steril.* and *Nat. Mul.* We are not, therefore, in a position to reconstruct with confidence precisely which treatises Soranus took to be genuine works of Hippocrates himself.

which he cites more often to criticise than to endorse,[209] and the point extends to members of his own sect, the Methodists,[210] with whose beliefs or practices he frequently takes issue. Wherever and for whatever reason drastic treatments were used – whether as popular remedies or with the recommendations of particular theorists – Soranus tends to be critical of them.[211] Many common practices where symbolic factors play a part are rejected as useless or dangerous or both and he sometimes castigates the superstitious as such.

Thus far the record is a most impressive one. But there is, if not another side to the question, at least some more to be said about it. Hardly surprisingly, Soranus does not always see through and reject the merely symbolic or affective in beliefs and practices: nor is he always quite so forthright in his condemnation of such beliefs and practices as in some of the passages that have already been mentioned.

First there are occasions when Soranus mentions, but does not expressly refute, a folk-belief. When we bear in mind the scepticism he evinces about magical or symbolic notions in some of the passages we have considered, we might argue that he did not think it necessary *always* to state his condemnation. Sometimes, however, there appears to be a certain ambivalence in his position, as, for example, when he positively endorses aspects of a popular belief, while not necessarily doing so in full.

His discussion of whether the foetus is affected by the mother's psychological state, and by what she sees, in I 39, is a case in point. 'What is one to say', he begins (27.28ff),

> about various states of the soul also producing certain changes in the mould of the foetus? For instance, some women, seeing monkeys during intercourse, have borne children resembling monkeys. The tyrant of the Cyprians who was misshapen, compelled his wife to look at beautiful statues during intercourse and became the father of well-shaped children; and horse-breeders, during covering, place noble horses in front of the mares.

Soranus does not here comment directly one way or the other[212] on the particular stories about the tyrant of Cyprus and women producing babies like monkeys. On the other hand he undoubtedly

---

[209] See, e.g., I 45, 31.26ff and 32.1ff, and IV 13, 144.2ff, as well as III 29, 112.14ff and IV 14–15, 144.21ff, 145.14ff, cited in my text. Cf. also Caelius Aurelianus, *Morb. Acut.* II 59ff (sec. 64), 113ff (sec. 121ff), 154, III 25ff, 57ff, 74, 83ff, 153ff, 206f, *Morb. Chron.* I 131, III 139ff, IV 77, 112ff, V 24ff.

[210] See further below, pp. 186f.

[211] Sometimes, to be sure, Soranus himself has to recommend recourse to drastic remedies, as for instance in connection with the removal of a dead foetus, IV 9ff, 140.2ff.

[212] He opens his discussion of the topic with a *question* – what is one to say about . . .? – which does not receive a direct answer.

endorses the general point that the state of mind of the mother may have an important influence on the child produced.

Thus, in order that the offspring may not be rendered misshapen, women must be sober during coitus because in drunkenness the soul becomes the victim of strange fantasies; this furthermore, because the offspring bears some resemblance to the mother as well, not only in body but in soul. Therefore it is good that the offspring be made to resemble the soul when it is stable and not deranged by drunkenness. Indeed, it is utterly absurd that the farmer takes care not to throw seed upon very moist and flooded land, and that on the other hand mankind assumes nature to achieve a good result in generation when seed is deposited in bodies which are very moist and inundated ⟨by⟩ satiety.

Elsewhere he accepts a popular practice that was associated with symbolic assumptions, but provides it with a different, naturalistic, basis. Thus in II 6, 54.11ff, dealing with delivery, he stresses the importance of breathing.

One must advise her to drive her breath into the flanks without screaming, rather with groaning and detention of the breath. . . . Whence, for the unhindered passage of the breath, it is necessary to loosen their girdles as well as to free the chest of any binder, though not on account of the lay (ἰδιωτική) conception according to which womenfolk are unwilling to suffer any fetter and thus ⟨also⟩ loosen the hair; it is rather for the above-mentioned reason that even loosening the hair possibly effects good tonus of the head.

Two areas in particular where symbolic beliefs were especially widespread and deepseated[213] were in connection with assumptions about the superiority of right to left and of male to female, and on both Soranus's attitudes are complex. At II 20 he refutes one popular notion, that a wet-nurse who is to feed a male should herself have given birth to a male child: 'one should pay no heed to these people, for they do not consider that mothers of twins, the one being male and the other female, feed both with one and the same milk' (68.30ff). Again in II 48 (87.9ff) he rejects the doctrine of Mnesitheus and Aristanax that female babies should be weaned later because they are weaker: 'for they do not realise that some female infants are both stronger and fleshier than many males. One should not alienate the child from anything . . .' Elsewhere, however, even though Soranus rejects some current practices in swaddling the baby as causing discomfort or even cruelty,[214] and recommends that swaddling should be discontinued if the infant is chafed by the friction of the bandages,[215] he still endorses attempts to mould the baby by

---

[213] Cf. Lloyd 1966, pp. 41ff, and see above, pp. 34, 36f and 41 n. 167 in connection with Aristotle in particular, and Part II on the debate on the difference between the sexes.

[214] E.g. the rejection of Antigenes's adoption of the so-called Thessalian swaddling, II 14, 60.29ff.

[215] See II 42, 84.25ff.

swaddling[216] and indeed to mould the male baby differently from the female. In II 15, 61.30ff, we read: 'Having also swaddled the other arm in the same manner, she [the midwife] should then wrap one of the broader bandages circularly around the thorax, exerting an even pressure when swaddling males, but in females binding the parts at the breasts more tightly, yet keeping the region of the loins loose, for in women this form is more becoming.'

A similar ambivalence also characterises Soranus's views concerning aspects of the symbolic associations of right and left. In I 45, 31.26ff, he is categorical in his rejection of Hippocrates's account of how to tell whether a pregnant mother will have a boy or a girl. The signs of a male child were supposed to include not just the better colour of the mother, but also that her right breast is 'bigger, firmer, fuller and in particular the nipple is swollen. Whereas the signs with a female are that, together with pallor, the left breast is more enlarged and in particular the nipple.' Soranus comments: 'this conclusion he has reached from a false assumption. For he believed a male to be formed if the seed were conceived in the right part of the womb, a female, on the other hand, if in the left part. But in the physiological commentaries *On Generation* we proved this untrue.'[217] Again in IV 12, 143.11ff, he is equally clear in his rejection of the division of labour – on symbolic grounds – between the hands in delivering the child. 'It is, however, difficult to suppose why the left hand should be appropriate for pulling and to explain it on the grounds that serpents too are lifted with it – for both statements are untrue.' Rather, as Soranus had explained (IV 9, 140.18ff), the left, being softer, is more appropriate for internal manipulations (while the right is the hand that should be used to extract the embryo).

Yet once again we find that Soranus endorses one common practice concerning the right hand. In II 42, 84.17ff, he recommends that in unswaddling the child

one should first free one hand, after some days the other, and then the feet. And one should liberate the right hand first. For if it is restrained according to the practice of those who free the left hand first, it becomes comparatively weak, because it gets exercise later than the other, so that also for this reason some people become left-handed.

Where Plato had already complained that nurses were making Greek children 'lame, as it were, in their hands', by differentiating between

---

[216] Cf. also II 32–3, 77.3ff, for other practices of moulding the baby's limbs by massage which Soranus does not reject, and II 16, 63.2ff, mentioned in my text, p. 172.

[217] Soranus's *On Generation* has not survived. *Gyn.* I 45 continues with other criticisms of further notions about how to predict the sex of the child which also clearly presuppose assumptions about the superiority of the male.

the right and left hands in swaddling,[218] Soranus does not adopt such a radical stance[219] and does not dissent from what was still presumably the practice of the majority.[220]

These passages indicate that Soranus's rejection of certain popular symbolic beliefs was sometimes less than total. Some he reports without critical comment, and others with remarks that can be construed as an endorsement. In some cases, no doubt, Soranus saw no harm in common symbolic practices. In II 10, 57.18ff, he says that the first thing the midwife should do is to put the newborn on the earth, and announce the sex of the child by a sign 'as is the custom of women'. On occasions there could be a delicate balance between what the doctor thought good medical practice and the expectations of his women patients themselves. In a well-known passage, III 42, 121.26ff, he describes certain amulets used for haemorrhage of the womb.

> Some people say that some things are effective by antipathy,[221] such as the magnet and the Assian stone and hare's rennet and certain other amulets to which we on our own part pay no attention. Yet one should not forbid their use; for even if the amulet has no direct effect, still through hope it will possibly make the patient more cheerful.

In I 53, 38.21ff, the problem is not so straightforward. He recognises that pregnant women sometimes develop irrational desires for all sorts of things, including some that would harm them or the embryo. Soranus begins: 'One must oppose the desires of pregnant women for harmful things first by arguing that the damage from the things which satisfy the desires in an unreasonable way harms the foetus just as it harms the stomach . . .' But if reasoning with the expectant mother will not work, Soranus makes a concession which illustrates his concern for the psychological state[222] of the mother-to-be and his

---

[218] *Lg.* 794 d 8ff.

[219] There were, no doubt, certain practical considerations that helped to perpetuate and confirm a custom that was held to be appropriate for deepseated symbolic reasons. So far as males were concerned, at least, left-handers were clearly no use in the battle-line.

[220] Despite his reference to those who do the opposite and free the left hand first. Cf. also II 37, 80.10ff, where Soranus recommends that the baby should not always be put to lie on the right side, first 'in order to change about and feed it on each breast', and second 'lest the right hand, if not always exercised, remain inactive after the removal of the swaddling clothes'.

[221] Cf. further below, pp. 178ff.

[222] Soranus's concern for the psychology of the patient, of the expectant mother and of the newborn baby, emerges in many passages in the *Gynaecology*. See I 25, 16.18ff (when approaching their first menstruation, girls should be encouraged to take passive exercise and their minds should be diverted), I 34, 24.6ff (the psychological state of the woman affects whether she conceives), I 46, 32.22ff (once the woman has conceived, one must guard against all excess and change, both somatic and psychological), I 47, 34.30ff (encouragement is necessary to help ensure against a recurrence of the ejection of the seed), I 54, 39.10ff (the mind of the expectant mother should be diverted when she approaches parturition), II

readiness to compromise. 'If, however, they feel wretched, though one should offer them none of these things during the first days, some days later one should do so; ⟨for⟩ if they do not obtain what they want, even the body, through the despondency of the soul, grows thinner', and he makes certain suggestions about how the damage can be kept to a minimum.

Finally the most interesting and complex case which throws light on the problems Soranus faced in coming to terms with popular symbolic beliefs concerns the doctrines of sympathy and antipathy, which figure with some frequency in the *Gynaecology*.[223] The idea that there are connections and interactions or mutual influences between apparently unrelated objects takes an astonishing variety of forms. It was often cited to explain the supposed influence of the heavenly bodies, especially the moon, on human life and on events on earth in general.[224] In philosophy, the Stoics proposed the doctrine in a universal form, that is that everything has some connection with everything else. This was both a general physical doctrine concerning the plenum and the absence of void, and also the basis of specific explanations of a variety of effects.[225] Apparent cases of action at a distance, especially, tended to be referred to a supposed sympathetic bond between the objects affected, and in 'alchemy' and pharmacology the real or imagined effects of certain substances on one another, or of substances on parts of the body, were often put down to their sympathies or antipathies.[226]

5, 53.12ff, 54.8ff (on allaying the anxiety of the woman during delivery), ii 6, 54.22ff (the midwife should be careful not to cause the woman shame by staring at her genitals), ii 18, 65.16ff (on the link of affection between mother and child created by breast-feeding), ii 40, 83.9ff (on avoiding frightening the baby if it keeps crying), iii 16, 104.22ff (divert the mind of the patient in cases of retention of the menses), iii 25, 109.6ff (the psychological effects of satyriasis in women), iii 46, 125.3ff (avoid sexual arousement in cases of 'gonorrhoea'), iii 47, 126.5ff (the psychological side-effects to be expected in cases of atony of the womb) and a whole series of passages in iv dealing with difficult labour, e.g. iv 2, 131.11ff (difficult labour can be caused by the woman's own fears or anxieties, or by her inexperience, see also iv 4, 134.1ff, iv 6, 135.7ff, iv 7, 136.8ff), iv 9, 140.6ff (it is necessary to warn the expectant mother of the dangers of complications when extraction of the foetus by forcible methods becomes necessary) and iv 35, 148.3ff (prolapse of the womb can be caused by psychological factors). Cf. also ii 19, 68.2ff, on the wet-nurse.

[223] Cf. also Caelius Aurelianus, *Morb. Acut.* i 71, iii 140, *Morb. Chron.* i 62, ii 25, 27, 94, iii 69.

[224] As indeed in *Gyn.* i 41, 28.25ff, quoted above, p. 171. From the time of Seleucus (second century B.C.) at least, a connection between the moon and tides was known. Préaux 1973, pp. 9ff, 64ff, 103ff, 288ff, provides extensive documentation on ancient ideas concerning the sympathetic influence of the moon.

[225] See, e.g., Cicero, *N.D.* ii 7.19ff, *Div.* ii 14.33ff, Sextus, *M.* v 4ff, ix 75ff, especially 79ff, Cleomedes i 1, 4.1ff, 8.15ff, Alexander, *Mixt.* 216.14ff, 226.30ff, 227.5ff and cf. Ptolemy, *Tetrabiblos* ii 1. Cf. Weidlich 1894, K. Reinhardt 1926, Sambursky 1959, pp. 9ff, 41ff, 108ff, Préaux 1973.

[226] As can be extensively documented from Pliny, for example: see *HN* xx 1f, xxii 106, xxiv 1ff, xxxvii 59ff, especially.

In Soranus some such beliefs get short shrift, but at the same time the notion of sympathy is retained in modified form and has an important role to play in his own theories and explanations. To consider the negative or critical side first, there is nothing to suggest that he endorsed the doctrine in the universal form in which it was proposed by the Stoics.[227] Again he certainly explicitly rejects a number of particular beliefs about the supposed sympathetic or antipathetic connections between objects. Apart from I 41 (28.25ff) and III 42 (121.26ff) already mentioned (above, pp. 171 and 177),[228] in I 63, 47.16ff, he refutes those practitioners who had used certain kinds of amulets as contraceptives for their supposed antipathetic effects. 'Others, however, have even made use of amulets which on grounds of antipathy they believe to have great effect; such are wombs of mules and the dirt in their ears and more things of this kind which according to the outcome reveal themselves as falsehoods.'

Positively, however, Soranus uses συμπάσχειν, συμπάθεια and their cognates in a variety of ways. First there is a psychological use, as when he requires that the midwife and the wet-nurse should be συμπάσχουσα or συμπαθής, that is, kind and sensitive, or, as we say, 'sympathetic'.[229] But he uses these terms also of certain physiological connections or interactions. Often when he remarks that a certain type of treatment, for instance, carries with it the risk of συμπάθεια, he does not specify the effects he anticipates or does so only very generally by the addition of such a term as νευρική.[230] Thus in I 63, 47.16, certain contraceptives are rejected as causing congestion of the head and bringing on συμπάθεια. In II 11, 58.19ff (see above, pp. 169f) incorrect cutting of the navel cord may give rise to συμπάθεια. In II 16, 63.9 (above, p. 172) moulding of the head is said to be possible without the drastic measures adopted by the Thracians and Macedonians, and can be carried out without danger and ἀσυμπαθῶς. In II 49, 88.22, he discusses how to deal with greater συμπάθεια – as we might say, in this case, sympathetic disturbances – in teething. In III 41, 120.13f (cf. 121.12) he speaks of trying to avoid causing συμπάθειαι and inflammations in the womb which may arise from blood-clots, and in IV 7, 137.7, he says that a shock to the womb may cause συμπάθειαι.[231]

---

[227] Cf. Temkin 1956, p. xxxi.

[228] Cf. also I 21, 14.6ff (above, pp. 170f) and Caelius Aurelianus, *Morb. Chron.* III 78.

[229] See I 4, 5.21, and II 19, 66.11 and 68.10f. At II 18, 65.18, when he says that mothers who breast feed their own babies become συμπαθέστεραι, he probably has psychological factors chiefly in mind. Cf. also Caelius Aurelianus, *Morb. Chron.* I 156.

[230] See IV 9, 140.7, IV 15, 145.16, cf. 145.18 and 145.29.

[231] Cf. also I 65, 48.24ff (only non-pungent vaginal suppositories should be used for fear of

We gain a clearer idea of the type of connection and interaction Soranus has in mind where he gives more specific indications of the parts affected. In III 25, 109.7f, he speaks of the sympathetic relation between the meninges (of the brain)[232] and the womb in his account of the alienation of mind that accompanies satyriasis. In III 20, 106.19ff, he specifies certain parts of the body that are affected when the neck of the womb is inflamed ('if the right part is inflamed the leg on the same side is affected – συμπάσχει – and the groin swollen; and if the left, then things are reversed') and III 22, 107.17ff, follows this up: 'if the whole womb is inflamed all signs are present together; the sympathetic reactions are severe and there is a greater swelling of the abdomen. . . . As a rule, in inflammations of the womb the head and neck are sympathetically affected, while in inflammation of the abdomen and the peritoneum they are little affected or not at all.[233] In I 15, 10.27ff, especially, he specifies that when the womb is diseased 'it influences the στόμαχος [here probably the cardia of the stomach] and the meninges by sympathy. It also has a kind of natural sympathy with the breasts. Thus when the womb becomes bigger in puberty, the breasts become enlarged with it.'

This provides us with the richest example of the complexity of Soranus's response to what was, in this case, a combination of both popular and philosophical beliefs. His generally critical attitude is clear: the more extreme type of sympathetic or antipathetic connection is rejected.[234] Yet he still has use for the idea of such connections. Some of his applications, such as, for instance, the proposed connection between the meninges of the brain and the womb in I 15 and III 25, appear to be largely imaginary – although according to his own methodological principles he ought to have been able to claim that such applications are suggested directly by the 'phenomena'

---

greater συμπάθεια and heat), IV 2, 131.21ff (according to Demetrius, difficult labour may be the result of lack of tonus, when the body is very relaxed and so cannot respond – οὐ . . . δύνασθαι συμπαθεῖν) and IV 8, 139.26ff (one should do everything gently and without bruising, so that the woman giving birth remains ἀσυμπαθής).

[232] That by μήνιγγες here Soranus indicates the meninges of the brain seems clear from the reference to mind at 109.7.

[233] Cf. also III 17, 105.18ff (which refers to sympathetic affection of the στόμαχος, and other complications – hiccups, pains in the throat, jaws, bregma and eyes, hindrance of urine and faeces – in inflammation of the womb), III 29, 113.6f (συμπάθεια between the στόμαχος and the womb), III 31, 114.6ff (συμπάθεια between certain tendons and the head with the womb) and III 49, 127.11f (sympathetic effects of paralysis of the womb – involuntary discharge of urine and faeces and heaviness in the rectum).

[234] The one possible exception, where Soranus appears to accept a popular and presumably purely symbolic belief in an antipathy, is in II 49, 88.5ff, where, in the text as we have it, he speaks of the effect of the brain of a hare on teething gums. The authenticity of this passage has, however, been doubled: see Temkin 1956, p. xxxii and p. 120 n. 74, following Ermerins, but contrast Ilberg ad loc.

themselves.[235] On the other hand, as the example of the 'sympathetic' interaction of the womb and the breasts in puberty shows, some of the connections he proposes are real enough, even though they would now be explained, not in terms of the direct influence of one part of the body on another, but as the joint effect – on both the parts affected – of certain hormonal changes or (in other cases) of nervous disturbances.

No modern, let alone any ancient, writer on gynaecology could be said to have eradicated *all* traces of doubtful popular beliefs and practices from his work. As we have seen, Soranus's views are rather ambivalent on certain topics where – with some hindsight – we detect the influence of symbolic or affective assumptions. Moreover – unsurprisingly – many of the treatments he takes over from his predecessors seem today to be of dubious value – and many are likely to have been quite ineffective.[236]

Nevertheless his caution and scepticism are strongly marked. He is on the look-out for superstitious beliefs and practices – whether of popular origin or the work of rationalising medical or philosophical writers – both on the score of their irrationality and pointlessness and, more especially, on that of the pain and positive harm they may cause. In this he is greatly helped by his sceptical epistemology, which had well developed critical and destructive tendencies, even though (as we shall see[237]) it was a difficult position to sustain consistently throughout his practice. Soranus was also, as we noted at the outset, following a long tradition of the criticism of popular assumptions and of speculative theories that goes back to the Hippocratics. Although much of that tradition is now lost, the probability is that Soranus added to it, and that some, perhaps even a large number, of his critical points are original. So far as our extant evidence goes, this is certainly true of many of them, and it could be argued that Soranus showed greater originality as a critic of received opinions than in his own constructive formulation of new theories, explanations, remedies and practices.

However, the accommodation of amulets for psychological reasons in III 42, and the discussion of how to deal with the irrational desires of pregnant women in I 53, show that Soranus is prepared to compromise in response to his patients' own beliefs. Some interpreters

---

[235] See below, section 6, especially pp. 184 and 189.
[236] This is true, for example, of many of the long list of contraceptives recommended in I 61ff, 45.20ff (even after Soranus himself had rejected the use of amulets in this connection, I 63, 47.16ff, above, p. 179), cf. Hopkins 1965–6, p. 150.
[237] See below, section 6.

might see Soranus's position here as a sign of weakness. Despite the critical tradition of which we have spoken and of which – in his own time – Soranus was himself a notable spokesman, 'superstition' showed no signs of diminishing, and may even have been on the increase, in the second century A.D. Certainly it too had some articulate representatives in the first three or four centuries A.D., even though some of these would not have seen themselves in that light.[238] Yet Soranus's accommodations should rather be seen as a mark of realism. He has not just some of the best Hippocratics,[239] but also Plato,[240] behind him in his view that the doctor should take his patients' own attitudes into account and should, so far as possible, *persuade* them to accept the course of treatment recommended. There were plenty of hard heads among Greek medical theorists, who were prepared to go ahead and implement some extreme ideas.[241] By contrast, it is a strength rather than a weakness of Soranus's gynaecology that he puts his concern for his patients' feelings and their psychological state[242] above his own conception of the futility of superstitious belief.

6. THE EPISTEMOLOGICAL THEORY AND PRACTICE OF SORANUS'S METHODISM

In a famous passage in the *Outlines of Pyrrhonism* (*P.* I 236ff) Sextus Empiricus asserts that the Sceptic has more affinity with the Methodists than with any other medical school – more so than with the Empiricists. 'For the Method alone is agreed (δοκεῖ) to avoid rashness concerning things that are unclear in the making of presumptuous claims as to whether they are apprehensible or not: but following appearances it grasps from these what is agreed to be expedient in accordance with the practice of the Sceptics.'

At least since Wellmann (1922, especially pp. 403f), the idea that

---

[238] From the first century A.D. I may instance Pliny, from the second Aelius Aristides, from the third and fourth the upsurge of neo-Platonism in such versions of it as that of Iamblichus. On the whole topic, see L. Edelstein (1937) 1967, pp. 205ff, Dodds 1951, pp. 283ff and Dodds 1968.

[239] For example the author of *Prog.* ch. 1, L II 110.1ff, and cf. *Morb.* I ch. 1, L VI 140.1ff, *VM* ch. 2, *CMG* I, 1 37.9ff, and *Decent.* ch. 12, *CMG* I, 1 28.23ff.

[240] *Lg.* 720b–e.

[241] This is a criticism already levelled against Herodicus in *Epid.* VI sec. 3 ch. 18, L V 302.1ff, cf. Plato, *R.* 406a ff, and it becomes a stock objection to Greek medicine in certain Roman writers, see especially Pliny, *HN* XXIX 6ff, 12ff, who also gives it as one reason for the rapid success and popularity of Asclepiades in Rome in the first century A.D. that he prescribed mainly pleasant remedies and identified the easy with the true (*HN* XXVI 12ff, cf. Celsus, *De Medicina* III 4.1–3).

[242] See the passages cited in n. 222 above.

there is a close connection between the Pyrrhonean scepticism of Sextus and Methodist medicine has been much canvassed, and this link has variously been seen as fundamental to our understanding of Methodism, of Sextus's scepticism, or of both. Thus in an influential discussion, Edelstein asserted that 'Methodist medicine must be interpreted as a transposition of Aenesidemean Skepticism', that 'the philosophical basis of Methodism is . . . Skepticism',[243] and that, in what he saw as an epistemological crisis created by Asclepiades's attack on the repeatability of observations and by the confrontation with Hippocratic scepticism and empiricism,[244]

no solution of the difficulties could possibly come from Dogmatism or Empiricism. Skepticism offered a way out, for in Skepticism there was the same rejection of all general principles, the same limitation to the here and now, as in Hippocratic empiricism . . . If the physician acted on Skeptical principles and made the afflictions of the human body the law governing his treatment, he was not letting himself be directed by a principle derived from his experience, or from his intellect, and then applied to his patient; on the contrary, each case suggested to the physician a suitable individual treatment.'[245]

Although with the authority of Sextus himself behind him Edelstein was on firm ground in claiming a link between scepticism and Methodism,[246] other aspects of his interpretation of Methodism were less secure, indeed less clear. One central problem concerns how certain fundamental notions of Methodism are supposed to be compatible with, let alone to be entailed by, scepticism. All our chief ancient secondary sources – Celsus, Galen, Sextus – are agreed that the doctrine of the three general or common conditions or states (κοινότητες, *communia*) of the body, the constricted (στεγνόν, στέγνωσις, *adstrictum*), the lax (ροῶδες, ῥύσις, *fluens*) and the mixed (ἐπιπεπλεγμένον, *mixtum*) was a basic, even the basic teaching of the Methodists. Galen makes a certain amount of play with the different interpretations of these three adopted by different members of the Methodist school.[247] But the chief difficulty does not lie in the varying application of this idea, so much as in the question of how any such notion can be squared with the sceptics' insistence on withholding judgement.

[243] L. Edelstein (1935) 1967, pp. 186 and 187.
[244] Certain aspects of Edelstein's views of the antecedents of Methodism, for example what it owes to Hippocratic ideas, are not fundamental to his understanding of Methodism as it became established from the beginning of the first century A.D.
[245] Edelstein (1935) 1967, p. 189.
[246] Contrast, however, Deichgräber's assimilation of Sextus with the Empiricist sect (1930), 1965, pp. 19, 216ff.
[247] See, e.g., Galen's presentation of what the Dogmatist would say in criticism of the Methodists at *Sect. Intr.* ch. 9, *Scr. Min.* III 23.4ff and 25.17ff, K I 93.12ff, 96.15ff. Cf. also Celsus, *De Medicina* I, Proem 66f, below, p. 197.

The problem can be highlighted by juxtaposing two passages from Edelstein. Writing of the connection between Methodism and scepticism, he puts it:

> concerning everything but phenomena the Skeptic withholds judgement: he does not claim that the hidden is unknowable, but he has as yet no knowledge of it and it does not concern him . . . Thus the Methodist leaves unanswered the question whether the hidden can be apprehended or not; he does not deny the possibility, as does the Empiricist . . ., for it is of no consequence to him.[248]

Yet earlier in his article Edelstein had said:

> The Methodists believed that all the fundamentals of treatment could be represented as knowledge (ἔνδειξις), not merely as observation (τήρησις). They agreed with the Dogmatists that experience was not enough for the physician, and for this reason they opposed the Empiricists. On the other hand, they did not, like the Dogmatists, derive their knowledge from logical deliberations but from the very phenomena from which the Empiricists gained their experience; they claimed an ἔνδειξις τῶν φαινομένων . . . They rely on the absolute validity of their knowledge . . .[249]

Hardly surprisingly, in view of these contrasting statements, Edelstein wrote: 'the mixture of Dogmatist and Empiricist principles is unclear . . . Above all, the fundamental principle of Methodism, the ἔνδειξις τῶν φαινομένων, seems full of contradictions.'[250] Edelstein did not attempt a detailed analysis of the Methodist ἔνδειξις and his interpretation of it as *knowledge* (*Wissen*) is obviously open to challenge.[251] Yet it is enough for us at this stage to note that the contrast between the Empiricists' reliance on observation alone and the Methodists' view that ἔνδειξις is possible is explicitly drawn not only in the probably spurious Galenic *Introduction or the Doctor*,[252] but also in the clearly authentic *On Sects for Beginners*[253] and is indeed

---

[248] L. Edelstein (1935) 1967, p. 186.

[249] L. Edelstein (1935) 1967, p. 184.

[250] L. Edelstein (1935) 1967, p. 185.

[251] Edelstein himself was aware ((1935) 1967, p. 186) that Sextus at least had insisted (*P.* 1 240) that the Methodist ἔνδειξις is undogmatic. Some confusion arises, and already arose in the ancient world, from the fact that ἔνδειξις is also a term used to describe the Dogmatists' claim that it is possible for the causes of diseases to be 'indicated', see, e.g., Galen, *Sect. Intr.* chh. 4f, *Scr. Min.* III 7.19ff, 10.18 (K I 73.3ff, 77.2) (cf. 10.22, K 77.6 where this possibility is denied by the Empiricist). At *Sect. Intr.* ch. 6, *Scr. Min.* III 13.19ff (K I 81.5ff) Galen raises the question of why the Methodists do not call themselves Dogmatists, given their use of the notion of ἔνδειξις, and replies, on behalf of the Methodists, that they do not investigate what is hidden but 'spend their time' with the phenomena.

[252] K XIV 677.12ff, cf. 682.17ff.

[253] *Sect. Intr.* ch. 6, *Scr. Min.* III 12.19f, 13.12, 13.19ff (K I 79.16f, 80.14, 81.5ff). These passages show that the main context in which the notion of ἔνδειξις was used relates to treatment: the claim was that the common states themselves indicate the therapies (the common states being described as φαινόμεναι, 13.24, 14.1f, 14.5f, K I 81.9, 10f, 15). This suggests that in such expressions as ἔνδειξις τῶν κοινοτήτων (e.g. K XIV 677.13, 683.1, cf. 680.13ff) the genitive is to be understood as subjective rather than objective.

represented, in the latter work, as one of the two chief marks that distinguish the Methodists from the Empiricists.[254]

One of the principal issues that Edelstein was concerned with was that of when, and by whom, the Methodist school was founded. Throughout his discussion he drew more on such secondary sources as Celsus and Galen[255] than on the main primary texts that are extant from the Methodists themselves, chief among which are the works of Soranus, who was active some 100 years after the founding of the school, that is in the second century A.D. To be sure, Soranus alludes to differences of opinion among the Methodists ('our people') and himself expresses his disagreement with some of the views he ascribes to Themison and others.[256] But even if we must, accordingly, renounce any ambition to reconstruct the teachings of the school as a whole[257] on the basis of what we have in Soranus, he remains, nevertheless, our most valuable original source from among those who considered themselves Methodists.

My aim in this study is to try, through an examination of Soranus himself, to get clearer the answers to certain questions both about the interactions of scepticism and Methodism, and on the relation between theory and practice within Methodist medicine itself. How far can we define the epistemological foundations of Soranus's medicine? How important is the rejection of Dogmatist or Empiricist principles to him and how coherent is his own alternative position? How do his own Methodist views compare with the reports on that school, and on scepticism, in our secondary sources? The problems concern not just his explicit epistemology but also how that is applied in his work. How far does his actual practice in argument, including the methods and criteria he uses in dealing with the issues he discusses, reflect, or how far does it appear to conflict with, such epistemological positions as he explicitly commits himself to? What light does Soranus throw on the question of the practicality of sceptical principles when applied to medicine? For our purposes the extant original Greek of

---

[254] *Sect. Intr.* ch. 6, *Scr. Min.* III 14.10ff, 16ff, K I 82.2ff, 7ff. The other difference (*Scr. Min.* 14.14ff, K I 82.6ff) is that the Empiricists treat what is hidden (τὰ ἄδηλα) as ἄγνωστα (unknown/unknowable) whereas the Methodists treat them as useless, ἄχρηστα. Cf. also Celsus I, Proem 57, where the Methodists complain, against the Empiricists, that there is little 'art' (*ars*) in the observation of experience.

[255] Both these authors, especially Galen, are critical of Methodist medicine and at many points their reports may be suspected of a certain bias: cf. further below, n. 285.

[256] See below, p. 186 on I 27, 17.17ff, p. 197 on III 24, 108.15ff and pp. 197–8 on III 42, 121.14ff; cf. also Caelius Aurelianus, e.g. *Morb. Acut.* II 46. On whether Themison himself was the founder or merely the forerunner of the Methodist school, compare Wellmann 1922, pp. 396ff, with L. Edelstein (1935) 1967, pp. 174ff.

[257] The Methodists were, indeed, careful to describe themselves as an ἀγωγή, a training or a tendency, rather than as a sect, αἵρεσις.

the *Gynaecology* is both more reliable and more interesting than the paraphrastic Latin versions of his *Acute* and *Chronic Diseases* that we have from Caelius Aurelianus,[258] and I shall accordingly concentrate on the *Gynaecology*.

One of the most impressive features of this work is its severely practical orientation. On such questions as the characteristics to be looked for in the ideal midwife, on how to deal with faulty presentation, on the care of the expectant mother, of the new-born baby, even of the wet-nurse, Soranus's discussion is, as we have seen in the last section, not just detailed and comprehensive, but also full of common sense, qualities that no doubt contributed largely to its survival.[259] Yet there are plenty of signs, throughout the work, of his awareness of theoretical and second-order debates in contemporary medicine, and on many occasions he directly or obliquely criticises Dogmatist and Empiricist theories, including their foundational, epistemological, positions.

Thus at 1 4, *CMG* IV 5. 1 off, in his description of the best midwife, he says that she must be trained in all branches of therapy. She should, moreover, be 'able to prescribe hygienic regulations for her patients, to observe the general (κοινόν) and the proximate (προσεχές) features of the case, and from these to find out what is expedient, not from the causes or from the repeated observations of what usually occurs or something of the kind' – a clear enough allusion to Dogmatist and Empiricist methodologies. At first sight it might seem strange that Soranus should take the trouble to suggest that the midwife should not be contaminated by the theories of other schools. We should, however, remember that one of his requirements for the ideal midwife is that she should be 'literate in order to be able to comprehend the art through theory too' (1 3, 4. 18f).

In 1 4 he does not mention any schools or individuals by name. But in dealing with a wide range of disputed questions it is characteristic of his method that he begins by reporting the views of the contending schools or of named individuals, and then criticises them before giving his own opinion. A classic example of this is in 1 27–9, 1 7. 1 7ff, when he discusses whether menstruation serves any useful purpose, where he cites Herophilus, Themison ('and the majority of our people', 17.25f), Mnaseas and Dionysius, as well as other unidentified groups, setting out systematically the various positions that had been

---

[258] Although Caelius Aurelianus makes it clear that he is drawing on Soranus and presenting his ideas in a Latin version (e.g. *Morb. Acut.* II 8, 65, 147), his own interspersed comments on Soranus himself show that what he gives us is a report of Soranus's views rather than a verbatim translation.

[259] Cf., however, on aspects of this question, Manuli 1982.

adopted, namely that the menses are useful for childbearing only, for health in general as well, and for neither. In this instance he does not confine his critical comments to Dogmatists, for – although he here comes down on the same side as Themison, the forerunner, if not the founder, of the Methodist school – he rejects the views of Mnaseas and of Dionysius, both of whom were Methodists.[260]

Arguing on both sides of the question – *in utramque partem* – which is mentioned by Celsus as a characteristic of the Empiricist sect,[261] was certainly not confined to them. We should, however, note that it is far from always the case that Soranus canvasses the alternatives merely in order to reduce the discussion to an aporia, and to instil in his reader an attitude of ἐποχή on the subject. Although this would be what we would expect of a sceptic of Sextus's persuasion, Soranus far more often ends his account of competing views by himself taking up a definite position (though this may not coincide exactly with any of those he has described). Thus in his discussion in 1 27–9 he ends by asserting, against Herophilus and others, that 'in regard to health, menstruation is harmful for all' (19.26f) and that it is useful only for childbearing (19.35f). Equally in his discussion of whether permanent virginity is healthful in 1 30–2, 20.1ff, he comes down on the side of those who argued that it is (21.23ff), and many other examples could be given.[262]

On many occasions the positions adopted on – broadly – methodological issues in the *Gynaecology* correspond closely to the reports of Methodist views in Celsus, Galen or Sextus. Thus destructively, Soranus is forthright in his rejection of humoral pathology in 1 52, for instance.[263] Some had argued that in cases of 'pica' different remedies are to be prescribed depending on whether the fluid present is 'pungent and burning' or 'thick and viscous' (38.9ff). 'This is absolutely non-methodic', Soranus comments (38.16ff): 'for one must not consider the variety of the humours, but the condition of the body.' Again in 1 28, 18.9ff, he brings a battery of often effective arguments to bear against teleology, notably that to appeal to teleology on the question of whether menstruation is useful is a case of *obscurum per obscurius*. 'In opposition to these people, one must say that

---

[260] On Mnaseas and Dionysius, see [Galen] K xiv 684.5 and cf. K x 52.16ff. It is notable that according to Soranus (17.25f) it is only 'most' of our people (not all Methodists) who side with Themison on this topic. In Caelius Aurelianus, too, criticisms of other Methodists are common, e.g. *Morb. Acut.* ii 24, iii 47, 172–4, 189–90, *Morb. Chron.* ii 16f, iii 137f.

[261] 1 Proem 39. The use of arguments *in utramque partem* in late Greek medicine has been discussed by Kudlien 1974.

[262] Two such are cited below, pp. 190f, on 1 58, 43.7ff, and ii 18, 64.21ff.

[263] See further below, n. 277.

the providence of nature has been disputed and that this proposition involves a decision which is more difficult than our problem.' Again constructively, Soranus makes extensive use, throughout the work, of the key Methodist notion of the common conditions, at least of the two basic opposed ones, the constricted and the lax.[264]

Nevertheless on a number of important points related to method he expresses views that diverge to a greater or less extent from those associated with the Methodists in our secondary sources, and this raises difficult questions concerning the reasons for such departures. While in some cases we may entertain the possibility that Soranus deviated from the teachings of the school,[265] or that those teachings were subject to development[266] or were otherwise more flexible than some of our sources appear to concede, that is, as we shall see, far from providing a complete solution to our problem.

Take, first, Soranus's explicit position on dissection. That the Methodist school as a whole rejected dissection emerges from both Celsus's account and passages in Galen. It is true that the most elaborate arguments designed to prove the uselessness of dissection, and the positive cruelty of vivisection, occur in Celsus when he is reporting the views of the Empiricists (1, Proem 36ff, 40ff). But he makes it clear (Proem 57) as does Galen (e.g. *Sect. Intr.* chh. 6f *Scr. Min.* III 13.21ff, 17.3ff, 18.1ff, K 1 81.6ff, 85.14ff, 86.17ff) that the Methodists too rejected conjecture about hidden things of any kind.

Soranus prefaces his discussion of female anatomy with these remarks (1 5, 6.6ff).

Some of this [the anatomy of the female parts] can be learned directly, some from dissection. And since dissection, although useless, is nevertheless employed for the sake of profound learning, we shall also teach what has been discovered by it. For we shall easily be believed when we say that dissection is useless, if we are first found to be acquainted with it, and we shall not arouse the suspicion that we reject through ignorance something which is accepted as useful.

---

[264] See further below, pp. 196ff. While Soranus often speaks of the constricted (στεγνόν) and the lax (ῥοῶδες) and of counteracting each of these, he does not, in the *Gynaecology*, expressly mention the third 'mixed', ἐπιπεπλεγμένον, state or condition. However Caelius Aurelianus not only uses the usual three-fold doctrine extensively in *Morb. Acut.* and *Morb. Chron.* in passages where he purports to be basing his ideas on Soranus, but also expressly attributes to Soranus (and to Mnaseas) the view that flux (*catarrhon*) is a 'mixed' (*complexa*) state (*Morb. Chron.* II 97).

[265] In any case 'orthodoxy' for a Methodist was a different matter from what it would represent for an Empiricist or for Dogmatists who aligned themselves with particular theorists – not a question of adherence to specific doctrines concerning the origins of diseases, since in principle there were no such doctrines, but at most one of acceptance of certain Methodist principles.

[266] This possibility is discussed by Drabkin 1951, pp. 516ff, and cf. Meyer-Steineg 1916, pp. 38ff, Wellmann 1922, pp. 396ff.

We shall be returning later to the questions of how much use Soranus actually makes of the findings of dissection, and for what purposes, but a certain ambivalence in his attitude appears already in this statement about this method of investigation. It looks, at first sight, as if all Soranus is interested in is in showing up the uselessness of anatomical dissection while establishing his own familiarity with the method. Yet if that had been all he was concerned with, he could have illustrated, and indeed demonstrated, his acquaintance with the method far more economically than he does. The 'uselessness' of dissection must be understood in the light of the general distinction between theory and practice:[267] the characterisation of anatomy as 'useless' is a characterisation of it as *merely* theoretical. The claim is that theoretical knowledge – including that deriving from dissection – is no help in therapy. But the findings of the anatomists are to be noted nevertheless. The subject is included 'for the sake of profound learning', and though there may well be more than a touch of irony in the term he uses here (χρηστομάθεια), the care and detail he devotes to his anatomical descriptions both here and elsewhere would not have disgraced a committed proponent of the method.

My second example concerns Soranus's references to what in Hellenistic epistemology were called the 'criteria'. The sceptical position of Sextus is that neither reason (λόγος) nor experience (πεῖρα, or observation, τήρησις) provides grounds for claims to knowledge. The sceptic refrains, therefore, from asserting any propositions about what really exists – and Sextus is careful to point out that even the proposition that knowledge is not possible is held undogmatically – ἀδοξάστως (e.g. *P.* 1 13ff). Rather the sceptic confines himself to what appears, the φαινόμενα[268] (e.g. *P.* 1 19ff, 21ff, *M.* vii 29ff), allowing himself to be guided not only by such affections of the body as thirst and hunger, but also by the conventional beliefs of the society he lives in (*P.* 1 23ff). If Soranus had rigorously adhered to such an epistemology, we should have expected him to rely simply on the phenomena, to make no appeal to 'reason', nor to 'observation' or 'experience', at least not with any intention of establishing what exists or of laying any claims to knowledge. In fact, however,

---

[267] Thus in 1 2, 4.6f, he remarks that the theoretical part of the subject is useless 'although it enhances profound learning' (χρηστομάθεια). He has in mind, there, such topics as the nature of the seed: it is, however, clear from 1 12, 9.18, that he wrote a treatise on that question, though we do not know whether it was entirely negative in its conclusions. Cf. also Galen, *Sect. Intr.* ch. 6, *Scr. Min.* III 14.15f, K 1 82.7, on the uselessness of the 'hidden' in the Methodist view.

[268] As already in Aristotle, the φαινόμενα will include more than just objects of sense-perception and comprise more generally what appears to be the case: see Burnyeat 1980, pp. 33ff.

some of his references to 'reason' and to the 'phenomena' appear to reflect a position that is a good deal less strict than this.

Thus in his discussion in I 41, 28.25ff, of the question of whether the periods that are favourable for conception are determined by external factors (such as the phases of the moon), he remarks: 'But even without submitting the matter to reason, the evidence from phenomena is sufficient to put these ideas to shame' (29.4f). From this it appears, first, that the possibility of an appeal to reason or argument (λόγος) is not ruled out, even though it is not necessary in this instance. Now as an *ad hominem* device this would be both legitimate and effective against his opponents, for example to show their inconsistency in the use of reason. Yet it is not that Soranus makes it clear that that would be the sole purpose and justification of such an appeal in this instance, and he introduces his remark without any qualifying comment to the effect that the sceptic himself would not endorse the use of reason as a criterion.[269]

Secondly, the phenomena that he in fact cites as the chief grounds for rejecting the doctrine of the influence of external factors turn out to be more complex than such paradigm cases of direct experience as hunger and thirst. He proceeds:

For we see (θεωροῦμεν) conception taking place in all seasons as well as being brought to a successful end . . . And if at the changes of the moon some modification took place also in our bodies, we should in any event have observed it (τετηρήκειμεν) just as in mice and oysters. If, on the other hand, nothing of this kind has been observed (τετήρηται) to take place in our bodies, all such talk will be plausible but false. (29.5–6, 10–15).

Here, clearly, it is not just a matter of an appeal to the immediate particular affections of the body, the hunger and thirst that Sextus refers to as constraining a certain response in the individual.[270] Rather the conclusion that conception takes place at any season of the year depends upon repeated observations – on experience built up over a period of time – and is, of course, a generalisation that goes beyond what is immediately given to sense-perception.[271]

This second point can be made more clearly in relation to a second passage in which Soranus appeals directly to 'phenomena'. In I 58, 43.7ff, he discusses the problem of whether the amniotic membrane exists in humans, and as usual he states both the opinion for and the opinion against that theory. In particular those who denied the

---

[269] Cf. also the appeal to *ratio* in Caelius Aurelianus, *Morb. Acut.* II 160, 206, III 122, 137.

[270] See, e.g., *P.* I 24 and 238: hunger 'leads' us (ὁδηγεῖ) to food, and thirst to drink. Evidently it is thought that no process of inference or reasoning about the underlying causes or realities is involved.

[271] Cf. I 44, 31.6ff, on the signs by which conception is to be recognised.

existence of such a membrane in humans asserted that it is 'not found in parturition' (43.17), though those – the majority – who asserted its existence had an account they could give of the rupturing of the membranes and the discharge of fluids which enabled them to evade the arguments of their opponents. Soranus ends his discussion by agreeing with this majority. 'We too agree with them, since above all the phenomena have testified to the structure of the amniotic membrane' (44.2ff). Here, even more clearly than in 1 41, the 'phenomena' appealed to are at some remove from the direct experiences of the body in the paradigm cases of hunger and thirst, and the inferential nature of the conclusion drawn is indicated by Soranus's use of the term 'testify to', μεμαρτύρηκεν, 44.4.

Finally in his discussion of whether the new-born baby should be given the mother's milk immediately, 11 18, 64.21ff, Soranus is prepared to use and, it seems, endorse the notion of 'manifest evidence', ἐνάργεια, the term itself being one that was often used in relation to an epistemological position far removed from that of Pyrrhonean scepticism. At 65.1ff he criticises first Damastes and then those who followed him, such as Apollonius called Biblas, who had argued that nature had provided the milk in the mother's breasts beforehand 'so that the newborn may have food straightaway'. 'By plausible sophistry', Soranus says (65.6f), 'they attempt to confuse clear evidence' – that is what Soranus himself takes to be the obvious facts that just after childbirth the maternal milk is 'in most cases unwholesome, being thick, too caseous, and therefore hard to digest, raw, and not prepared to perfection', and being, furthermore, 'produced by bodies which are in a bad state, agitated and changed to the extent we see the body altered after delivery' (64.22ff, 25ff). Here too, evidently, Soranus believes he has clear grounds for his conclusions and, so far from playing off one opinion against another with the aim of encouraging ἐποχή, he is prepared to assert his own position without apparent reservations. Moreover he does so with the help of one of the key terms used by such Dogmatists as the Epicureans (though admittedly it was not confined to them).[272] Even though Soranus's own conclusions, in this case, do not concern underlying realities or hidden causes, so much as points which he would no doubt claim to be matters of tried and tested medical experience, it is still remarkable that he employs the term ἐνάργεια

---

[272] For the Epicurean use, see, e.g., D.L. x 33, 52 and 146 (*Principal Doctrine* 22), Sextus, *M*. VII 203. Sextus also uses the term of Peripatetic views (*M*. VII 217–18), of the Stoic φαντασία καταληπτική where there is no impediment (*M*. VII 257, cf. 403 on Carneades's criticisms) and of the notion of self-evidence (*M*. VII 364ff).

which Dogmatists had used to express *their* views about the reliability of the evidence for their – dogmatic – assertions.[273]

Most of the texts we have considered so far refer directly or indirectly to methodological issues. Naturally enough, in a treatise such as the *Gynaecology*, Soranus does not engage in detailed theoretical discussions of epistemological problems. Nevertheless certain aspects of his views emerge from the passages we have mentioned. His *general* adherence to Methodist principles is clear: at the same time some of his methodological pronouncements manifest a certain ambivalence or otherwise fail to tally precisely with the expectations generated by Celsus's report on the Methodist school or by Sextus's account of the sceptical Methodist doctor. We may now broaden the basis of our discussion and take into account further aspects of Soranus's actual practice of argumentation. Let us begin by recalling that the strictly sceptical doctor – at least in Sextus's view – will allow himself to be guided only by the phenomena and will withhold judgement about any underlying realities. According to Celsus also, the Methodists do not engage in speculation about what is hidden (I, Proem 57), and further they contend that 'there is no cause whatever, the knowledge of which has any bearing on treatments' (I, Proem 54). Such principles effectively rule out not just anatomical and physiological theorising, but also aetiology, the attempt to infer the causes of diseases from diagnostic signs. The question we must now pose is how far in practice Soranus kept to such a methodology.

We may begin with anatomy, where we have already noted his justification for the inclusion of the findings of dissection and remarked that his anatomical descriptions are quite detailed. What is chiefly remarkable, here, is his readiness not just to report the discoveries of the anatomists, but to use points derived from dissection in the context of his own resolution of particular problems. Thus in I 35, 24.24ff, he argues against the view of Euenor and Euryphon that fumigation can indicate whether a woman is capable of conceiving. 'All this is wrong . . . The substances made into suppositories and fumigations will be carried up through certain invisible ducts (literally 'ducts visible to reason') even ⟨if⟩ a person is unable to conceive.' This idea of sub-sensible ducts – which manifestly breaks the sceptic's rule prohibiting speculation about the hidden – was the view of, among others, Asclepiades, who is indeed mentioned in the immediately following sentence (25.1ff). Yet there is no indication whatsoever that Soranus himself has any doubts or reservations

---

[273] Cf. also I 45, 32.12, and I 55, 40.2f, and the adjective ἐναργής used at I 42, 30.5f.

concerning it.[274] Moreover the point at issue here is not just a theoretical matter (included for the sake of 'profound learning') but one that has a bearing on medical practice.

Again in I 14, 10.14ff, he quotes and rejects Diocles's opinion that there are, in the womb, cotyledons or suckers, tentacles and antennae which are similar to breasts. 'But these statements are proved wrong by dissection – for one finds no suckers.' In I 16–17, too, he contradicts the opinion of those who claimed that there is, in virgins, a membrane that grows across the vagina, and the first consideration he offers is that 'this membrane is not found in dissection' (12.3) – the second is that the probe ought to meet resistance, whereas it penetrates to the deepest point. It is notable that in these last two passages he is using dissection for destructive purposes, to refute an opinion, not to establish one of his own. Yet we may still contrast Soranus's emphatic *denial* of the doctrines he is overturning with the *indifference* which Sextus recommends the sceptic should adopt concerning the whole topic of the hidden structures of the body.

In what we should term physiology, too, Soranus does not always refrain from theorising about what is hidden. Thus at II 39, 81.20ff, he argues that crying is, sometimes at least, beneficial for the new-born baby, and therefore should not always be stopped by giving the child the breast. 'For it is a natural exercise to strengthen the breath and the respiratory organs, and by the tension of the dilated ducts the distribution (ἀνάδοσις) of the food is more readily effected.'[275] Again in I 40, 28.6ff, justifying the view that the best time for intercourse is after a rubdown, Soranus says that this helps the reception and retention of the seed, just as it 'naturally aids the distribution (ἀνάδοσις) of the food'.

In pathological aetiology we may distinguish two main types of case. First there are those passages where Soranus expresses the indifference we expect concerning the causes of a particular condition and concentrates, in true Methodist spirit, on what is necessary for treatment. In III 17, 105.3ff, for instance, he comments on the diversity of the conditions that precede the inflammation of the womb. 'There are many conditions which precede inflammation of the womb, but the more frequent are cold, likewise pain, miscarriage, and a badly managed delivery, none of which makes any difference in the treatment.'[276] Again in III 43, 122.2ff, he lists various earlier views

---

[274] Cf. Soranus's use of the notion of πόροι in the body at II 19, 67.23ff, II 22, 69.30ff, II 35, 79.15ff, and with ἀραιώματα at II 46, 85.29ff. Cf. Temkin 1956, pp. xxxiii f and cf. further below on II 39, 81.20ff.

[275] Temkin 1956, pp. xxxiv, commented that here Soranus 'indulges in downright physiology'.

[276] Cf. also III 19, 106.16ff.

on the different kinds of flux and then breaks off (122.20ff): 'it is tedious as well as useless to set forth these differences, for in every flux one must treat the whole body and the womb locally'.

Yet in contrast with these instances there are occasions when aetiology plays a part in his argument or where a diagnosis of the underlying causes of a complaint has to be made in order to arrive at a decision concerning the correct course of treatment. In III 6ff, 97.7ff, for example, he recognises that there may be different reasons for a woman not menstruating, for this may be 'physiological' ('according to nature') or 'pathological' ('contrary to nature'). Thus in 7, 97.21ff, he writes:

Now of those who do not menstruate, some have no ailment and it is physiological – φυσικῶς – for them not to menstruate: either because of their age . . . or because they are pregnant, or mannish, or barren singers and athletes in whom nothing is left over for menstruation . . . Others, however, do not menstruate because of a disease of the womb, or of the rest of the body, or of both.

The next chapter offers advice first about the signs that will help the doctor to recognise the various kinds of 'physiological' cases and the 'pathological' ones. At 98.14ff he comments,

when . . . there is at the same time [as the pathological complaint] lack of menstruation from one of the physiological causes (e.g. if pregnancy is present . . .), we discover from the additional signs that the retention has not come about by reason of the disease. If, however, this escapes us there is no harm done, since we do not do anything specific about the retention of the menses, but remove the whole underlying disease directly, whether it checks the menstrual flux or not.

That seems reassuring, and in line with the Methodist principle that it is treatment that counts. Yet the reassurance has a somewhat superficial, not to say specious, air. As he goes on to note, cases of physiological non-menstruation should not be treated at all, for the danger is that a physiological state, if interfered with, will indeed be turned into a pathological one (9, 98.22ff). In the mixed case, where retention is due to both physiological and pathological factors, the treatment will be directed at the latter only, and so the presence of the former will not affect therapy. So far, perhaps, so good. But the problem that Soranus does not follow up is that of the possible confusion between a physiological and a pathological condition. A comparison between the signs by which pathological retention of the menses is to be recognised and those of pregnancy shows that there is a good deal of overlap between them. 'Heaviness of the loins' figures in both accounts (III 8, 98.10, cf. I 44, 31.16) and so too does an upset stomach (III 8, 98.11, cf. I 44, 31.17f). Soranus would, no doubt, claim that while individual signs may not be distinct, nevertheless when taken as a whole, they allow a differential diagnosis to be made. But that does not affect the point that in this case such a diagnosis is crucial in determining treatment, or rather whether to treat or not. Here is an instance where the doctor must be clear not only about the immediate symptoms of the condition he has to treat, but also about their underlying causes.

Again in III 40, 119.2ff, when he discusses haemorrhage of the womb, Soranus first lists the different causes. 'Haemorrhage of the womb occurs as a result of difficult labour, or miscarriage, or erosion by ulceration, or a porous condition, or from the bursting of blood-vessels from whatever cause.' The haemorrhage itself, he proceeds, 'is clearly recognised from the sudden and excessive rush of blood, and, besides, the patients become weak, shrunken, thin, pale, and if the condition persists, suffer from anorexia'. The treatment for the general condition is set out in the next chapter: however, once again a differential diagnosis is involved. The blood, he says at the end of III 40, 119.10ff, 'flows not only from the womb but from the vagina too, and some people in diagnosing the seat say that the blood flowing from the vagina is thin, yellowish, and warm, while that from the womb is thicker, darker and colder'. Where Soranus might have been expected to refrain from the further investigation of what is obscure if not totally hidden, in this instance he proceeds: 'But one can determine the affected part more safely by using a speculum (διοπτρισμός)' (119.14f).

Moreover the point is one that has an important bearing on treatment. After his general recommendations about ensuring that the patient is kept quiet, bandaged and bathed, he goes on:

And a soft piece of wool soaked in any one of the said juices [i.e. those which he has just described] should be inserted into the orifice of the uterus with a finger or a probe, particularly if the haemorrhage comes from there. For if the haemorrhage comes from the parts above, the wedged-in piece of wool hinders the flux, but retains the discharged blood in the cavity. In such a case a soft clean sea sponge which is small and oblong and soaked with the same substances should be inserted as far inside as possible, so that the discharged blood may be absorbed and may not clot and thus cause sympathetic reactions with inflammations. (120.6ff)

Furthermore in this case the correct diagnosis that the haemorrhage proceeds from or is accompanied by erosion of the womb will also affect treatment. 'If, besides, there is an erosion, one should also use the "black remedy" made of papyrus, together with vinegar, or any of the troches which are prescribed for dysentery' (121.1ff).

In theory, the Methodist doctor is supposed to refrain from conjectures about what is hidden and is indifferent to the aetiology of diseases. Soranus's discussions suggest, however, that in practice treating the effects on their own is not always enough. This point can be developed in connection with the central Methodist notion of the three common conditions, the constricted, the lax and the mixed. There is no doubt that a pathological theory that referred to these three main states stayed a good deal closer to fairly directly observable appearances than such traditional Dogmatist doctrines as that based on the four humours.[277] The idea of the three common conditions could be, and no doubt usually was, introduced and explained with some simple examples, the kind of cases where, as Celsus puts it, 'even the most inexperienced person can see whether the disease is constricted or relaxed'.[278] Among the more obvious instances from Soranus himself are the classification of 'gonorrhoea' as a 'lax' condition (III 45, 124.15) and that of the retention of the menses as a 'constricted' one (III 9–10, see 99.15). Moreover the rationale of the treatment of the two extreme common conditions is, in principle at least, nothing if not clear and straightforward. The constricted condition should be countered by remedies inducing laxity, and *vice versa*.

Yet although the notion of the common conditions originates in readily identifiable states, it was far from being always simply a matter of direct observation. The reasons for which Soranus categorises certain conditions as either constricted or lax are sometimes far from transparent. We can perhaps understand why flexion of the womb is considered a constricted condition (III 50, 128.3 and 7) and also why air in the womb also is (III 32, 114.16f and III 33, 115.33f). But in some cases there is some conflict between individual signs and the condition as a whole. Thus paralysis of the womb is classified as a constricted condition in III 49, 127.12. Yet one of the signs is that the neck of the womb is relaxed.[279]

Not surprisingly, there were disputes among different members of the school about the categorisation of certain conditions. These were, as we noted before, exploited by their opponents as one of the

[277] That is when the four humours are treated as the constituent elements of the body and the sources of diseases, as for example in the Hippocratic *On the Nature of Man*. The substances phlegm and bile are, however, often obvious enough, for instance in excreta, and phlegm appears in some of Soranus's lists of symptoms, e.g. at II 54, 91.8ff, despite his objections to humoral pathology in general.

[278] Celsus I, Proem 63, cf. 65. Cf. also the famous Methodist reversal of the Hippocratic aphorism, when they asserted that the art is short and life long, and their notorious claim that the whole art can be learnt in six months (see, e.g., Galen, *Sect. Intr.* ch. 6, *Scr. Min.* III 14.22ff, 15.5ff, K I 82.13ff, 83.4ff, cf. ch. 9, 24.22ff, K I 95.15ff).

[279] χαλᾶσθαι, 127.5. Exacerbations, too, according to 127.14f, are to be recognised by 'increased flux' (ῥύσις) (though Temkin, ad loc., notes that this 'does not agree with the picture of the condition').

weaknesses of Methodist medicine. Celsus (1, Proem 66f) remarks that

indeed these very same men [the Methodists], even within their own profession, cannot in any way be consistent, if there are different kinds of constricted and of lax diseases and this can be observed more easily in those where there is a flux. For it is one thing to vomit blood, another bile, another food; it is one thing to suffer from diarrhoea, another from dysentery; one thing to be relaxed through sweating, another to be wasted by consumption. Also humour may break out into particular parts, such as the eyes or the ears, and no member of the human body is free from such a danger. No one of these complaints is treated in the same way as another.

There is certainly an element of unfair polemic in this text, notably in the tacit use of humoral theory. Yet it is clear from passages in Soranus himself that disputes between the Methodists on this topic were not merely a figment of their opponents' imaginations. Thus Themison[280] is taken to task in III 24, 108.15ff. While for inflammations without fever he approved of relaxing remedies, for those accompanied by fever he advised astringent remedies, such as the juice of στρύχνος – black nightshade. 'He is deceived by the concomitant heat into prescribing cooling remedies . . . without realising that things which increase inflammation also heighten the heat.' Despite the concomitant presence of heat, Soranus seems to be arguing, the inflammations in question should not be categorised as 'lax' and so in need of 'constriction': rather, like all inflammations they are 'constrictions' in need of relaxing remedies.

Again in I 29 (19.10ff, 16ff), in a chapter we have mentioned already, Mnaseas and Dionysius are attacked for, among other things, considering as 'natural' certain kinds of constriction and laxity which are not healthy. Here Soranus also objects, more generally, that venesection was sometimes misused as a way of dealing with a constricted condition. Although it achieved the release of the constriction itself, it did so at the cost of seriously weakening the patient – an example that shows that, according to Soranus at least, determining the correct treatment could involve other factors besides a simple decision to counter constriction with laxity or *vice versa*. Similarly in III 44, 124.2ff, dealing with flux, Soranus rejects venesection, this time on the grounds that 'the disease needs contraction, not relaxation which the removal of blood by its very nature effects', and in III 42, 121.14ff, Themison is again criticised for

---

[280] The question of whether Themison founded the school itself, or was merely thought of as a forerunner, is controversial (see above, n. 256), but does not affect my point here, since he certainly proposed the notion of the three common conditions and may therefore be taken to illustrate the divergences in their interpretation. Disputes on the interpretation of 'lax' and 'constricted' conditions are also reported in Caelius Aurelianus, e.g. *Morb. Chron.* II 16, 145ff.

using bloodletting in haemorrhage of the womb 'in order to divert the sanguineous material. For bloodletting relaxes, ⟨whereas⟩ haemorrhage demands condensation and contraction; and one should not divert the material, but stop it.'

The problem here is rather different from those we have encountered before. As we have seen, at a number of points Soranus diverges from the line we would expect a pure Methodist to take, at least according to the accounts in Celsus and Galen, let alone that in Sextus. The possibility of developments within the school, or of Soranus's own departure from standard Methodist positions,[281] cannot be ruled out, though the question of why these developments or divergences occurred would still remain. Yet with the notion of the common conditions, the problem does not lie solely or even principally in the possible atypicality of Soranus's position, for this is a view that is, according to all our evidence, central to Methodist medicine of any kind.

The difficulties here lie, rather, at the heart of Methodism itself. On the one hand the Methodist was enjoined to refrain from theorising about causes: indeed if true to sceptical principles, he was to practise ἐποχή and to be guided by the appearances alone. On the other, the notion of the three common conditions, applied as a general account of diseases, clearly goes beyond what can, even on a charitable construal, be said to be included in the 'appearances' and clearly involves not just inference and interpretation, but inference and interpretation concerning the hidden internal states and processes of the body. On general philosophical grounds we might argue that the Methodist-sceptical enterprise was doomed to failure: no therapeutics and no pathology can be totally theory-free, since to a greater or lesser extent all observation-statements, let alone generalisations, in these as in every other domain, presuppose interpretation.[282] In practice, the elaboration of the notion of the common conditions illustrates that this was indeed the case, even though – to repeat an earlier point – we should still recognise that the Methodist view stayed a good deal closer to what is directly observable than did most of the therapeutic and pathological theories of the Dogmatists.

Scepticism and Methodism offer one of the best opportunities to study the interaction of philosophy of science and its practice in the

---

[281] Though cf. above, n. 265, on the question of what 'orthodoxy' would have meant for a Methodist.

[282] Frede has, however, recently argued strongly for the possibility, within Methodism, of the deployment of reason and even of theoretical beliefs provided they are recognised as speculative, see 1982.

Hellenistic period. Sextus Empiricus is both articulate on the problems of sceptical epistemology and well informed about medical practice. Moreover medicine is often cited as one, and perhaps the best, example of the arts that the sceptic can and should engage in and to which he can and should apply his sceptical principles.[283]

It is certainly fair to say that for the doctor to adopt such principles made an important difference. The load of theoretical preconceptions that Soranus carries is markedly lighter than those of Herophilus and Erasistratus before him, let alone that of his younger contemporary Galen. Speculation about such issues as the fundamental constituents of the human body, or on the origin of diseases in general, could be dismissed as unnecessary and pointless. So too could the investigation of final causes. So too – as we have seen – could much in the popular tradition that seemed useless or even positively harmful. Destructively, there is the rejection of Dogmatism, and positively and constructively there is the fruitful concentration on the patient's condition and on the problems of treatment. In all these respects the Methodist doctor could be described as less pretentious, more modest, more cautious and more pragmatic than his Dogmatist, and even to some extent also his Empiricist,[284] rivals.

On the other hand anyone who looks for a fully elaborated and coherent implementation of scepticism in Soranus will be disappointed. Four principal points stand out. (1) While he often argues *in utramque partem*, this does not always lead – in fact it rarely leads – to sceptical withholding of judgement. (2) Whereas the sceptic Methodist should refrain from anatomy and physiology insofar as they dealt with what is hidden, Soranus uses both and not just for the purpose of scoring *ad hominem* points against his opponents. (3) Although the sceptic is not concerned with the causes of any condition, it turns out in Soranus that aetiology is sometimes an essential prerequisite to determining treatment. (4) Above all the notion of the common conditions goes beyond the phenomena and depends in many cases upon reason and judgement concerning the hidden.

Certain of these divergences may well be peculiar to Soranus himself,[285] though how far this is the case is hard to determine since

[283] See especially *P.* 1 236ff. Medical and physiological examples punctuate Sextus's arguments in both *P.* and *M.*: some of the principal texts are collected in Deichgräber (1930), 1965, pp. 216ff.

[284] At least if we allow the sceptic argument that in positively denying that the hidden can be known the Empiricist is being dogmatic, see Sextus, *P.* 1 236.

[285] Some of the divergences between what we find in Soranus and the reports in our secondary sources could, however, be put down to a tendency in the latter, especially in polemical contexts, to represent Methodism as more radical and extreme than it was in practice.

he is the only early Methodist author represented by an extended text extant in the original. At the same time some of the problems appear to relate not just to Soranus's version of Methodism, but to Methodism as a whole. In the last of my four examples, especially, we have reason to believe we are dealing not with idiosyncratic views of Soranus, so much as with a difficulty that arises for any radically sceptical Methodist when confronted with a practical situation.

When tensions between Methodist or sceptical principles and actual medical practice arise, they are resolved by Soranus, in several of the cases we have considered, in favour of practice, in the sense that the purity of some of the principles is sacrificed, or the principles more or less drastically modified, in the course of his discussion of what were, after all, often obscure and complex issues. This makes Soranus a better gynaecologist, but a less interesting exponent of a particular philosophy of science. Sceptical Methodism, if applied according to the letter of Sextus's recommendation, would, in any event, have provided a starkly impoverished framework for tackling many of the problems that Soranus was interested in, and as a practising gynaecologist it is as well that he does not withhold judgement as doggedly as Sextus would demand.

Yet it is not that Soranus simply abandons Methodist or sceptical principles entirely. What he could and did retain is a certain pragmatism, a certain resistance to wild speculation, that is characteristic both of the sceptic and of the Methodist. One might offer as a conclusion of our examination of his practice that it is here, rather than in the ideal analysis of the conditions of knowledge – just as it may be in some of the pragmatic ethical advice rather than in the account of the foundations of morality – that the principal strengths of the sceptical position lie.

CONCLUSION: SCIENCE,
FOLKLORE AND IDEOLOGY

The studies we have been engaged on have attempted to investigate aspects of the relationship between the life sciences and traditional belief in ancient Greece. What did Greek medicine and biology owe to popular notions and how successful were they in evaluating them critically? How far did their growth depend upon that critical evaluation or on achieving some kind of emancipation from traditional lore? What was distinctive about Greek medicine and biology and what claims have they to be called scientific? We may now return to these and the other general issues we have raised on the comparison and contrast between primitive thought and early Greek science, on the role of literacy in the development of Greek science, and on the ideological factors in that development.

Our case-studies show that at times the distinctions between the type of idea found in writings often hailed as making an important contribution to the development of science on the one hand, and those that formed part of traditional lore on the other, are very slight, not to say imperceptible. On such questions as how to test whether a woman can conceive, or whether a pregnant woman will bear a boy or a girl, the 'scientific' literature from the Hippocratic authors, through Aristotle, down to the end of antiquity contains many recommendations that correspond closely to what we can confidently infer to have been widespread popular beliefs.[1] Similar testing procedures are not only common in 'primitive' societies in general, but can be attested from Greeks' ancient Near Eastern neighbours. Some of the suggestions to be found in our extant gynaecological treatises of the fifth and fourth centuries B.C. are closely comparable with those contained in much earlier Egyptian texts. Again early Greek pharmacology bears many resemblances, and may in some cases be directly indebted, to ancient Near Eastern, especially Babylonian, lore,[2] and here too the

---

[1] Cf, above, p. 65 (and n. 21), p. 83 (and n. 93), p. 176 and p. 192.
[2] The most complete study is Goltz 1974, who has, however, insisted on many differences between Greek, and Near Eastern, pharmacologies, in both the structure and the contents of the recipes. Cf. Harig 1975, who has challenged the usefulness of comparisons between individual items in otherwise contrasting medical traditions.

ethnographic literature confirms that broadly similar techniques and recipes are widespread, if not universal.[3]

A very considerable body of evidence can be assembled to show how much of Greek science consists in the rationalisation of popular belief. Time and again Greek scientific writings reflect or are based on traditional ideas, with or without the addition of some kind of explanation or justification. Where this is so we have to ask whether there are any good grounds for speaking of this work as *science* as such at all. It would doubtless be wise to speak of the *literate* representation of Greek folklore: and it was not only in Greece, but also in Egypt and Babylon, that our evidence for folk beliefs generally comes from written sources and often from literary texts. The very writing down of popular beliefs, recipes, tests and the like, is, no doubt, important. As Goody has insisted,[4] once recorded the ideas are static, not so vulnerable to modification as in the oral tradition, and they acquire or can acquire a different kind of authority. Goody also argued that they are open to revision – though to this one must add that whether they will be scrutinised critically will depend on other factors besides their having been written down, since that method of recording can lead not to the release, but to the paralysis, of new thought. That has already been suggested by one ancient Near Eastern specialist, A.L. Oppenheim, in connection with Mesopotamian medicine in particular.[5] But leaving aside what might be argued concerning the pre-Greek evidence, we have found ample confirmation, in the history of later Greco-Roman science, of what we may call the ambivalence of literacy. The development of a literate elite represented in some cases a barrier to communication within ancient society that could damage the growth or even the continued existence of science. Learning was evidently sometimes bought at a price: and the prestige of the written authority could, and often did, become inflated. I shall return to that issue later, but for the moment the fundamental point is clear, that the mere recording of popular belief cannot by itself be deemed to constitute science.

No doubt at one stage it would have been fashionable to respond to

---

[3] The point is clear enough even though until comparatively recently far more attention was paid, in the ethnographic literature, to the more dramatic or sensational aspects of medicine (views on and treatment of epilepsy or abnormal psychological states) than on its more mundane features: see, e.g., Lewis 1975, pp. 1ff. Thanks partly to the connections between pharmacopoeia and magic, substances used as drugs have, however, often been reported.

[4] See Goody 1977, pp. 36ff.

[5] See Oppenheim 1962, p. 104. Cf. Shirokogoroff 1935, p. 108 (cf. pp. 340ff) who remarks that written records in general receive more credit (with the Tungus) for in a great number of cases they are supported by the authority of the authors whose names are preserved or by the name of the emperor who ordered the translation or composition of the work.

that challenge by the counterclaim that what Greek medicine and biology owed to folk belief forms some kind of residuum. Such debts or similarities would, on this view, be evidence of where science came from, and of its incomplete emancipation from its origins, but should be seen as throw-backs, appendices, blemishes on an otherwise new – genuinely scientific – approach to the problems.

But the first difficulty for any such hypothesis is that the beliefs in question are often firmly embedded in the ('scientific') writing, that so far from being anomalous, they may be characteristic of the texts concerned. We can see this especially clearly when a traditional belief is given some kind of rational basis within a would-be scientific system, as when differences between man and the animals, or between males and females, are explained in part by the theory that man, and males, are hotter, itself part of a comprehensive physical doctrine purporting to provide a framework of explanation for a wide variety of phenomena. It is not as if the folk beliefs can be excised surgically from the Hippocratic writers, from Aristotle, Theophrastus, Rufus and Soranus – let alone from such as Pliny – to leave the scientific elements in their work isolated in their purity.

But, the question becomes more urgent, what are those scientific elements? On what valid grounds can the term 'scientific' be applied to their work at all? The star examples brought to support the thesis of Greek achievement in science are generally drawn from the mathematised physical sciences, from acoustics and optics, statics and hydrostatics, and especially astronomy. In those fields Greek scientists eventually systematised a body of knowledge and produced theories that could be, and were, used predictively. Ptolemy's *Syntaxis*, which not only collects a mass of empirical data, but also develops mathematical theories from which conclusions can be deduced that can be tested again against fresh data, has as much claim to be called scientific as the work that so much resembles it, Copernicus's *De Revolutionibus*.

Yet that example is, from many points of view, quite exceptional, and of course comparatively late, and the very contrasts between the *Syntaxis* and the characteristic products of the life sciences in Greece might be thought to tell strongly against the claim of the latter to be scientific. The categorisation of the latter is obviously a more complex and delicate matter and any expectations of a clear-cut answer should be suspended. While no claim can be made that our case-studies do more than merely illustrate aspects of the problem – and some of its complexities – we can attempt here to take stock of some of the conclusions they suggest.

In the first place there is the point we began with, the very large
role played by traditional or popular beliefs in the life sciences.
Whether it is in the interest shown in the social behaviour of animals,
or physiognomical speculation, or the use of herbal remedies in the
Hippocratic writers, what can broadly be called popular motifs bulk
large in medicine and zoology. These are particularly distinctive
examples which we have documented in some detail, but many others
could be added. Hippocratic surgical techniques draw on earlier, in
some cases much earlier, procedures (including, for instance, trepanning). Many Hippocratic pathological doctrines, including humoral
theories and theories that refer to the interaction of primary elements
or opposites, are speculative developments, but they take as their
explananda disease entities that had, in many cases, been identified – even if not necessarily unambiguously – in Greek popular
vocabulary (φθίσις, στραγγουρία, δυσεντερία).[6] Even more
obviously Greek zoological and botanical taxonomy generally took
the natural species picked out in ordinary language as given.

The presence of traditional elements in the writers we have been
studying is very prominent. So much is clear, but the crux of the
matter is the way in which the traditional material is used, and here
the pattern is very mixed. Alongside the examples we began with,
where traditional material figures more or less intact in the writers we
are concerned with, there are others where such writers modify what
they adopt, producing their own versions of popular ideas, and
introducing new points and criticisms.

The development of zoological taxonomy illustrates very clearly
the continued influence of widely held Greek beliefs about the animal
kingdom and about man's position in relation to it. But it also
exemplifies how Aristotle, deeply influenced as he was by such beliefs,
adapted or even transformed what he took over. Not only does he
establish firm boundaries to the domain to be investigated, the animal
world, but in many cases his descriptions imply criticisms of popular
assumptions about particular species. This is not just a matter of his
being confident that whales are not fish, but also, for example, of his
identifying the cephalopods as a clearly marked natural group with
certain distinctive characteristics in common. Although much of his
discussion is influenced by, for instance, his preoccupation with the
special position of man, his research has been extensive. It has been
carried out under the influence of those preoccupations, to be sure,

---

[6] The use of these and many other such terms outside, and sometimes before, Hippocratic
medical writings is well attested: for these three, see, e.g., Hdt. vii 88 (cf. Pi. *Pae.* 9.14), Ar. *V.*
810, Hdt. viii 115.

and they often affect its quality, in that he jumps too quickly to his preconceived conclusion, or fails to take into account, or dismisses too easily, apparent counter-evidence. Nevertheless, many of his zoological descriptions áre exact. He has, in fact, not just brought together what others had observed – fishermen, hunters, bee-keepers (though no one before him had encompassed the whole range of material found in the *Historia Animalium*) – but also added to what was known, particularly in the field of anatomy.

The example of zoological taxonomy shows both the strengths and the limitations of what has been called 'concrete science'[7] and again both the strengths and the limitations of Aristotle's attempts to do something that he would certainly have wished to contrast with 'concrete science' and to claim for science proper, that is, for him, knowledge not merely of the fact, but of the explanation. First on the side of 'concrete science': evidently here, as in many other areas corresponding to other areas in the life sciences such as anatomy and pathology, the fruits of long experience are embedded in popular beliefs. Thus in ancient Greece, as elsewhere, ideas about anomalous species of animals presuppose a firm and intelligible classificatory framework. Yet that framework remains implicit. It is assumed and goes unchallenged: it is not the subject of deliberate inquiry or critical reflection. What Aristotle, for his part, began to do was to attempt to collect, and at the same time to analyse, the similarities and differences between species of animals as a preliminary to a comprehensive, certainly an explicit, explanatory account of them. The grounds on which he proposes his principal groups often appear and are thin. Yet the point is that, being explicit, they are open to criticism, as his work is on other scores as well. Zoological taxonomy becomes a *problem*, with the possibility of further critical discussion – the evaluation of the grounds for theories and beliefs – and of research.

In other areas of the life sciences, too, the claim of Greek work to be more than recorded popular notions must chiefly rest on the same two elements we have identified – of critical analysis and of research. Yet we must both refine these two criteria and mark the limitations of the Greek performance, when they are applied. To begin with, not only is learning from experience a universal feature of human behaviour, but trial and error procedures are common in a wide range of contexts some of which are relevant to the acquisition of understanding about what we should call natural phenomena.[8] Research implies a more

[7] See especially Lévi-Strauss (1962a) 1966.
[8] Cf. Lloyd 1979, pp. 222ff.

deliberate inquiry, often one carried out to test a well-defined idea or theory. But if we allow, as we surely should, that research may have practical, not just theoretical, ends – for example in medicine – then the distinctions between those who first tried out trepanning, or hellebore, to see whether they would help in therapy, and those (like Galen) who investigated the nervous system in detail by dissection, are matters of degree rather than of kind, a question of how systematic and how sustained the investigation was.

When we turn to the Greek performance in research, the actual practice of many writers falls far short of the ideals they profess when they describe their aims and methods. To listen to some Hippocratic writers, the practice of medicine depended on the most wide-ranging and meticulous collection of data and the scrupulous avoidance of preconceived opinions.[9] Yet not only are their theoretical preconceptions often much in evidence, but their observations in some fields are unimpressive, not to say slap-dash. While their clinical records provide full evidence on such issues as the periodicities of diseases, they entirely omit many other factors. The most famous of them, in *Epidemics* I and III, do not systematically record how patients responded to treatment, nor even give precise details of that treatment.[10] Again Aristotle's expressed ideal was to investigate every one of the species of animals – however unimportant or ignoble it might appear. That was a vital factor in his development of the use of dissection.[11] Even so that use was still very limited by comparison with that of some of his ancient Greek successors, such as Herophilus and Erasistratus, let alone by more modern standards.[12]

The very variable record of Greek life scientists, in practice, in research reflects in part, to be sure, the practical difficulties of certain investigations. It is generally much more difficult to determine precisely what effect, if any, a particular drug has had on a patient than to produce careful accounts of whether the patient was hungry, went to stool, felt feverish and so on over the course of a number of days. In anatomy, the finer the structure the more difficult it is to investigate – though the history of the subject shows that accurate

[9] The latter point is especially prominent in *On Ancient Medicine*. Recommendations concerning how the doctor should proceed in examining the patient are set out in *Prognosis* (passim) and *Epidemics* I ch. 10 (L II 668.14ff) especially.

[10] Treatment is rarely mentioned in the case-histories and not often in the 'constitutions', and the writers are evidently not usually concerned to investigate how the course of a disease was affected by the therapy adopted, although they do note on several occasions that no treatment tried was of any help, e.g. *Epid.* III First series, case 9, and Second series, case 5, L III 58.7 and 118.8.

[11] See especially *PA* I ch. 5, 644b22ff, 645a6ff, 21ff.

[12] Cf. Lloyd 1975a and 1979, pp. 16off, 164ff.

knowledge of grosser structures did not always precede that of finer ones: Aristotle's account of the chambers of the heart is wider of the mark than his description of some more minute parts of the blood-vascular system.[13]

But, as that last example shows,[14] an even more important factor is the role of the guiding theory, which takes us back to our second main criterion and to the issues of the character and limits of the critical spirit displayed in Greek medicine and biology. Here too it would be quite incorrect to suppose that criticism is totally absent from traditional or popular thought. On the contrary, the ethnographic literature provides plenty of evidence that, for example, individuals with claims to special knowledge, such as diviners and shamans, are often criticised, and doubts are expressed about those claims or about their ideas, explanations and predictions.[15] In Greece itself, popular notions are far from entirely static. Of the different strands of medicine, that which was practised in the shrines of Asclepius evidently underwent certain changes, including incorporating a good deal from the tradition of rational, naturalistic medicine represented by many of the Hippocratic writers.[16] It is not just that some of the Hippocratic writers are critical of other kinds of medicine. It is clear from the Epidaurus inscriptions of the fourth century B.C. and from Aelius Aristides in the second century A.D. that temple medicine sometimes returned the compliment and implied and expressed criticisms of the recommendations of ordinary doctors.[17] The Epidaurus inscription that rejects cauterisation in one case had just as good grounds for doing so, in terms of the pain caused (even if those

---

[13] Aristotle's chief discussions of the anatomy of the heart are in *HA* I ch. 17, *HA* III ch. 3, *PA* III ch. 4 and *Somn. Vig.* 458a15ff. It is notable that although he continued to hold, in all four accounts, that the heart has three chambers, the identification of these three appears to shift: see Shaw 1972, pp. 355ff, Harris 1973, pp. 121ff. By contrast some parts of the accounts of the main blood-vessels in the arm and shoulder at *HA* 513b32ff are accurate enough, see Harris 1973, pp. 147ff.

[14] It is particularly striking that the notion that the central chamber of the heart is the ἀρχή for the other two persists even when his views on the identity of the three cavities changed (see Lloyd 1978, pp. 227f, and more generally on Aristotle's preconceptions about the value of μεσότης, Byl 1980, pp. 238ff, developing points from the more general studies of Vernant (1963a) 1965 and (1963b) 1965).

[15] This has been pointed out both in Shirokogoroff's classic study of the Tungus (1935 e.g. pp. 332ff, 389ff) and in Evans-Pritchard's of the Azande (1937, e.g. pp. 183ff), cf. also Lévi-Strauss (1958) 1968, pp. 175ff, citing Boas's account of the Kwakiutl shaman Qā'selīd, Boas 1930, II pp. 1–41, and cf. also Lienhardt 1961, p. 73.

[16] This has been pointed out by E.J. Edelstein and L. Edelstein 1945, II p. 112 n. 4 for the cult of Asclepius and by Ilberg 1931, p. 32, for the first century A.D. Cf. also Lloyd 1979, pp. 40ff.

[17] See, e.g., case 48, Herzog 1931, p. 28, in the Epidaurus inscriptions. Aelius Aristides provides many examples where the god overrules the diagnoses or therapies of ordinary physicians: see *Or.* XLVII 61–4, 67–8, cf. 54–7, XLIX 7–9.

grounds are not themselves expressed), as Soranus had for criticising popular practices that harmed the new-born child.[18]

The situation is more complex still. Within the material we have been discussing in these studies, the response to traditional beliefs and the extent to which they were exposed to critical examination are very variable. The first question we face is that of characterising the nature of the criticisms offered. The second concerns why it is that some popular notions were scrutinised and rejected, while others were not and were even incorporated into research programmes. The answers are bound to involve large elements of conjecture, but certain features of the sociological background may be considered relevant.

First where there is professional rivalry and competition for a clientèle, this clearly provides one context that may stimulate criticism. In medicine, many of the Hippocratic writers were evidently keen to differentiate themselves from other types of practitioner, and from the ordinary lay individual: the layman is expected to be intelligent, to be able to describe his symptoms, and to be likely to be eager, too, to ask the doctor questions, but not to possess the specialised knowledge and experience that the art, *techne*, itself conveys.[19] But it is notable that different Hippocratic authors express criticisms not just of priests, or of the sellers of charms and incantations, but also of the theories and practices of other doctors like themselves. The authors of the surgical treatises, especially, repeatedly criticise bad surgical practice on the part of their colleagues, as careless, useless, damaging and painful.[20] The tradition continues – with Soranus damning many of the ideas he attributes to 'Hippocrates' as categorically as he rejects certain folk practices or the practices of superstitious midwives.

At the point where a sick man or woman seeks treatment, those who offered it – and not just our Hippocratic authors – would no doubt cultivate their reputations carefully and engage, at times, in undermining those of their rivals. This could involve a display of knowledge and learning not just in the domain of pathology and therapeutics, but in every branch of understanding in which it might

---

[18] The Epidaurus case is that cited in the last note. For Soranus, see above p. 169 on *Gyn.* II 11, 58.12ff, p. 172 on II 16, 63.2ff, and, especially, p. 170 on II 12, 59.10ff.

[19] The relationship between the doctor and the patient, and the distinction between the doctor and the layman, are both recurrent themes in the Hippocratic Corpus, not only in such works as *de Arte, Decent.* and *Praec.*, but also, e.g., *Acut.* (e.g. ch. 1, L II 224.3ff, ch. 2, 234.2ff, ch. 11, 316.13ff), *VM* (e.g. ch. 2, *CMG* I, 1 37.7ff, and 17ff, ch. 9, 42.6ff, ch. 21, 52.17ff) and *Morb.* I (ch. 1, L VI 140.1ff).

[20] See, e.g., *Art.* ch. 1, L IV 78.5ff, ch. 11, 104.20ff, ch. 14, 120.7ff, *Fract.* ch. 2, L III 416.1ff, ch. 3, 422.12ff, ch. 25, 496.11ff, ch. 30, 518.1ff, ch. 31, 524.17ff. Other treatises, too, are quick to bring the charge of quackery, e.g. *Acut.* ch. 2, L II 236.4ff, *VM* ch. 9, *CMG* I, 1 41.25ff.

pay the doctor or healer to appear wise. The rivalry thus extended far beyond disputes about what treatment to recommend in particular cases, or about the theoretical justification of a whole style of treatment, to include anatomical and physiological issues, even – in some of our Hippocratic texts – issues in general element theory and in cosmology. It might well be easier to score a victory in debate on some more abstract topic than in the area of the justifications for the treatment prescribed, where, as we can see from the case-histories in the *Epidemics*, the failure rate was high and the difficulties in claiming credit for the few successes were probably considerable. Again the continued validity of the point in later Greek medicine can be documented. Soranus, we saw, describes dissection as useless, but is careful not to reject it too quickly, in case he appeared to do so from a position of ignorance,[21] and Galen shows that the public dissection was used by some of his contemporaries – and by himself – as an important means of building up a reputation.[22]

The negative potential of this rivalry is obvious. Debate for debate's sake very easily became sterile.[23] The competitiveness shown in literate Greek medicine often led to blinkered partisanship.[24] The elements of bluff in many of the criticisms expressed, and in the counter-claims to superior knowledge or skill, are large. One further negative aspect that can be seen in our case-studies concerns the history of anatomical terminology. The difficulties encountered in the standardisation of anatomical terms, which are illustrated so clearly by Rufus, stem in part from the desire of individual investigators to develop and impose their own coinages.

At the same time there could be and often were positive features to this competitiveness. It encouraged the close scrutiny of many (though certainly not all) prominent assumptions, including not just common beliefs, but also the views of other theorists – the exploration of the weaknesses of rivals' ideas and practices. There is no reason to think that our would-be scientific or rational doctors had a monopoly of well-founded criticism, but they certainly scored some successes in its deployment, notably the rejection of the idea of supernatural intervention in diseases,[25] as well as of a good many superstitious beliefs and practices.

[21] See above, p. 188 on *Gyn.* 1 5, 6.6f.
[22] See above the texts discussed on p. 166 and p. 167 n. 190.
[23] I attempted to document this in Lloyd 1979, pp. 86ff.
[24] This appears to be especially true in the Hellenistic period, with the development of the medical sects or schools, whose methodological and other polemics are recorded in Celsus, *De Medicina*, 1, Proem, and Galen's *On Sects for Beginners*.
[25] The chief text is *On the Sacred Disease*, discussed at some length in Lloyd 1979, ch. 1, but cf. also *Aër* ch. 22, *CMG* 1, 1,2 72.10–76.4 and see above, p. 69 on *Virg.*, L VIII 466–70.

The rivalry in philosophy was different in one respect, in that it was conducted by individuals who in one respect had less at stake in terms of their means of livelihood, in that they competed for pupils, not also for patients. Yet it was often intense none the less, with reputations, if not always also livelihoods, at risk. Both Aristotle and Theophrastus seldom miss an opportunity to attack their predecessors and contemporaries. Indeed Aristotle considers the common opinions on a topic, and those of the accepted authorities, systematically as part of his usual method of setting out the problems. Theophrastus, too, is more articulate in his criticisms of the ideas of the root-cutters and the drug-sellers than the Hippocratic pharmacological writings, which adopt what appears to be the somewhat ambivalent tactic of simply ignoring the mystical and the superstitious in the use of certain plants. Here the natural philosopher engaged in Aristotelian-style ἱστορία spends more time trying to come to terms with current practices, and shows an open-mindedness about their possible efficacy, even if sometimes also his bewilderment about what to believe on that score: the doctors in, as it were, the field concentrated exclusively on drawing up a list of what they hope – and claim – will be effective remedies.

As in medicine, so too in natural philosophy, there could be substantial elements of bluff in both the constructive and the destructive arguments deployed. But again some criticisms were well founded. If popular assumptions often formed the starting-point in zoology and botany, Aristotle and Theophrastus were nevertheless successful in at least giving the problems clear definition, even if some of their proposed solutions were premature.

Yet if some features of what had commonly been believed came under attack from one direction or from the other, many others, we said, did not. Some never came under close scrutiny; but the most striking instances we must now consider are those where such modifications as were introduced had the effect of providing some kind of justification or rational basis for what was commonly assumed, the two most important examples being, of course, the notions of man as supreme in the animal kingdom, and of the innate superiority of the male sex.

In these two instances it is evident that the underlying beliefs correspond to deep-seated value-judgements and reflect what always remained the dominant ideology in Greece. The distinction that this suggests appears to offer a rather clear-cut solution to the problem of the limits of the criticism of popular assumption in the 'scientific' literature: the question of whether such assumptions will be liable to revision and attack will depend largely on the extent to which aspects of the dominant ideology are implicated. Where that is the case – on this hypothesis – criticism of traditional positions will stop short, however much other popular beliefs – as it might be some practice connected with gathering a particular plant medicine or a belief about the instrument to be used to cut the navel-string of a new-born baby – may, at one period or another, be exposed to reasoned rejection or to ridicule. The appearance of the uninhibited scrutiny of popular assumptions that the critical tone of many of the characteristic products of the life sciences in Greece gives will be to some extent misleading – as directed only at a carefully (though of course not consciously) circumscribed set of such assumptions.

This hypothesis contains much that must surely be retained, but it should be both developed and qualified since in one respect it appears too weak, in another too strong. The respect in which it might be described as too weak relates to the contribution that the philosophers themselves made to the construction and support of what I have called the dominant ideology. The belief in the inferiority of the female sex is widespread and takes many forms in Greek thought and culture. But we should not underestimate the extent to which that belief was positively fortified when theories were developed that appeared to give it a rational basis. Aristotle defines females in terms of an incapacity, and provides something of a list of what purport to be anatomical and physiological differences between the sexes. Where he finds exceptions, in certain species, to the general rules he propounds concerning manifestations of male superiority, he explains these sometimes in terms of the deformed or degenerate character of the species in question. While he certainly did not invent the idea of the superiority of the male sex, he just as certainly subsequently reinforced it. Similarly the belief in man's distinctiveness and superiority to other animals was given far stronger expression in Aristotle's even more detailed review of the topic than in any earlier author. Aristotle's role in both cases is not one of simply failing to scrutinise critically a traditional position (in fact he does, as we saw, introduce modifications to particular items among the accepted assumptions): it is rather one of providing such a position with an elaborate and detailed would-be rational justification.

On the other hand the hypothesis of an immunity to scrutiny of popular assumptions where the dominant ideology is implicated appears also in certain other respects to be too strong. First – a point that would have to be followed up within the philosophical debate itself – in the spheres of moral philosophy and cosmology most aspects of that ideology came under challenge at one period or another. There was no unanimity among Greek philosophers on such questions as whether the world is under the guidance of a benevolent craftsmanlike deity, nor on whether or how teleological explanations are appropriate or applicable to natural phenomena.[26] There was no unanimity either even on an issue that was fundamental to the established order of ancient society, namely whether the institution of slavery is natural or not[27] – even though that debate remained an entirely theoretical or intellectual one with no important consequences in terms of practical social reform.[28] As that last example illustrates, there were more, and less, well-entrenched items in the package of beliefs, assumptions and value-judgement in the prevailing ideology – and the degree of exposure to criticism, and the character of the criticism, varied correspondingly. But the ferment of disagreement that characterised discussion not just of peripheral or detailed topics, but of questions of central social and political importance, undermines the simple hypothesis that *all* that the Greek intellectual elite was doing was (consciously or unconsciously) providing support for that ideology, even though *much* of the time *many* of them were doing precisely that.

Secondly, on one of the specific issues from the life sciences we have considered, namely the position of women, there is a little more to be said. While Aristotle throws his weight behind the widespread and traditional view, the notion of the inferiority of the woman's role in one biological context – namely as providing merely the matter, or merely the place, for the developing embryo – was contested, and among the rival views that were expressed on that topic, some emphasise not just that the woman produces seed as the man does, but also that that seed is strictly comparable with that of the man, so that the mother may be just as responsible for the characteristics, including the sex, of the child as the father.

Again some of the Hippocratic writers (including some of those whose attitude towards popular beliefs about plant drugs may be somewhat ambivalent) make some effort to overcome some of the barriers to communication that existed between them and their female patients. First they recognise that there is a problem, and they

---

[26] The chief opponents of teleology and of the belief in a benevolent deity in the Hellenistic period were the Epicureans, but the contributions they made to concrete natural scientific research (as opposed, for example, to element theory, where the issues were generally debated at an abstract level) were minor.

[27] Aristotle, who argues that the institution of slavery is natural, implies that the contrary view had been put forward, see *Pol.* 1 chh. 2–7, especially ch. 3, 1253b20ff.

[28] See, e.g., Finley 1980, pp. 120ff.

criticise those of their colleagues who tended to ignore it. Secondly they try to enlist the cooperation and help of their female patients in their own treatment, not just in entering into dialogue with them but also, on occasion, inviting them to conduct their own internal examinations. However we also noted that there may be negative aspects to both these features, in that (1) it was always possible for criticism of other doctors to be offered merely in a spirit of rivalry, and (2) trusting a patient's own report might well be an evasive tactic, a substitute for a personal examination.

More importantly we must add that what is at issue here is a matter of the best medical treatment. Even if it is only fair to acknowledge that some of these writers are anxious to break down some of the barriers imposed by social structures in ancient Greece, that by itself hardly constituted a serious threat to the prevailing ideology. As for the writers who claimed that the woman's contribution to reproduction is strictly equal to that of the man, they certainly offered an alternative to biological theories that underpinned the prevailing assumptions. Yet in their Hippocratic form, at least, those alternatives were open to attack on the score both of the weakness of the evidence adduced in their support and of the apparent arbitrariness of the interpretations of that evidence they gave – a vulnerability that was exploited to the full by Aristotle, even if *his* views in turn were criticised and rejected by prominent later biologists.

A review of the possible range of motivations of ancient scientists will help to throw light on further aspects of the issue of the role of ideology. One of the chief weaknesses of ancient science as a whole (not just of the life sciences) was the lack of any explicit institutional recognition of the scientific endeavour as such. There were doctors, philosophers, mathematicians and engineers, not to mention more peripheral figures such as root-cutters, drug-sellers and midwives. Their work sometimes overlapped, and some of them were well aware of one another's approach. Yet there was no role for the scientist as a separate category, and no institutional backing for science as such. Not even the Museum at Alexandria where – quite exceptionally – many individuals who engaged in scientific inquiries received considerable financial and other support from the first three Ptolemies,[29] was devoted to that as its explicit aim. The lack of any

---

[29] The Museum supported poets and philologists and many others besides those who made contributions to natural scientific debate: see in general Fraser 1972. The point that the help the Ptolemies gave to Herophilus and Erasistratus in particular was not merely financial emerges from the report in Celsus, *De Medicina* 1, Proem 23f, that they practised vivisection on human subjects, said to be criminals whom they obtained from the 'kings'. Celsus does not specify the Ptolemies, but they must clearly be meant in the case of Herophilus, at least,

equivalent to a scientific research institution, combined with the very
modest degree to which the potentialities for the application of
science in technology were explored, had far-reaching consequences
for the level of scientific activity as a whole, and those who pursued
the different branches of what *we* include under the general heading
of natural science engaged in different occupations between which
greater, or less strongly marked, contrasts always existed.

Among those who, as *we* see it, contributed to the early development of the life sciences in particular, the tension between a
predominantly theoretical, and a predominantly practical, motivation is especially clear. These two motivations were not, to be sure,
mutually exclusive. There were doctors who combined both, and
Galen, for one, in late antiquity, devoted one of his shorter treatises to
the thesis of the title: *That the best doctor is also a philosopher.*[30]
Nevertheless the point remains valid as a broad generalisation.
Ultimately, if not also immediately, what concerned the doctors was
healing the sick: that was principally what they were paid for. The
philosophers could and did cultivate the idea that philosophy is an
end in itself, that the philosophical life is not just a constituent of, but
is, the good life. But although the philosophers spoke of theory, of
contemplation and speculation, their work was, in many cases,
anything but dispassionate or merely the pursuit of abstractions.
Indeed the more it was linked to a notion of the good life, the greater
the role of value-judgements was likely to be.

We have studied the normative role of the concept of φύσις, nature,
in Aristotle. Although he is one of the most eloquent spokesmen for
the superiority of theoretical to practical (including, in his view,
ethical and political) inquiries, and for the notion that the supreme
human activity, and the essential ingredient in happiness, εὐδαιμονία,
is contemplation, θεωρία, large areas of his speculative philosophy are
strongly and explicitly value-laden. The three notions of (1) teleo-

---

although whether this is so also in the case of Erasistratus is disputed: see Lloyd 1975*c* against
Fraser 1969 and 1972, 1 pp. 347ff.

[30] Galen's attempt to assimilate the doctor to the philosopher is, in part, a bid for higher status:
the social status of doctors (often Greeks) at Rome in the second century A.D. was, in general,
probably lower than it had been in Athens in the fifth and fourth centuries B.C., though Galen
himself, as physician to Marcus Aurelius, was in a favoured position. He argues that the
doctor must be trained in scientific method, that the task of philosophy is to study nature (this
will include the investigation of the constituent elements of the body and the functions of the
organs) and that there is an ethical motive for the doctor to study philosophy, in that he must
learn to despise money – the profit motive being incompatible with a serious devotion to the
art. For Galen, philosophy is the supreme study in part because it is supremely
unselfinterested: the more philosophical the doctor appears, the less he will be open to the
charge of avarice (a charge which, however, Galen frequently brings against his colleagues);
cf. Vegetti 1981*b*.

logy, (2) hierarchical differentiation, and (3) the superiority of form to matter, permeate his thought as a whole, for they influence his ethics and politics, and his religious beliefs, as well as his natural philosophy and his cosmology. It is therefore clear that the value-laden-ness, including at times the ideological slant, of much of his work in the life sciences, so far from being fortuitous, or a mere residue from traditional assumptions, corresponds to one of the primary motivations of the Aristotelian enterprise. The chief benefit for the natural philosopher in the study of animals, is, in Aristotle's view – as he expressly claims in the *De Partibus Animalium* – the discovery of form and finality in nature, and this will involve appreciating that animals manifest a lower grade of finality than man, and that the relationship between male and female exemplifies that between form and matter.

At the same time the distinctive features of what is true about Aristotle and some other areas of natural philosophy show how dangerous it would be to generalise these claims to apply to the whole of ancient scientific thought. All ancient science is, no doubt, ideological in the sense that the different groups of those who engaged in various types of inquiry were more or less actively engaged in legitimating their own positions. But not all of ancient science was seen as in the service of a morality[31] or directly linked to a notion of the good life, let alone geared to underpinning the moral and political attitudes implied in the dominant ideology.

The social and occupational barriers between the various groups we have been concerned with are especially prominent where we come to the literate/non-literate divide – not that that was a *single* clearly-marked boundary. The self-defining and self-justifying endeavours of the various *literate* groups are well attested in their extant works. The points of view of the midwife and of the root-cutter are not directly represented: worse still, much of the evidence about them comes from literate sources that are more or less hostile, critical or contemptuous – from authors who may be keen to differentiate themselves from these other groups. The superstitious beliefs and practices of midwives and root-cutters often, as we have seen, attract adverse comments from writers who thereby demonstrate their own allegiance to a naturalistic, rational tradition. What the peripheral groups could contribute from their not inconsiderable experience is

---

[31] Moral issues and questions of etiquette are, of course, often discussed in medical literature, especially in the so-called deontological treatises in the Hippocratic Corpus, such as *Decent.*, *Jusj.*, *Lex*, *Medic.*, *Praec.* and *Prorrh.* II. But these are concerned with the relationship between doctors and patients, not with moral, let alone political, philosophy in general.

far less often noticed. Even when he draws fairly systematically on the information available from fishermen, bee-keepers and the like, Aristotle is careful to contrast their practical interests in the data with his own research.

The closeness of the ancient life sciences to traditional belief has been one of our recurrent themes. But those beliefs were often, even usually, handed down principally in the oral tradition. When the barriers between learned and illiterate became marked, that could be much to the disadvantage of science – as the case of Pliny seems to illustrate. In some areas, such as pharmacology or *materia medica*, the emerging life sciences needed a symbiosis with folklore, the sympathetic evaluation of its potentialities, even if also the critical scrutiny of accepted beliefs. But that was not the only field in which the ancient world never acquired a very solid basis for that scrutiny, and in its absence the difficulties encountered in coming to terms with the oral tradition can be seen in all our literary sources. Their response is very mixed, and we should recognise that the pressure was often to reject too much, rather than too little, to dismiss too easily, or to fail to investigate further, what the 'illiterate country-folk' said or claimed to know. In late antiquity the ever-present dangers of the substitution of an appeal to authority for original research were much exacerbated by the increase in the use and availability of written texts, even though here, once again, the great works of the past were viewed very differently by a Soranus and by a Pliny.

Ancient science has sometimes been described as a series of brilliant taxiing runs, with the plane never actually taking off. Our verdict will depend, of course, on our view of what it takes for science to be air-borne. The vulnerability of ancient science, in its lack of an institutional framework, reflecting its lack of social or even conceptual recognition, is evident. Yet not just in what we call the exact sciences, but also in some of the separate branches of what we group together as the life sciences, Greco-Roman antiquity made important démarches, in defining the problems and in establishing methods, including not just the theoretical analysis of those methods, but also, occasionally, their successful application.

Even if traditional thought is not entirely static, it possesses no built-in stimulus to growth such as the methodology of ancient science eventually provided. Many investigators implicitly shared the same ideals – of research, of open-mindedness, of the critical approach, of the importance of being able to give an account of a theory or belief adopted. The very disagreements that were expressed on the nature of the correct method – between doctors and philosophers or within either group – contributed to the advance of awareness of methodological issues.

There was, to be sure, often a shortfall between the ideals expressed and the actual practice of inquiry: this too, no doubt, is a fundamental weakness of large areas of ancient science. The elements of bluff and of wishful thinking in some writers when they set out the correct method – and the one they say they will themselves follow – are strong. Yet that was not always the case. In certain limited investigations, the research is as meticulous as is claimed, and it led to results that did not simply confirm preconceived ideas, but in some instances ran counter to them and in others yielded quite unexpected discoveries. There was no Copernican revolution in the life sciences, no major paradigm shift. But there was the discovery of the nervous system and its detailed investigation through the use of dissection.[32] Much exact descriptive work was done in other areas of anatomy, in zoology and in botany. Even in the medical sciences, we may mention the development of surgical techniques,[33] and the discovery of the diagnostic value of the pulse.[34]

Many of the problems correspond to what are already implicit concerns in popular or traditional thought (though this is less true of physiology or of embryology than of zoological taxonomy). But they had to be brought out into the open, made explicit and become the subject-matter of deliberate inquiry. Most importantly, even though the methods used often in practice fall far short of the expressed ideals, the ideals themselves contained an immense potential for future development – such as traditional lore did not expressly provide. What our particular case-studies reveal is the very variable performance and success in different fields of different groups and sometimes even of the same individuals: but there is some fruitful, if complex, interaction of tradition and innovation, and an occasional, even if sometimes only temporary, emergence not just of an ideal of critical inquiry, but of its effective actual practice.

[32] The discovery of the nervous system had important practical, as well as theoretical, consequences, especially in surgery: see Galen, *AA* II chh. 2f, K II 283.7ff.

[33] One example which has been mentioned above in connection with Celsus is the techniques used to couch a cataract. Though we have no means of dating the introduction of this or many other surgical procedures, the innovatory ambitions of the Hippocratic surgical authors are well documented, and the development of surgical instrumentation can be traced in the archaeological record. In the Hippocratic Corpus, indeed, some writers warn against excessive striving after new effects, in the use of mechanical devices or even in that of fancy, new-fangled bandaging, see, e.g., *Art.* ch. 42, L IV 182.14ff, cf. ch. 14, 120.15ff, ch. 44, 188.13ff, ch. 62, 268.3ff.

[34] Attributable to Praxagoras of Cos, the teacher of Herophilus, in the late fourth century B.C.

BIBLIOGRAPHY

The bibliography includes details of all the books and articles cited in my text, together with a very selective list of other studies which, though not mentioned in my discussion, bear directly on the issues raised.

Ackerknecht, E.H. (1971) *Medicine and Ethnology* (Johns Hopkins, Baltimore).

Adelmann, H.B. (1966) *Marcello Malpighi and the Evolution of Embryology*, 5 vols. (Cornell University Press, Ithaca, New York).

Agassiz, L. (1857) 'The glanis of Aristotle', *Proceedings of the American Academy of Arts and Sciences* III (1852–7), 1857, pp. 325–33.

Ahern, E.M. (1981) *Chinese Ritual and Politics* (Cambridge).

Althusser, L. (1969) *For Marx* (trans. B. Brewster of *Pour Marx*, Paris, 1966) (London).

Altman, P.L. and Dittmer, D.S. (1972–4) *Biology Data Book*, 2nd ed., 3 vols. (Bethesda, Maryland).

André, J. (1955) 'Pline l'ancien botaniste', *Revue des études latines* XXXIII, 297–318.

Angel, J.L. (1972–3) 'Ecology and population in the Eastern Mediterranean', *World Archaeology* IV, 88–105.

(1975) 'Paleoecology, paleodemography and health', in *Population, Ecology, and Social Evolution*, ed. S. Polgar (The Hague and Paris), pp. 167–90.

Annas, J. (1976) 'Plato's *Republic* and feminism', *Philosophy* LI, 307–21.

Arber, A. (1938) *Herbals, Their Origin and Evolution* (1st ed. 1912), 2nd ed. (Cambridge).

Ardener, E. (1975) 'Belief and the problem of women' and 'The problem revisited', in *Perceiving Women*, ed. S. Ardener (London), pp. 1–17 and 19–27.

Armstrong, A. MacC. (1958) 'The methods of the Greek physiognomists', *Greece and Rome* V, 52–6.

Artelt, W. (1937) *Studien zur Geschichte der Begriffe 'Heilmittel' und 'Gift'* (Leipzig).

Arthur, M.B. (1976) 'Classics', *Signs* II, 2, 382–403.

Aubert, H. and Wimmer, F. (1868), *Aristoteles Thierkunde*, 2 vols. (Leipzig).

Bachelard, G. (1972) *La Formation de l'esprit scientifique* (1st ed. 1947), 8th ed. (Paris).

Balme, D. M. (1961/1975) 'Aristotle's use of differentiae in zoology' (in *Aristote et les problèmes de méthode*, ed. S. Mansion (Louvain and Paris, 1961), 195–212) in Barnes, Schofield, Sorabji 1975, pp. 183–93.

(1962a) 'γένος and εἶδος in Aristotle's biology', *Classical Quarterly* NS XII, 81–98.

(1962b) 'Development of biology in Aristotle and Theophrastus: theory of spontaneous generation', *Phronesis* VII, 91–104.

(1970) 'Aristotle and the beginnings of zoology', *Journal of the Society for the Bibliography of Natural History* V (1968–71) 4, 1970, 272–85.

(1980) 'Aristotle's biology was not essentialist', *Archiv für Geschichte der Philosophie* LXII, 1–12.

(unpublished) 'Aristotle's *Historia Animalium*: date and authorship.'

Balss, H. (1923) 'Praeformation und Epigenese in der griechischen Philosophie', *Archivio di Storia della Scienza* IV, 319–25.

(1936) 'Die Zeugungslehre und Embryologie in der Antike', *Quellen und Studien zur Geschichte der Naturwissenschaften und der Medizin* V,2, 193–274.

Barb, A. A. (1950) 'Birds and medical magic', *Journal of the Warburg and Courtauld Institutes* XIII, 316–22.

Barnes, J. (1979) *The Presocratic Philosophers*, 2 vols. (London).

Barnes, J., Schofield, M. and Sorabji, R. (edd.) (1975) *Articles on Aristotle, I Science* (London).

Barnes, S. B. (1969) 'Paradigms, scientific and social', *Man* NS IV, 94–102.

(1972) 'Sociological explanation and natural science: a Kuhnian reappraisal', *Archives Européennes de sociologie* XIII, 373–93.

(1973) 'The comparison of belief-systems: Anomaly versus falsehood', in Horton and Finnegan 1973, pp. 182–98.

(1974) *Scientific Knowledge and Sociological Theory* (London).

Barthes, R. (1953/1967a) *Writing Degree Zero* (trans. A. Lavers and C. Smith of *Le Degré zéro de l'écriture*, Paris, 1953) (London, 1967).

(1964/1967b) *Elements of Semiology* (trans. A. Lavers and C. Smith of *Éléments de sémiologie*, Paris, 1964) (London, 1967).

(1970/1975) *S/Z* (trans. R. Miller of *S/Z*, Paris, 1970) (London, 1975).

Bateson, W. (1899/1900) 'Hybridisation and cross-breeding as a method of scientific investigation' (read 11 July 1899), *Journal of the Royal Horticultural Society* XXIV, 59–66.

Beaujeu, J. (1950) *Pline l'Ancien, Histoire Naturelle Livre II* (Paris).

Below, K.-H. (1953) *Der Arzt im römischen Recht* (Münchener Beiträge zur Papyrusforschung und antiken Rechtsgeschichte 37, München).

Benveniste, E. (1945) 'La doctrine médicale des Indo-Européens, *Revue de l'histoire des religions* CXXX, 5–12.

Berger, P. L. and Luckmann, T. (1967) *The Social Construction of Reality* (London).

Berthelot, M. (1885) *Les Origines de l'alchimie* (Paris).

Bertier, J. (1972) *Mnésithée et Dieuchès* (Philosophia Antiqua 20, Leiden).

Birchler, U.B. (1975) 'Die Rolle der Frau bei der Liebeskrankheit und den Liebestränken', *Sudhoffs Archiv* LIX, 311–20.

Bloor, D. C. (1971) 'Two paradigms for scientific knowledge?', *Science Studies* I, 101–15.

Boas, F. (1930) *The Religion of the Kwakiutl Indians* (Part II) (Columbia University Contributions to Anthropology 10, Columbia University Press, New York).

Bodson, L. (1978) ΙΕΡΑ ΖΩΙΑ (Académie Royale de Belgique, Mémoires de la Classe des Lettres, 2nd ser. 63, 2, Bruxelles).

Bollack, J. (1965–9) *Empédocle*, 3 vols. in 4 (Paris).

Bonnet, E. (1903) 'Essai d'identification des plantes médicinales mentionnées par Dioscoride', *Janus* VIII, 169–77, 225–32, 281–5.

(1909) 'Étude sur les figures de plantes et d'animaux peintes dans une version arabe, manuscrite, de la matière médicale de Dioscoride', *Janus* XIV, 294–303.

Bottéro, J. (1974) 'Symptômes, signes, écritures en Mésopotamie ancienne', in *Divination et Rationalité*, J. P. Vernant et al. (Paris) pp. 70–197.

(1977) 'Les noms de Marduk, l'écriture et la "logique" en Mésopotamie ancienne', in *Essays on the Ancient Near East*, ed. M. de Jong Ellis (Memoirs of the Connecticut Academy of Arts and Sciences 19, Hamden, Connecticut), pp. 5–28.

Bourdieu, P. (1972/1977) *Outline of a Theory of Practice* (trans. R. Nice of *Esquisse d'une théorie de la pratique*, Genève, Paris, 1972) (Cambridge, 1977).

Bourgey, L. (1953) *Observation et expérience chez les médecins de la collection hippocratique* (Paris).

(1955) *Observation et expérience chez Aristote* (Paris).

Bourgey, L. and Jouanna, J. (edd.) (1975) *La Collection hippocratique et son rôle dans l'histoire de la médecine* (Leiden).

Brannigan, A. (1981) *The Social Basis of Scientific Discoveries* (Cambridge).

Breasted, J. H. (1930) *The Edwin Smith Surgical Papyrus*, 2 vols (University of Chicago Press).

Bretzl, H. (1903) *Botanische Forschungen des Alexanderzuges* (Leipzig).

Brisson, L. (1973) 'Bisexualité et médiation en Grèce ancienne', *Nouvelle revue de psychanalyse* VII, 27–48.

(1976) *Le mythe de Tirésias* (Leiden).

Broneer, O. (1958) 'Excavations at Isthmia, Third Campaign 1955–1956', *Hesperia* XXVII, 1–37.

Bronn, H. G. (1850) *Allgemeine Zoologie* (originally in *Neuen Encyklopädie der Wissenschaften und Künste*, Band III) (Stuttgart).

Brothwell, D. and Sandison, A. T. (edd.) (1967) *Diseases in Antiquity* (Springfield, Illinois).

Buberl, P. (1936) 'Die antiken Grundlagen der Miniaturen des Wiener Dioskurideskodex', *Jahrbuch des deutschen archäologischen Instituts* LI, 114–36.

Buchholz, E. (1871–85) *Die homerischen Realien*, 3 vols. (Leipzig).

Bulmer, R. (1967) 'Why is the cassowary not a bird? A problem of zoological taxonomy among the Karam of the New Guinea highlands', *Man* NS II, 5–25.

Burckhardt, R. (1904) 'Das koische Tiersystem, eine Vorstufe der zoologischen Systematik des Aristoteles', *Verhandlungen der Naturforschenden Gesellschaft in Basel* XV,3, 377–414.

Burke, K. (1957) *The Philosophy of Literary Form* (New York).

(1966) *Language as Symbolic Action* (University of California Press, Berkeley and Los Angeles).

Burke, P. (1978) *Popular Culture in Early Modern Europe* (London).

Burkert, W. (1972) *Lore and Science in Ancient Pythagoreanism*, revised translation, E. L. Minar, of *Weisheit und Wissenschaft* (1962) (Harvard University Press, Cambridge, Mass.).

(1977) *Griechische Religion der archaischen und klassischen Epoche* (Stuttgart).

Burnyeat, M.F. (1980) 'Can the Sceptic live his Scepticism?' in *Doubt and Dogmatism*, edd. M. Schofield, M. Burnyeat, J. Barnes (Oxford), pp. 20–53.

Bussemaker, U. C. and Daremberg, C. V. (1851–76) *Oeuvres d'Oribase*, 6 vols. (Paris).

Byl, S. (1980) *Recherches sur les grands traités biologiques d'Aristote: sources écrites et préjugés* (Académie Royale de Belgique, Mémoires de la Classe des Lettres, 2nd ser. 64, 3, Bruxelles).

Cain, A. J. (1956) 'The genus in evolutionary taxonomy', *Systematic Zoology* V, 97–109.

(1958) 'Logic and memory in Linnaeus's system of taxonomy', *Proceedings of the Linnean Society of London* CLXIX, 144–63.

(1963) 'The natural classification', *Proceedings of the Linnean Society of London*, CLXXIV, 115–21.

Callaway, H. (1978) 'The most essentially female function of all: giving birth', in *Defining Females*, ed. S. Ardener (London), pp. 163–85.

Calvert, B. (1975) 'Plato and the equality of women', *Phoenix* XXIX, 231–43.

Capitani, U. (1972) 'Celso, Scribonio Largo, Plinio il Vecchio e il loro atteggiamento nei confronti della medicina popolare', *Maia* XXIV, 120–40.

Cassirer, E. (1946) *Language and Myth* (trans. S. K. Langer of *Sprache und Mythos*, Berlin, 1925) (New York).

(1963–7) *The Philosophy of Symbolic Forms* (trans. R. Mannheim of *Philosophie der symbolischen Formen*, Berlin, 1923–9), 3 vols. (New Haven).

Chamfrault, A. (1954–9) *Traité de médecine chinoise*, 3 vols. (Angoulême).

Chantraine, P. (1975) 'Remarques sur la langue et le vocabulaire du *Corpus Hippocratique*', in Bourgey and Jouanna, 1975, pp. 35–40.

Cherniss, H. (1935) *Aristotle's Criticism of Presocratic Philosophy* (Baltimore).

(1944) *Aristotle's Criticism of Plato and the Academy*, Vol. 1 (Baltimore).

Choulant, L. (1855) 'Ueber die Handschriften des Dioskorides mit Abbildungen', *Archiv für die zeichnenden Künste* 1, 56–62.

Clark, S. (1975) *Aristotle's Man* (Oxford).

Clarke, E. (1963) 'Aristotelian concepts of the form and function of the brain', *Bulletin of the History of Medicine* XXXVII, 1–14.

Cohn-Haft, L. (1956) *The Public Physicians of Ancient Greece* (Smith College Studies in History 42, Northampton, Mass.).

Cole, F. L. (1930) *Early Theories of Sexual Generation* (Oxford).

Cole, T. (1967) *Democritus and the sources of Greek Anthropology* (American Philological Association, Philological Monographs 25, Western Reserve University Press).

Cornford, F. M. (1950) *The Unwritten Philosophy and Other Essays* (Cambridge).

(1952) *Principium Sapientiae* (Cambridge).

Daremberg, C. V. (1865) *La Médecine dans Homère* (Paris).

(1879) *Oeuvres de Rufus d'Éphèse*, continuée par C. E. Ruelle (Paris).

Daudin, H. (1926) *Les Méthodes de la classification et l'idée de série en botanique et en zoologie de Linné à Lamarck* (1740–1790) (Paris).

Davison, J. A. (1962) 'Literature and literacy in ancient Greece', *Phoenix* XVI, 141–56 and 219–33.

Debus, A. G. (1978) *Man and Nature in the Renaissance* (Cambridge).

Deichgräber, K. (1930/1965) *Die griechische Empirikerschule: Sammlung der Fragmente und Darstellung der Lehre* (Berlin, 1930) (repr. Berlin and Zürich, 1965).

(1933) *Die Epidemien und das Corpus Hippocraticum* (Abhandlungen der preussischen Akademie der Wissenschaften, Jahrgang 1933, 3, phil.-hist. Kl., Berlin).

(1935) *Hippokrates, Über Entstehung und Aufbau des menschlichen Körpers* (περὶ σαρκῶν) (Leipzig).

(1973) *Pseudhippokrates Über die Nahrung* (Akademie der Wissenschaften und der Literatur, Mainz, Abhandlungen der geistes- und sozialwissenschaftlichen Klasse, Jahrgang 1973, 3, Wiesbaden).

De Jong, H.W.M. (1959) 'Medical prognostication in Babylon', *Janus* XLVIII, 252–7.

Delatte, A. (1961) *Herbarius: Recherches sur le cérémonial usité chez les anciens pour la cueillette des simples et des plantes magiques* (Académie Royale de Belgique, Mémoires de la Classe des Lettres, 2nd ser. 54, 4, 3rd ed., Bruxelles).

De Ley, H. (1980) 'Pangenesis versus panspermia', *Hermes* CVIII, 129–53.

Derrida, J. (1967a/1976) *Of Grammatology* (trans. G. C. Spivak of *De la grammatologie*, Paris, 1967) (Johns Hopkins, Baltimore, 1976).

(1967b/1978) *Writing and Difference* (trans. A. Bass of *L'Ecriture et la différence*, Paris, 1967) (London, 1978).

(1972/1981) *Dissemination* (trans. B. Johnson of *La Dissémination*, Paris, 1972) (London, 1981).

Detienne, M. (1967) *Les Maîtres de vérité dans la Grèce archaïque* (Paris).

(1971/1981) 'The myth of "Honeyed Orpheus"' (originally 'Orphée au miel', *Quaderni Urbinati di Cultura Classica* XII (1971), 7–23, reprinted in *Faire de l'histoire*, edd. J. Le Goff and P. Nora, vol. 3 (Paris, 1974), pp. 56–75), in Gordon 1981, pp. 95–109.

(1972*a*/1977) *The Gardens of Adonis* (trans. J. Lloyd of *Les Jardins d'Adonis*, Paris, 1972) (Hassocks, Sussex, 1977).

(1972*b*/1981) 'Between beasts and gods' (originally 'Entre Bêtes et dieux', *Nouvelle revue de psychanalyse* VI (1972), 231–46, reprinted in a revised version in *Dionysos mis à mort*, Paris, 1977, pp. 135–60) in Gordon 1981, pp. 215–28.

(1977/1979) *Dionysos slain* (trans. M. and L. Muellner of *Dionysos mis à mort*, Paris, 1977) (Johns Hopkins, Baltimore, 1979).

(1981) *L'Invention de la mythologie* (Paris).

Detienne, M. and Vernant, J. P. (1974/1978) *Cunning Intelligence in Greek Culture and Society* (trans. J. Lloyd of *Les Ruses de l'intelligence: la mètis des grecs*, Paris, 1974) (Hassocks, Sussex, 1978).

Deubner, L. (1910) 'Charms and amulets (Greek)', in *Encyclopaedia of Religion and Ethics*, ed. J. Hastings, Vol. III (Edinburgh), pp. 433–9.

Di Benedetto, V. (1966) 'Tendenza e probabilità nell' antica medicina greca', *Critica Storica* V, 315–68.

Dickison, S. K. (1973) 'Abortion in antiquity', *Arethusa* VI, 159–66.

Diels, H. (1879) *Doxographi Graeci* (Berlin).

(1893*a*) 'Über die Excerpte von Menons Iatrika in dem Londoner Papyrus 137', *Hermes* XXVIII, 407–34.

(1893*b*) *Anonymi Londinensis ex Aristotelis Iatricis Menoniis et aliis medicis Eclogae* (Supplementum Aristotelicum III, 1, Berlin).

(1905) *Die Handschriften der antiken Ärzte, Theil I, Hippokrates und Galenos* (Abhandlungen der königlich preussischen Akademie der Wissenschaften zu Berlin, phil.-hist. Kl., III, Berlin 1905).

(1906) *Die Handschriften der antiken Ärzte, Theil II, Die übrigen griechischen Ärzte ausser Hippokrates und Galenos* (Abhandlungen der königlich preussischen Akademie der Wissenschaften zu Berlin, phil.-hist. Kl., I, Berlin 1906).

Diepgen, P. (1920) 'Die Betätigung des Mannes als Frauenarzt von den ältesten Zeiten bis zum Ausgang des Mittelalters', *Zentralblatt für Gynäkologie*, Jahrgang 44, XXVII, 725–9.

(1937) *Die Frauenheilkunde der alten Welt* (München).

(1949) 'Die Lehre von der leibseelischen Konstitution und die spezielle Anatomie und Physiologie der Frau im Mittelalter', *Scientia* LXXXIV, 97–103 and 132–4.

Dierauer, U. (1977) *Tier und Mensch im Denken der Antike* (Amsterdam).

Dierbach, J. H. (1824/1969) *Die Arzneimittel des Hippokrates* (Heidelberg, 1824) (repr. Hildesheim, 1969).

(1833/1970) *Flora Mythologica* (Frankfurt am Main, 1833) (repr. Wiesbaden, 1970).

Diller, H. (1932) 'ὄψις ἀδήλων τὰ φαινόμενα', *Hermes* LXVII, 14–42 (reprinted in *Kleine Schriften zur antiken Literatur* (München, 1971), pp. 119–43).

(1934) *Wanderarzt und Aitiologe* (Philologus Suppl. Bd 26, 3, Leipzig).

(1936–7) 'Eine stoisch-pneumatische Schrift im Corpus Hippocraticum', *Sudhoffs Archiv für Geschichte der Medizin und der Naturwissenschaften* XXIX, 178–95 (reprinted in Diller 1973, pp. 17–30).

(1964) 'Ausdrucksformen des methodischen Bewusstseins in den hippokratischen Epidemien', *Archiv für Begriffsgeschichte* IX, 133–50 (reprinted in Diller 1973, pp. 106–23).

(1970) *Hippocratis, De Aere Aquis Locis* (Corpus Medicorum Graecorum I 1, 2, Berlin).

(1973) *Kleine Schriften zur antiken Medizin* (Berlin).

Dirlmeier, F. (1937) *Die Oikeiosis-Lehre Theophrasts* (Philologus Suppl. Bd 30, 1, Leipzig).

Dittmeyer, L. (1887) 'Die Unechtheit des IX. Buches der Aristotelischen Tiergeschichte', *Blätter für das Bayerische Gymnasialschulwesen* XXIII, 16–29, 65–79, 145–62.

Dodds, E. R. (1951) *The Greeks and the Irrational* (University of California Press, Berkeley and Los Angeles).

(1968) *Pagan and Christian in an Age of Anxiety* (Cambridge).

Dolby, R. G. A. (1971) 'Sociology of knowledge in natural science', *Science Studies* I, 3–21.

Douglas, M. (1966) *Purity and Danger* (London).

(1970) *Natural Symbols* (London).

(1975) *Implicit Meanings* (London).

(1978) *Cultural Bias* (Royal Anthropological Institute of Great Britain and Ireland, Occasional Paper 35, London).

Douglas, M. (ed.) (1973) *Rules and Meanings* (London).

Drabkin, I. E. (1944) 'On medical education in Greece and Rome', *Bulletin of the History of Medicine* XV, 333–51.

(1951) 'Soranus and his system of medicine', *Bulletin of the History of Medicine* XXV, 503–18.

(1957) 'Medical education in ancient Greece and Rome', *Journal of Medical Education* XXXII, 286–95.

Ducatillon, J. (1977) *Polémiques dans la Collection Hippocratique* (Lille and Paris).

Duckworth, W. L. H. (1962) *Galen On Anatomical Procedures, The Later Books*, trans. W. L. H. Duckworth, edd. M. C. Lyons and B. Towers (Cambridge).

Düring, I. (1961) 'Aristotle's method in biology', in *Aristote et les problèmes de méthode*, ed. S. Mansion (Louvain and Paris), pp. 213–21.

(1966) *Aristoteles: Darstellung und Interpretation seines Denkens* (Heidelberg).

Dulière, W.-L. (1965) 'Les "Dictyaques" de Denys d'Égée ou les dilemmes du "sic et non" de la médecine antique. Histoire d'un procédé dialectique', *L'Antiquité Classique* XXXIV, 506–18.

Dumont, L. (1967/1970) *Homo hierarchicus* (trans. M. Sainsbury of *Homo hierarchicus*, Paris, 1967) (London, 1970).

Dundes, A. (1975) *Analytic Essays in Folklore* (The Hague and Paris).

Dupré, J. (1981) 'Natural kinds and biological taxa', *Philosophical Review* XC, 66–90.

Durand, J. L. (1979) 'Bêtes grecques', in *La Cuisine du sacrifice en pays grec*, M. Detienne, J. P. Vernant et al. (Paris), pp. 133–65.

Durkheim, E. (1912/1976) *The Elementary Forms of the Religious Life* (trans. J. W. Swain of *Les Formes élémentaires de la vie religieuse*, Paris, 1912), 2nd ed. (London, 1976).

Durkheim, E. and Mauss, M. (1901–2/1963) *Primitive Classification* (trans. R. Needham of 'De quelques formes primitives de classification', *L'Année sociologique* VI (1901–2) 1–72) (London, 1963).

East, S. P. (1958) 'De la méthode en biologie selon Aristote', *Laval Théologique et Philosophique* XIV, 213–35.

Ebbell, B. (1937) *The Papyrus Ebers* (Copenhagen and London).

Edelstein, E. J. and Edelstein, L. (1945) *Asclepius*, 2 vols. (Johns Hopkins, Baltimore).

Edelstein, L. (1931) ΠΕΡΙ ΑΕΡШΝ *und die Sammlung der hippokratischen Schriften* (Problemata 4, Berlin).

(1932–3/1967) 'The history of anatomy in antiquity' (originally 'Die Geschichte der Sektion in der Antike', *Quellen und Studien zur Geschichte der Naturwissenschaften und der Medizin* III, 2 (1932–3), 100–56), in L. Edelstein 1967, pp. 247–301.

(1935/1967) 'The Methodists' (originally 'Methodiker', *Pauly-Wissowa Real-Encyclopädie der classischen Altertumswissenschaft*, Suppl. Bd VI (Stuttgart, 1935), cols. 358–73), in L. Edelstein 1967, pp. 173–91.

(1937/1967) 'Greek medicine in its relation to religion and magic' (*Bulletin of the Institute of the History of Medicine* v (1937), 201–46), in Edelstein 1967, pp. 205–46.

(1967) *Ancient Medicine*, edd. O. and C. L. Temkin (Johns Hopkins, Baltimore).

Eliade, M. (1963) *Myth and Reality* (trans. W. R. Trask of *Aspects du mythe*, Paris, 1963) (New York, 1963).

Evans, E. C. (1941) 'The study of physiognomy in the second century A.D.' *Transactions and Proceedings of the American Philological Association* LXXII, 96–108.

Evans-Pritchard, E. E. (1937) *Witchcraft, Oracles and Magic among the Azande* (Oxford).

Fasbender, H. (1897) *Entwickelungslehre, Geburtshülfe und Gynäkologie in den hippokratischen Schriften* (Stuttgart).

Festugière, A. J. (1948) *Hippocrate, L'Ancienne médecine* (Études et Commentaires 4, Paris).

Feyerabend, P. K. (1961) *Knowledge without Foundations* (Oberlin).

(1975) *Against Method* (London).

Finley, M. I. (1973) *Democracy Ancient and Modern* (London).

(1975) *The Use and Abuse of History* (London).

(1980) *Ancient Slavery and Modern Ideology* (London).

Firatli, N. and Robert, L. (1964) *Les stèles funéraires de Byzance Gréco-Romaine* (Bibliothèque archéologique et historique de l'Institut français d'archéologie d'Istanbul 15, Paris).

Flashar, H. (ed.). (1971) *Antike Medizin* (Darmstadt).

Förster, R. (1893) *Scriptores Physiognomonici Graeci et Latini*, 2 vols. (Leipzig).

Fortenbaugh, W. W. (1971) 'Aristotle: animals, emotion, and moral virtue', *Arethusa* IV, 137–65.

(1975) 'On Plato's feminism in *Republic* V', *Apeiron* IX,2, 1–4.

Foucault, M. (1963/1973) *The Birth of the Clinic* (trans. A. M. Sheridan Smith of *Naissance de la clinique*, Paris, 1963), (London, 1973).

(1966/1970) *The Order of Things* (trans. of *Les Mots et les choses*, Paris, 1966), (London, 1970).

(1969/1972) *The Archaeology of Knowledge* (trans. A. M. Sheridan Smith of *L'Archéologie du savoir*, Paris, 1969), (London, 1972).

(1976/1978) *The History of Sexuality* (trans. R. Hurley of *La Volonté de savoir*, Paris, 1976), (New York, 1978).

Fraenkel, E. (1922) *Plautinisches im Plautus* (Philologische Untersuchungen 28, Berlin).

(1950) *Aeschylus, Agamemnon*, 3 vols. (Oxford).

Fränkel, H. (1921) *Die homerischen Gleichnisse* (Göttingen).

(1960) *Wege und Formen frühgriechischen Denkens* (1st ed. 1955), 2nd ed. (München).

(1962/1975) *Early Greek Poetry and Philosophy* (trans. M. Hadas and J. Willis of 2nd ed. of *Dichtung und Philosophie des frühen Griechentums*, München, 1962) (Oxford, 1975).

Frankfort, H. (ed.) (1949) *Before Philosophy* (1st ed. *The Intellectual Adventure of Ancient Man*, Chicago, 1946), 2nd ed. (London).

Fraser, P. M. (1969) 'The career of Erasistratus of Ceos', *Rendiconti del Istituto Lombardo*, Classe di Lettere e Scienze Morali e Storiche CIII, 518–37.

(1972) *Ptolemaic Alexandria*, 3 vols. (Oxford).

Frazer, J. G. (1911–15), *The Golden Bough*, 12 vols., 3rd ed. (London).

Frede, M. (1981) 'On Galen's epistemology', in *Galen: Problems and Prospects*, ed. V. Nutton (Wellcome Institute for the History of Medicine), pp. 65–86.

(1982) 'The method of the so-called Methodical school of medicine', in *Science and Speculation*, edd. J. Barnes, J. Brunschwig, M. Burnyeat, M. Schofield (Cambridge), pp. 1–23.

Fritz, H. von (1971) *Grundprobleme der Geschichte der antiken Wissenschaft* (Berlin and New York).

Gasking, E. B. (1959) 'Why was Mendel's work ignored?', *Journal of the History of Ideas* xx, 60–84.

Geddes, A. (1975) 'The philosophic notion of women in antiquity', *Antichthon* IX, 35–40.

Geertz, C. (1973) *The Interpretation of Cultures* (New York).

Gellner, E. (1962/1970) 'Concepts and society' (from *The Transactions of the Fifth World Congress of Sociology*, 1962), in *Rationality*, ed. B. R. Wilson (Oxford, 1970), pp. 18–49.

(1973) 'The savage and the modern mind', in Horton and Finnegan 1973, pp. 162–81.

Gernet, L. (1968/1981) *The Anthropology of ancient Greece* (trans. J. Hamilton, and B. Nagy of *Anthropologie de la Grèce antique*, Paris, 1968) (Johns Hopkins, Baltimore, 1981).

Gerstinger, H. (1970) *Dioscurides Codex Vindobonensis Med. Gr. 1 der österreichischen Nationalbibliothek: Kommentarband zu der Faksimileausgabe* (Graz).

Gigon, O. (1946) 'Die naturphilosophischen Voraussetzungen der antiken Biologie', *Gesnerus* III, 35–58.

(1966) 'Plinius und der Zerfall der antiken Naturwissenschaft', *Arctos* NS IV, 23–45.

Gohlke, P. (1924) 'Die Entstehungsgeschichte der naturwissenschaftlichen Schriften des Aristoteles', *Hermes* LIX, 274–306.

Goltz, D. (1972) *Studien zur Geschichte der Mineralnamen in Pharmazie, Chemie und Medizin von den Anfängen bis Paracelsus* (Sudhoffs Archiv Beiheft 14, Wiesbaden).

(1974) *Studien zur altorientalischen und griechischen Heilkunde, Therapie, Arzneibereitung, Rezeptstruktur* (Sudhoffs Archiv Beiheft 16, Wiesbaden).

Gomperz, H. (1943) 'Problems and methods of early Greek science', *Journal of the History of Ideas* IV, 161–76.

Goody, J. (1977) *The Domestication of the Savage Mind* (Cambridge).

(unpublished) 'Literacy and achievement in the ancient world.'

Goody, J. and Watt, I. P. (1968) 'The consequences of literacy', in *Literacy in Traditional Societies*, ed. J. Goody (Cambridge), pp. 27–68.

Gordon, R. L. (ed.) (1981) *Myth, Religion and Society*, Structuralist essays by M. Detienne, L. Gernet, J.-P. Vernant and P. Vidal-Naquet (Cambridge).

Gossen, H. (1914) 'Rufus (18)', *Pauly-Wissowa Real-Encyclopädie der classischen Altertumswissenschaft*, 2nd ser. 1 Halbband, I,1, cols. 1207–12.

Gould, J. P. (1980) 'Law, custom and myth: Aspects of the social position of women in Classical Athens', *Journal of Hellenic Studies* C, 38–59.

Green, P. M. (1954) 'Prolegomena to the Study of Magic and Superstition in the *Natural History* of Pliny the Elder, with special reference to book XXX and its sources' (unpubl. Ph.D. dissertation, Cambridge, 1954).

Grensemann, H. (1968a) *Die hippokratische Schrift 'Über die heilige Krankheit'* (Ars Medica, Abt. II Bd 1, Berlin).

(1968b) *Hippocratis, De Octimestri Partu, De Septimestri Partu* (Corpus Medicorum Graecorum I 2,1, Berlin).

(1975a) *Knidische Medizin I. Die Testimonien zur ältesten knidischen Lehre und Analysen knidischer Schriften im Corpus Hippocraticum* (Ars Medica, Abt. II Bd 4,1, Berlin).

(1975b) 'Eine jüngere Schicht in den gynäkologischen Schriften', in Bourgey and Jouanna 1975, pp. 151–69.

Griffith, F. L. (1898) *The Petrie Papyri. Hieratic Papyri from Kahun and Gurob* (London).

Grmek, M. D. (ed.). (1980) *Hippocratica* (Actes du Colloque hippocratique de Paris) (Paris).

von Grot, R. (1889) 'Ueber die in der hippokratischen Schriftensammlung enthaltenen pharmakologischen Kenntnisse', in *Historische Studien zur Pharmakologie der Griechen, Römer und Araber*, ed. R. Kobert (1889–96), Bd I (Halle, 1889), pp. 58–133.

Habermas, J. (1968/1978) *Knowledge and Human Interests* (trans. J. J. Shapiro of *Erkenntnis und Interesse*, Frankfurt am Main, 1968) (new ed. London, 1978).

(1971/1974) *Theory and practice* (trans. J. Viertel of *Theorie und Praxis*, Frankfurt am Main, 1971) (London, 1974).

Halleux, R. (1974) *Le Problème des métaux dans la science antique* (Bibliothèque de la Faculté de Philosophie et Lettres de l'Université de Liège 209, Paris).

Hamelin, O. (1931) *Le Système d'Aristote* (1st ed. 1920), 2nd ed. (Paris).

Hanson, A. E. (1975) 'Hippocrates: *Diseases of Women* I', *Signs* 1,2, 567–84.

Harig, G. (1974) *Bestimmung der Intensität im medizinischen System Galens* (Berlin).

(1975) Review of Goltz 1974, *Deutsche Literaturzeitung* XCVI, cols. 654–8.

(1977a) 'Bemerkungen zum Verhältnis der griechischen zur altorientalischen Medizin', in Joly 1977, pp. 77–94.

(1977b) 'Die antike Auffassung vom Gift und der Tod des Mithridates', *NTM* (Schriftenreihe für Geschichte der Naturwissenschaften, Technik und Medizin) XIV, 104–12.

(1980) 'Anfänge der theoretischen Pharmakologie im Corpus Hippocraticum', in Grmek 1980, pp. 223–45.

Harig, G. and Kollesch, J. (1973–4) 'Arzt, Kranker und Krankenpflege in der griechisch-römischen Antike und im byzantinischen Mittelalter', *Helikon* XIII–XIV, 256–92.

(1974) 'Diokles von Karystos und die zoologische Systematik', *NTM* (Schriftenreihe für Geschichte der Naturwissenschaften, Technik und Medizin) XI, 24–31.

(1977) 'Neue Tendenzen in der Forschung zur Geschichte der antiken Medizin und Wissenschaft', *Philologus* CXXI, 114–36.

Harris, C.R.S. (1973) *The Heart and the Vascular System in Ancient Greek Medicine from Alcmaeon to Galen* (Oxford).

Harvey, F. D. (1966) 'Literacy in the Athenian democracy', *Revue des études grecques* LXXIX, 585–635.

Havelock, E. A. (1971) *Prologue to Greek Literacy* (University of Cincinnati).

(1976) *Origins of Western Literacy* (Ontario Institute for Studies in Education 14, Toronto).

Heidel, W. A. (1941) *Hippocratic Medicine: its spirit and method* (New York).

Heinimann, F. (1945) *Nomos und Physis* (Schweizerische Beiträge zur Altertumswissenschaft 1, Basel).

Herzog, R. (1931) *Die Wunderheilungen von Epidauros* (Philologus Suppl. Bd 22,3, Leipzig).

Heusch, L. de (1964/1981) 'Social structure and praxis among the Lele of the Kasai' (originally 'Structure et praxis sociales chez les Lele du Kasai', *L'Homme* IV,3 (1964) 87–109) in *Why Marry Her? Society and Symbolic Structures* (trans. J. Lloyd) (Cambridge, 1981), pp. 82–106.

Höffe, O. (1976) 'Grundaussagen über den Menschen bei Aristoteles', *Zeitschrift für philosophische Forschung* XXX, 227–45.

Holton, G. (1978) *The Scientific Imagination* (Cambridge).

Hopfner, T. (1938) *Das Sexualleben der Griechen und Römer*, vol. 1 (Prague).

Hopkins, K. (1965–6) 'Contraception in the Roman Empire', *Comparative Studies in Society and History* VIII, 124–51.

Horowitz, M. C. (1976) 'Aristotle and woman', *Journal of the History of Biology* IX, 183–213.

Hort, A. (1916) *Theophrastus, Enquiry into Plants*, 2 vols., Loeb ed. (London and Cambridge, Mass.).

Horton, R. (1973) 'Lévy-Bruhl, Durkheim and the scientific revolution', in Horton and Finnegan 1973, pp. 249–305.

Horton, R. and Finnegan, R. (edd.) (1973) *Modes of Thought* (London).

Huby, P.M. (unpublished) 'Theophrastus in the Aristotelian *Corpus*, with particular reference to biological problems.'

Hull, D. L. (1964–5) 'The effect of essentialism on taxonomy – two thousand years of stasis, I', *British Journal for the Philosophy of Science* XV, 314–26.

(1965–6) 'The effect of essentialism on taxonomy – two thousand years of stasis, II', *British Journal for the Philosophy of Science* XVI, 1–18.

(1966–7) 'The metaphysics of evolution', *British Journal for the History of Science* III, 309–37.

Humphreys, S. C. (1978) *Anthropology and the Greeks* (London).

(1983) *The Family, Women and Death* (London).

Ilberg, J. (1913) Review of Wellmann 1913, *Neue Jahrbücher für das klassische Altertum, Geschichte und deutsche Literatur* XXXI, 692–6.

(1927) *Soranus, Gynaeciorum Libri* IV (Corpus Medicorum Graecorum IV, Berlin).

(1931) *Rufus von Ephesos. Ein griechischer Arzt in trajanischer Zeit* (Abhandlungen der phil.-hist. Klasse der sächsischen Akademie der Wissenschaften XLI, 1, 1930, Leipzig, 1931).

Irigoin, J. (1980) 'La formation du vocabulaire de l'anatomie en grec: du mycénien aux principaux traités de la Collection hippocratique', in Grmek 1980, pp. 247–56.

Irmer, D. (1980) 'Die Bezeichnung der Knochen in *Fract.* und *Art.*', in Grmek 1980, pp. 265–83.

Iversen, E. (1939) *Papyrus Carlsberg No. VIII* (Det kgl. Danske Videnskabernes Selskab. Historisk-filologiske Meddelelser XXVI, 5, Copenhagen).

Jackson, B. P. and Berry, M. I. (1973) 'Hydroxytropane Tiglates in the roots of *Mandragora* Species', *Phytochemistry* XII, 1165–6.

Jacobsen, T. (1949) 'Mesopotamia', in Frankfort 1949, pp. 137–234.

Jaeger, W. (1938) *Diokles von Karystos. Die griechische Medizin und die Schule des Aristoteles*, 2nd ed. (Berlin).

Jenner, E. (1798/1801) *An Inquiry into the causes and effects of the variolae vaccinae* (1st ed. 1798) 3rd ed. (London, 1801).

Joachim, H. (1892) *De Theophrasti Libris ΠΕΡΙ ΖΩΙΩΝ* (Bonn).

Johnson, J. de M. (1912–13) 'A botanical papyrus with illustrations', *Archiv für die Geschichte der Naturwissenschaften und der Technik* IV, 403–8.

Joly, R. (1960) *Recherches sur le traité pseudo-hippocratique Du Régime* (Bibliothèque de la faculté de philosophie et lettres de l'Université de Liège, 156, Paris).

(1962) 'La caractérologie antique jusqu'à Aristote', *Revue Belge de Philologie et d'Histoire* XL, 5–28.

(1966) *Le Niveau de la science hippocratique* (Paris).

(1968) 'La biologie d'Aristote', *Revue philosophique de la France et de l'Étranger* CLVIII, 219–53.

(1975) 'Remarques sur le "De Alimento" pseudo-hippocratique', in *Le Monde grec*, edd. J. Bingen, G. Cambier, G. Nachtergael (Bruxelles), pp. 271–6.

Joly, R. (ed.) (1977) *Corpus Hippocraticum* (Actes du Colloque hippocratique de Mons, Editions Universitaires de Mons, Série Sciences Humaines IV, Université de Mons).

Jones, W. H. S. (1923–31) *Hippocrates*, Loeb ed. 4 vols. (London and Cambridge, Mass.).

(1947) *The Medical Writings of Anonymus Londinensis* (Cambridge).

(1951–63) *Pliny, Natural History*, Vols. 6–8 (Books xx–xxiii, xxiv–xxvii, xxviii–xxxii) Loeb ed. (London and Cambridge, Mass.).

Jouanna, J. (1974) *Hippocrate: pour une archéologie de l'école de Cnide* (Paris).

(1975) *Hippocratis, De Natura Hominis* (Corpus Medicorum Graecorum 1 1,3, Berlin.

Justesen, P. T. (1928) *Les principes psychologiques d'Homère* (Copenhagen).

Kalinka, E. (ed.) (1920) *Tituli Asiae Minoris*, Vol. ii (Wien).

Keller, O. (1877) *Rerum Naturalium Scriptores Graeci Minores*, Vol. i (Leipzig).

(1909–13) *Die antike Tierwelt*, 2 vols. (Leipzig).

Kember, O. (1973) 'Anaxagoras' theory of sex differentiation and heredity', *Phronesis* xviii, 1–14.

Kind, E. (1929) 'Soranus', *Pauly-Wissowa Real-Encyclopädie der classischen Altertumswissenschaft*, 2nd ser. 5 Halbband, iii, 1, cols. 1113–30.

Kirchner, O. (1874*a*) 'Die botanischen Schriften des Theophrast von Eresos', *Jahrbücher für classische Philologie*, Suppl. Bd vii (1873–5), 3, 6 (Leipzig, 1874), pp. 449–539.

(1874*b*) *De Theophrasti Eresii Libris Phytologicis* (Bratislava).

Knutzen, G. H. (1964) *Technologie in den hippokratischen Schriften* περὶ διαίτης ὀξέων, περὶ ἀγμῶν, περὶ ἄρθρων ἐμβολῆς (Akademie der Wissenschaften und der Literatur, Mainz, Abhandlungen der geistes- und sozialwissenschaftlichen Klasse, Jahrgang 1963, 14, Wiesbaden, 1964).

Koelbing, H. M. (1977) *Arzt und Patient in der antiken Welt* (Zürich and München).

Körner, O. (1917) *Das homerische Tiersystem und seine Bedeutung für die zoologische Systematik des Aristoteles* (Wiesbaden).

(1929) *Die ärztlichen Kenntnisse in Ilias und Odyssee* (München).

(1930) *Die homerische Tierwelt* (1st ed. 1880), 2nd ed. (München).

Kollesch, J. (1974) 'Die Medizin und ihre sozialen Aufgaben zur Zeit der Poliskrise', in *Hellenische Poleis*, Vol. iv, ed. E. C. Welskopf (Berlin), pp. 1850–71.

(1979) 'Ärztliche Ausbildung in der Antike', *Klio* lxi, 507–13.

Krell, D. F. (1975) 'Female parts in *Timaeus*', *Arion* N.S. ii, 400–21.

Kroll, W. (1930*a*) *Die Kosmologie des Plinius* (Abhandlungen der Schlesischen Gesellschaft für vaterländische Cultur, Geisteswissenschaftliche Reihe 3, Breslau).

(1930*b*) 'Plinius und die Chaldäer', *Hermes* lxv, 1–13.

(1940) *Zur Geschichte der aristotelischen Zoologie* (Akademie der Wissenschaften in Wien, phil.-hist. Kl., Sitzungsberichte 218, 2, Wien).

Kudlien, F. (1962) 'Poseidonios und die Ärzteschule der Pneumatiker', *Hermes* xc, 419–29.

(1963) 'Probleme um Diokles von Karystos', *Sudhoffs Archiv für Geschichte der Medizin und der Naturwissenschaften* xlvii, 456–64.

(1967) *Der Beginn des medizinischen Denkens bei den Griechen* (Zürich and Stuttgart).

(1968*a*) 'Der Arzt des Körpers und der Arzt der Seele', *Clio Medica* iii, 1–20.

(1968*b*) 'Early Greek primitive medicine', *Clio Medica* iii, 305–36.

(1970) 'Medical education in classical antiquity', in *The History of Medical Education*, ed. C. D. O'Malley (University of California Press, Berkeley and Los Angeles), pp. 3–37.

(1974) 'Dialektik und Medizin in der Antike', *Medizinhistorisches Journal* ix, 187–200.

(1976) 'Medicine as a "Liberal Art" and the question of the physician's income', *Journal of the History of Medicine and Allied Sciences* xxxi, 448–59.

(1979) *Der griechische Arzt im Zeitalter des Hellenismus* (Akademie der Wissenschaften und der Literatur, Mainz, Abhandlungen der geistes- und sozialwissenschaftlichen Klasse, Jahrgang 1979, 6, Wiesbaden).

Kühn, J.-H. (1956) *System- und Methodenprobleme im Corpus Hippocraticum* (Hermes Einzelschriften 11, Wiesbaden).

Kuhn, T. S. (1962/1970a) *The Structure of Scientific Revolutions* (1st ed. 1962) 2nd ed. (University of Chicago, 1970).

(1970b) 'Postscript – 1969', in *The Structure of Scientific Revolutions*, 2nd cd. (University of Chicago), pp. 174–210.

(1970c) 'Reflections on my critics', in *Criticism and the Growth of Knowledge*, edd. I. Lakatos and A. Musgrave (Cambridge), pp. 231–78.

(1974) 'Second thoughts on paradigms', in *The Structure of Scientific Theories*, ed. F. Suppe (University of Illinois, Urbana, Chicago), pp. 459–82.

Kullmann, W. (1974) *Wissenschaft und Methode: Interpretationen zur aristotelischen Theorie der Naturwissenschaft* (Berlin and New York).

(1979) *Die Teleologie in der aristotelischen Biologie* (Sitzungsberichte der Heidelberger Akademie der Wissenschaften, phil.-hist. Kl., Jahrgang 1979, 2, Heidelberg).

(1980) 'Der Mensch als politisches Lebewesen bei Aristoteles', *Hermes* CVIII, 419–43.

Labat, R. (1951) *Traité Akkadien de Diagnostics et Pronostics Médicaux* (Paris and Leiden).

Laín Entralgo, P. (1970) *The Therapy of the Word in Classical Antiquity* (trans. L. J. Rather and J. M. Sharp of *La curacíon por la palabra en la Antigüedad clásica*, Madrid, 1958) (New Haven and London).

Lanata, G. (1967) *Medicina Magica e Religione Popolare in Grecia* (Roma).

Landels, J. G. (1979) 'An ancient account of reproduction', *Biology and Human Affairs* XLIV, 94–113.

Lang, P. (1911) *De Speusippi Academici Scriptis* (Bonn) (reprinted Hildesheim, 1965).

Langkavel, B. (1866/1964) *Botanik der spaeteren Griechen* (Berlin, 1866) (repr. Amsterdam, 1964).

Lanza, D. and Vegetti, M. (1975) 'L'ideologia della città', *Quaderni di Storia* II, 1–37.

Leach, E. R. (1964) 'Anthropological aspects of language: animal categories and verbal abuse', in *New Directions in the Study of Language*, ed. E. H. Lenneberg (Cambridge, Mass.), pp. 23–63.

Le Blond, J. M. (1939) *Logique et méthode chez Aristote* (Paris).

(1945) *Aristote, Philosophe de la vie* (Paris).

Lefebure, G. (1956) *Essai sur la médecine Égyptienne de l'époque pharaonique* (Paris).

Lefkowitz, M. (1981) *Heroines and Hysterics* (London).

Lehman, H. (1967) 'Are biological species real?' *Philosophy of Science* XXXIV, 157–67.

Lennox, J. G. (1980) 'Aristotle on Genera, Species, and "the More and the Less"', *Journal of the History of Biology* XIII, 321–46.

Lenoble, R. (1952) 'Les obstacles épistémologiques dans l'"histoire naturelle" de Pline', *Thalès* VIII, 87–106.

Le Page Renouf, P. (1873) 'Note on the medical papyrus of Berlin', *Zeitschrift für ägyptische Sprache und Alterthumskunde* XI Jahrgang, 123–5.

Lesky, E. (1951) *Die Zeugungs- und Vererbungslehren der Antike und ihr Nachwirken* (Akademie der Wissenschaften und der Literatur, Mainz, Abhandlungen der geistes- und sozialwissenschaftlichen Klasse, Jahrgang 1950, 19, Wiesbaden).

Lévi-Strauss, C. (1958/1968) *Structural Anthropology* (trans. C. Jacobson and B. G. Schoepf of *Anthropologie structurale*, Paris, 1958) (London, 1968).

(1962a/1966) *The Savage Mind* (trans. of *La Pensée sauvage*, Paris, 1962) (London, 1966).

(1962b/1969) *Totemism* (revised trans. R. Needham of *Le Totémisme aujourd'hui* Paris, 1962) (London, 1969).

(1973/1976) *Structural Anthropology*, Vol. 2 (trans. M. Layton of *Anthropologie structurale Deux*, Paris, 1973) (New York, 1976).

Lewes, G. H. (1864) *Aristotle: A chapter from the history of science* (London).

Lewis, G. (1975) *Knowledge of Illness in a Sepik Society* (London).

Lichtenthaeler, C. (1948) *La Médecine Hippocratique I: Méthode expérimentale et méthode hippocratique* (Lausanne).

Lienau, C. (1973) *Hippocratis. De Superfetatione* (Corpus Medicorum Graecorum I 2,2, Berlin).

Lienhardt, G. (1961) *Divinity and Experience: The Religion of the Dinka* (Oxford).

Lipinska, M. (1900) *Histoire des femmes médecins depuis l'antiquité jusqu'à nos jours* (Paris).

Lisowski, F. P. (1967) 'Prehistoric and early historic trepanation', in Brothwell and Sandison 1967, pp. 651–72.

Littré, E. (1839–61) *Oeuvres complètes d'Hippocrate*, 10 vols. (Paris).

Lloyd, G. E. R. (1961) 'The development of Aristotle's theory of the classification of animals', *Phronesis* VI, 59–81.

(1966) *Polarity and Analogy* (Cambridge).

(1975a) 'Alcmaeon and the early history of dissection', *Sudhoffs Archiv* LIX, 113–47.

(1975b) 'The Hippocratic Question', *Classical Quarterly* NS XXV, 171–92.

(1975c) 'A note on Erasistratus of Ceos', *Journal of Hellenic Studies* XCV, 172–5.

(1978) 'The empirical basis of the physiology of the *Parva Naturalia*', in *Aristotle on Mind and the Senses*, edd. G. E. R. Lloyd and G. E. L. Owen (Cambridge), pp. 215–39.

(1979) *Magic, Reason and Experience* (Cambridge).

(1982) 'Observational error in later Greek science', in *Science and Speculation*, edd. J. Barnes, J. Brunschwig, M. Burnyeat, M. Schofield (Cambridge), pp. 128–64.

Longrigg, J. (1963) 'Philosophy and medicine, some early interactions', *Harvard Studies in Classical Philology* LXVII, 147–75.

(1975) 'Elementary physics in the Lyceum and Stoa', *Isis* LXVI, 211–29.

(1981) 'Superlative achievement and comparative neglect: Alexandrian medical science and modern historical research', *History of Science* XIX, 155–200.

Lonie, I. M. (1973) 'The paradoxical text "On the Heart"', *Medical History* XVII, 1–15 and 136–53.

(1978) 'Cos versus Cnidus and the historians', *History of Science* XVI, 42–75 and 77–92.

(1981) *The Hippocratic Treatises 'On Generation' 'On the Nature of the Child' 'Diseases IV'* (Ars Medica Abt. II Bd 7, Berlin).

Loraux, N. (1978/1981a) 'Sur la race des femmes et quelques-unes de ses tribus' (*Arethusa* XI (1978), 43–87), in Loraux 1981a, pp. 75–117.

(1981a) *Les enfants d'Athéna: idées athéniennes sur la citoyenneté et la division des sexes* (Paris).

(1981b) *L'Invention d'Athènes: histoire de l'oraison funèbre dans la "cité classique"* (Paris).

Louis, P. (1955) 'Remarques sur la classification des animaux chez Aristote', in *Autour d'Aristote* (receuil d'études ... offert à M. A. Mansion) (Louvain), pp. 297–304.

(1961) *Aristote: De la Génération des animaux* (Paris).

(1964–9) *Aristote: Histoire des animaux*, 3 vols. (Paris).

(1967) 'Les animaux fabuleux chez Aristote', *Revue des études grecques* LXXX, 242–6.

(1975) 'Monstres et monstruosités dans la biologie d'Aristote', in *Le Monde grec*, edd. J. Bingen, G. Cambier, G. Nachtergael (Bruxelles), pp. 277–84.

Lovejoy, A. O. (1936) *The Great Chain of Being* (Cambridge, Mass.).

Lovejoy, A. O. and Boas, G. (1935) *Primitivism and Related Ideas in Antiquity* (Johns Hopkins, Baltimore).

Lukes, S. (1973) 'On the social determination of truth', in Horton and Finnegan 1973, pp. 230–48.

Maclean, I. (1980) *The Renaissance Notion of Woman* (Cambridge).

Majno, G. (1975) *The Healing Hand* (Cambridge, Mass.).

Mannheim, K. (1936) *Ideology and Utopia* (trans. L. Wirth and E. Shils) (London).

Manquat, M. (1932) *Aristote naturaliste* (Paris).

Mansfeld, J. (1971) *The Pseudo-Hippocratic Tract* ΠΕΡΙ ʽΕΒΔΟΜΑΔΩΝ *ch. 1–11 and Greek Philosophy* (Assen).

　(1975) 'Alcmaeon: "Physikos" or Physician?', in *Kephalaion*, edd. J. Mansfeld and L. M. de Rijk (Assen), pp. 26–38.

Mansion, A. (1946) *Introduction à la physique aristotélicienne* (1st ed. 1913), 2nd ed. (Louvain and Paris).

Mansion, S. (ed.) (1961) *Aristote et les problèmes de méthode* (Louvain and Paris).

Manuli, P. (1980) 'Fisiologia e patologia del femminile negli scritti ippocratici dell' antica ginecologia greca', in Grmek 1980, pp. 393–408.

　(1982) 'Elogio della castità', *Memoria* III, 39–49.

Manuli, P. and Vegetti, M. (1977) *Cuore, sangue e cervello* (Milano).

Margetts, E. L. (1967) 'Trepanation of the skull by the medicine-men of primitive cultures, with particular reference to present-day native East African practice', in Brothwell and Sandison 1967, pp. 673–701.

Masterman, M. (1970) 'The nature of a paradigm', in *Criticism and the Growth of Knowledge*, edd. I. Lakatos and A. Musgrave (Cambridge), pp. 59–89.

May, M. T. (1968) *Galen On the Usefulness of the Parts of the Body*, 2 vols. (Cornell University Press, Ithaca, New York).

Mayr, E. (1969) *Principles of systematic zoology* (New York and London).

Merton, R. K. (1968) *Social Theory and Social Structure*, enlarged ed. (New York and London).

Meyer, J. B. (1855) *Aristoteles Thierkunde: ein Beitrag zur Geschichte der Zoologie, Physiologie und alten Philosophie* (Berlin).

Meyer-Steineg, T. (1916) *Das medizinische System der Methodiker* (Jenaer medizinhis-torische Beiträge 7–8, Jena).

Michler, M. (1962a) 'Das Problem der westgriechischen Heilkunde', *Sudhoffs Archiv für Geschichte der Medizin und der Naturwissenschaften* XLVI, 137–52.

　(1962b) 'Die praktische Bedeutung des normativen Physis-Begriffes in der hippokratischen Schrift De fracturis – De articulis', *Hermes* LX, 385–401.

Migne, J. P. (1860) *Patrologiae Cursus Completus*, Vol. 103 (Paris).

Mignucci, M. (1965) *La teoria aristotelica della scienza* (Firenze).

　(1975) *L'argomentazione dimostrativa in Aristotele* (Padova).

Moreau, J. (1959) 'L'éloge de la biologie chez Aristote', *Revue des études anciennes* LXI, 57–64.

Morel, W. (1938) 'Pharmakopoles', in *Pauly-Wissowa Real-Encyclopädie der classischen Altertumswissenschaft*, 38 Halbband, XIX,2, cols. 1840–1.

Morsink, J. (1979) 'Was Aristotle's biology sexist?', *Journal of the History of Biology* XII, 83–112.

Mulkay, M. J. (1972) *The Social Process of Innovation* (London).

Murr, J. (1890) *Die Pflanzenwelt in der griechischen Mythologie* (Innsbruck).

Nachmanson, E. (1917) *Erotianstudien* (Uppsala and Leipzig).

Nardi, E. (1971) *Procurato aborto nel mondo greco-romano* (Milano).

Needham, J. (1954–) *Science and civilisation in China* (in progress) (Cambridge).

　(1959) *A History of Embryology* (1st ed. 1934), 2nd ed. (Cambridge).

Neugebauer, O. (1975) *A History of Ancient Mathematical Astronomy*, 3 vols. (Berlin and New York).

Nickel, D. (1972) 'Ärztliche Ethik und Schwangerschaftsunterbrechung bei den Hippokratikern', *NTM* (Schriftenreihe für Geschichte der Naturwissenschaften, Technik und Medizin) IX, 73–80.

(1979) 'Berufsvorstellungen über weibliche Medizinalpersonen in der Antike', *Klio* LXI, 515–18.

Nussbaum, M. C. (1978) *Aristotle's De Motu Animalium* (Princeton University Press, Princeton).

(1982) 'Saving Aristotle's appearances', in *Language and Logos*, edd. M. Schofield and M. C. Nussbaum (Cambridge), pp. 267–93.

Oehler, J. (1909) 'Epigraphische Beiträge zur Geschichte des Aerztestandes', *Janus* XIV, 4–20 and 111–23.

Ogle, W. (1882) *Aristotle on the Parts of Animals* (London).

(1897) *Aristotle on Youth and Old Age, Life and Death and Respiration* (London).

Olby, R. C. (1966) *Origins of Mendelism* (London).

(1979) 'Mendel no Mendelian?', *History of Science* XVII, 53–72.

O'Neill, Y. V. and Chan, G. L. (1976) 'A Chinese coroner's manual and the evolution of anatomy', *Journal of the History of Medicine and Allied Sciences* XXXI, 3–16.

Onians, R. B. (1951) *The Origins of European Thought* (Cambridge).

Oppenheim, A. Leo (1962) 'Mesopotamian medicine', *Bulletin of the History of Medicine* XXXVI, 97–108.

(1964) *Ancient Mesopotamia, Portrait of a Dead Civilisation* (Chicago).

Orel, V. (1973) 'Response to Mendel's Pisum experiments in Brno since 1865', *Folia Mendeliana* VIII, 199–211.

Owen, G. E. L. (1961/1975) 'Tithenai ta phainomena' (*Aristote et les problèmes de méthode*, ed. S. Mansion (Louvain and Paris, 1961), pp. 83–103), in Barnes, Schofield, Sorabji 1975, pp. 113–26 (also in *Aristotle*, ed. J. M. E. Moravcsik, London, 1968, pp. 167–90).

(1970) 'Aristotle: method, physics and cosmology', in *Dictionary of Scientific Biography*, ed. C. C. Gillispie (New York), Vol. I, pp. 250–8.

Pack, R. A. (1941) 'Artemidorus and the Physiognomists', *Transactions and Proceedings of the American Philological Association* LXXII, 321–34.

Pagel, W. (1958) *Paracelsus: An introduction to philosophical medicine in the era of the Renaissance* (Basel and New York).

Pearson, A. C. (1917) *The Fragments of Sophocles*, 3 vols. (Cambridge).

Peck, A. L. (1937) *Aristotle, Parts of Animals*, Loeb ed. (London and Cambridge, Mass.).

(1943) *Aristotle, Generation of Animals*, Loeb ed. (London and Cambridge, Mass.).

(1965) *Aristotle, Historia Animalium*, Books I–III, Loeb ed. (London and Cambridge, Mass.).

(1970) *Aristotle, Historia Animalium*, Books IV–VI, Loeb ed. (London and Cambridge, Mass.).

Pembroke, S. (1967) 'Women in charge: the function of alternatives in early Greek tradition and the ancient idea of matriarchy', *Journal of the Warburg and Courtauld Institutes* XXX, 1–35.

Peruzzi, E. (1956) 'Sulle denominazioni della retina', *La Parola del Passato* XI, 89–109.

Phillips, E. D. (1973) *Greek Medicine* (London).

Plamböck, G. (1964) *Dynamis im Corpus Hippocraticum* (Akademie der Wissenschaften und der Literatur, Mainz, Abhandlungen der geistes- und sozialwissenschaftlichen Klasse, Jahrgang 1964, 2, Wiesbaden).

Plamenatz, J. (1970) *Ideology* (London).

Platt, A. (1912) *Aristotle, De Generatione Animalium*, Oxford trans. in *The Works of*

Aristotle translated into English, ed. W. D. Ross, Vol. v (Oxford).

(1921) 'Aristotle on the heart', in *Studies in the History and Method of Science*, ed. C. Singer, Vol. ii (Oxford), pp. 521–32.

Plochmann, G. K. (1953) 'Nature and the living thing in Aristotle's biology', *Journal of the History of Ideas* xiv, 167–90.

Pohlenz, M. (1938) *Hippokrates und die Begründung der wissenschaftlichen Medizin* (Berlin).

Poirier, J.-L. (1978) 'Éléments pour une zoologie philosophique', *Critique* ccclxxv-ccclxxvi, 673–706.

Polanyi, M. (1958) *Personal Knowledge* (London).

(1967) *The Tacit Dimension* (London).

Poliakov, L. (ed.) (1975) *Hommes et bêtes: entretiens sur le racisme* (Paris and The Hague).

Pollak, K. (1968–9) *Wissen und Weisheit der alten Ärzte*, 2 vols. (Düsseldorf and Wien).

Pomeroy, S. B. (1973) 'Selected bibliography on women in antiquity', *Arethusa* vi, 125–52.

(1975) *Goddesses, Whores, Wives, and Slaves* (New York).

(1977) 'Technikai kai mousikai', *American Journal of Ancient History* ii, 51–68.

(1978a) 'Plato and the female physician (*Republic* 454d2)', *American Journal of Philology* xcix, 496–500.

(1978b) 'Supplementary notes on Erinna', *Zeitschrift für Papyrologie und Epigraphik* xxxii, 17–22.

Popper, K. R. (1963) *Conjectures and Refutations* (London).

Poschenrieder, F. (1887) *Die naturwissenschaftlichen Schriften des Aristoteles in ihrem Verhältnis zu den Büchern der hippokratischen Sammlung* (Bamberg).

Potter, P. (1976) 'Herophilus of Chalcedon: An assessment of his place in the history of anatomy', *Bulletin of the History of Medicine* l, 45–60.

Préaux, C. (1973) *La Lune dans la pensée grecque* (Académie Royale de Belgique, Mémoires de la Classe des Lettres, 2nd ser. 61, 4, Bruxelles).

Preus, A. (1975a) *Science and Philosophy in Aristotle's Biological Works* (Hildesheim and New York).

(1975b) 'Biomedical techniques for influencing human reproduction in the fourth century B.C.', *Arethusa* viii, 237–63.

(1977) 'Galen's criticism of Aristotle's conception theory', *Journal of the History of Biology* x, 65–85.

Provine, W. S. (1971) *The Origins of Theoretical Population Genetics* (University of Chicago Press, Chicago and London).

Puelma, M. (1972) 'Sänger und König. Zum Verständnis von Hesiods Tierfabel', *Museum Helveticum* xxix, 86–109.

Rahn, H. (1967) 'Das Tier in der homerischen Dichtung', *Studium Generale* xx, 90–105.

Randolph, C. B. (1904–5) 'The mandragora of the ancients in folk-lore and medicine', *Proceedings of the American Academy of Arts and Sciences* xl, 485–537.

Redfield, J. M. (1975) *Nature and Culture in the* Iliad (University of Chicago Press, Chicago and London).

Redfield, R. (1956) *Peasant Society and Culture* (University of Chicago Press, Chicago and London).

Regenbogen, O. (1931) *Eine Forschungsmethode antiker Naturwissenschaft* (Quellen und Studien zur Geschichte der Mathematik, Astronomie und Physik, B, 1, 2 (1930) Berlin, 1931), pp. 131–82 (reprinted in *Kleine Schriften* (München, 1961), pp. 141–94).

(1937) 'Eine Polemik Theophrasts gegen Aristoteles', *Hermes* LXXII, 469–75 (reprinted in *Kleine Schriften* (München, 1961), pp. 276–85).

(1940) 'Theophrastos', *Pauly-Wissowa Real-Encyclopädie der classischen Altertumswissenschaft*, Suppl. Bd VII (Stuttgart, 1940), cols. 1354–1562.

Reinhard, F. (1915–16) 'Gynäkologie und Geburtshilfe der altägyptischen Papyri I', *Archiv für Geschichte der Medizin* IX, 315–44.

(1916–17) 'Gynäkologie und Geburtshilfe der altägyptischen Papyri II', *Archiv für Geschichte der Medizin* X, 124–61.

Reinhardt, K. (1926) *Kosmos und Sympathie* (München).

Renehan, R. (1981) 'The Greek anthropocentric view of man', *Harvard Studies in Classical Philology* LXXXV, 239–59.

Reymond, E. A. E. (1976) *A Medical Book from Crocodilopolis* (Mitteilungen aus der Papyrussammlung der österreichischen Nationalbibliothek NS X Folge) (Wien).

Richardson, W. F. (1976) '"Acromion" in ancient Greek medical writers', *Medical History* LXX, 52–8.

Riddle, J. M. (1971) 'Dioscorides', in *Dictionary of Scientific Biography*, ed. C. C. Gillispie (New York), Vol. IV, pp. 119–23.

Riezler, K. (1936) 'Das homerische Gleichnis und der Anfang der Philosophie', *Die Antike* XII, 253–71.

Rivier, A. (1952) *Un Emploi archaïque de l'analogie* (Lausanne).

Roberts, H. F. (1929) *Plant Hybridization before Mendel* (Princeton, New Jersey).

Rosaldo, M. Z. and Lamphere, L. (1974) *Woman, Culture, and Society* (Stanford University Press, Stanford, California).

Rosenthal, C. O. (1923) 'Zur geburtshilflich-gynäkologischen Betätigung des Mannes bis zum Ausgange des 16 Jahrhunderts', *Janus* XXVII, 117–48 and 192–212.

Rousselle, A. (1980) 'Images médicales du corps en Grèce: Observation féminine et idéologie masculine', *Annales* XXXV,5, 1089–1115.

Rudberg, G. (1911) *Zum sogenannten zehnten Buche der aristotelischen Tiergeschichte* (Uppsala and Leipzig).

Ruelle, C. E. (1879) 'Préface' in Daremberg 1879, pp. i–lvi.

Ruse, M. (1969) 'Definitions of species in biology', *British Journal for the Philosophy of Science* XX, 97–119.

Sabbatucci, D. (1965) *Saggio sul misticismo greco* (Roma).

Sachs, J. von (1890) *History of Botany* (trans. H. E. F. Garnsey and I. B. Balfour) (Oxford).

Sambursky, S. (1956) *The Physical World of the Greeks* (trans. M. Dagut) (London).

(1959) *Physics of the Stoics* (London).

(1962) *The Physical World of Late Antiquity* (London).

Saunders, J. B. de C. M. (1963) *The Transitions from ancient Egyptian to Greek Medicine* (University of Kansas Press, Lawrence).

Savage Smith, E. (1971) 'Galen's account of the cranial nerves and the autonomic nervous system', *Clio Medica* VI, 77–98 and 173–94.

Scarborough, J. (1978) 'Theophrastus on herbals and herbal remedies', *Journal of the History of Biology* XI, 353–85.

Scheffler, I. (1967) *Science and Subjectivity* (Indianopolis and New York).

Schnapp-Gourbeillon, A. (1981) *Lions, héros, masques* (Paris).

Schofield, M. (1978) 'Aristotle on the imagination', in *Aristotle on Mind and the Senses*, edd. G. E. R. Lloyd and G. E. L. Owen (Cambridge), pp. 99–140.

Schuhl, P. M. (1949) *Essai sur la formation de la pensée grecque* (1st ed. 1934), 2nd ed. (Paris).

Senn, G. (1929) 'Über Herkunft und Stil der Beschreibungen von Experimenten im Corpus Hippocraticum', *Sudhoffs Archiv für Geschichte der Medizin* XXII, 217–89.

(1933) *Die Entwicklung der biologischen Forschungsmethode in der Antike und ihre grundsätzliche Förderung durch Theophrast von Eresos* (Veröffentlichungen der schweizerischen Gesellschaft für Geschichte der Medizin und der Naturwissenschaften 8, Aarau and Leipzig).

(1956) *Die Pflanzenkunde des Theophrast von Eresos* (Basel).

Seymer, L. R. (1957) *A General History of Nursing* (1st ed. 1932), 4th ed. (London).

Shapere, D. (1964) 'The structure of scientific revolutions', *Philosophical Review* LXXIII, 383–94.

Shaw, J. R. (1972) 'Models for cardiac structure and function in Aristotle', *Journal of the History of Biology* V, 355–88.

Sherwin-White, S. M. (1978) *Ancient Cos* (Hypomnemata 51, Göttingen).

Shirokogoroff, S. M. (1935) *Psychomental Complex of the Tungus* (London)

Sigerist, H. E. (1951–61) *A History of Medicine*, 2 vols. (Oxford).

Simon, M. (1906) *Sieben Bücher Anatomie des Galen*, 2 vols. (Leipzig).

Simpson, G. G. (1961) *Principles of Animal Taxonomy* (Columbia University Press, New York and London).

Singer, C. (1927) 'The herbal in antiquity and its transmission to later ages', *Journal of Hellenic Studies* XLVII, 1–52.

Sissa, G. (1981) 'La Pizia delfica: Immagini di una mantica amorosa e balsamica', *Aut Aut* CLXXXIV-CLXXXV, 193–213.

Skorupski, J. (1976) *Symbol and Theory* (Cambridge).

Sloan, P. R. (1972) 'John Locke, John Ray and the Problem of the Natural System', *Journal of the History of Biology* V, 1–53.

(1979) 'Buffon, German biology, and the historical interpretation of biological species', *British Journal for the History of Science* XII, 109–53.

Smith, W. D. (1973) 'Galen on Coans versus Cnidians', *Bulletin of the History of Medicine* XLVII, 569–85.

(1979) *The Hippocratic Tradition* (Cornell University Press, Ithaca and London).

Snell, B. (1948/1953) *The Discovery of the Mind* (trans. T. G. Rosenmeyer of *Die Entdeckung des Geistes*, 2nd ed. Hamburg, 1948) (Oxford, 1953).

(1975) *Die Entdeckung des Geistes*, revised 4th ed. (Göttingen).

Sober, E. (1980) 'Evolution, population thinking and essentialism', *Philosophy of Science* XLVII, 350–83.

Solmsen, F. (1955) 'Antecedents of Aristotle's psychology and scale of beings', *American Journal of Philology* LXXVI, 148–64.

(1960) *Aristotle's System of the Physical World* (Cornell University Press, Ithaca, New York).

(1961) 'Greek philosophy and the discovery of the nerves', *Museum Helveticum* XVIII, 150–67 and 169–97.

Souques, A. (1935) 'Connaissances neurologiques d'Hérophile et d'Erasistrate', *Revue neurologique* LXIII, 145–76.

Spencer, W. G. (1935–8) *Celsus, De Medicina*, 3 vols. Loeb ed. (London and Cambridge, Mass.).

Sperber, D. (1975) *Rethinking Symbolism* (trans. A. L. Morton) (Cambridge).

Sprengel, K. (1818) *Geschichte der Botanik* (revised ed. Leipzig).

Staden, H. von (1975) 'Experiment and experience in Hellenistic medicine', *Bulletin of the Institute of Classical Studies* XXII, 178–99.

(forthcoming) *The Art of Medicine in Ptolemaic Alexandria: Herophilus and his School* (Cambridge).

Stannard, J. (1961) 'Hippocratic pharmacology', *Bulletin of the History of Medicine* xxxv, 497–518.

(1962) 'The plant called Moly', *Osiris* xiv, 254–307.

(1965) 'Pliny and Roman botany', *Isis* lvi, 420–5.

(1969) 'The herbal as a medical document', *Bulletin of the History of Medicine* xliii, 212–20.

Staub, H. (1962) 'Über die chemischen Bestandteile der Mandragorawurzel 2. Die Alkaloide', *Helvetica Chimica Acta* xlv,7, 2297–2305.

Stearn, W. T. (1959) 'The background of Linnaeus's contributions to the nomenclature and methods of systematic biology', *Systematic Zoology* viii, 4–22.

(1976) 'From Theophrastus and Dioscorides to Sibthorp and Smith: the background and origin of the *Flora Graeca*', *Biological Journal of the Linnean Society* viii, 285–98.

Steinmetz, P. (1964) *Die Physik des Theophrastos von Eresos* (Bad Homburg, Berlin, Zürich).

Stemplinger, E. (1919) *Sympathieglaube und Sympathiekuren in Altertum und Neuzeit* (München).

(1925) *Antike und moderne Volksmedizin* (Das Erbe der Alten 10, Leipzig).

Stéphanidès, M. (1925) 'La terminologie des anciens: note introductive', *Isis* vii, 468–77.

Steuer, R. O. and Saunders, J. B. de C. M. (1959) *Ancient Egyptian and Cnidian Medicine* (University of California Press, Berkeley and Los Angeles).

Stiebitz, F. (1930) 'Über die Kausalerklärung der Vererbung bei Aristoteles', *Sudhoffs Archiv für Geschichte der Medizin* xxiii, 332–45.

Strömberg, R. (1937) *Theophrastea. Studien zur botanischen Begriffsbildung* (Göteborg).

(1940) *Griechische Pflanzennamen* (Göteborgs Högskolas Årsskrift xlvi, 1, Göteborg).

(1944) *Griechische Wortstudien. Untersuchungen zur Benennung von Tieren, Pflanzen, Körperteilen und Krankheiten* (Göteborgs Kungl. Vetenskaps- och Vitterhets-Samhälles Handlingar, Sjätte Följden Ser. a Bd 2, 2, Göteborg).

Tambiah, S. J. (1968) 'The magical power of words', *Man* ns iii, 175–208.

(1969) 'Animals are good to think and good to prohibit', *Ethnology* viii, 423–59.

(1973) 'Form and meaning of magical acts: a point of view', in Horton and Finnegan 1973, pp. 199–229.

(1977) 'The galactic polity', *Annals of the New York Academy of Sciences* ccxciii, 69–97.

Temkin, O. (1935) 'Celsus' "On Medicine" and the ancient medical sects', *Bulletin of the Institute of the History of Medicine* iii, 249–64.

(1956) *Soranus' Gynecology* (Johns Hopkins, Baltimore).

(1973) *Galenism: The Rise and Decline of a Medical Philosophy* (Cornell University Press, Ithaca and London).

Theiler, W. (1924) *Zur Geschichte der teleologischen Naturbetrachtung bis auf Aristoteles* (Zürich).

Thompson, A. R. (1952) 'Homer as a surgical anatomist', *Proceedings of the Royal Society of Medicine* xlv (Section of the History of Medicine), 765–7.

Thompson, D'A. W. (1910) *Aristotle, Historia Animalium*, in *The Works of Aristotle* translated into English (ed. W. D. Ross), Vol. iv (Oxford).

(1936) *A Glossary of Greek Birds* (1st ed. 1895), 2nd ed. (Oxford).

(1945) 'ὄνος – ἄνθρωπος', *Classical Quarterly* xxxix, 54–5.

(1947) *A Glossary of Greek Fishes* (Oxford University Press, London).

Thorndike, L. (1923–58) *A History of Magic and Experimental Science*, 8 vols. (New York).

Todorov, T. (1977) *Théories du symbole* (Paris).

(1978a) *Symbolisme et interprétation* (Paris).

(1978b) *Les Genres du discours* (Paris).

Trapp, H. (1967) *Die hippokratische Schrift DE NATURA MULIEBRI. Ausgabe und textkritischer Kommentar* (Hamburg).

Treggiari, S. (1976) 'Jobs for women', *American Journal of Ancient History* I, 76–104.

Turner, E. G. (1951) 'Athenian books in the fifth and fourth centuries B.C.' (Inaugural lecture, University College London).

Turner, V. (1970) *The Forest of Symbols* (Cornell University Press, Ithaca, New York and London).

Vegetti, N. (1973) 'Nascita dello scienziato', *Belfragor* XXVIII, 641–63.

(1979) *Il Coltello e lo Stilo* (Milano).

(1981a) 'Lo spettacolo della natura. Circo, teatro e potere in Plinio', *Aut Aut* CLXXXIV–CLXXXV, 111–25.

(1981b) 'Modelli di medicina in Galeno', in *Galen: Problems and Prospects* ed. V. Nutton (Wellcome Institute for the History of Medicine), pp. 47–63.

Veith, I. (1965) *Hysteria, The history of a disease* (University of Chicago Press, Chicago and London).

(1979–80) 'The history of medicine dolls and foot-binding in China', *Clio Medica* XIV, 255–67.

Vernant, J. P. (1963a/1965) 'Hestia-Hermès: sur l'expression religieuse de l'espace et du mouvement chez les Grecs' (*L'Homme* III, 3 (1963), 12–50), in Vernant 1965, pp. 97–143.

(1963b/1965) 'Géométrie et astronomie sphérique dans la première cosmologie grecque' (*La Pensée* CIX (1963), 82–92), in Vernant 1965, pp. 145–58.

(1965) *Mythe et pensée chez les grecs*, 2nd ed. (Paris).

(1972/1980) 'Between the Beasts and the Gods' (originally 'Entre bêtes et dieux', introduction to M. Detienne, *Les Jardins d'Adonis* (Paris, 1972) pp. i–xlvii, in *Myth and Society in Ancient Greece* (trans. J. Lloyd of *Mythe et Société en Grèce ancienne*, Paris, 1974) (Hassocks, Sussex, 1980), pp. 130–67.

(1974) 'Parole et signes muets', in *Divination et Rationalité*, J. P. Vernant et al. (Paris, 1974), pp. 9–25.

(1977/1981) 'Sacrificial and alimentary codes in Hesiod's myth of Prometheus' (originally 'Sacrifice et alimentation humaine: à propos du *Prométhée d'Hésiode*', *Annali della Scuola Normale di Pisa* VII, 3 (1977), 905–40, reprinted as 'À la table des hommes' in *La Cuisine du sacrifice en pays grec*, M. Detienne, J. P. Vernant et al. (Paris, 1979), pp. 37–132) in Gordon 1981, pp. 57–79.

Vidal-Naquet, P. (1970a/1981) 'Land and sacrifice in the Odyssey: a study of religious and mythical meanings' (originally 'Valeurs religieuses et mythiques de la terre et du sacrifice dans l'Odyssée', *Annales* XXV, 5 (1970), 1278–97, reprinted in *Problèmes de la terre en Grèce ancienne*, ed. M. I. Finley (Paris, The Hague, 1973), pp. 269–92) in Gordon 1981, pp. 80–94.

(1970b/1981) 'Slavery and the rule of women in tradition, myth and utopia' (originally 'Esclavage et gynécocratie dans la tradition, le mythe, l'utopie', in *Recherches sur les structures sociales dans l'antiquité classique*, edd. C. Nicolet and C. Leroy (Paris, 1970), pp. 63–80, reprinted in a revised version in Vidal-Naquet 1981, pp. 267–88), in Gordon 1981, pp. 187–200.

(1974/1981) 'Recipes for Greek adolescence' (originally 'Le cru, l'enfant grec et le cuit', in *Faire de l'histoire*, edd. J. Le Goff and P. Nora, Vol. 3 (Paris, 1974), pp. 137–68, reprinted in Vidal-Naquet 1981, pp. 177–207), in Gordon 1981, pp. 163–85.

(1975) 'Bêtes, hommes et dieux chez les Grecs', in Poliakov 1975, pp. 129–42.

(1981) *Le Chasseur noir: formes de pensée et formes de société dans le monde grec* (Paris).

Vlastos, G. (1975) *Plato's Universe* (Oxford).

Vygotsky, L. S. (1962) *Thought and Language* (trans. E. Hanfmann and G. Vakar) (Cambridge, Mass.).

Weidlich, T. (1894) *Die Sympathie in der antiken Literatur* (Stuttgart).

Weinreich, O. (1909) *Antike Heilungswunder* (Religionsgeschichtlichen Versuche und Vorarbeiten VIII, 1 (1909–10), Giessen, 1909).

Weinstein, A. (1977) 'How unknown was Mendel's paper?', *Journal of the History of Biology* x, 341–64.

Wellmann, M. (1889) 'Sextius Niger: eine Quellenuntersuchung zu Dioscorides', *Hermes* XXIV, 530–69.

(1895) *Die pneumatische Schule* (Philologische Untersuchungen 14, Berlin).

(1897) *Krateuas* (Abhandlungen der königlichen Gesellschaft der Wissenschaften zu Göttingen, Phil.-hist. Kl., NF II (1897–9), 1 Berlin, 1897).

(1898) 'Die Pflanzennamen des Dioskurides', *Hermes* XXXIII, 360–422.

(1901) *Die Fragmente der sikelischen Ärzte Akron, Philistion und des Diokles von Karystos* (Berlin).

(1906–14) *Pedanii Dioscuridis Anazarbei, De Materia Medica Libri Quinque*, 3 vols. (Berlin).

(1912) 'Zur Geschichte der Medicin im Altertum', *Hermes* XLVII, 1–17.

(1913) *A. Cornelius Celsus. Eine Quellenuntersuchung* (Philologische Untersuchungen 23, Berlin).

(1922) 'Der Verfasser des Anonymus Londinensis', *Hermes* LVII, 396–429.

(1925) 'A. Cornelius Celsus', *Archiv für Geschichte der Medizin* XVI, 209–13.

(1929) 'Spuren Demokrits von Abdera im Corpus Hippocraticum', *Archeion* XI, 297–330.

West, M. L. (1977) 'Erinna', *Zeitschrift für Papyrologie und Epigraphik* XXV, 95–119.

Westermann, A. (1839) ΠΑΡΑΔΟΖΟΓΡΑΦΟΙ *Scriptores rerum mirabilium Graeci* (Braunschweig).

Wieland, W. (1970) *Die aristotelische Physik*, 2nd ed. (Göttingen).

Wilamowitz-Moellendorff, U. von (1881) *Antigonos von Karystos* (Philologische Untersuchungen 4, Berlin).

Wilhelm, A. (1932) 'Ärzte und Ärztinnen in Pontos, Lykien und Ägypten', *Jahreshefte des österreichischen archäologischen Institutes in Wien* XXVII, Beiblatt, pp. 72–95.

Wilson, J. A. (1949) 'Egypt', in Frankfort 1949, pp. 39–133.

Withington, E. T. (1928) *Hippocrates*, Loeb ed. Vol. III (London and Cambridge, Mass.).

Wittern, R. (1974) *Die hippokratische Schrift De morbis I* (Hildesheim and New York).

Yates, F. A. (1964) *Giordano Bruno and the Hermetic Tradition* (London).

(1979) *The Occult Philosophy in the Elizabethan Age* (London).

Zilsel, E. (1941–2) 'The sociological roots of science', *American Journal of Sociology* XLVII, 544–62.

Zirin, R. A. (1980) 'Aristotle's biology of language', *Transactions and Proceedings of the American Philological Association* CX, 325–47.

Zirkle, C. (1951) 'Gregor Mendel and his precursors', *Isis* XLII, 97–104.

Zuckerman, S. (1961) *A New System of Anatomy* (London).

Zuntz, G. (1971) *Persephone* (Oxford).

INDEX OF PASSAGES REFERRED TO

AELIAN
  NA (I 32), 20 n. 38; (III 22), 20 n. 38; (IV 5), 20 n. 38; (V 48), 20 n. 38; (VI 22), 20 n.
    38; (XII 20), 156 n. 136
AESCHYLUS
  Eu. (658ff), 86 n. 109
  Pr. (484ff), 20 n. 38
AETIUS
  V (3.6), 88 n. 116; (5.1), 87 n. 114, 88 n. 116, 108 n. 189; (5.2), 108 n. 189; (5.3), 87
    n. 112; (11.1), 87 n. 114; (11.3), 108 n. 189; (11.4), 108 n. 189
ALEXANDER OF APHRODISIAS
  Fat. (6), 24 n. 50
  Mixt. (216.14ff), 178 n. 225; (226.30ff), 178 n. 225; (227.5ff), 178 n. 225
ARISTIDES
  XLVII (54–7), 207 n. 17; (61–4), 207 n. 17; (67–8), 207 n. 17
  XLIX (7–9), 207 n. 17
ARISTOPHANES
  V. (810), 204 n. 6; (1194f), 155 n. 124
  Scholia *Eq.* (1159), 156 n. 134
ARISTOTLE
  APr. (II 27, 70b7ff), 22, 23 n. 47; (70b11ff), 22; (70b32ff), 23 n. 47
  APo. (71b33ff), 27 n. 58
  Top. (117b17ff), 46 n. 186
  Ph. (184a16ff), 27 n. 58; (205a25ff), 48–9; (259a23ff), 48
  Cael. (II 2, 285b14ff), 28 n. 62
  GC (I 10, 328b8ff), 49
  Mete. (384a26ff), 33 n. 113
  de An. (403a8f), 28 n. 68; (409a9ff), 40 n. 153; (411b19ff), 40 n. 153; (413b16ff),
    40 n. 153; (413b21ff), 28 n. 65; (II 7ff, 418a26ff), 28 n. 63; (421a18ff), 31 n.
    95; (425a10ff), 40 n. 154; (428a8ff), 28 n. 65; (428a16ff), 28 n. 68; (431a16f),
    28 n. 68; (433a10ff), 28 n. 68
  Sens. (436a1–11), 28 n. 63; (440b31ff), 31 n. 95; (444a10ff), 100 n. 158;
    (444a28ff), 30 n. 87
  Mem. (453a6ff), 28 n. 66
  Somn. Vig. (457b29ff), 38 n. 144; (458a13ff), 100 n. 158; (458a15ff), 207 n. 13
  Div. Somn. (463b12ff), 29 n. 69
  Long. (464b26ff), 44 n. 172; (466a1ff), 31 n. 93; (466a4–9), 31 n. 94; (466a9f),
    30 n. 92; (466a11ff), 30 n. 92; (466a13ff), 31 n. 93; (466b7ff), 31 n. 94;
    (466b9ff), 103 and n. 171, 104 n. 174; (466b12ff), 103 n. 169; (466b14ff), 101
    n. 160; (467a18ff), 40 n. 153
  Juv. (468a13ff), 38–9; (468a26ff), 40 n. 153; (469b3ff), 38 n. 146
  Resp. (475b7ff), 39 n. 150; (476b30ff), 39 n. 150; (479a3ff), 40 n. 153
  HA (487a11ff), 19, 21; (487a15ff), 51 n. 205; (487a23ff), 47 n. 191; (487b9f), 28

ARISTOTLE (*cont.*)

n. 64; (487b23f), 46 n. 183; (488a2), 49 n. 200; (488a7), 49; (488a7ff), 25 n. 53; (488b13–24), 19, 22; (488b24f), 25 n. 54; (488b25f), 28 n. 66; (488b27f), 22; (488b29ff), 39 n. 147; (489a8ff), 39 n. 147; (489a20ff), 38 nn. 139 and 142; (488a23ff), 38 n. 143; (490b7ff), 16 n. 29, 17 n. 30; (I 6, 491a19ff), 27, 35 n. 120; (I 7ff), 27; (491b2ff), 102 n. 165; (491b9ff), 30 n. 73; (I 8, 491b12ff), 23, 24 n. 52; (491b15ff), 23; (491b24ff), 23; (491b25), 23 n. 49; (491b27ff), 40 n. 154; (492a5f), 30 n. 75; (492a8ff), 23, 24 n. 52; (492a10ff), 23, 24 n. 52; (492a22f), 30 n. 76; (492a28), 30 n. 76; (492a32ff), 23; (492a34ff), 23; (492b30f), 24 n. 52; (493a3f), 163 n. 179; (493b7), 160 n. 156; (494a26ff), 41 n. 167; (494a33ff), 41 n. 167; (494b16–18), 31 n.95; (I 16, 494b21ff), 27 and n. 60; (494b27ff), 30 n. 87, 39 n. 149; (495b19ff), 162 n. 172; (I 17), 207 n. 13; (497b31), 30 n. 81; (497b34ff), 30 n. 79; (498a16ff), 49; (498a31ff), 46 n. 183; (498b21ff), 30 n. 74; (498b24f), 30 n. 74; (499a31ff), 30 n. 91; (499b11ff), 47 n. 189; (500a15ff), 30 n. 79; (501a21ff), 44 n. 172, 46 n. 181; (501b19ff), 102; (502a16–b26), 47 n. 187; (II 8–9), 31–2; (502a20f), 32 n. 102; (502a22ff), 32 n. 101; (502a23), 32 n. 106; (502a27ff), 32 n. 102; (502a31ff), 32 n. 100; (502a34ff), 32 n. 101; (502a35ff), 32 n. 103; (502b1ff), 32 n. 104; (502b3ff), 32 nn. 103 and 109; (502b5ff), 32 n. 109; (502b10ff), 32 n. 109; (502b14ff), 32 n. 106; (502b16ff), 32 n. 109; (502b20f), 32 n. 107; (502b21f), 32 n. 105; (502b22f), 32 n. 105; (503a18f), 32 n. 102; (505b25ff), 16 n. 29; (505b29f), 17 n. 30; (506a21ff), 46 n. 182; (508a23ff), 29 n. 72; (511b4ff), 38 n. 143; (511b13ff), 27 n. 60; (III 3), 207 n. 13; (513a12ff), 27 n. 60; (513b7ff), 34 n. 116, 153 n. 117; (513b26ff), 152 n. 115; (513b32ff), 207 n. 13; (515b33ff), 33 n. 113; (516a18ff), 102 n. 165; (519b26ff), 38 nn. 137 and 143; (520b10ff), 38 n. 139; (520b23ff), 33 n. 113; (520b26f), 33 n. 112; (521a2ff), 33, 100 n. 157; (521a3f), 33 n. 112; (521a4ff), 100 n. 158; (521a21ff), 100 nn. 153 and 157; (521a26f), 30 n. 85, 100 n. 154; (523a15), 30 n. 86; (523a17ff), 55 n. 222; (523a26f), 55 n. 222; (IV 1–7), 39 and n. 149; (523a31ff), 16 n. 29; (523b1ff), 45 n. 177; (523b21ff), 45 n. 177; (524a2ff), 45 n. 176; (524a8f), 45 n. 175; (524b4), 39 n. 149; (524b20ff), 39 n. 150; (524b32), 39 n. 149; (527b4ff), 36 n. 126; (529b19ff), 47 n. 190, 50 n. 202; (530a2f), 39; (531a12ff), 39; (531b30ff), 40 n. 153; (IV 8, 532b29ff), 28 n. 63; (533a2ff), 40 n. 154; (534b12ff), 16 n. 29, 45 n. 177; (535a27ff), 29 n. 70; (536a20ff), 29 n. 71; (536a32ff), 29 n. 70; (538a10ff), 104; (538a22ff), 103; (IV 11, 538b2–15), 101; (V 1, 539a6ff), 35 n. 120, 37; (539a8ff), 16 n. 29; (540b15ff), 103 n. 168; (541b1ff), 45 n. 175; (541b8ff), 45 n. 175; (542a1ff), 97 n. 146; (544a12f), 45 n. 175; (545a14ff), 101 n. 161; (545b6ff), 31 n. 97; (545b18ff), 103 n. 170; (546a20ff), 34 n. 119; (548a14ff), 47 n. 190; (548b10ff), 28 n. 64; (553a17ff), 25 n. 53; (V 27, 555b14f), 100; (556a27f), 97 n. 146; (566b27ff), 46; (567a3ff), 34 n. 119; (572a5ff), 34 n. 119; (572a8ff), 103 n. 172; (572b29ff), 30 n. 85; (573a5ff), 34; (574a20ff), 31 n. 97; (574b29ff), 103; (575a3ff), 103 n. 169; (575a25ff), 31 n. 98; (575b30ff), 103 n. 172; (575b33ff), 31 n. 99; (576a26ff), 103 n. 170; (576b20f), 34 n. 119; (577b4ff), 103 n. 171; (578a17ff), 31 n. 98; (578b23ff), 55 n. 221; (579a2), 30 n. 73; (579a20ff), 31 n. 99; (579b2ff), 55 n. 221; (579b16ff), 55 n. 221; (580a14ff), 55 n. 221; (580a21f), 55 n. 221; (582a29ff), 95 n. 139; (582a34ff), 83 n. 91, 171 n. 198; (582b2f), 83 n. 92; (582b28ff), 30 n. 85; (582b32ff), 103 n. 168; (582b34ff), 31 n. 95; (583a4ff), 30 n. 86; (583a17f), 72 n. 52; (583a21ff), 85 n. 103; (583b14ff), 27 n. 59; (584a33ff), 30 n. 83; (584b26ff), 30 n. 84, 49–50; (585b14ff), 95 n. 139; (585b24ff), 95 n. 139; (586a2ff), 106 n. 181; (587b11ff), 30 n. 88; (587b13ff), 30 n. 77; (VIII 1, 588a17ff), 19; (588a18ff), 25 n. 55; (588a23ff), 28 n. 67;

(588a29ff), 28 n. 67; (588b4ff), 28 n. 64, 35 n. 121, 51 n. 207; (588b12ff), 51 n. 208; (588b16ff), 47 n. 191; (588b2of), 28 n. 64; (589a1ff), 25 n. 53; (VIII 2, 589a1off), 48 n. 196; (589a2of), 48 n. 196; (589b29ff), 53 n. 213; (590a8f), 48 n. 196; (590a13ff), 48 n. 196, 51 n. 205; (598a13ff), 48 n. 195; (602a15ff), 48 n. 195; (606a8ff), 55 n. 222; (VIII 29, 607a9ff), 19 n. 37; (608a11ff), 20, 25 n. 55; (608a15), 28 n. 67; (IX 1, 608a21–8), 36 n. 130, 98–9; (608a33–b18), 98–9; (608a35–b2), 99; (608b4ff), 36 n. 130; (608b19ff), 20; (608b27f), 20 n. 38; (609a4ff), 20; (609a8ff), 20 n. 40; (609a28ff), 20; (609b11ff), 20 n. 39; (610a8), 20 n. 41; (612b18ff), 28 n. 67; (613a16ff), 104; (613a25ff), 103 n. 171; (613a32ff), 103 n. 171; (IX 13, 616a6ff), 20; (616b27), 28 n. 67; (IX 37, 620b11ff), 20; (620b19ff), 20; (621a1of), 47 n. 192; (621a2off), 21, 99; (IX 39, 623a23f), 100; (623b8ff), 25 n. 53; (631a5f), 30 n. 73; (IX 50, 632a21ff), 108 n. 186; (632a27ff), 108 n. 186; (636b15ff), 96 n. 140; (637a35ff), 96 n. 140; (637b30ff), 96 n. 140; (x 7, 638a5ff), 68 n. 36

PA (12–4), 16; (642b7ff), 18 n. 32; (642b15f), 15 n. 22, 17 n. 31; (642b18ff), 51 n. 206; (642b31ff), 18 n. 33, 51 n. 209; (643a3f), 51 n. 206; (643a13ff), 18 n. 33, 51 n. 209; (643b9ff), 18 n. 32; (643b28ff), 18 n. 32; (644b7ff), 18 n. 36; (15), 206 n. 11; (644b24ff), 37 n. 134; (645a6ff), 37 n. 134, 206 n. 11; (645a15ff), 37 n. 134; (645a21ff), 56, 206 n. 11; (645a26ff), 37 n. 134; (645b6ff), 38 n. 137; (645b8ff), 38 n. 142; (647a30f), 38 n. 146; (647a35ff), 38 n. 140; (647b29ff), 32; (647b34f), 34 n. 115, 100 n. 158; (648a1ff), 38 n. 142; (II 2, 648a2ff), 22, 33; (648a5ff), 28 n. 67; (648a9ff), 33, 100 n. 153; (648a11f), 100 n. 158; (648a12f), 100 n. 159; (648a19ff), 38 nn. 137 and 142; (648a25ff), 100 n. 156; (648a28ff), 33 n. 114; (648a33–649b8), 33 n. 110; (648b35ff), 33 n. 111; (649a17), 33 n. 111; (649b2off), 33 n. 110; (649b23f), 33 n. 111; (650a2ff), 39 n. 147; (650b14ff), 33 n. 113; (650b27ff), 22; (651a2ff), 33 n. 112; (651a14f), 38 n. 140; (652a6f), 38 n. 140; (652b23ff), 39 n. 149; (653a1off), 38 n. 144; (653a27ff), 30 n. 87, 102 n. 167; (653a30f), 30 n. 78; (653a33ff), 30 n. 88; (653a37ff), 102 n. 165; (653b2f), 102 n. 166; (653b2off), 38 n. 143; (654a9ff), 45 n. 177; (655a12ff), 102 n. 167; (655b29ff), 38–9; (656a3ff), 28, 35 n. 120; (656a1off), 41 n. 167; (656a12f), 30 n. 78; (II 1off, 656b26ff), 28 n. 63; (657a12ff), 41 n. 158; (657a22ff), 46 n. 183; (657a35ff), 30 n. 75; (658a14f), 30 n. 74; (658a24f), 30 n. 74; (658a25f), 30 n. 74; (658b7ff), 30 n. 87; (659b30ff), 29; (660a11ff), 31 n. 95; (660a17ff), 29; (660a29ff), 29; (660a30ff), 29; (660b3ff), 29 and n. 72; (660b5ff), 29 n. 72; (661b13f), 29; (661b26ff), 98 n. 147, 101; (661b31–4), 101; (661b34ff), 102 n. 164; (661b36–662a6), 101; (662b17ff), 30 n. 73; (662b2off), 30 n. 78; (664a16ff), 162 n. 171; (III 4), 207 n. 13; (665a30ff), 15 n. 22; (665b5f), 38 n. 140; (665b11ff), 38 nn. 139 and 145; (665b2off), 36 n. 128; (666a34), 28 n. 64; (666b6ff), 36 n. 128; (666b35ff), 33 n. 111, 100 n. 159; (667a1f), 34 n. 115; (667b15ff), 34 n. 116; (668a19ff), 38 n. 140; (669a6ff), 48 n. 196; (669b5ff), 30 n. 78; (669b13ff), 49 n. 198; (669b2off), 36 n. 127; (669b26ff), 49 n. 198; (670a23ff), 33 n. 111; (670b18ff), 34 n. 115; (672b1off), 152 n. 109; (678a8f), 38 n. 142; (678a26ff), 16 n. 29; (678a31ff), 38 n. 140; (678b1ff), 38 n. 146; (678b24ff), 45 n. 177; (680a24ff), 36 n. 126; (681a9ff), 28 n. 64; (681a12ff), 28 n. 64, 35 n. 121, 51 n. 207; (681a15ff), 28 n. 64; (681a25ff), 51 n. 208; (681a35ff), 47 n. 191; (681b12ff), 39 n. 151; (681b26ff), 39 n. 151; (681b33ff), 39; (682a6ff), 36 n. 129; (IV 5, 682a31ff), 35 n. 120, 37; (683b18ff), 41 nn. 162 and 163; (684a26ff), 36 n. 126; (684a32ff), 40 n. 155; (684b6ff), 45 n. 177; (685b27ff), 16 n. 29; (686a27ff), 29 n. 69, 30 n. 78; (686a31ff), 41 n. 158; (686b2ff), 41 n. 165; (686b2off), 41 n. 165; (686b31ff), 41 n. 163; (687a4ff), 30 n. 78; (687a5ff), 30 n. 80; (687a9ff), 32 n. 108;

ARISTOTLE (*cont.*)

(688a18ff), 30 n. 79; (689b5ff), 30 n. 91; (689b11ff), 30 n. 78; (689b14ff), 30 n. 91; (689b25ff), 41 n. 165; (689b31ff), 47 n. 187; (689b33f), 32 n. 105; (690a27f), 30 n. 90; (690a28f), 30 n. 78; (691a5ff), 29 n. 72; (693b2–15), 41 n. 160; (693b2ff), 51 n. 206; (695a3ff), 41 n. 159; (695a8ff), 41 n. 165; (695b2ff), 41 n. 161; (697b1ff), 45; (697b1–13), 46; (697b5), 46 n. 180; (697b10ff), 46 n. 185; (697b13ff), 47 n. 188

MA (703a14ff), 38 n. 146

IA (705b2ff), 41 n. 163; (705b25ff), 36 n. 126; (706a10ff), 36 n. 126; (706a16ff), 41 n. 167; (706a20ff), 36 n. 125, 41 n. 167; (706a29ff), 41 n. 158; (706b5ff), 41 n. 163; (706b9f), 41 n. 167; (707a16ff), 51 n. 206; (707a27ff), 40 n. 153; (710b9ff), 30 n. 78; (710b12ff), 41 n. 165; (710b17ff), 41 n. 159; (710b30ff), 41 n. 159; (12f, 711a8ff), 32 n. 104; (712b22ff), 41 n. 160; (712b30ff), 41 n. 159; (713a26ff), 49 n. 199; (714a6ff), 40 n. 156; (714b8ff), 41 n. 164; (714b10ff), 41 n. 164; (714b12f), 46 n. 183; (714b14ff), 41 n. 164; (714b16ff), 36

GA (715a18ff), 36 n. 131; (715b19ff), 36 n. 131; (716a17ff), 95 n. 139; (717a34ff), 109 n. 192; (720b15ff), 45 nn. 175 and 177; (720b32ff), 45 n. 175; (721a17ff), 103 n. 168; (117–18), 96; (721b11ff), 88 n. 116; (721b17ff), 106 n. 180; (721b13ff), 96 n. 141; (721b29ff), 106 n. 180; (722a8ff), 106 n. 181; (722a16ff), 96; (722b3ff), 88 n. 117; (722b6ff), 88 n. 115, 97; (722b17ff), 97 n. 144; (723a26ff), 92 n. 127; (723b9ff), 97 n. 146; (724a3ff), 96, 106 n. 180; (725a21ff), 97; (726b3ff), 38 n. 140; (726b30ff), 97, 101; (727a2ff), 34 n. 118; (727a22f), 30 n. 85; (727a25ff), 34 n. 118, 97; (728a18ff), 95 n. 139; (728a20f), 38 nn. 140 and 142; (728a26ff), 96 n. 140; (728b14f), 30 n. 85; (728b15f), 30 n. 86; (729a4ff), 97 n. 146; (729a6ff), 98; (729a9ff), 97 n. 145; (729a28ff), 97 n. 145; (729a34ff), 97, 109 n. 192; (729b12ff), 97 n. 145; (729b22ff), 97 n. 145; (729b33ff), 97 n. 146; (730b5ff), 97 n. 145; (731a24ff), 36 n. 131; (731b8ff), 36 n. 131, 47 n. 191; (11 1, 731b18ff), 95 n. 138; (732a3ff), 98; (732b15), 44 n. 172, 51; (732b28–733b16), 16 n. 29, 18 n. 35, 35 n. 122, 36 n. 124; (732b32ff), 33 n. 111; (733a2ff), 36 n. 124; (733a27ff), 44 n. 172; (733a32ff), 33 n. 111; (733a33ff), 36 n. 124; (733b7ff), 35; (733b13ff), 35 n. 123; (735a22ff), 38 n. 146; (736a2ff), 55 n. 222; (736a10ff), 55 n. 222; (736b27ff), 29 n. 69; (737a7ff), 109 n. 193; (737a10), 29 n. 69; (737a12ff), 97 n. 145; (737a27ff), 96 n. 140; (737b25ff), 35 n. 120; (738a16ff), 83 n. 91, 171 n. 198; (738b4ff), 30 n. 85; (738b16f), 38 n. 146; (738b27ff), 106 n. 178; (739b2off), 97 n. 145; (741b15ff), 38 n. 146; (742b35ff), 38 n. 146; (744a24ff), 30 n. 88; (744a26ff), 30 n. 87; (745b9ff), 30 n. 77; (745b15ff), 31 n. 95; (745b17f), 30 n. 82; (746a29ff), 106 n. 178; (747a7ff), 65 n. 21; (753a11ff), 28 n. 67; (756a33ff), 149 n. 103; (756b5ff), 55 n. 222; (757b31ff), 45 n. 177; (759b1ff), 102 n. 162; (759b5ff), 99 n. 152; (760b27ff), 102 n. 162; (761a4f), 29 n. 69; (761a15ff), 47 n. 191; (763b30ff), 87 n. 113; (764a6ff), 88 n. 116; (764b1ff), 97 n. 144; (764b15ff), 88 n. 115; (765a21ff), 82 n. 90; (765b8ff), 95 n. 139, 101 n. 160; (765b16ff), 101 n. 160; (765b17ff), 100 n. 153; (765b18ff), 100 n. 154; (766a30ff), 95 n. 139; (766b29ff), 95 n. 139; (766b31ff), 95 n. 139; (767a1ff), 83 n. 91, 171 n. 198; (767a33ff), 95 n. 139; (767b10ff), 95 n. 139; (769a15ff), 97 n. 144; (769b2off), 23 n. 50; (770b5ff), 44 n. 172; (771b18ff), 97 n. 145; (772a37ff), 30 n. 84, 49–50; (772b7ff), 30 n. 83; (772b8ff), 77 n. 74; (773b29ff), 103 n. 172; (774b17ff), 31 n. 99, 44 n. 172, 47 n. 189; (774b23ff), 31 n. 99; (775b2ff), 30 n. 85; (777b3ff), 30 n. 92; (779a26ff), 30 n. 75; (781a20ff), 38 n. 146; (781b17ff), 31 n. 95; (781b21f), 31 n. 95; (781b22ff), 46 nn. 182 and 183; (783b8ff), 30 n. 89; (785b8f), 31 n.

95; (786b17ff), 101 n. 161; (786b18ff), 29 n. 70; (787b19ff), 109 n. 192; (788a3ff), 109 n. 192

Phgn. (807a31ff), 24; (809b36ff), 99 n. 150; (810a28ff), 24; (811b21f), 24 n. 52; (811b24f), 24 n. 52; (811b29f), 23 n. 48, 24 n. 52

Metaph. (980a27ff), 28 n. 66; (980b21ff), 28 n. 67; (980b25ff), 28 n. 66; (1016b31ff), 38 n. 136; (1018a12ff), 38 n. 136

EN (1111b4ff), 25 n. 53; (1116b24f), 25 n. 53; (1116b30ff), 25 n. 53; (1118a23ff), 25 n. 53; (1134b33ff), 30 n. 81; (1141a26ff), 28 n. 67; (1144b1ff), 25 n. 53; (1147b5), 28 n. 66

MM (1194b33ff), 30 n. 81; (1197a31), 49 n. 197

EE (1236b6ff), 20 n. 38

Pol. (1 2–7), 212 n. 27; (1253b20ff), 212 n. 27; (1254b13ff), 98 n. 147; (1256b15ff), 56 n. 224; (1259b1ff), 98 n. 147; (1332b1ff), 49 n. 197; (1336a12ff), 170 n. 196; (1337b21ff), 49 n. 197

ATHENAEUS

(105b), 15 n. 25; (452cd), 46 n. 184

CAELIUS AURELIANUS

Morb. Acut.

I (71), 178 n. 223; (103), 169 n. 193

II (8), 186 n. 258; (24), 187 n. 260; (46), 185 n. 256; (59ff), 174 n. 209; (64), 174 n. 209; (65), 186 n. 258; (113ff), 174 n. 209; (121ff), 174 n. 209; (147), 186 n. 258; (154), 174 n. 209; (160), 190 n. 269; (206), 190 n. 269

III (25ff), 174 n. 209; (47), 187 n. 260; (57ff), 174 n. 209; (74), 174 n. 209; (83ff), 174 n. 209; (122), 190 n. 269; (137), 169 n. 193, 190 n. 269; (140), 178 n. 223; (153ff), 174 n. 209; (172–4), 187 n. 260; (189–90), 187 n. 260; (206f), 174 n. 209

Morb. Chron.

I (1), 169 n. 193; (62), 178 n. 223; (119f), 169 n. 193; (131), 174 n. 209; (156), 179 n. 229

II (16), 197 n. 280; (16f), 187 n. 260; (25), 178 n. 223; (27), 178 n. 223; (94), 178 n. 223; (97), 188 n. 264; (145ff), 197 n. 280

III (69), 178 n. 223; (78), 179 n. 228; (137ff), 187 n. 260; (139ff), 174 n. 209

IV (77), 174 n. 209; (112ff), 174 n. 209

V (24ff), 174 n. 209

CELSUS

I Proem. (23f), 213 n. 29; (27ff), 165 n. 187; (36ff), 188; (39), 187 n. 261; (40ff), 188; (45ff), 149 n. 104; (50ff), 149 n. 104; (54), 192; (57), 165 n. 187, 185 n. 254, 188, 192; (62ff), 165 n. 187; (63), 196 n. 278; (65), 196 n. 278; (66f), 183 n. 247, 197; (74f), 149 n. 104

III (4.1–3), 182 n. 241; (4.3), 149 n. 104; (5.6), 149 n. 104; (11.2), 149 n. 104; (24.3), 149 n. 104

IV (26.4), 149 n. 104

VII (7), 149 n. 104, 159 n. 147; (7.6c), 149 n. 104; (7.13b), 158 n. 144; (12.4), 149 n. 104

CENSORINUS

de Die Nat. (5,4, 10.3f), 108 n. 189; (5,4, 10.4ff), 87 n. 112; (6,5, 11.7ff), 88 n. 116

CICERO

Div. II (14.33ff), 178 n. 225

Fat. (5.10), 24 n. 50

N.D. II (7.19ff), 178 n. 225

Tusc. IV (37.80), 24 n. 50

CLEOMEDES
 I (1, 4.1ff), 178 n. 225; (1, 8.15ff), 178 n. 225

DEMOSTHENES
 LIX (55ff), 79 n. 78, 120 n. 19
DIOGENES OF APOLLONIA
 fr. (6), 153 n. 116
DIOGENES LAERTIUS
 I (112), 120 n. 18
 V (43), 21; (49), 21
 VII (159), 108 n. 189
 VIII (28), 87 n. 114
 IX (46ff), 15 n. 22
 X (33), 191 n. 272; (52), 191 n. 272; (146), 191 n. 272
DIOSCORIDES
 de Materia Medica Proem. (1, 1 1.12f), 120 n. 20; (3, 1 2.10f), 137 n. 66; (4f, 1 2.16ff),
  137 n. 66; (1 3.6ff), 137 n. 66
  IV (22, II 186.5), 144 n. 92; (75, II 233.11ff), 132 n. 57; (II 235.6ff), 132 n. 57; (II
  237.8ff), 132 n. 57

EMPEDOCLES
 fr. (57–60), 54 n. 214; (61), 54 n. 214; (62), 54 n. 214; (105), 158 n. 142
EPICRATES
 fr. (11), 16 n. 26
EROTIAN
 fr. (40, 111.10ff), (Nachmanson), 156 n. 131; (42, 112.2ff), 156 n. 134
EURIPIDES
 HF (1095), 155 n. 124
 Hipp. (293–6), 78 n. 76

GALEN
 Libr. Propr. (*Scr. Min.* II) (11, 120.9f), 150 n. 106; (120.15f), 150 n. 106
 Sect. Intr. (*Scr. Min.* III) (4f, 7.19ff), 184 n. 251; (10.18), 184 n. 251; (10.22), 184 n.
  251; (6, 12.19f), 184 n. 253; (13.12), 184 n. 253; (13.19ff), 184 nn. 251 and 253;
  (13.21ff), 188; (13.24), 184 n. 253; (14.1f), 184 n. 253; (14.5f), 184 n. 253;
  (14.10ff), 185 n. 254; (14.14ff), 185 n. 254; (14.15f), 189 n. 267; (14.16ff), 185
  n. 254; (14.22ff), 196 n. 278; (15.5ff), 196 n. 278; (17.3ff), 188; (18.1ff), 188; (9,
  23.4ff), 183 n. 247; (24.22ff), 196 n. 278; (25.17ff), 183 n. 247
 UP (II 2, I 65.27ff), 159 n. 147; (I 67.4ff), 154 n. 120; (II 14, I 104.10ff), 155 n. 129;
  (II 15, I 104.22ff), 156 n. 134; (I 108.15ff), 156 n. 132; (II 16, I 113.25ff), 159 n.
  147; (IV 1, I 195.10ff), 162 n. 172; (IV 9, I 213.9ff), 150 n. 106; (V 3, I 253.19ff),
  158 n. 141; (VI 16, I 356.4ff), 150 n. 106; (VII 5, I 381.21ff), 162 n. 171; (VIII 1, I
  443.13ff), 162 n. 171; (VIII 7, I 472.25ff), 164 n. 184; (VIII 11, I 483.4ff), 150 n.
  106; (IX), 159 n. 152; (IX 17, II 49.26ff), 102 n. 165; (X 2, II 61.22ff), 161 n. 164;
  (XI 4, II 120.21ff), 157 n. 138; (XI 12, II 150.14), 164 n. 184; (XI 14, II 154.20ff),
  110 n. 197; (XII 7, II 198.16f), 155 n. 127; (XII 8f, II 203.9ff), 159 n. 147; (XIII 11, II
  273.8ff), 47 n. 187; (XIV 3, II 288.9ff), 109 n. 196; (II 290.17ff), 162 n. 172; (XIV
  5, II 295.27ff), 110 n. 197; (XIV 6, II 299.5ff), 110 n. 198; (II 299.19ff), 110 nn.
  200 and 202; (II 301.3ff), 110 nn. 198 and 199; (XIV 7, II 308.19ff), 110 n. 201
  (XIV 10, II 317.5ff), 110 n. 199; (II 318.1ff), 110 n. 199; (II 318.8ff), 109 n. 195;
  (XIV 11, II 321.6ff), 162–3 n. 175; (II 323.18ff), 108 n. 187; (XV 8, II 366.5ff), 159
  n. 147; (II 366.26 ff), 47 n. 187; (XVI), 159 n. 152

CMG v, 2, 1 (48.17ff), 109 n. 195

CMG v, 4, 1, 2 (86.24ff), 164 n. 184

CMG v, 4, 2 (24.21ff), 170 n. 196

CMG v, 8, 1 (110.13ff), 78 n. 76

CMG v, 9, 1 (69.29ff), 113 n. 2; (70.10ff), 113 n. 2; (137.17ff), 162 n. 172

K I (73.3ff), 184 n. 251; (77.2), 184 n. 251; (77.6), 184 n. 251; (79.16f), 184 n. 253; (80.14), 184 n. 253; (81.5ff), 184 nn. 251 and 253; (81.6ff), 188; (81.9), 184 n. 253; (81.10f), 184 n. 253; (81.15), 184 n. 253; (82.2ff), 185 n. 254; (82.6ff), 185 n. 254; (82.7), 189 n. 267; (82.7ff), 185 n. 254; (82.13ff), 196 n. 278; (83.4ff), 196 n. 278; (85.14ff), 188; (86.17ff), 188; (93.12ff), 183 n. 247; (95.15ff), 196 n. 278; (96.15ff), 183 n. 247

K II (263.16ff), 159 n. 147; (280.1ff), 113 n. 2; (283.7ff), 113 n. 2, 217 n. 32; (306.1ff), 159 n. 147; (346.12ff), 162 n. 169; (347.1ff), 162 n. 169; (421.7ff), 157 n. 138; (422.2ff), 157 n. 138; (572.13ff), 158 n. 141; (578.2), 158 n. 141; (581.1ff), 150 n. 106; (619.16ff), 166; (636.3ff), 167 n. 190; (642.3ff), 166–7; (669.4ff), 167 n. 190; (677.1ff), 167 n. 190; (690.3ff), 167 n. 190; (719.14ff), 158 n. 143; (762.15ff), 160 n. 159; (771.7ff), 158 n. 142; (780.13ff), 158 n. 141; (900.8ff), 109 n. 195

K III (90.8ff), 159 n. 147; (92.2ff), 154 n. 120; (142.6ff), 155 n. 129; (142.17ff), 156 n. 134; (147.18ff), 156 n. 132; (155.4ff), 159 n. 147; (267.2ff), 162 n. 172; (290.16ff), 150 n. 106; (346.1ff), 158 n. 141; (488.15ff), 150 n. 106; (525.9ff), 162 n. 171; (611.11ff), 162 n. 171; (652.2ff), 164 n. 184; (665.16ff), 150 n. 106; (751.7ff), 102 n. 165; (768.14ff), 161 n. 164; (853.3ff), 157 n. 138; (894.13), 164 n. 184; (900.10ff), 110 n. 197

K IV (24.3f), 155 n. 127; (30.12ff), 159 n. 147; (126.1ff), 47 n. 187; (147.9ff), 109 n. 196; (150.8ff), 162 n. 172; (157.12ff); 110 n. 197; (161.13ff), 110 n. 198; (162.10ff), 110 nn. 200 and 202; (164.1ff), 110 nn. 198 and 199; (173.18ff), 110 n. 201; (184.16ff) 110 n. 199; (185.18ff), 110 n. 199; (186.6ff), 109 n. 195; (190.1ff), 162–3 n. 175; (193.2ff), 108 n. 187; (250.6ff), 159 n. 147; (251.7ff), 47 n. 187; (516.5ff), 109 n. 193; (518.7ff), 109 n. 193; (527.17ff), 109 n. 196; (529.15ff), 109 n. 196; (536.16ff), 110 n. 199; (548.6ff), 110 n. 199; (558.11ff), 109 n. 192; (570.1ff), 108 n. 186; (573.14ff), 109 n. 192; (574.13ff), 109 n. 192; (582.12ff), 162 n. 175; (595.13ff), 109 n. 194; (596.4ff), 108 n. 187, 109 n. 195; (596.8ff), 108 n. 188; (596.11ff), 161 n. 168; (596.17), 108 n. 188; (597.7–8), 108 n. 188; (597.9ff), 108 n. 188; (598.5ff), 109 n. 195; (599.11ff), 109 n. 191; (604.4ff), 106 n. 178; (612.3ff), 109 n. 191; (613.8ff), 109 nn. 193 and 196; (616.5ff), 88 n. 115; (616.11ff), 88 n. 115; (617.13ff), 88 n. 115; (622.7ff), 108 n. 186; (623.3ff), 109 n. 196

K V (195.4ff), 164 n. 184

K VI (51.7ff), 170 n. 196

K VIII (396.6f), 158 n. 141; (414.6ff), 76 n. 66; (425.1f), 72 n. 54, 76 n. 66; (433.15ff), 72 n. 54

K X (52.16ff), 187 n. 260; (1020.10ff), 161 n. 164

K XI (187.1ff), 79 n. 77; (188.5ff), 79 n. 77

K XII (403.16), 60 n. 6; (416.3ff), 63 n. 11; (446.1), 60 n. 6

K XIII (250.3), 63 n. 11; (341.2), 63 n. 11

K XIV (2.3ff), 126 n. 32; (641.5ff), 78 n. 76; (677.12ff), 184 n. 252; (677.13), 184 n. 253; (680.13ff), 184 n. 253; (682.17ff), 184 n. 252; (683.1), 184 n. 253; (684.5), 187 n. 260

K XV (135.14ff), 113 n. 2; (136.10ff), 113 n. 2; (460.7ff), 162 n. 172

K XVIII A (380.6ff), 152 n. 112; (428.7ff), 157 n. 138; (429.7ff), 157 n. 138

K XVIII B (926.1ff), 113 n. 2

GALEN (*cont.*)

K xix (44.11f), 150 n. 106; (44.17f), 150 n. 106; (87.15), 156 n. 134
De Anat. Admin. ix (9, 9 Duckworth), 164 n. 185; (13), 159 n. 152
   x (1, 31), 150 n. 106; (3, 42), 150 n. 106; (9, 65), 150 n. 106
   xii (1, 109), 108 n. 186; (2, 115), 151 n. 106, 164 n. 184; (5, 118), 150 n. 106; (7,
      128), 164 n. 184
   xiii (4, 154), 150 n. 106
   xiv (1, 183–4), 113 n. 2; (2, 185ff), 152 n. 112; (4, 196), 164 n. 185; (7, 210–12),
      164 n. 184; (7, 212), 167 n. 190
   xv (1, 224), 151 n. 106; (2, 229), 155 n. 130

GELLIUS

iv (11.12–13), 48 n. 194

HERODOTUS

i (34ff), 170 n. 195
iii (111), 123 n. 27
vii (88), 204 n. 6
viii (115), 204 n. 6

HESIOD

Op. (41), 144 n. 90; (60ff), 95 n. 132; (276ff), 11; (780–1), 120; (824), 120
Th. (211ff), 11; (265ff), 11; (585ff), 95 n. 132

HIPPOCRATIC CORPUS

Acut. (περὶ διαίτης ὀξέων) (1, L ii 224.3ff), 208 n. 19; (2, 234.2ff), 208 n. 19; (2,
   236.4ff), 208 n. 20; (11, 316.13ff), 208 n. 19
Acut. (Sp.) (περὶ διαίτης ὀξέων (νόθα)) (38, L ii 526.3f), 128 n. 41
Aër. (περὶ ἀέρων ὑδάτων τόπων) (3, CMG i,1,2 28.8ff), 65 n. 22; (4, 30.22ff), 65 n.
   22; (5, 32.24), 65 n. 22; (7, 36.13f), 65 n. 22; (7, 36.16f), 65 n. 22; (7, 36.20ff), 65
   n. 22; (9, 44.19), 162 n. 172; (9, 44.22ff), 162 n. 172; (9, 44.28ff), 162 n. 172; (10,
   48.11), 65 n. 22; (10, 48.15), 65 n. 22; (10, 48.19), 65 n. 22; (10, 48.21), 65 n. 22;
   (10, 52.4), 65 n. 22; (14, 58.20ff), 88 n. 118; (17, 64.11ff), 65 n. 22; (18, 66.10ff),
   65 n. 22; (21, 72.1ff), 65 n. 22; (22, 72.10–76.4), 209 n. 25
Aff. (περὶ παθῶν) (4, L vi 212.7ff), 155; (4, 212.8), 155 n. 126; (38, 248.5), 128 n. 41
Alim. (περὶ τροφῆς) (31, CMG i,1 82.13f), 153 n. 117
Anat. (περὶ ἀνατομῆς) (L viii 538.6), 156 and n. 136
Aph. (ἀφορισμοί) (i 2, L iv 458.9f), 67 n. 31; (ii 34, 480.7ff), 67 n. 31; (iii 11,
   490.2ff), 65; (iii 14, 492.3ff), 65; (v 28–62, 542.5–556.2), 65 n. 20; (v 38,
   544.11ff), 65 n. 21; (v 41, 546.1ff), 65 n. 21; (v 42, 546.4f), 65 n. 21; (v 48,
   550.1f), 65 n. 21; (v 59, 554.3ff), 65 n. 21, 83 n. 98, 88 n. 118; (v 62, 554.12ff),
   88 n. 118; (v 63, 556.3ff), 88 n. 118; (v 69, 560.6ff), 66 n. 26; (vii 43, 588.14), 65
   n. 21
Art. (περὶ ἄρθρων ἐμβολῆς) (1, L iv 78.5ff), 208 n. 20; (4, 86.9f), 64 n. 16; (8,
   94.2ff), 64 n. 17; (8, 94.10ff), 64 n. 13; (8, 98.8f), 64 n. 13; (8, 98.13f), 64 n. 13;
   (11, 104.17f), 64 n. 16; (11, 104.18f), 64 n. 16; (11, 104.20ff), 208 n. 20; (11,
   108.15), 152 n. 112; (11, 110.3), 152 n. 112; (14, 120.7ff), 208 n. 20; (14,
   120.15ff), 217 n. 33; (18, 132.4), 155; (29, 140.4), 64 n. 12; (30, 140.10), 155–6;
   (30, 140.12), 157; (37, 166.1ff), 74 n. 62; (37, 166.7), 74 n. 61; (37, 166.12ff), 64
   n. 19; (41, 180.15ff), 64 n. 12; (42, 182.14ff), 82 n. 88, 217 n. 33; (44, 188.13ff),
   217 n. 33; (45, 190.4), 157; (45, 194.8), 157; (50, 218.18), 152 n. 112; (52,
   228.6ff), 74 n. 62; (52, 230.9ff), 64 n. 12; (53, 232.12ff), 64 n. 12; (55, 238.21ff),
   64 n. 12; (55, 240.19ff), 64 n. 12; (55, 242.12ff), 64 n. 12; (56, 242.19ff), 64 n.
   15; (58, 248.4), 64 n. 12; (58, 252.17ff), 64 nn. 12 and 15; (60, 256.10ff), 64 n.
   12; (60, 258.13ff), 64 n. 12; (62, 262.10ff), 64 n. 15; (62, 268.3ff), 217 n. 33; (70,

288.18), 159 n. 150; (71, 292.5ff), 64 n. 17; (79, 316.11f), 156; (85, 324.1f), 64 n. 15

de Arte (περὶ τέχνης) (10, *CMG* I,1, 15.21ff), 155 n. 125; (10, 15.27), 155

Carn. (περὶ σαρκῶν) (19, L VIII 610.3ff), 77; (19, 610.10ff), 77; (19, 614.8ff), 70 n. 46

Coac. (Κωακαὶ προγνώσιες) (IV 163, L v 618.17ff), 65; (xx 394, 672.5), 153 n. 118; (XXXII 503–44, 700.13–708.8), 65 n. 20

Cord. (περὶ καρδίης) (2, L IX 80.12), 156 n. 137

Decent. (περὶ εὐσχημοσύνης) (12, *CMG* I,1 28.23ff), 182 n. 239; (14, 29.3ff), 68 n. 37

Epid. I (ἐπιδημίαι) (8, L II 646.9), 67 n. 31; (9, 656.6ff), 67 n. 31; (10, 668.14ff), 67 n. 31, 206 n. 9

Epid. II (2,24, L v 96.2ff), 155; (4,2, 124.9ff), 152 n. 112

Epid. III (1st series, case 9, L III 58.7), 206 n. 10; (14, 98.1), 67 n. 31; (16, 102.2ff), 67 n. 31; (2nd series, case 5, 118.8), 206 n. 10; (case 14, 140.18), 68 n. 38; (case 14, 140.22), 68 n. 38; (case 14, 142.3), 68 n. 38

Epid. IV (6, L v 146.11f), 68 n. 36; (20, 160.6), 68 n. 37; (22, 162.5), 68 n. 37

Epid. v (12, L v 212.5ff), 84 n. 102; (25, 224.6ff), 75; (25, 224.10f), 71; (25, 224.11ff), 75; (32, 230.1ff), 68 n. 35; (45, 234.4ff), 68 n. 35; (74, 246.21ff), 68 n. 35; (103, 258.9ff), 64 n. 18

Epid. VI (3,18, L v 302.1ff), 182 n. 241; (4,21, 312.10f), 82 n. 90; (8,28, 354.4ff), 64 n. 18

Epid. VII (36, L v 404.14ff), 68 n. 35; (49, 418.1ff), 64 n. 18; (79, 436.2f), 130 n. 50

Fist. (περὶ συρίγγων) (3, L VI 448.22), 128 n. 42; (7, 454.23), 128 n. 41; (7, 456.2f), 128 n. 43

Flat. (περὶ φυσῶν) (8, *CMG* I,1 96.23), 153 n. 116; (10, 97.12ff), 153 n. 116; (10, 97.15ff), 153 n. 116

Foet. Exsect. (περὶ ἐγκατατομῆς ἐμβρύου) (1, L VIII 512.1ff), 74 n. 60, 82 n. 87; (1, 512.3f), 74 n. 60; (1, 512.4), 85 n. 105; (4, 514.14ff), 81 n. 82; (4, 514.17f), 74; (4, 516.7f), 127 nn. 35 and 37; (5, 516.12ff), 82 n. 84

Fract. (περὶ ἀγμῶν) (2, L III 416.1ff), 208 n. 20; (2, 420.7f), 156; (2, 420.8), 156 n. 134; (3, 422.12ff), 208 n. 20; (4, 428.1), 154 n. 120; (4, 428.2ff), 154; (4, 428.9ff), 64 n. 12; (11, 452.17), 152 n. 112; (12, 460.1ff), 154; (18, 478.23ff), 154; (19, 482.9ff), 64 n. 19; (25, 496.11ff), 208 n. 20; (30, 518.1ff), 208 n. 20; (31, 524.17ff), 208 n. 20; (36, 538.14ff), 64 n. 14; (37, 540.18ff), 154, 156 n. 134; (37, 542.3f), 154; (41, 548.1), 154 n. 120; (42, 552.1), 154; (44, 554.16), 154; (44, 554.17ff), 154

Genit. (περὶ γονῆς) (1, L VII 470.1ff), 89; (2, 472.16ff), 153 n. 116; (2, 472.20ff), 153 n. 116; (4, 474.16f), 89; (4, 476.8ff), 84 n. 102; (5, 476.18), 89; (5, 476.23ff), 77; (6, 478.1ff), 89; (6, 478.5–11), 89; (6, 478.8), 89 n. 121; (6, 478.11ff), 93 n. 128; (7, 478.16ff), 89–90; (8, 480.10ff), 90, 97 n. 144; (8, 480.16ff), 90; (9, 482.3ff), 90

Gland. (περὶ ἀδένων) (6, L VIII 560.13ff), 153; (10, 564.8ff), 153

Haem. (περὶ αἱμορροΐδων) (9, L VI 444.1ff), 66 n. 24

Int. (περὶ τῶν ἐντὸς παθῶν) (1, L VII 168.14), 128 n. 41; (10, 190.17), 128 n. 41; (18, 210.21), 130 n. 50; (25, 232.5ff), 66 n. 23; (27, 238.3ff), 128 nn. 41 and 44; (28, 240.21), 66 n. 23; (30, 246.14ff), 66 n. 23; (40, 266.9), 129 n. 49; (42, 272.15), 130 n. 50

Jusj. (ὅρκος) (6, *CMG* I,1 5.3f), 67 n. 32

Liqu. (περὶ ὑγρῶν χρήσιος) (2, *CMG* I,1 87.14), 155 n. 123; (4, 88.14f), 66 n. 25; (6, 89.3), 66 n. 25

Loc. Hom. (περὶ τόπων τῶν κατὰ ἄνθρωπον) (4, L VI 284.1ff), 152 n. 114; (5,

HIPPOCRATIC CORPUS (*cont.*)

284.9ff), 152 n. 114; (14, 306.13), 153 n. 118; (39, 328.17), 130; (39, 328.19), 130; (47, 344.3ff), 84 n. 100

Medic. (περὶ ἰητροῦ) (1, *CMG* 1,1 20.20ff), 67 n. 32

Mochl. (μοχλικόν) (1, L ɪᴠ 340.5ff), 154; (1, 340.10ff), 156; (1, 340.11), 156; (1, 340.14f), 157; (1, 344.10f), 156 n. 135; (1, 344.11), 155 n. 129, 156 n. 134; (1, 344.12), 152 n. 113, 157; (5, 350.1), 64 n. 13; (5, 350.9ff), 64 n. 15; (5, 350.15ff), 64 n. 12; (5, 352.6f), 74 n. 62; (11, 356.1), 64 n. 15; (18, 360.1f), 64 n. 15; (18, 360.2f), 64 n. 12; (19, 360.7), 64 n. 15; (20, 360.16), 64 n. 15; (20, 360.21ff), 64 n. 12; (21, 364.6), 64 n. 15; (21, 364.10), 64 n. 12; (23, 366.8ff), 64 n. 12; (23, 366.13), 64 n. 15; (24, 368.3ff), 64 n. 12; (24, 368.7), 64 n. 15; (29, 372.2f), 64 n. 15; (37, 380.15ff), 64 n. 12; (40, 388.6ff), 64 n. 15; (40, 390.7f), 152 n. 114

Morb. ɪ (περὶ νούσων) (1, L ᴠɪ 140.1ff), 76 n. 67, 182 n. 239, 208 n. 19; (3, 144.6), 66 n. 28; (3, 144.19), 66 n. 28; (5, 146.19), 66 n. 28; (7, 152.20), 66 n. 28; (7, 152.22), 66 n. 28; (8, 154.7f), 66 n. 28; (22, 182.22ff), 66

Morb. ɪɪ (13, L ᴠɪɪ 24.12), 66 n. 23; (28, 46.2), 156; (28, 46.11), 156; (43, 60.10f), 130, 132 n. 57; (47, 68.2), 129 n. 48; (49, 76.5), 66 n. 23; (54, 82.14), 153 n. 118; (66, 100.22ff), 66 n. 23; (70, 106.10f), 66 n. 24; (73, 112.8), 66 n. 23; (73, 112.9), 66 n. 23

Morb. ɪɪɪ (1, L ᴠɪɪ 118.14), 128 n. 41; (8, 128.1), 130 n. 50; (15, 140.22), 130 n. 50; (16, 146.17), 130 n. 50; (16, 152.5), 155 n. 123

Morb. ɪᴠ (32, L ᴠɪɪ 542.3ff), 90 n. 122; (38, 554.21ff), 153 n. 116; (39, 558.6ff), 153 n. 116

Morb. Sacr. (περὶ ἱερῆς νούσου) (1, L ᴠɪ 352.1ff), 69 n. 42; (2, 364.19ff), 88 n. 118; (4, 368.1ff), 153 n. 116; (6, 370.18ff), 153 n. 116; (7, 372.10ff), 153 n. 116; (7, 372.22ff), 153 n. 116; (17, 392.5ff), 152 n. 109

Mul. ɪ (γυναικεια) (2, L ᴠɪɪɪ 20.14ff), 80, 81 n. 81; (6, 30.12f), 76 n. 68; (8, 34.9f), 88 n. 118; (8, 36.4ff), 85 n. 104; (10–20), 84 n. 101; (10, 40.12ff), 76 n. 68; (11, 44.15), 85 n. 104; (11, 46.10ff), 82 n. 83; (13, 50.14ff), 82 n. 83; (13, 52.1), 74 n. 63; (17, 56.1ff), 84 n. 101; (17, 56.15ff), 83 n. 92; (17, 56.21ff), 83 n. 97, 88 n. 118; (18, 58.5), 162 n. 172; (20, 58.16f), 72, 73 n. 55; (21, 60.15ff), 71, 75, 76 n. 68; (22–4), 84 n. 101; (24, 62.19ff), 83 n. 92; (24, 62,20f), 88 n. 118; (24, 64.3f), 83 n. 97; (25, 64.13ff), 81 n. 79; (25, 68.14ff), 85 n. 106; (29, 72.7), 83 n. 97; (29, 74.3), 68 n. 38; (34, 78.11ff), 81 n. 79; (34, 80.20ff), 80; (36, 84.23), 162 n. 172; (37, 92.6f), 74 n. 63, 84 n. 102; (38, 94.7–10), 84 n. 99; (40, 96.16ff), 70; (40, 98.1), 70; (41, 100.12ff), 81 n. 79; (46, 106.1), 127 n. 35; (46, 106.7), 70 n. 46; (59, 118.3), 72 n. 53; (59, 118.9f), 82 n. 86; (59, 118.18), 84 n. 102; (60, 120.7ff), 72, 73 n. 55; (60, 120.16), 81 n. 79; (60, 120.17f), 129 n. 45; (61, 122.17), 83 n. 97; (61, 126.1ff), 81 n. 79; (62, 126.5ff), 78–9, 81 n. 79; (62, 126.6), 78; (62, 126.11f), 76; (62, 126.12ff), 78; (62, 126.14–19), 78; (62, 126.17ff), 76 n. 68; (63, 128.19ff), 80; (63, 130.16f), 84 n. 102; (65, 134.9ff), 80; (66, 138.6ff), 81 n. 81; (66, 138.14f), 74 n. 63; (67, 140.14ff), 80; (67, 140.15f), 70 n. 46; (68, 142.13ff), 75; (68, 142.20ff), 81 n. 82; (68, 144.13), 74; (68, 144.22ff), 75–6; (70, 146.19ff), 74 n. 60, 82 n. 87; (71, 150.12), 81 n. 79; (71, 150.18f), 127 nn. 35 and 37; (74, 154.19), 129 n. 46; (74, 156.9), 83 n. 95; (74, 160.1), 82 n. 89; (74, 160.12), 130 n. 51; (74, 160.15), 130 n. 51; (74, 160.17), 128 n. 41; (75, 164.22ff), 84 n. 101; (75, 166.15), 83 n. 95; (76, 170.7f), 85 n. 103; (77, 170.11), 127 n. 35; (77, 170.14), 127 n. 35; (77, 172.9), 127 nn. 35 and 37; (78, 180.15f), 127 nn. 35 and 37; (78, 182.7f), 82 n. 89; (78, 182.24). 82 n. 89; (78, 184.15), 127 n. 35; (78, 192.6), 130 n. 50; (78, 194.17f), 130 n. 50; (78, 196.11), 128 n. 41; (78, 196.12ff), 81 n. 81; (78, 196.18), 128 n. 41; (80, 202.1), 130 n. 51; (81, 202.10), 83 n. 95; (81, 202.11ff), 129 n. 45; (81, 202.18), 128 n. 41; (84, 206.2ff), 83 n. 95; (84,

206.16), 129 n. 45; (84, 208.17ff), 82 n. 86; (84, 210.1ff), 82 n. 86; (88, 212.11f),
74 n. 63; (91, 220.1), 83 n. 95; (92, 220.20ff), 62 n. 9; (92, 222.1), 130 n. 50; (109,
230.15), 130 n. 50

Mul. II (110, L VIII 236.3), 152 n. 112; (110, 236.5ff), 81 n. 79; (110, 236.21ff), 82 n.
85; (113, 244.4f), 81 n. 79; (115, 248.9), 81 n. 79; (118, 256.17), 130 n. 50; (118,
258.1ff), 81 n. 79; (119, 260.7), 130 n. 50; (119, 260.10f), 71, 76 n. 68; (119,
260.21f), 81 n. 79; (121, 264.19f), 81 n. 79; (123–31, 266.11–280.3), 84 n. 100;
(125, 270.4f), 82 n. 86; (127, 274.4f), 84 n. 102; (128, 276.8), 84 n. 102; (129,
278.4ff), 81 n. 79; (131, 280.1ff), 84 n. 102; (133, 282.21ff), 81 n. 79; (133,
286.15f), 82 n. 85; (133, 286.16f), 71, 75; (133, 288.8ff), 71 n. 50, 81 n. 81, 82 n.
85; (133, 288.12ff), 82 n. 83; (133, 294.7ff), 71; (133, 296.12ff), 81 n. 81; (133,
298.3f), 76 n. 68; (134, 302.22ff), 74, 82 n. 85; (134, 304.1–6), 74–5; (135,
306.17ff), 82 n. 86; (139, 312.19f), 81 n. 79; (139, 312.20f), 84 n. 102; (141,
314.16), 72 n. 53; (141, 314.17f), 81 n. 79; (141, 314.19f), 84 n. 102; (143,
316.3f), 84 n. 103; (143, 316.12), 84 n. 103; (144, 316.13ff), 73 n. 59; (144,
316.17f), 84 n. 103; (144, 318.4f), 82 n. 84; (144, 318.5ff), 81 n. 82; (145,
320.20), 68 n. 38; (146, 322.12ff), 83 n. 98; (146, 322.15ff), 71; (149, 324.20f),
81 n. 79; (149, 324.21ff), 84 n. 103; (153, 328.6f), 68 n. 38; (155, 330.13f), 72, 73
n. 55; (155, 330.15), 129 n. 48; (156, 330.21f), 72, 73 n. 55; (156, 332.5ff), 82 n.
83; (157, 332.16ff), 71; (157, 334.3), 129 n. 48; (158, 334.17ff), 82 n. 83; (160,
338.5), 73 n. 55; (162, 340.5), 129 n. 48; (163, 342.13f), 73 n. 55; (165, 344.7),
129 n. 48; (167, 346.1), 73 n. 55; (168, 346.20), 73 n. 55; (169, 350.9f), 81 n. 79,
84 n. 102; (171, 352.5), 68 n. 38; (171, 352.8f), 81 n. 79; (174bis, 356.2), 85 n.
104; (174bis, 356.16f), 81 n. 79; (175, 358.3), 129 n. 45; (175, 358.4f), 82 n. 86;
(181, 364.3f), 81 n. 81; (182, 364.12ff), 85 n. 104; (185, 366.19f), 82 n. 89; (199,
382.6), 130 n. 51; (201, 384.1ff), 84 n. 100; (201, 386.1), 131, 133; (201, 386.6),
131, 133; (203, 386.21ff), 84 n. 100; (203, 390.8f), 82 n. 89; (205, 396.13f), 129
n. 48; (206, 398.9ff), 81 n. 81; (206, 400.17), 130–1; (206, 402.1f), 82 n. 89; (207,
402.11), 129 n. 48; (208, 406.3), 129 n. 48; (209, 404.1ff), 81 n. 81

Nat. Hom. (περὶ φύσιος ἀνθρώπου) (9, *CMG* I,1,3 188.10ff), 66 n. 29; (11, 194.9),
157 n. 139

Nat. Mul. (περὶ γυναικείης φύσιος) (2, L VII 314.13, Trapp), 84 n. 102; (3, 316.5ff),
84 n. 102; (4, 316.19), 84 n. 103; (5, 316.20ff), 73 n. 59; (5, 318.1ff), 85 n. 103;
(5, 318.10ff), 82 n. 84; (5, 318.11ff), 81 n. 82; (6, 320.7ff), 74 n. 64; (6, 320.9ff),
75 n. 65, 129 n. 49; (6, 320.16), 129 n. 47; (8, 322.13), 73 n. 55; (8, 324.1ff), 82 n.
86; (8, 324.2), 129 n. 49; (8, 324.9), 84 n. 102; (9, 324.15), 129 n. 47; (10,
326.3ff), 76 n. 68; (12, 330.1), 84 n. 103; (13, 330.14), 73 n. 55; (21, 340.10f), 72
n. 53; (25, 342.14), 129 n. 49; (29, 344.14), 128 n. 41; (32, 346.14ff), 82 n. 86;
(32, 348.11), 128 n. 39; (32, 348.17), 127 nn. 35 and 37; (32, 348.19f), 82 n. 86;
(32, 348.20), 74 n. 63; (32, 350.5), 130; (32, 350.6), 129 n. 49; (32, 352.7), 129 n.
49; (32, 352.10), 129 n. 49; (32, 352.17–18), 129 n. 49; (32, 358.2), 127 nn. 35
and 36; (32, 358.7), 129 n. 49, 130, 133; (32, 358.10), 129 n. 49; (32, 358.18), 129
n. 49; (32, 360.1), 129 n. 49; (32, 362.16ff), 83 n. 95, 129 n. 47; (32, 364.5), 128
n. 41; (32, 364.10), 82 n. 89; (33, 368.19), 130 n. 50; (33, 370.9ff), 128 nn. 41 and
43; (34, 372.13ff), 130; (34, 376.8), 128 n. 41; (35, 376.23f), 73 n. 55; (35,
378.11), 129 n. 47; (36, 378.22ff), 73 n. 55; (36, 380.1), 129 n. 47; (37, 380.6ff),
73 n. 55; (37, 380.12ff), 82 n. 83; (38, 382.12ff), 81 n. 79; (39, 382.15f), 73 n. 55;
(39, 382.22f), 82 n. 83; (40, 384.10ff), 74 n. 64, 82 n. 83; (40, 384.12f), 81 n. 79;
(42, 386.8), 73 n. 55; (42, 386.10), 129 n. 47; (42, 386.15f), 82 n. 84; (44,
388.4ff), 84 n. 100; (44, 388.18f), 81 n. 79; (45, 390.4f), 73 n. 55; (46, 390.17f),
73 n. 55; (48, 392.9ff), 84 n. 100; (49, 392.15ff), 84 n. 100; (58, 398.1ff), 84 n.
100; (62, 400.3ff), 84 n. 100; (67, 402.8), 73 n. 55; (68, 402.14), 82 n. 89; (75,

HIPPOCRATIC CORPUS (*cont.*)

404.18), 83 n. 95; (92, 410.7), 129 n. 47; (96, 412.19ff), 83 n. 93; (96, 412.20), 72 n. 53; (98, 414.20f), 85 n. 103; (101, 416.7f), 82 n. 89; (103, 418.4), 83 n. 95; (109, 424.11ff), 83 n. 95; (109, 426.17), 83 n. 95; (109, 428.2ff), 82 n. 86; (109, 430.4), 74 n. 63

Nat. Puer. (περὶ φύσιος παιδίου) (12, L VII 486.1ff), 90 n. 122; (13, 490.5ff), 78; (15, 494.13ff), 153 n. 116; (15, 494.23ff), 153 n. 116; (18, 498.27ff), 91 n. 124; (21, 510.22ff), 91 n. 124; (21, 512.18ff), 153 n. 116; (29, 530.3ff), 92; (30, 532.14ff), 78; (30, 534.8ff), 78; (31, 540.16ff), 90 n. 122

Oct. (περὶ ὀκταμήνου) (1, *CMG* 1,2,1 78.16ff), 83 n. 91, 171 n. 198; (4, 88.4ff), 84 n. 101; (4, 88.11ff), 83 n. 92; (6, 92.4ff), 76; (6, 92.7ff), 76 n. 70; (7, 92.15), 77; (7, 92.16–21), 77 n. 74; (9, 94.15ff), 77 n. 75

Oss. (περὶ ὀστέων φύσιος) (14, L IX 188.5f), 162

Prog. (προγνωστικόν) (1, L II 110.1ff), 182 n. 239; (20, 172.2ff), 66 n. 27; (23, 174.14ff), 162 n. 171; (23, 176.11ff), 162 n. 171; (23, 178.9), 155; (24, 184.8ff), 66 n. 26

Salubr. (περὶ διαίτης ὑγιεινῆς) (6, L VI 82.2ff), 66 n. 25

Steril. (περὶ ἀφόρων) (213, L VIII 408.17), 72 and n. 54; (213, 410.3f), 72 and n. 54; (213, 410.13), 72 n. 52; (213, 410.20f), 72 n. 52; (213, 410.23), 72 n. 52; (213, 412.17), 76 n. 68; (213, 414.11ff), 76 n. 68; (213, 414.15f), 85 n. 106; (214, 414.17ff), 83 n. 93; (214, 414.20ff), 83 n. 98; (214, 416.2ff), 65 n. 21, 83 n. 98; (215, 416.8ff), 83 n. 93; (216, 416.18ff), 83 n. 93; (217, 418.3), 162 n. 172; (217, 418.23ff), 74 n. 64, 82 n. 83; (217, 422.3), 162 n. 172; (217, 422.7), 162 n. 172; (217, 422.13), 162 n. 172; (218, 422.18ff), 84 n. 101; (219, 422.23ff), 83 nn. 93 and 98, 162 n. 172; (220, 424.14ff), 84 n. 101; (221, 426.9ff), 82 n. 83; (221, 428.8ff), 74 n. 63; (222, 428.17), 81 n. 79; (222, 428.25ff), 75; (222, 430.11f), 75; (223, 432.4f), 81 n. 79; (223, 432.6), 83 n. 95; (224, 434.11), 83 n. 95; (225, 434.15f), 83 n. 95; (227, 436.11ff), 74 n. 63, 75 n. 65; (230, 438.11), 72 n. 53; (230, 442.9), 83 n. 95; (230, 442.19ff), 81 n. 81; (230, 442.22), 81 n. 81; (230, 442.24ff), 81 n. 81; (230. 442.27ff), 85 n. 108; (230, 444.1ff), 81 n. 81; (230, 444.2ff), 81 n. 79; (230, 444.17f), 84 n. 103; (232, 446.1ff), 81 n. 79; (233, 448.3f), 127 nn. 35 and 37; (241, 454.23ff), 81 n. 81; (244, 458.4ff), 81 n. 79; (248, 460.14ff), 73 n. 59; (248, 462.2), 82 n. 84; (249, 462.16ff), 74 n. 60

Superf. (περὶ ἐπικυήσιος) (4, *CMG* 1,2,2 74.7), 73 n. 58; (4, 74.14), 73 n. 58; (5, 74.20ff), 73 n. 58; (6, 74.24), 73 n. 58; (6, 74.25ff), 73 n. 58; (7, 74.28ff), 74 n. 60, 82 n. 87; (18, 80.8ff), 83 n. 94; (25, 80.28ff), 83 nn. 93 and 98; (26, 82.12ff), 84 n. 101; (28, 84.19), 128 n. 41; (30, 90.8ff), 84 n. 101; (31, 90.12ff), 82 n. 90, 83 n. 92; (32, 90.27), 130 n. 50; (32, 90.28), 128 n. 41; (33, 92.4), 130 n. 50

Ulc. (περὶ ἑλκῶν) (11, L VI 410.16), 128 n. 41; (15, 418.13), 128 n. 38; (17, 422.8), 128 n. 38

VC (περὶ τῶν ἐν κεφαλῇ τρωμάτων) (1, L III 182.1ff), 102 n. 165; (2, 188.12ff), 64 n. 16; (3, 192.16ff), 64 n. 16

VM (περὶ ἀρχαίης ἰητρικῆς) (2, *CMG* 1,1 37.7ff), 208 n. 19; (2, 37.9ff), 182 n. 239; (2, 37.17ff), 208 n. 19; (9, 41.25ff), 208 n. 20; (9, 42.6ff), 208 n. 19; (19, 50.22), 155 n. 123; (21, 52.17ff), 208 n. 19

Vict. I (περὶ διαίτης) (3, L VI 472.12ff), 90; (9, 482.13ff), 90; (27ff, 500.1ff), 90, 92 and n. 125; (27, 500.5ff), 90–1; (27, 500.7f), 92 n. 126; (28, 500.23ff), 91; (29, 502.24ff), 91; (32, 506.14ff), 91; (34, 512.13ff), 91, 92 n. 125

Vict. II (46–9, L VI 544.17ff), 14 n. 21

Virg. (περὶ παρθενίων) (L VIII 466–70), 209 n. 25; (466.4ff), 69 n. 43; (468.17ff), 69 n. 43; (468.19), 69 n. 44; (468.21ff), 69 n. 44, 84 n. 102

HOMER
Iliad III (35), 160; (292), 162 n. 172
    IV (191), 119 n. 16; (218), 119 n. 16
    V (305ff), 154; (307), 152 n. 112; (900ff), 119
    XI (844ff), 119
    XIII (546f), 152 n. 115
    XVI (481ff), 152; (502ff), 152
    XXII (324f), 160
Odyssey III (449), 152 n. 112
    IV (404ff), 45 n. 178
    X (302ff), 119
    XVII (225), 159 n. 150
HYGINUS
Fab. 274 (171–2), 70 n. 47

IAMBLICHUS
Protr. (21,8), 170 n. 195
ISOCRATES
    XII (240), 44 n. 172

LUCRETIUS
    IV (1209ff), 108 n. 189

ORIBASIUS
    XXII (3), 72 n. 54

PARMENIDES
    fr. (18), 87 n. 114
PHERECRATES
    fr. (19), 44 n. 172
PHILOSTRATUS
    *Im.*1 (24), 156 n. 134
    VA V (5), 156 n. 134
PINDAR
    Pae. (9,14), 204 n. 6
PLATO
    Epin. (980c ff), 54 n. 217; (981b–e), 54 n. 217; (984b–d), 54 n. 217
    Lg. (720 b–e), 182 n. 240; (794d8 ff), 177 n. 218; (823b), 15 n. 23; (903d), 95 n.
        136; (909a ff), 69 n. 41; (933a ff), 69 n. 41
    Phdr. (248e ff), 95 n. 136; (257b), 44 n. 172
    Plt. (264d ff), 15 n. 23
    R. (364b ff), 69 n. 41; (406a ff), 182 n. 241; (451c ff), 107 n. 183; (451e1 f), 107 n.
        185; (454b ff), 107 n. 183; (455ef), 70 n. 47, 107 nn. 184 and 185; (456a 11), 107
        n. 185; (479b11), 44 n. 172; (479c3), 44 n. 172, 46 n. 184; (619b ff), 95 n. 136
    Sph. (220ab), 15 n. 23
    Ti. (69e4), 155 n. 124; (70a), 152 n. 109; (70d ff), 84 n. 100; (90e ff), 15, 42, 95 nn.
        135 and 136; (91c), 84 n. 100; (91d ff), 15, 54 n. 215; (91e), 41 n. 158
PLATO COMICUS
    fr. (174.13), 162 n. 174
PLINY
    HN I (Pref. 12ff), 135; (Pref. 17), 135; (Pref. 22), 135
    II (1ff), 147 n. 100; (28), 140 n. 76; (34ff), 140 n. 76; (46), 147 n. 100; (56ff), 147 n.

PLINY (*cont.*)

100; (59ff), 147 n. 100; (72ff), 147 n. 100; (87ff), 147 n. 100; (101); 138; (105ff), 140 n. 76; (117), 137

III (136), 138 n. 68

VII (75), 138; (97), 138 n. 68

VIII (43f), 136

IX (133), 148 n. 102; (136), 138; (151), 148 n. 102

XI (16), 148 n. 102; (57), 138

XIII (83), 138 n. 68

XIV (2ff), 136

XV (1), 147 n. 99

XVI (64), 139 n. 70; (251), 141 n. 76

XVII (42), 137

XVIII (55), 139; (128), 138; (160), 139 n. 70; (205), 137; (209), 139; (280–9), 140 n. 76; (317), 139

XIX (19), 139; (81), 139

XX (1f), 178 n. 226; (74), 141 n. 76; (174), 140 n. 73; (215), 137; (226), 63 n. 11; (261), 140 n. 73

XXI (42), 144; (44), 145 n. 94; (57), 146–7; (60), 144; (61), 144 n. 87; (64ff), 144 n. 91; (66), 141 n. 76; (67), 144; (67f), 144 n. 91; (74), 137; (90), 144 n. 85; (94ff), 144 n. 88; (97), 144 n. 86; (104), 144 n. 89; (108), 144 n. 90; (144), 148 n. 102; (145), 145; (166), 141 n. 76

XXII (11), 137; (61), 141 n. 76; (94), 148; (95), 148 n. 101; (106), 134 n. 61, 178 n. 226

XXIII (112), 136; (141), 137

XXIV (1ff), 178 n. 226; (12), 170 n. 195; (68), 170 n. 195; (72), 141 n. 76; (103), 170 n. 195; (160–6), 144 n. 84; (176), 170 n. 195; (177), 138 n. 67

XXV (1ff), 136–7; (2), 136; (5ff), 136; (8f), 114 n. 4, 139; (9), 114 n. 5, 139; (15ff), 140 n. 75; (16), 136 and n. 64, 139 n. 70, 147–8; (18f), 138; (24f), 136; (26) 141 and n. 79; (29), 145, 146 n. 97; (30), 145 nn. 94 and 95; (48), 142; (49), 142; (50), 145; (92–4), 142–4; (98), 138 n. 69; (148), 145; (150), 132 n. 57; (174), 148 n. 102

XXVI (5), 139; (10f), 137; (12ff), 182 n. 241; (18ff), 141 n. 76; (24), 148 n. 102; (99), 146–7

XXVII (1ff), 136 n. 64; (4), 136 n. 64; (39), 138 n. 67; (67), 148 n. 102; (85), 145; (99), 138 n. 68; (102–3), 138 n. 67; (141), 138 n. 67

XXVIII (38), 63 n. 11; (65), 137; (66), 63 n. 11; (67), 148 n. 102; (81), 63 n. 11; (82), 63 n. 11; (83), 63 n. 11; (85), 141 n. 76; (104), 141 n. 76; (151), 137; (215), 141 n. 76; (226), 141 n. 76; (228–9), 146 n. 98; (246), 63 n. 11; (253), 63 n. 11; (262), 63 n. 11

XXIX (1ff), 141 n. 76; (6ff), 182 n. 241; (12), 182 n. 241; (14ff), 141 n. 76; (18), 136; (53), 138; (81), 146 n. 98

XXX, 141 n. 76; (13), 145 n. 95; (103), 138 n. 67

XXXI (45), 148 n. 102; (60), 138

XXXII (34), 141 n. 76; (61), 148 n. 102; (135), 63 n. 11; (140), 63 n. 11; (154), 138 and n. 67

XXXIII (90), 148 n. 102

XXXIV (108), 137 n. 65; (138ff), 170 n. 195; (151ff), 170 n. 195

XXXVII (59ff), 178 n. 226

PLINY THE YOUNGER

Ep. III (5), 145 n. 93

VI (16), 140 n. 74

PLUTARCH
 De curiositate (7, 518cd), 78 n. 76
 De invidia et odio (537bc), 20 n. 38
POLLUX
 II (85f, 109.17ff), 159 n. 148; (131, 124.1ff), 155 n. 127; (174, 137.2ff), 162 n. 174;
  (183, 139.20f), 160 n. 159; (189, 141.14f), 156 n. 131; (189, 141.21), 159 n. 150;
  (202, 145.13f), 162 n. 175
PORPHYRY
 VP (42), 170 n. 195; (45), 48 n. 194
PTOLEMY
 Tetr. II (1), 178 n. 225
RUFUS
 Anat. (170.9ff), 151 n. 107, 161 n. 163; (171.1ff), 161 n. 164; (171.3), 161 n. 164;
  (171.9ff), 161 n. 165; (172.1ff), 161 n. 166; (173.6f), 160 n. 157; (173.8f), 151 n.
  107, 160 n. 157, 163 n. 180; (174.7ff), 162 n. 171; (174.10), 162 n. 172;
  (174.14ff), 162 n. 171; (176.14ff), 151 n. 107; (181.8f), 151 n. 107; (182.1ff),
  151 n. 107; (183.12ff), 151 n. 107, 160 n. 154; (184.15ff), 159 n. 151;
  (184.15–185.7), 152 n. 111
 Onom. (134.9ff), 151 n. 107; (134.12ff), 160 n. 153; (135.2ff), 161 n. 167; (136.8f),
  161 n. 164; (137.8f), 163 n. 176; (137.10), 163 n. 176; (138.6ff), 159 n. 148;
  (139.3ff), 160 n. 155; (139.8ff), 159 n. 149; (139.12ff), 162 n. 171; (140.11), 156
  n. 137; (141.2f), 160 n. 158; (141.3ff), 160 n. 157; (141.5f), 151 n. 107, 163 n.
  179; (141.6ff), 162 n. 171; (141.7ff), 152 n. 108; (142.5f), 152 n. 108, 160 n. 156;
  (142.8ff), 161 n. 168; (143.10f), 163 n. 176; (143.12f), 154 n. 120; (144.1), 158
  n. 142; (144.2f), 162 n. 169; (145.12ff), 159 n. 150; (146.12ff), 151 n. 107, 163 n.
  181; (147.10f), 163 n. 177; (147.12f), 152 n. 108; (148.1ff), 160 n. 159; (148.2),
  158 n. 142; (148.10), 159 n. 150; (148.11), 156 n. 131; (149.12ff), 151 n. 107;
  (151.1ff), 158 n. 146, 163 n. 177; (151.10ff), 163 n. 183; (152.2ff), 157 n. 138;
  (152.6ff), 164 n. 185; (153.9f), 158 n. 143; (153.10ff), 152 n. 111; (153.13ff),
  161 n. 160; (154.1ff), 151 n. 107; (154.2f), 161 n. 162; (154.3ff), 161 n. 164;
  (154.7ff), 161 n. 165; (154.9f), 158 n. 144; (154.11ff), 161 n. 166; (154.13f),
  155; (155.1ff), 162 n. 168; (155.4f), 162 n. 175; (155.7f), 162 n. 172; (155.10f),
  161 n. 161; (155.11), 153 n. 118; (156.4), 158 n. 142; (157.5f), 152 n. 108;
  (157.7ff), 163 n. 177; (157.14ff), 162 n. 168; (158.5ff), 159 n. 149; (158.11ff),
  162 n. 168; (158.15ff), 151 n. 107, 162 n. 175; (159.1), 163 n. 177; (159.4ff), 162
  n. 175; (159.13–160.5), 157; (160.9ff), 161–2 n. 168; (161.2f), 160 n. 154;
  (161.4ff), 160 n. 154; (161.6ff), 162 n. 173; (162.5ff), 153 n. 117; (163.3ff), 160
  n. 154, 163 n. 178; (163.5ff), 153 n. 118; (163.9ff), 164 n. 184; (163.12ff), 159 n.
  151; (164.5ff), 162 n. 170; (164.9ff), 161 n. 160; (167.6ff), 160 n. 154
 Ren. Ves. (23, *CMG* III,1 116.4), 163 n. 182
 Syn. Puls. (222.11f), 151 n. 107

SEMONIDES
 (7), 46 n. 186, 95 n. 133
SEXTUS EMPIRICUS
 M. V (4ff), 178 n. 225
 VII (29ff), 189; (203), 191 n. 272; (217–18), 191 n. 272; (257), 191 n. 272; (364ff),
  191 n. 272; (403), 191 n. 272
 IX (75ff), 178 n. 225; (79ff), 178 n. 225
 P. I (13ff), 189; (19ff), 189; (21ff), 189; (23ff), 189; (24), 190 n. 270; (236ff), 182,
  199 nn. 283 and 284; (238), 190 n. 270; (240), 184 n. 251

SORANUS

Gyn. I (2, *CMG* IV 4.6f), 189 n. 267; (3, 4.18f), 186; (4, 5.10ff), 79 n. 77, 186; (4, 5.21), 179 n. 229; (4, 5.28ff), 168; (5, 6.6ff), 188, 209 n. 21; (8, 7.18ff), 172; (12, 9.18), 189 n. 267; (14, 10.14ff), 193; (15, 10.27ff), 180; (16–17), 193; (17, 12.3), 193; (21, 14.6ff), 170–1, 179 n. 228; (25, 16.18ff), 177 n. 222; (27–9, 17.17ff), 185 n. 256, 186–7; (27, 17.25ff), 186, 187 n. 260; (28, 18.9ff), 187–8; (29, 19.10ff), 197; (29, 19.16ff), 197; (29, 19.26f), 187; (29, 19.35f), 187; (30–2, 20.1ff), 85 n. 103, 187; (32, 21.23ff), 187; (34, 24.6ff), 177 n. 222; (35, 24.24ff), 192; (35, 25.1ff), 192; (39, 27.28ff), 174–5; (40, 28.6ff), 193; (41, 28.25ff), 171, 178 n. 224, 179, 190; (41, 29.4f), 190; (41, 29.5f), 171, 190; (41, 29.10ff), 171, 190; (42, 29.16ff), 85 n. 103; (42, 30.5f), 192 n. 273; (44, 31.6ff), 190 n. 271; (44, 31.16), 194; (44, 31.17f), 194; (45, 31.26ff), 174 n. 209, 176; (45, 32.1ff), 174 n. 209; (45, 32.12), 192 n. 273; (46, 32.22ff), 177 n. 222; (47, 34.30ff), 177 n. 222; (52, 38.9ff), 187; (52, 38.16ff), 187; (53, 38.21ff), 177; (54, 39.10ff), 177 n. 222; (55, 40.2f), 192 n. 273; (58, 43.7ff), 187 n. 262, 190; (58, 43.17), 191; (58, 44.2ff), 191; (58, 44.4), 191; (60, 45.6ff), 173 n. 208; (61ff, 45.20ff), 181 n. 236; (63, 47.16ff), 179, 181 n. 236; (65, 48.13ff), 173 n. 208; (65, 48.24ff), 179 n. 231

II (5, 53.12ff), 74 n. 61, 178 n. 222; (5, 54.8ff), 178 n. 222; (6, 54.11ff), 175; (6, 54.22ff), 178 n. 222; (8, 56.24ff), 173 n. 207; (10, 57.18ff), 177; (11, 58.12ff), 169, 208 n. 18; (11, 58.19ff), 179; (12, 59.10ff), 170, 172 n. 203, 208 n. 18; (14, 60.29ff), 175 n. 214; (14, 61.4ff), 173 n. 207; (15, 61.30ff), 176; (16, 63.2ff), 172, 176 n. 216, 208 n. 18; (16, 63.9), 179; (18, 64.21ff), 187 n. 262, 191; (18, 64.22ff), 191; (18, 64.25ff), 191; (18, 65.1ff), 191; (18, 65.6f), 191; (18, 65.16ff), 178 n. 222; (18, 65.18), 179 n. 229; (19, 66.11), 179 n. 229; (19, 67.23ff), 193 n. 274; (19, 68.2ff), 178 n. 222; (19, 68.10f), 179 n. 229; (19, 68.15ff), 168–9; (20, 68.30ff), 175; (22, 69.30ff), 193 n. 274; (32–3, 77.3ff), 176 n. 216; (35, 79.15ff), 193 n. 274; (37, 80.10ff), 177 n. 220; (39, 81.20ff), 193 and n. 274; (40, 83.9ff), 178 n. 222; (41, 83.29ff), 173 n. 206; (42, 84.17ff), 176; (42, 84.25ff), 175 n. 215; (46, 85.29ff), 193 n. 274; (47, 87.1ff), 173 n. 207; (48, 87.9ff), 175; (49, 88.5ff), 180 n. 234; (49, 88.22), 179; (50, 88.29ff), 172; (51, 89.23ff), 173; (54, 91.8ff), 196 n. 277; (54, 91.10ff), 173 n. 207

III (3, 95.6ff), 79 n. 77; (3, 95.7), 69 n. 39; (6ff, 97.7ff), 194; (7, 97.21ff), 194; (8, 98.10), 194; (8, 98.11), 194; (8, 98.14ff), 194; (9, 98.22ff), 194; (9–10), 196; (10, 99.15), 196; (12, 101.28ff), 173 n. 207; (12, 102.9ff), 173 n. 206; (16, 104.22ff), 178 n. 222; (17, 105.3ff), 193; (17, 105.18ff), 180 n. 233; (19, 106.16ff), 193 n. 276; (20, 106.19ff), 180; (22, 107.17ff), 180; (24, 108.15ff), 185 n. 256, 197; (25, 109.6ff), 178 n. 222; (25, 109.7f), 180; (29, 112.10ff), 172; (29, 112.14ff), 173, 174 n. 209; (29, 113.1ff), 173; (29, 113.3ff), 172; (29, 113.6f), 180 n. 233; (31, 114.6ff), 180 n. 233; (32, 114.16f), 196; (33, 115.28ff), 173 n. 207; (33, 115.33f), 196; (39, 118.15ff), 173 n. 207; (40, 119.2ff), 195; (40, 119.10ff), 195; (40, 119.14f), 195; (41, 120.6ff), 195; (41, 120.13f), 179; (41, 121.1ff), 195; (41, 121.12), 179; (42, 121.14ff), 185 n. 256, 197–8; (42, 121.26ff), 177, 179; (43, 122.2ff), 193–4; (43, 122.20ff), 194; (44, 124.2ff), 197; (45, 124.15), 196; (46, 125.3ff), 178 n. 222; (47, 126.5ff), 178 n. 222; (49, 127.5), 196 n. 179; (49, 127.11f), 180 n. 233; (49, 127.12), 196; (49, 127.14f), 196 n. 179; (50, 128.3), 196; (50, 128.7), 196

IV (2, 131.11ff), 178 n. 222; (2, 131.21ff), 180 n. 231; (4, 134.1ff), 178 n. 222; (6, 135.7ff), 178 n. 222; (7, 136.8ff), 178 n. 222; (7, 137.6ff), 173 n. 207; (7, 137.7), 179; (8, 139.26ff), 180 n. 231; (9ff, 140.2ff), 174 n. 211; (9, 140.6ff), 178 n. 222; (9, 140.7), 179 n. 230; (9, 140.18ff), 176; (12, 143.11ff), 176; (13, 144.2ff), 174 n. 209; (14–15, 144.21ff), 173, 174 n. 209; (15, 145.14ff), 173, 174 n. 209; (15,

145.16), 179 n. 230; (15, 145.18), 179 n. 230; (15, 145.29), 179 n. 230; (35, 148.3ff), 178 n. 222; (36, 149.11ff), 173 n. 207; (36, 149.21ff), 172

SPEUSIPPUS
fr. (8), 15 n. 25

STRABO
IX (3.3), 142 n. 80

THEOPHRASTUS
CP I (5.5), 113 n. 3; (8.2), 121 n. 21
II (6.4), 121 n. 22; (11.7ff), 121 n. 21; (19.6), 43 n. 170
VI (6.1), 121 n. 21; (17.11), 121 n. 21
HP I (1.5), 43 n. 170; (1.11), 43 n. 170; (3.1), 43 n. 170; (3.2), 43 n. 170; (4.3), 43 n. 170
III (1.1–6), 113 n. 3; (18.6–8), 43 n. 170
VI (2.4), 147; (4.3), 144 n. 88; (4.5–6), 144 n. 85; (4.10–11), 144 n. 86; (7.3), 144; (7.4), 144 n. 87; (7.6), 144 n. 87; (8.1ff), 144 n. 91; (8.3), 145
VII (7.2), 128 n. 40; (13.3), 144 n. 90; (14.3), 144 n. 89; (15.4), 128 n. 40
IX (4), 122; (4.8), 122 n. 25; (5.1), 123; (5.2), 123; (8.2), 128; (8.5ff), 122–3, 130; (8.6), 133, 145; (8.7), 124, 131, 144, 145 n. 94; (8.8), 130, 145; (9.1), 130; (9.2), 131; (9.3), 129; (9.5f), 130; (10.2f), 142; (10.3), 142; (10.4), 142; (11.1–3), 131; (11.4), 131; (11.5–9), 128 n. 40; (12.1), 128; (14.1), 123 n. 26; (14.4), 122; (15.2), 124; (15.3), 124; (15.7), 141 and n. 79; (16.1ff), 126 n. 31, 127, 142–4; (16.6), 122; (16.8), 122; (16.9), 122; (17), 122; (17.1ff), 122, 125; (17.2f), 122; (18.2), 124; (18.4), 122; (18.9), 146; (18.10), 121 n. 22; (19), 125; (19.2), 145 and n. 94; (19.2–3), 123, 125; (19.4), 125; (20.3), 130

THUCYDIDES
VIII (85), 44 n. 172

XENOPHON
Oec. (7.37), 79 n. 78

GENERAL INDEX

abnormalities, congenital distinguished from acquired, 64; *see also* deformities, mutilations
abortion, 62 n. 7, 68 n. 37, 136
Academy, 16–17
Aelian, 56
Aeschylus, 86, 136
Agassiz, L., 21
alchemy, 178
Alcmaeon, 87
Alexandria, 158, 165, 167, 213
amulets, 123, 125–6, 129, 131, 145, 177, 179, 181
analogy, 36, 38–9, 93, 97, 106, 108 n. 188, 109 n. 191, 158, 171
Anaxagoras, 32 n. 108, 87, 88 n. 116
anomaly, 7–8, 10–11, 45–6, 48, 50, 52–3, 205
anthropocentricity, 3, 27, 35, 42, 55
anthropology, 2–3, 7–10, 17, 48, 65, 202, 207
ape, 31–2, 41, 46–7, 51
appearances, *see phainomena*
Aristides, Aelius, 182 n. 238, 207
Aristotle, 3–4, 13–57, 60–1, 86–8, 94–106, 108–11, 113–14, 122, 135–6, 148–50, 153 n. 117, 201, 203–7, 210–16; authenticity of works in Aristotelian Corpus, 21, 24, 43, 96 n. 140
ἀρτηρία, 153
Asclepiades, 173, 182 n. 241, 183, 192
Asclepius, 69, 79, 207
astrology, 20 n. 38, 118, 140
astronomy, 60, 112, 147 n. 100, 203

Babylonia, 65 n. 21, 201–2
Balme, D.M., 16 n. 27
bat, 11, 46, 51, 53
Bateson, W., 105 n. 177
bear, 31, 98–9
bees, 22, 25 n. 53, 28 n. 65, 29 n. 69, 33, 99, 102
birds, 15–17, 20, 24, 29, 41, 47, 51, 95, 104
blood, 86, 124, 195, 197–8; analogues to, 33, 38; concoction of, 95, 97–8, 101; quality of, associated with character and intelligence, 22, 26, 32–4, 38, 100
blooded and bloodless groups of animals, 15 n. 22, 16–17, 31, 33, 37, 45, 51, 103

blood-vascular system, 34, 152–4, 159–60, 164–8
boar, 19, 22, 24
bones, terminology for, 153–6, 158, 163
book-learning, 116–17, 136–7, 148–9, 202; *see also* literacy
boundary-crossing, 3, 7–8, 10–11, 44–8, 50–2
brain, 30, 36 n. 127, 38–9, 102, 108, 153, 158, 180
breast-feeding, 178 n. 222, 179 n. 229, 191, 193
breasts, 30, 32, 109 n. 191, 176, 180–1
bull, 22, 33, 83, 101
Burckhardt, R., 14 n. 21

Caelius Aurelianus, 186, 187 n. 260, 188 n. 264
cantharides, 82
carotids, 164
Castor, Antonius, 114 n. 5, 139–41
cataract, 145, 149 n. 104, 159 n. 147
causation, 125, 132, 134, 166; in Aristotle, 13, 18, 56, 86, 96 n. 143, 109; in Methodist medicine, 186, 191–5, 198–9
cautery, 207
Celsus, 149, 183, 185, 187–9, 192, 196–8
cephalopods, 16–17, 39, 45, 99, 204
Cesalpino, 44 n. 171
character, animal, 10, 19–26, 36, 98–105
charms, 123, 125, 129, 131, 133, 145, 208
childbirth, 30–1, 50, 64–6, 68, 73–4, 76–7, 79–81, 129, 133, 175, 177–8 n. 222, 180 n. 231, 191, 193, 195
China, 73 n. 56
cinnamon, 20, 123
clientèle of doctors, 63, 67–8, 73 n. 57, 132, 208
cold, harm caused by, 170, 193; *see also* hot
common conditions (κοινότητες), 183, 188, 196–9
competitiveness, in medicine, 69, 79, 81, 118–19, 131–2, 166, 208–9, 213; in philosophy, 118, 210
conception, 65, 77–8, 83–5, 171, 177 n. 222, 190, 192, 201; *see also* pregnancy, sterility
consensus, 5, 117, 166

256

contraception, 62 n. 7, 85 n. 103, 179, 181 n. 236
Copernicus, 203
Cos, 165
cow, 31 n. 98, 34, 101
crabs, 36, 39, 47–8
Crateuas, 114, 120 n. 20
Crete, 127, 142–4
criticism, of popular assumptions, 1, 4–5, 14, 52, 55, 80–1, 123, 168–82, 204, 207–12, 215–17
Ctesias, 55

Daremberg, C.V., 151 n. 107, 164
Darwin, C., 26, 88
deer, 10, 19, 33, 83, 102
deformities, 40–2, 46, 48, 50, 52–4, 90, 95, 103–4, 110, 211
deliberation, 24–5
delivery, *see* childbirth
Democritus, 14, 15 n. 22, 87 n. 114, 88, 93, 107, 121 n. 21, 156
Detienne, M., 10–11
dichotomy, 15–18, 51 n. 206
Diepgen, P., 62
diet, 46, 66; *see also* regimen; dietary proscriptions, 7–9, 13
Diocles, 15 n. 21, 120, 171, 173, 193
Diogenes of Apollonia, 87 n. 112, 107 n. 182, 153 n. 116
Dionysius, (Methodist), 186–7, 197
Dioscorides, 114, 137 n. 66, 144, 149
dissection, 27, 113, 157, 165–7, 188–9, 192–3, 206, 209, 217
dittany, 127, 142–4
Dittmeyer, L., 21 n. 44
divination, 20 n. 38, 159 n. 149, 207
dog, 19, 31, 52 n. 212, 98, 103
Dogmatists, 165–6, 183–8, 191–2, 196, 198–9
Douglas, M., 7–8
drug-sellers, 116, 120–3, 125–6, 137 n. 65, 210, 213
Druids, 138, 141 n. 76
dry/wet, 14 n. 21, 18, 90–2, 110, 126
ducts, sub-sensible, 192–3
Durkheim, E., 9

ear, 46 n. 183, 159, 163
Edelstein, L., 183–4
education: medical, 165, 167; scientific, 116
eel, 104
efficacy, 81 n. 79, 83, 132–3, 181, 210
egg, 18, 35, 44 n. 172, 92, 97
Egypt, 65 n. 21, 82, 84 n. 100, 158, 201–2
eighth-month child, 76–8
elephant, 19, 30, 31 n. 98, 166
embryo, 27, 78, 91 n. 124, 92
Empedocles, 53–4, 87–8, 97, 158 n. 142, 171

Empiricists, 165, 182–8, 199
Epicureans, 108 n. 189, 110 n. 204, 191, 212 n. 26
Epicurus, 87 nn. 112 and 114
Epidaurus, 69 nn. 40 and 45, 79, 207
Epimenides, 120 n. 18
ἐποχή, *see* withholding judgement
Erasistratus, 40 n. 152, 113, 150, 157, 159, 166, 199, 206, 213 n. 29
Ethiopia, 82, 124
Euclid, 116
Euryphon, 173 n. 208, 192
evolution, 13, 18, 26, 57
excreta, 83, 179
eye, membranes of, 158, 161, 165

female: deemed inferior to male, 3, 59, 61, 68, 87, 94–5, 104–5, 107, 110–11, 210–11, defined by incapacity, 86, 95, 98, 101, 107, 211, as natural deformity, 41, 95, 110; as providing place in reproduction, 66, 86, 87 n. 113, 93, 97, 107, 212, as matter, 86, 93, 97, 107, 109, 212, 215, as producing seed, 66, 87–94, 96–7, 109–10, 212, as not producing concocted seed, 96 and n. 140, 109–10; /male, correlated with cold/hot, 33–4, 90–1, 97, 100–2, 104, 107, 110, 203, and wet/dry, 90–1, 110; differentiated in swaddling, 175–6

fishing-frog, 20
foetus, removal of dead, 74–5, 82, 174 n. 211, 178 n. 222
friendships/enmities between animals, 20
front/back, 28 n. 62, 36, 41, 101
fumigation, 65 n. 21, 71, 74, 82, 130, 172, 192

Galen, 24 n. 51, 105, 108–10, 113, 116, 150–60, 162 n. 172, 164, 166–7, 170 n. 196, 183–5, 186–9, 198–9, 206, 209, 214
gardens, botanical, 114 n. 5, 140
glands, 153
glanis, 20, 99
glycyside, 124, 129–30, 133, 145
goat, 83, 102, 142–4
Goody, J., 52 n. 211, 115–16, 202
gregariousness, 19, 49

habitat: animal, 19 n. 37, 31, 46, 48; plant, 144, 146
habituation, 122, 125, 136
Hagnodice, 70 n. 47
hands, 32
heart, 33 n. 111, 36 n. 128, 38–40, 49, 100, 108, 153 n. 117, 166, 207
hellebore, 82, 122, 124, 126–7, 142, 145, 206
hemlock, 122
heredity, 3, 86–91, 96, 105–6

hermit-crab, 39, 47, 50 n. 202
Herodicus, 182 n. 241
Herodotus, 55, 122 n. 24
Herophilus, 40 n. 152, 108–9, 113, 150, 153 n.
    117, 157–9, 161–2, 164 n. 185, 166, 186–7,
    199, 206, 213 n. 29
Hesiod, 11–12, 14, 53, 94–5, 119–20, 136, 144
    n. 90, 145
hidden, the, 165–6, 184, 185 n. 254, 188–9,
    191–3, 195, 198–9
hierarchy, 15, 35–7, 42–3, 56–7, 95, 103, 111,
    215; *see also* perfection
Hipparchus, 112
Hippocrates, 109, 173, 176, 208
Hippocratic Corpus, 3–4, 14, 58–9, 62–86,
    88–94, 106–7, 109, 116, 118, 121, 126–30,
    150, 152–7, 159, 166, 168, 171, 181–3, 201,
    203–4, 206–10, 212–13, 217
Hippon, 87 n. 112, 107 n. 182
Homer, 10, 12, 14, 24, 45, 52, 119, 136, 141,
    152, 154, 160
horticulture, 105
hot/cold, 18, 22, 32–4, 38 n. 144, 39, 90–2, 97,
    100–2, 104, 107, 110, 126, 197, 203
Huby, P.M., 21
humours, 126, 153, 187, 196–7, 204
hybrids, 8, 13 n. 19, 52 n. 212, 105–6

Iamblichus, 182 n. 238
illustration, botanical, 114, 139
immunisation, 125, 136; *see also* habituation
incurable cases, 78, 81 n. 79
India, 82 n. 89, 124, 139
inhibitions, in doctor-patient relationships,
    78, 80
institutional organisation of science, 118, 165,
    167, 213–14, 216
intelligence, animal, 19–22, 24–6, 28, 32–3,
    38
intercourse, sexual, 174–5, 193; pleasure in,
    89 n. 120, 96 n. 141; prescribed, 69, 84–5
intermediates, 3, 7, 10, 40, 44–7, 51–3; *see also*
    boundary-crossing
iron, 169–70
ἱστορία, 60, 122; *see also* research

Jenner, E., 117 n. 12

Kuhn, T.S., 117

land-animals/water-animals, 14, 15 n. 23, 19,
    31, 45–6, 48, 51 n. 205, 53 n. 213, 95
Leach, E.R., 8, 10 n. 10, 83 n. 95
leopard, 98–9
Leophanes, 82 n. 90
Lesky, E., 86
Lévi-Strauss, C., 8–9, 24 n. 51, 116 n. 11
Linnaeus, C., 17, 44 n. 171

lion, 10, 19, 22–4
literacy, 2, 5, 60 n. 6, 115–17, 186, 202, 215;
    literary versus oral sources, 4, 60 n. 6, 116,
    120, 135–8, 146–9, 202, 215–16
liver, 49, 159 n. 149, 171
lobsters, 40
locomotion, modes of, in classification of
    animals, 26, 39–41, 49, 51
longevity, 19–20, 30–1, 103–4
Loraux, N., 12
lungs, 33 n. 111, 39, 152, 156, 161
Lycus, 113 n. 2

Macedonia, 172, 179
Magi, 138, 141 n. 76, 146
magic, 48, 140, 168, 174
magnet, 177
man: in relation to animals, 11–12, 25, 42,
    55–6, 204, as model and supreme animal, 3,
    26–43, 49, 52–3, 99, 105, 210, 215; in
    relation to gods, 11–12, 53–4
mandragora, 124, 130, 132–3, 145
Manuli, P., 62
mare, 31 n. 99, 103
Marinus, 113 n. 2
mathematics, 6, 60, 112, 116, 118, 203
Mendel, J.G., 105
menses, 30, 33–4, 65, 68 n. 35, 72, 96 n. 140,
    97–8, 100–1, 107, 109, 129–30, 170–1, 177
    n. 222, 186–7, 194
Methodists, 165, 174, 182–200
methodology, 1, 4–5, 55–6, 113–15, 135,
    180–1, 187–92, 216–17
midwives, 3, 63 n. 11, 70, 72 n. 54, 78 n. 76,
    148 n. 102, 168–9, 176–9, 186, 208, 213,
    215; *see also* women as healers
milk, 175, 191
mirabilia, 56 n. 226, 139
miscarriage, 64–5, 68 nn. 35 and 37, 71, 76,
    85, 193
Mithridates, 126 n. 32, 136
Mnaseas, 186–7, 188 n. 264, 197
Mnesitheus, 15 n. 21, 175
mole, 40
moly, 118, 141
monkey, 31, 47 n. 187, 174
monsters, 40, 45, 53–4
moon, 83, 147 n. 100, 170–1, 178, 190
morphology, 18, 45–6, 48, 98, 101
motivations of ancient science, 213–15
moulding of the new-born baby, 172, 179
mule, 52 n. 212, 103, 179
muscles, 39, 113 n. 2, 154–5, 157, 159–60, 165
Museum, Alexandrian, 167, 213
mushrooms, 148
mutilations, 40–2, 96, 106, 110; *see also* defor-
    mities

myth, 4, 11, 13, 42, 54–5, 94, 123–4, 132 n. 55, 133, 135, 173, 210

nature: craftsmanship of, 56, 110, disputed, 188, 212, (*see also* teleology); versus culture, 9–10; normative conception of, 41–2, 55, 214–15
navel-string, cutting of, 70 n. 46, 169–70, 179, 211
nerves, 40, 108, 152, 157, 159–60, 164–5, 206, 217
νεῦρον, 152, 157, 159, 165
Numisianus, 113 n. 2
nurses, 168–9, 172–3, 175, 178 n. 222, 179, 186

Oppenheim, A.L., 202
ostrich, 47, 51
ovaries, 108–9, 153 n. 119
ovovivipara, 17–18, 35, 51 n. 210

pain-killing properties of plants, 119, 128, 132
πάνακες ('all-heal'), 124, 130–1, 133
pangenesis, 88–90, 93, 96–8, 106–7, 108 n. 189
Paracelsus, 116 n. 12
Parmenides, 87
past: critical attitude towards, 173–4, 216; deference to, 116, 136–7, 147, 173, 216
Peck, A.L., 44
Pelops, 113 n. 2
perfection, 18, 35–7, 47, 56, 98–9, 110
pessary, 71, 74, 80, 129–31
phainomena – the appearances, 54, 171, 180–2, 184, 189–92, 198–9
philosophers, natural, 2, 4, 56, 86–8, 107–9, 118, 121, 139, 168–70, 178, 180–1, 210–11, 213–15
φλέβες, 83, 152–4, 162–3
physiognomy, 10, 22–5, 204
plants, 2–3, 28, 30 n. 92, 31, 36, 39, 41, 43, 47, 51, 56, 105; medical uses of, 4, 119–36, 139–48, 197, 210–11; poisonous, 124–5, 132, 137–8, 148; powers of, 119, 123–8, 132, 139, 143, 146; problems of identification of, 127–9, 133–4, 139, 141, 146
Plato, 15–16, 42, 52, 54, 70 n. 47, 94–5, 107–8, 171, 176–7, 182
Pliny, 4–5, 24 n. 51, 56, 60 n. 6, 114, 116, 135–49, 168, 173, 182 n. 238, 203, 216
Plutarch, 24 n. 51, 78 n. 76
Praxagoras, 157, 162, 166, 217 n. 34
prayer, 124, 131
pregnancy, 65, 68 n. 35, 69, 76–9, 83–5, 194, 201; desires in, 177, 181
presentation, faulty, 73, 85 n. 107, 186
priests, 80, 208; *see also* seers
prognosis, 69

psychological factors in medical practice, 5, 74, 85, 132, 177 n. 222, 181–2; in pregnancy, 174–5, 177–8
Ptolemy, 112, 203
pulse, 217
purifications, 69, 120 n. 18, 131–3
Pyrrho, 183, 191
Pythagoreans, 48, 87 n. 114, 170 n. 195

questioning of patients, 71–2, 76, 80–1
Quintus, 113 n. 2

regimen, 84 n. 101, 90–2; *see also* diet
reproduction: modes of, appeal to in classification of animals, 18, 25–6, 33 n. 111, 35–7, 39, 45–8, 51; theories of, 3–4, 61, 84, 86–98, 105–111
reproductive capacities of female, male concern with, 84–5
research, 4, 55, 60, 92, 95, 104, 106, 112–15, 122, 133–40, 147, 149, 204–8, 210, 216–17
resemblances, argument from, in debate on reproduction, 87 n. 114, 89–90, 96–8, 106
residues, 39, 47, 97
riddles, 11, 46
right/left, 28 n. 62, 34, 36, 41 n. 167, 82, 86, 100, 175–7
rites, 168, 173; in plant collection, 123, 129–33, 145
root-cutters, 116, 120–3, 125–6, 134, 148, 210, 213, 215
Rousselle, A., 62
Ruelle, C.E., 151 n. 107
Rufus, 5, 150–67, 203, 209

Sappho, 59–60
Satyrus, 113 n. 2
Scala Naturae, 35, 42
Scepticism, 182–5, 187, 189–92, 198–200
Scythia, 124, 170
seal, 11, 45–6, 51, 53, 82
secretiveness, 136, 148
seed: dispute whether both parents produce, 66, 87–94, 96–7, 109–10; male/female, 89, 93, 96, 110; strong/weak, 89–93, 106
seers, 69; *see also* priests
Seleucus, 178 n. 224
semen, 30, 38 n. 140, 109; considered analogue of menses, 34 n. 118, 96 n. 140, 97–8, 101, 107
Semonides, 12, 94, 95 n. 133
sex: determination, 65–6, 83–4, 90–2, 176, 201; differentiation, taken as a mark of superiority, 36, 95, 98–9, in plants, 43–4 n. 171
Sextus Empiricus, 182–3, 187, 189–90, 192–3, 198–9
shame, 64, 70 n. 47, 78, 178 n. 222

Sicily, 144, 163 n. 176
signs, 22–4, 65, 190 n. 271, 194–6
snake, 10–11, 19, 24, 29, 83, 103, 138, 139 n.
   70, 148 n. 101, 176
Sophocles, 120, 136
Soranus, 5, 58 n. 4, 69 n. 39, 85 n. 103,
   115–16, 118, 168–200, 203, 208–9, 216
Spain, 138
species: fixity of natural, 52 n. 212, 106;
   notion of, 13
Speusippus, 15–17
spider, 100, 103
sterility, 64, 71, 84
Stoics, 87 n. 112, 108, 153 n. 117, 178–9, 191
   n. 272
στόμαχος, 162, 180
Strato, 55 n. 221
στρύχνος, 128, 197
styptic effects of plants, 119, 124
succussion, 64, 74–5, 81, 82 n. 88
superstition, 4–5, 131, 141 n. 76, 168–9, 174,
   181–2, 208–10, 215
surgery, 64, 73–5, 81–2, 85, 149 n. 104, 152,
   159 n. 147, 204, 208, 217
sutures, 102, 104, 158
swaddling, 175–7
swine, 31, 47 n. 189, 50 n. 204, 102, 108 n. 186
symbolic factors, 2–3, 7–9, 13–14, 83, 132 n.
   56, 168, 170, 172–7, 180–1
sympathetic communication, 83–4, 134 n. 61,
   169, 171–2, 177–81, 195
Syria, 131, 173

taboo, 7, 48
Tambiah, S.J., 8–9
tame/wild, 14, 19
teeth, 29–30, 39, 46, 102, 104
teething, 179
teleology, 15, 56, 110–11, 187–8, 199, 212,
   214–15
temple medicine, 69, 79, 131, 133, 207
testacea, 16–17, 36, 41, 47
testicles, 108–9, 153 n. 119, 162

text-books, 116
Themison, 185–7, 197–8
Theophrastus, 4, 21, 43, 113–14, 118, 121–36,
   141–8, 203, 210
Thrace, 124, 172, 179
Thrasyas of Mantinea, 122
tongue, 29, 39
totemism, 9
transmigration, 15, 54, 95
treatments, criticised as harmful, 80–1,
   169–73, 181, 194, 197–9, 207–8
trepanning, 85 n. 107, 204, 206

ὑοσκύαμος, 130, 132
up/down, 28, 32, 36, 41–2, 47, 49, 100–1
ureter, 151 n. 107, 163
urethra, 163
uvula, 151 n. 107, 155, 160, 163

venesection, 197–8
Vernant, J.P., 11
Vidal-Naquet, P., 11
virginity, 85 n. 103, 187, 193
vivisection, 188, 213 n. 29
voice, 29, 101

water-animals, *see* land-animals
weaning, 175
Wellmann, M., 182
wet-nurses, *see* nurses
whales, 17, 204
withholding judgement (ἐποχή), 183–4, 187,
   191–2, 198–200
Withington, E.T., 154
womb, 70–5, 80–3, 90, 109, 130, 177, 179–81,
   193–8; believed to move round body, 83–4,
   131, 133, this belief rejected, 171–2; prolapse of, 73, 81, 172
women, 12, 15, 94–5; as healers, 60 n. 6, 61,
   69–73, 75–6, 79–80, 169, (*see also* midwives,
   nurses); as patients, 63–86, 172–4, 177–81,
   194–7, internal examination of, 62, 70–4,
   79–81, 213, veracity of reports, 68, 76–8